D1074131

William Henry Fox Talbot

*Pioneer of photography and
man of science*

W. H. F. Talbot from a Daguerreotype taken at the Royal Polytechnic Institution, London. This previously unpublished portrait may be dated approximately to the mid – 1840s

William Henry Fox Talbot

*Pioneer of photography and
man of science*

H. J. P. ARNOLD

HUTCHINSON BENHAM
LONDON

Hutchinson Benham Ltd
3 Fitzroy Square, London WIP 6JD

An imprint of the Hutchinson Group

London Melbourne Sydney Auckland
Wellington Johannesburg and agencies
throughout the world

First published 1977
© Kodak Limited 1977

Set in Monotype Bembo

Printed in Great Britain by The Anchor Press Ltd
and bound by Wm Brendon & Son Ltd
both of Tiptree, Essex

ISBN 0 09 129600 5

With love and thanks to
Audrey, Ann Helen and Dolly –
who lived through it with me

Contents

Permission to quote from letters and other documents in the possession of the following institutions and individuals is acknowledged with thanks:

The Talbot Museum; the Science Museum; the Royal Society; the Royal Institution; the Royal Botanic Garden, Edinburgh; the Royal Botanic Gardens, Kew; the Royal Greenwich Observatory; the Wiltshire County Record Office, Trowbridge; the Royal Photographic Society; the Master and Fellows of Trinity College, Cambridge; Mr Anthony Burnett-Brown; Mr A. C. Davidson; and Mr Christopher Methuen Campbell.

Sources of Illustrations

The illustrations have been drawn from the following museums, institutions and individuals, whose permission to reproduce them is gratefully acknowledged.

FRONTISPIECE

Lacock Collection

BETWEEN PAGES 96 AND 97

The Trustees of the British Museum, 14
Earl of Mount Edgecumbe, 10
Kodak Museum, 9
Lacock Collection, 1*, 2, 3, 7, 8, 12, 20*, 21, 23, 24*
Science Museum, London; Fox Talbot Collection, 4, 5, 17, 22
   Crown Copyright, 15, 16, 18, 19
Miss Thelma Vernon, 13
Harold White, 6
Dowager Viscountess Wimborne, 11

BETWEEN PAGES 160 AND 161

The Trustees of the British Museum, 28
Lacock Collection, 30, 33, 34, 35, 41, 42*, 43, 45, 46, 47, 48, 49, 50, 51, 52, 53, 54, 55, 56, 58, 59, 60, 61, 62, 63, 64, 67, 69, 72, 75, 76, 77
Richard Morris, 70
Scottish National Portrait Gallery, 73, 74
Science Museum, London; Fox Talbot Collection, 25†, 26†, 27†, 29†, 31†, 32†, 36†, 37†, 38†, 39†, 40†, 44†, 57, 65†, 66†, 68†, 71, 78

* Bromide reproductions from Lacock originals, courtesy of the Kodak Museum.
† Modern Calotype process positives produced by B. W. Coe, Curator of the Kodak Museum, from original negatives in the possession of the Science Museum.

BETWEEN PAGES 288 AND 289

Kodak Museum, 82
Lacock Collection, 79, 80, 81, 83, 84, 85, 86, 87, 88, 90, 91, 96, 97, 98, 100, 101, 102, 103, 104, 105, 106
Science Museum, London, 89, 92, 93, 94, 95, 99†

Acknowledgements

This biography is the result of eighteen months' full-time research and writing. The opportunity to devote myself in this manner to a project which was surely long overdue was made possible by my former employers and colleagues at Kodak Limited who agreed to sponsor the biography as the company's major contribution to the commemoration of Talbot's memory on the occasion of the one hundredth anniversary of his death. In today's economic conditions it seems likely that a full-length biography might have been delayed indefinitely but for the Kodak support and, accordingly, I write first of all to express my sincere and deep gratitude to the company for making my work possible. All of those interested in the study of British scientific development in the nineteenth century will, I am sure, share that sense of gratitude.

In preparing a biography the full cooperation of the subject's family is a precious advantage. From the moment some years ago when I first expressed the hope of writing Henry Talbot's biography I have had the pleasure of a friendly and fruitful contact with his great-great-grandson and great-great-grand-daughter, Anthony and Janet Burnett-Brown. They gave constant support and help to me and I hope they will consider the result does justice to their distinguished ancestor. The same sentiments are extended to my good friend and former Kodak colleague Robert E. Lassam, who has been Curator of the Talbot Museum in Lacock since its inception and who over the months of my research and writing was always prepared to help in countless ways no matter the many demands upon his time. For the hospitality during my visits to Lacock I thank Margaret Lassam, as well as the kind hosts at the Abbey itself.

Readers of the pages that follow will realize that Henry Talbot was a man of genius and many talents. In telling his story and assessing his achievements it was vital to be able to call upon the knowledge and help of scholars in various disciplines. Those whom I approached were generous in their assistance and it is no exaggeration whatsoever to state that without their help the comprehensive nature of the biography would not have been possible. Thus I am happy to record my most sincere thanks to John C. E. Wren, Dr Antony F. Anderson, Andrew Sugden, Victor E. Watts, Dr Jennifer Moore-Blunt, Christopher B. F. Walker and Colin A. Ronan. These and other scholars were also good enough to read various parts of the text before publication and it benefited greatly from their suggestions. For any failings it still possesses I alone, of course, am responsible.

In telling the story of Talbot's photographic researches, I received help from a number of previous workers in the field whose generosity with their time and wisdom has been more than I could have expected. They included Harold White who over many years has researched and lectured on aspects of Talbot's life and work, has assisted other workers in the same area, and who in particular tackled the daunting task of arranging much of the correspondence in the Lacock Collection in a chronological sequence; Arthur T. Gill who needs no introduction as one of the most scholarly and reliable photographic historians in this country – and for whom nothing was too much trouble; Dr David Thomas and John P. Ward of the Science Museum in London who throughout my researches provided me with ready access to the Talbot Collection at the Museum and extended many kindnesses and words of advice; and my former colleague Brian Coe, Curator of the Kodak Museum, who is another leading British historian of photography and in addition now knows more about the practical preparation of sensitized papers by Talbot's processes than anybody else anywhere. There is also need to mention the aid and encouragement received from that doyen of photographic historians Beaumont Newhall and the guidance readily given by my former colleague (and managing director) Dr D. A. Spencer. Help with various aspects of the story was received from other members of the Kodak organization – these included Dr G. I. P. Levenson of the Research Laboratory at Harrow and Margaret Gauntlett and Sue Smith of the Research Laboratory Library, Christine Lucas (Assistant Curator of the Kodak Museum at Harrow), L. A. Trangmar of the Patents and Trade Marks Department, Franz Krpata of Kodak G.m.b.H., Vienna, Karl Steinorth and his colleagues of Kodak A.G. in Stuttgart and Jean Ganot and his staff of Kodak-

Pathé S.A. in Paris. Kodak staff at Ruislip and Hemel Hempstead gave valuable help generally. To all of these I extend my thanks.

My footsteps through the history of Lacock village and some passages of the Talbot family story received sound guidance from Miss Thelma Vernon, while study of the Fox-Strangways family history was made easier by the kindness of the Dowager Countess Wimborne. Both of these ladies have been a biographer's dream for their patient researches, the results of which were willingly passed on to me, saving many, many hours of original research.

The biographer's task would be impossible without the assistance and advice provided by librarians. Without doubt I asked more of my good friend Frank W. S. Baguley (Assistant County Librarian of Hampshire) than I had any right to expect would be fulfilled – but typically no request was too much. Similarly, Mr N. H. Robinson of the Royal Society and his colleagues were friendliness and helpfulness itself and I shall long look back with pleasure to my visits to Carlton House Terrace. It was Professor Sir George Porter who was kind enough in the first instance to secure my introduction to the Royal Society. The following persons and organizations all helped with the research task and will I hope accept my warm thanks: Alan Q. Morton of the Royal Scottish Museum, Edinburgh; Sara Stevenson of the Scottish National Portrait Gallery; M. V. Mathew, Librarian of the Royal Botanic Garden, Edinburgh; Mary Smyth, Crawford Librarian at the Royal Observatory, Edinburgh; R. Smart, Keeper of Archives of St Andrew's University; Irena M. McCabe, Librarian of the Royal Institution; Peter Wyld, Director of the General Synod Enquiry Centre; Jill Davies of the Royal Asiatic Society Library; John Palmer of the Research Division of the House of Commons; H. J. R. Wing of Christ Church, Oxford; Maurice G. Rathbone and his colleagues of the Wiltshire County Record Office at Trowbridge; Ann Shirley of the National Maritime Museum, Greenwich; and A. W. H. Pearsall, Historian at that Museum; Rosemary Graham, Manuscript Cataloguer at Trinity College Library, Cambridge; J. A. Edwards, Archivist at the University of Reading Library; Harry G. R. King of the Scott Polar Research Institute, Cambridge; P. S. Laurie of the Royal Greenwich Observatory; Robert J. Doherty, Director of the International Museum of Photography at George Eastman House; R. E. Sandell of the Wiltshire Archaeological Society, Devizes; Miss E. Talbot Rice of the National Army Museum; W. H. Rutherford, Executive Secretary of the Royal Society of Edinburgh; and officials of Harrow School, the Linnean Society, the Royal Society of Literature, the Royal Society of Arts, the Wiltshire County Library,

Devizes, and the St Bride Printing Library in London. I also thank Anthony Burnett-Brown for securing my admission to the collection of the Royal Photographic Society.

There is one more long list. The compilation of a biography obviously takes the researcher well beyond the walls of libraries and academic institutions – and success depends upon the response from many individuals who can advise, make suggestions, and provide minute or major pieces of evidence. There are also those kind people who open doors previously closed and fully give of their ideas. I record the help of the following and extend my thanks: John Vivian Hughes, Gerald Bonner, A. F. Thompson and Mary Thompson, Kenneth Harper, Dr George Parker, Dr Brian Bowers, R. Derek Wood, Geoffrey Crawley, Otto M. Lilien, Eric Chambers, Derek J. Woods, Ann Turner, Katherine Michaelson, Michael Lansdowne, P. A. M. van der Helm, R. M. Strathdee, Graham Johnson, Christopher Methuen Campbell, E. A. Vauvelle, Professor Eric R. Laithwaite, Professor H. W. F. Saggs, Professor D. J. Wiseman, Professor Margaret Harker, the Earl of Mount Edgcumbe, Annita Christie, Phyllis Deane, Dr B. A. Sparkes, Eugene Ostroff, Richard Morris, Marie-Ange Baisbrown, Christopher Traves and Mary Uridge.

My brother John E. G. Arnold helped in many practical ways. Initially Pat Dixon and then Maureen Hawkins assisted me with typing the seemingly limitless number of letters of enquiry and once again it was my great good fortune that the wearisome and daunting task of converting my dictation from tape through the various stages of typing to a final version should be executed for me with dedication and a high degree of professional excellence by Arlene Clothier. I am very grateful.

Finally – my feelings towards the ladies of the Arnold household, who kept quiet and looked after the author whilst he worked (and fretted) over eighteen long months, are recorded in the dedication.

H. J. P. ARNOLD

Preface

As the first full-length study of William Henry Fox Talbot's life and work, and one based as extensively as possible upon original sources, this volume may be regarded as both an end and a beginning.

Hopefully it will reveal the substance behind the figure who has been little more than an outline shadow in the history books and also enable Talbot's position in nineteenth-century science and learning to be established. In that sense, the biography will be an end. But thereafter it is to be hoped earnestly that other scholars, perhaps starting from the basis of the biography, will move deeper into the disciplines in which Talbot researched and greatly increase our knowledge of his work. It is likely that as such research proceeds, the interpretations and even some of the facts in this volume will be modified: that is in the nature of things and will be genuinely welcomed by the present author, for thereby the biography will also mark a beginning. There is in the Talbot Museum at Lacock a natural point of focus for these future researches.

Some readers may be surprised that throughout this volume the subject is referred to as 'Talbot' and not 'Fox Talbot'. The latter has a traditional, not to say mellifluous, ring to it – and was used invariably by a number of Talbot's close family, including his mother who considered it distinguished him suitably from the numerous branches of the Talbot family. However, 'Fox' was not part of a surname but a third Christian name and though very occasionally Talbot himself used the form of 'Fox Talbot' the vast bulk of his letters and other documents were signed 'Henry F. Talbot' or 'H. F. Talbot'. Accordingly, throughout this biography he is referred to as 'Talbot'.

Finally – in recounting the story of a nineteenth-century scientist and his family, a modern audience may have difficulty in relating to many of the concepts and details of the period. Nowhere is this more the case than in the expression of monetary values. However, while an indication of precise values is fraught with problems and dangers, it may be taken that the purchasing power of money *circa* 1850 was between ten and fifteen times the mid-1977 level in the United Kingdom.

I

An Abbey and Ancestors

On 16 April 1232 Ela, Countess of Salisbury, laid the foundation stone of a nunnery for Augustinian canonesses at Snaylesmede in her manor of Lacock in Wiltshire. The foundation was in memory of her husband William Longespee – half brother of Richard I and King John – who was one of the most powerful barons of the early thirteenth century.

Ela was Countess of Salisbury in her own right and was evidently a formidable personality. For two years after her husband's death, she was Sheriff of Wiltshire – the only woman sheriff the county has ever had – at a time when the office carried far greater influence and power than it does today. She herself joined the Abbey in 1238, becoming the first abbess in 1241. She continued in that position until 1256 when she resigned, and died in 1261 at the ripe age of seventy-five. Throughout the Middle Ages, the Abbey flourished. There were normally between fifteen and twenty-five nuns in residence but although living under a rule of celibacy they did not take vows and often visited their families.

The peace of centuries, however, was not to last. In 1535 the commissioners of King Henry VIII visited the Abbey and extracted a fine. Four years later the Abbey was suppressed: the nuns were dispersed and the house and grounds were granted to one William Sharington in return for £783 13s. 10d. Thus began the Abbey's lay existence as 'Lacock House'.

The Talbot links with Lacock started with the marriage of Olive Sharington, William's niece, to 'John Talbotte esquire', a great-grandson of the second Earl of Shrewsbury, on 13 September 1574. Initially the marriage was against the family's wishes, for John Aubrey, the Wiltshire antiquarian, related how

B

Olive jumped from the 'battlements' to join her lover below. Fortunately her petticoats 'did somewhat break her fall' but despite this measure of aerodynamic braking, John Talbot was felled by the impact and lay 'as one dead'. He revived, whereupon Olive's father said 'since she made such leapes she should e'en marry him'.

Their grandson, Sharington Talbot, was Aubrey's 'honoured friend' and an ardent Royalist – he was at Nottingham in 1642 when the Royal Standard blew down from the Castle. (It was he who told John Aubrey of this event which was regarded as a bad omen for the King's cause at the outbreak of the hostilities.) At different periods during the war Lacock House was occupied by Parliamentary and Royalist forces, but the Talbots were constant to the Royalist cause.

On the day that Charles II landed at Dover, John Talbot, Sharington's son, was said to have been the first person on shore to greet the King. In June of 1660 he was knighted at Whitehall Palace and in 1663 the King dined with the family at Lacock. A few years later, Sir John acted as second to his kinsman – Francis Talbot, the eleventh Earl of Shrewsbury – in a duel with the Duke of Buckingham in which both principals and seconds fought. In a diary entry for 17 January 1668 Samuel Pepys recorded:

> Much discourse of the duel yesterday between the Duke of Buckingham, Holmes [Sir Robert Holmes], and one Jenkins [Captain William Jenkins], on one side and my Lord of Shrewsbury, Sir John Talbot, and one Bernard Howard [eighth son of the Earl of Arundel], on the other side; and all about my Lady Shrewsbury, who at this time, and hath for a great while been, a mistress to the Duke of Buckingham. And so her husband challenged him, and they met yesterday in a close near Barn-Elmes, and there fought: and my Lord Shrewsbury is run through the body, from the right breast through the shoulder; and Sir John Talbot all along up one of his armes; and Jenkins killed upon the place, and the rest all, in a little measure, wounded. This will make the world think that the King hath good councillors about him, when the Duke of Buckingham, the greatest man about him, is a fellow of no more sobriety than to fight about a mistress.

Unlike the Earl, Sir John Talbot recovered from his wounds and continued an active public life as Lord of the Manor of Lacock, Justice of the Peace and as a Member of Parliament. His loyalty to the Royalist cause and especially to the memory of Charles I never wavered. He wrote to his daughter Anne on 28 January 1706 (two days before the anniversary of the execution of Charles I fifty-seven years before):

Pray deliver the enclosed, and resolve to continue at Dunstable all Thursday the 30th & go everyone to church there both morning and evening service & fast till supper. I hope the time of your meeting was so fixed with intention to keep together that day & not to travel with carriers & waggoners. I had much rather pay the expense ten times over than that any of mine should profane that day with contempt. I have sealed up your sister's letter before this reflection came to my thoughts. Though I was jocular to her, I am serious in this to you all, & so expect a compliant.[1]

'A very fine, strong old gentleman', Sir John was eighty-four when he died in 1714, the last of the direct Talbot male line.

The Abbey then passed to his grandson, John Ivory, who assumed the name Talbot and presided at Lacock for almost sixty years. He too was a Tory M.P. and known as a Royalist: in 1721 his name was passed to the Pretender as a likely supporter in the event of a rising.[2] During his time the Abbey's formal gardens were replaced by parkland and parts of the house were rebuilt in the Gothick style.

Ivory Talbot's eldest son John succeeded him in 1772 but lived for only six more years and died childless. The Abbey and the estate passed to his sister Martha Davenport and, on her death in 1788, to her son William Davenport, who took the name of Talbot. On 17 April 1796 this Talbot married the Lady Elisabeth Fox-Strangways, and just under four years later on 11 February 1800, William Henry Fox Talbot was born.

There were some similarities between the background of the Talbots and the Fox-Strangways – fierce loyalty to the Royalist cause in the Civil War, for example, and participation in politics, although at opposite ends of the political spectrum. But the Talbots could not compare in terms of social eminence and political prominence.

Lady Elisabeth's great-grandfather was Stephen Fox. Born in 1627, he was reputed to have been on the scaffold at the execution of Charles I and to have helped the young Charles to escape to France. He raised money for the royal exiles and is reported to have been 'the first to bring his master the news of Cromwell's death and to salute him as the real King of Great Britain'. Stephen Fox was knighted in July 1665 and by 1680 – after fifteen more hard-working years as M.P. and in the King's service – Sir Stephen was said to be worth £200,000 'honestly got and unenvied, which is next to a miracle' according to Evelyn. On Queen Anne's succession in 1702, at the age of seventy-five,

Sir Stephen indicated a wish to retire, but by the Queen's express wish he led the Commons in procession at her coronation. He died in 1716 at the age of eighty-nine, safe in a reputation for 'courtesy, kindliness of disposition and generosity'.

Sir Stephen Fox had married twice. A son by his first marriage entered politics but predeceased him. He married again at the age of seventy-six and had two sons Stephen and Henry. Both became friends of the powerful political figure of the day, Lord Hervey, and it was he who converted Stephen as M.P. for Shaftesbury in Dorset from his Toryism to give support to the Whig administration of Robert Walpole.[3]

In 1736 Stephen Fox married Elizabeth Strangways Horner. Elizabeth was but thirteen at the time of the marriage and she and Stephen did not live together for some three years.

Stephen Fox's loyalty to Sir Robert Walpole continued and at the time of the Minister's downfall in 1740–1 he became one of Walpole's most rigorous and distinguished defenders. In 1741 Stephen acquired a peerage and became Lord Ilchester, largely by paying an appropriate sum of money to the King's mistress. He took the Strangways name when his wife inherited the Strangways estates in 1758. In 1776 he died, leaving a large family and considerable estates.

Stephen's brother Henry meantime was pursuing a career which led Sir Lewis Namier to call him the most rapacious statesman of the eighteenth century for the manner in which he acquired his wealth at the expense of King and country. He ran away with Caroline Lennox, daughter of the second Duke of Richmond and a great-granddaughter of Charles II, and they became the parents of Charles James Fox, one of the most charming, brilliant, liberal and yet controversial politicians of the century. Henry Fox was elected to Parliament in 1735. He became a leading figure in the House of Commons – making and breaking opportunistic alliances, entering the Cabinet (in 1755) and becoming Leader of the House and Secretary of State. He was created Baron Holland of Foxley in 1763, the name being taken from Holland House – the beautiful early-seventeenth-century property in Kensington which had been the family's London residence since 1749 – and he died in 1774.

His grandson, the third Baron Holland, was recognized as the exponent in the House of Lords of Charles James Fox's policies. He adopted 'liberal' views for his day – resisting suspension of the Habeas Corpus Act at the turn of the century, supporting the admission of Roman Catholics to Parliament and the emancipation of slaves, opposing the existence of capital punishment for stealing and in 1815 opposing the bill for the detention of Napoleon as a prisoner of war on the grounds that the detention must be justified by the 'Laws of Nations' or not at all.* When the Whigs returned to power in 1830 Lord Holland was made Chancellor of the Duchy of Lancaster in Lord Grey's Ministry and retained the post for most of the next decade till he died in 1840. The Holland title became extinct nineteen years later in 1859.

The family background of the Ilchesters and Hollands was thus one of high politics and frequent contact with members of the Royal Family. For instance, one of the first Earl of Ilchester's daughters – Lady Susan – was a bridesmaid at the wedding of George III to Charlotte of Mecklenburg and was herself at one time sought by the (Royal) Duke of Gloucester.

Henry Thomas Fox-Strangways, the second Earl of Ilchester (1747–1802), had numerous children by two wives. His first wife was Mary Theresa, daughter of Standish O'Grady of County Limerick in Ireland. She gave birth to a son Henry (who subsequently became the third Earl) followed by several daughters, the eldest of whom was the Lady Elisabeth Theresa (born in 1773).

Lady Elisabeth was not only highly intelligent, but a seeker after knowledge, a natural linguist, a sparkling conversationalist, a Whig throughout her entire life (frequently adopting the causes of her second cousin Charles James Fox), strongly willed, obstinate – and spoilt from her first year on. A mind such as Lady Elisabeth's must have rebelled at the typically restricted upbringing for a girl in the late eighteenth century. No wonder perhaps that one correspondent – writing to her in the last decade of that century and addressing her as 'My Dear little volatile friend' – continued:

Since you are so notorious for changing your plans with so much facility to yourself, & so little scruple respecting your friends, how can I flatter myself you will keep your appointment . . . How much I wish you were not like a pretty little feather floating in every wind, that with your excess of spirits there was a solidity in your affections that those who love you might never feel disappointed.[4]

Somewhat later another (political) correspondent wrote:

Don't write me in your *black book* when I confess I have not enrolled my name with the Whig Club . . . I look upon you as a meteor which appears for a moment to dazzle and entrance – and then vanishes below the horizon to act, to like purpose, on other beings in other spheres.[5]

* When young Henry Talbot was at Harrow, Dr George Butler, the headmaster, had strict instructions to allow the boy to go to Holland House whenever sent for.

Elisabeth first met William Davenport Talbot, it may be assumed, around
1794, when her younger sister Mary Lucy married Thomas Mansel Talbot of
Oxwich, Penrice and Margam, the grandson of John Ivory Talbot and thus
a cousin of Davenport Talbot. Lady Elisabeth apparently found some difficulty
in making up her mind about Davenport Talbot. In a delightful letter written
in March 1796 Lady Susan told her: 'The Eliza is aground on the shingles . . .
don't be shilly shally . . . I can find no *reasonable* cause for delay.'[6] Her advice
was taken and in just under three weeks the marriage was made.

Talbot was nine years older than Lady Elisabeth. He had left Christ Church,
Oxford in 1781 without a degree and was later commissioned in the Queen's
Dragoon Guards. Subsequently he transferred to the Royal Fusiliers and then
to the 88th Foot – being on active duty until shortly before his death in 1800.

Davenport Talbot was a handsome man – even if idealized, a miniature in
the Talbot Museum at Lacock is evidence of this – and he roused great affection
in those with whom he came into close contact. He moved in influential circles
and one of his most intimate friends during military service (they served
together in Europe, Gibraltar and Canada) was Prince Edward Augustus,
George III's fourth son and the man who as Duke of Kent was later to father
the girl destined to become Queen Victoria.

In their brief married life together of a little over four years in various
military postings Lady Elisabeth and Captain Davenport Talbot were well
suited and very much in love. Elisabeth was already an industrious and brilliant
letter writer and many letters to her younger sister Harriet and her Aunt
Susan still survive. Three months after the marriage in 1796, Lady Elisabeth
wrote to her sister:

Don't you wonder Harriet *how* he *could* leave me for so long a time? . . . what is still
worse I do not know when he will return . . . I am not well which is very unlucky in
Cimosco's[*] absence as I want very much to be soothed. I am expecting him à chaque
moment but the hour passes and he does not come! . . .[7]

On 6 September 1796 Elisabeth wrote happily to Harriet:

My dear little Harriet you cannot conceive *anything* so happy as we are. Cimosco desires
me to tell you he will kiss your dear little hand when he sees you if you will promise *to
keep it clean*. Is he not *very indelicate*? . . . He says . . . that he thinks it is very odd that you
do not *fete* him so much now he is *your brother* as you did when he was only en qualite

* 'Cimosco' was the pet name for Davenport Talbot which Lady Elisabeth always used in her letters.

d'amant . . . I can think of nothing all day long but my own happiness which is so much beyond what I feel I deserve.

On the state of her husband's indifferent health Lady Elisabeth adopted a somewhat bantering manner which may well have hidden deeper worries. In February 1798 she related how Talbot had sprained his ankle and would not be able to walk for a month. He was 'in a high fever yesterday . . . still very ill and fancies himself worse. At least he fancies that he has had so many violent illnesses that he may at any time succombé to a slight one'. References to a 'fever' occurred in a number of letters but in June 1799 Lady Elisabeth gave it as her opinion that he was perfectly well and 'if he would constantly take excessive exercise he would always continue so'[8] which helps little in the endeavour to diagnose his illness. The joyous occasion of the birth of a son on 11 February 1800 occupied the family for some weeks, but by April concern for Davenport Talbot was again evident. On 25 April Lady Susan, after expressing her delight at the progress of 'little Henry', her great-nephew, went on: 'I am very glad [Mr Talbot] is so much better tho' I don't like relapses, however as the Doc says they must be expected, they cease to be alarming . . .' But Davenport Talbot had just under three more months to live – he died on 31 July 1800, when Henry Talbot was but five months old.

2
Minority, Cambridge and the 1820s

When William Davenport Talbot died he left debts and liabilities in excess of £30,000. The precise origin and nature of much of the debt is not clear, although at least one third of the sum was not of his own making – the estate being subject to mortgages totalling £10,000 contracted by John Talbot and John Ivory Talbot his father prior to 1770, and charged with unpaid legacies from John Talbot's will.

As a serving army officer Davenport Talbot was not often in residence. His sister Barbara acted as his steward part of the time but in 1795 he had faced up to the situation and rented the Abbey to a kinswoman – the Dowager Countess of Shrewsbury – at £300 per annum. To Davenport Talbot's probable lack of interest in the estate must be added a nature which was doubtless generous and not inclined to accept the tedium of running an estate – features which were exacerbated when he married Lady Elisabeth in 1796, for it is unlikely that she then paid much attention to the estate or encouraged her husband so to do.

Be that as it may, the young widow faced a harsh awakening following Davenport Talbot's death in July 1800. Quite apart from the mortgages, interest payments due thereon and residual legacies still outstanding, there were even larger debts 'by bond and simple contract'. Nor was that all. Payments of taxes and rates 'were in great arrears' and the buildings on the estate were in a 'most dilapidated & ruinous condition'. It was indeed a situation 'to appal the stoutest heart'.[1]

The years from 1800 to 1804 were chaotic. Lady Elisabeth was largely absent from the estate and Barbara Davenport took its management upon herself with the best of intentions if without any authority. In 1804 matters came to a head and with no persons authorized to receive estate rents, or manage the estate, or to act as legal guardian to the infant Henry Talbot, reference to the law was long overdue. The immediate occasion was action by creditors and in July of 1804 the case was referred to Mr Campbell, one of the Masters in Chancery. The ensuing seventeen years were to be an excellent demonstration of the English law in action in defence of a minor.

In April 1805 Lady Elisabeth was appointed her son's legal guardian and allowed £500 per year from the estate. A few weeks later Joseph Pitt – one of the lawyers acting for the mortgagees – became receiver. It took somewhat longer to bring order to the chaotic accounts but by July 1806 the Master reported on rents received between July 1800 and 25 March 1805. The creditors pressed for the sale of Abbey furniture and contents, but this was fortunately avoided. Apparently Lady Elisabeth's father, Lord Ilchester, and her second husband, Charles Feilding, paid the Court's valuation to the creditors and were subsequently reimbursed from the estate.

With sensible management the condition of the young Henry Talbot's inheritance proved to be basically sound. By 1806 the estate was beginning 'to recover from embarrassments & to wipe off the heavy load of debt previously affecting it'. The Master next turned his attention to the dilapidated condition of the buildings, recouping the cost of repairs by selling timber from the estate. By 1810 the purchase money for the contents of the Abbey was repaid, all back interest was cleared and the position was further eased by the death of at least one of the beneficiaries under John Talbot's will. A minor setback in 1810 was the death of the Abbey's tenant, the Countess of Shrewsbury, but after standing empty for six months, the building was rented by John Rock Grosett who was subsequently to become M.P. for Chippenham.

In the years immediately after 1811, the net income from the estate varied between £500 and £1,000. In 1814 the £1,500 still due to Mary Davenport, Henry's aunt, under John Talbot's will was paid to her widower husband John Shakespeare. About this time steps for the positive expansion of the estate began with the purchase of numerous lots of the Montagu family property which adjoined the Lacock estate at Lackham. By 1817 the rentals and 'casual' profits had again increased and eventually the Court paid off the mortgages in 1819.

When Henry Talbot came of age on 11 February 1821, the Court transferred to him untouched investments, consols and annuities totalling around

£4,250. The estate was now well recovered, was in good repair, the whole of the debt was paid off and the net annual income after all outgoings (including repairs) was about £1,800 per annum. This financial stability has been stressed because critics of Henry Talbot's patenting and other activities in later life have attributed his actions to a desire to repair the financial excesses of his father and to recoup the family fortune. In the first place, the Talbots never had a 'family fortune'. In the second, whatever criticism might or might not be justified on account of his later activities, on his majority Henry Talbot inherited no debts and possessed a considerable property in a good state of repair and yielding a reasonable income.

It was no coincidence that Lady Elisabeth's marriage to Captain Charles Feilding, R.N.* on 24 April 1804 marked the beginning of the drive to bring order out of the chaos into which the estate had fallen. Although he was frequently at sea until 1809, many of the lawyers' letters of the period were addressed to Feilding. It was he too who, watchful for Henry Talbot's interest, wrote of his concern that too many trees were being felled on the estate.

Life must have been difficult for Charles Feilding at this time – returning from active duty in the Navy to deal with numerous problems on behalf of his young stepson in addition to his own affairs – but his affection for Henry Talbot was such that he gave Lacock matters some priority over his own and he acted with wisdom as well as energy. Lady Elisabeth was telling the plain truth when, in greeting her son on his coming of age in 1821, she observed that if Henry considered things were well managed it was due not to her but to his stepfather.[2]

Born in August 1780 Charles Feilding was thus some six years younger than Lady Elisabeth. Like many contemporaries, he first went to sea with the Royal Navy as a captain's secretary at the age of thirteen. This was a well established path for those with some influence and within two years – in 1795 – Feilding was a midshipman seeing service with the Channel Fleet. Promotion to the rank of lieutenant followed in 1799, and by 1801 Feilding was an acting captain in command of a 32-gun frigate. He served in the West Indies, later transferring to North Sea, Thames Estuary and Channel duties in command of a succession of frigates ending with the 38-gun *Revolutionnaire* from November

* In November 1807 a correspondent 'was quite in an agony when he found he had placed the "i" before the "e" ' in spelling Feilding's name. The person would not have felt so badly if he could have known how many correspondents during Feilding's lifetime (and how many writers touching upon Henry Talbot's family background since) were to make exactly the same error.

1806 to February 1808. Like many of his fellow officers Charles Feilding seems not to have been involved in any of the famous naval battles of the period – Cape St Vincent, The Nile, The Baltic and Trafalgar – but he was involved in patrol duties elsewhere. After 1809 Feilding saw no active service, remaining on half pay till his death (as a Rear-Admiral) in 1837.

It might be supposed that, in the absence of a permanent home, the early years of William Henry Fox Talbot would have been disturbed to say the least and possibly damaging psychologically. Nothing could have been further from the truth: he and his mother had a series of permanent homes – at Melbury in Dorset where Henry had been born and which was the seat of the third Earl of Ilchester, Lady Elisabeth's brother Harry; at Moreton House near Dorchester, and Bowood in Wiltshire, the homes of Lady Elisabeth's younger married sisters Harriet and Louisa; and most of all, Penrice on the beautiful Gower coast a few miles from Swansea where Lady Mary Lucy – as the wife of Thomas Mansel Talbot – had settled to rear a family. All but one of the eight Welsh Talbot children were girls and the welcome extended there to Henry in particular and to his mother when they came to stay may be imagined. While the warmth extended at the other homes was considerable, Penrice occupied a special place in Henry Talbot's childhood – providing happy memories he was never to forget and warm friendships with aunt and cousins which lasted throughout life. 'Aunt Mary' was very much a second mother.

During these early years then the young Talbot was a wanderer – a very privileged wanderer to be sure, but a wanderer nevertheless. He appeared to enjoy the experience greatly and it is easy to see in his youth the formation of attitudes to travel and to rented or purchased homes in Britain, attitudes which were to be with him throughout life. This situation is reflected in the frequency with which letters were sent to Lacock Abbey or his London address almost without exception beginning – 'Henry, where are you?'

Until he went to his first school in 1808, Henry Talbot's education was in the hands of Lady Elisabeth Feilding and tutors. His mother's strength was in languages – she had fluent French, some German and a reasonable grounding in the classics – but her greatest influence, apart from providing tutors of the right quality, was in shaping Henry's attitude to learning. The relationship between mother and son – as interpreted largely through the letters that they left – is a fascinating one. Lady Elisabeth felt an intense love for Henry and occasionally she expressed it in writing with an intensity which would be difficult to match. But it was a very demanding love: Lady Elisabeth seemingly from the very beginning recognized Henry's mental capabilities and she was determined that nothing (not even the boy himself) would stand in the way of the great achievements she resolutely expected. In this sense, there was a very hard side to her relationship with her son – she enveloped him with the inspiration of her own intellect but at the same time drove him on by encouragement and warning to horizons which she knew that she would never reach but which would be her son's natural domain. She was not prepared to accept anything less and when she considered that Henry was falling short of his rightful standard she told him so – whether child or man – with brutal frankness. Such a relationship might have done irreparable harm but Lady Elisabeth had judged his intellectual calibre, his resilience and strength of character well – and the young boy thrived. On the occasions when Henry satisfied his mother's standards, she radiated joy and immediately used the achievement for self-glorification as does any ambitious mother of a talented child.

But the demands did not all flow one way. What Lady Elisabeth expected of her son, she demanded of herself – as far as her situation would allow. A small notebook which she commenced in 1811 (Henry's first year at Harrow) contains definitions of scientific and mathematical terms, and meanings of obscure words in classical and modern languages, as though she were determined to stay level with Henry as long as possible since knowledge was a better position from which to inspire and to drive.

Thus mother and child were bound together in a close intellectual as well as emotional relationship. It was inevitable that Charles Feilding would not be able to enter into the intensity of that relationship but from the very beginning there was no doubting the warmth of his love for his young stepson. If he could not match the intellectual brilliance of wife or stepson he could contribute stability of character, experience of the world and the organizational skills and leadership of a naval officer to help bring order to the chaotic world in which they initially found themselves. Thereafter he was a source of judicious advice and guidance, based upon deep Christian beliefs, which was always available to Henry as he faced the increasing responsibilities of life. Above all, he counselled that the young man should not only be true to his own potential and achievements but also to his responsibilities to those around him – a reminder about the dangers of selfishness and self-gratification that was well made, since Lady Elisabeth could not escape some criticism on this count.

For his part, Henry Talbot had a considerable regard for his stepfather and the relationship was a close one. But it is doubtful whether Henry's affection for Charles Feilding matched the depth of that of Feilding for his stepson – and this was a product of Henry's make-up. Feilding found Henry somewhat reserved at all times and therefore not infrequently committed his thoughts and advice at important periods of his stepson's life to paper which is fortunate for the biographer. All in all, Charles Feilding comes down through the years as a delightful personality – the very antithesis of the stepfather as portrayed in some Victorian literature – who provided a large measure of the balance and solidness largely missing from his wife's character.

We have only glimpses of Henry Talbot in the first years of his life. The first anecdote about him – the recollection of which is attributed to an aunt, Lady Harriet Frampton – concerns the four-year-old Talbot whose nurse complained that 'Master Talbot was very naughty and nothing she could do would please him. I have sat down my Lady and stood up but nothing would satisfy him.' Upon which the child appealed to his mother, 'Mamma, Betty will not turn on her axis! I have begged her to do so over and over again but she will not understand.'

The earliest surviving letters sent over Henry's own name – though in his mother's handwriting – date from 1805. It is difficult of course to separate the amount of inspiration they drew from mother as distinct from son, but there are some topics – references to natural history, calculations, an awareness of the value of money, an interest in travel – which are recognizably the marks of Henry Talbot if his letters in more mature life are used as a guide.

In 1806, again initially via his mother's pen, Henry began keeping a journal. Although the final entry was dated 1811, the journal contained frequent entries only until mid-1808 but none the less it presents a graphic picture of Henry Talbot's last two pre-school years – his relations with his mother, their travels, his likes and dislikes and the famous people he met.

[Monday, 20 October 1806 at Penrice]
Wrote two tenses of the word *avoir*, & six Latin & French words. Did a sum in compound subtraction & another in compound multiplication & *proved* them. Read 2 chapters of the Roman History. Looked in the map of Ancient Italy for Latium and Hetruria. Counted in French up to 100. Wrote four lines in the Writing Book. Translated part of the French Fable about le garçon & le Papillon.

[Tuesday, 21 October]
Wrote 3 lines of the Multiplication Table [This was the first entry in Henry's own hand] ... Danced with Mr Hart extremely well.

[Wednesday, 29 April 1807 in the West Country]
Talked to Mamma about the Parliament being dissolved. Asked her a great many questions about it.

[Thursday, 9 July at Plymouth Docks]
Got up – not very well. Mr Little came & said I read too much & sat still too much.

[Sunday, 13 September]
Mr F went to Plymouth to sail away, perhaps to Cape Finisterre. Took a walk . . . through a kind of a Forest by the river & gathered water cresses, Nuts & Honeysuckles.

[Wednesday, 23 September]
Played at the Verb game, it was avoir & aimer & I won two pence halfpenny from Mamma.

[6 November]
Did a recreation in optics 3 times, it was to put a shilling in a glass of water & to turn it over upon a plate & there will be a half-crown at the bottom of the water and a shilling floating at the top.

[31 March 1808]
Went to Laycock[sic] Abbey. Did not like it. [He did not like Blenheim either but did like Windsor.]

[1 May at Oxford]
Saw All Souls library. Ran about in it. There was an orrery in it exactly like the real solar system, as the Moon went round the Earth in 28 Days. There was a large terrestrial & a large celestial Globe. Saw two very curious pieces of Papyrus with some Arabic written upon them.

[Wednesday, 4 May at Windsor]
Went to Dr Herschell's, he was at Bath. Saw his sister Miss Herschell. She shewed us his telescopes. They were exactly in my opinion like Cannons, only bigger. [This visit would have been to Slough, the home of William Herschel, the famous astronomer who in 1781 discovered the planet Uranus. He was knighted in 1816. His sister Caroline was an important collaborator in his work for many years.]

[22 June in London]
Cast up the number of miles I have travelled in my life to be 3219 & this is the three thousand and fifty second day of my life.

[Tuesday, 19 July]
Went with Mamma to Windsor. Walked on the Terrace & spoke to the King [George III] & the Princess Augusta & the Princess Sophia.

Within the covers of the journal are references to most of the subjects which were to figure in Henry Talbot's later life: languages (ancient and modern), mathematics, politics, natural history – particularly botany, optics, astronomy

(the contact with the Herschel family was to blossom into a scientific relationship with the brilliant Sir John Herschel, son of William Herschel), and of
course Lacock Abbey. There was a pointer to the future in the comment that
Henry 'read too much and sat still too much'. As a testimony to his application
and the seriousness with which he approached his studies, this and similar
comments that followed in later years are quite accurate. But it should not be
imagined that Henry was the archetypal 'swot' who lived only for work,
praise and achievement, made no friends, and had no regard for the somewhat
more enjoyable side of life. If he tackled work with verve and energy, so he
did buns, cakes, a game of bows and arrows or sea-bathing when the mood
took him and he had no problems in making friendships when schooldays
arrived. The small boy who went off to preparatory school in the spring of
1808 was to enjoy life and inevitably to do well.

The establishment of the Reverend Thomas R. Hooker at Rottingdean in
Sussex was a small school for boys where the classics, mathematics and French
were well taught. Starting school was a wrench for both Lady Elisabeth and
Henry, so Hooker made the change easier by allowing Henry for a few weeks
to go home to his mother in the evenings (Lady Elisabeth had taken a house
temporarily at Brighton) before coming into full-time residence. It did not
take the headmaster long to realize the calibre of his new student. On 20 May
1808 he wrote to Lady Elisabeth: 'He seems to be of a very sweet & amiable
disposition and . . . I have not a moment's hesitation in pronouncing him to
be of very superior capacity . . .' – but then, apparently somewhat apprehensive at Henry's intense application to his work, added: '. . . everything should
be done to induce him to play more and think less'.[3] Henry Talbot was never
one of those intellectually gifted people who coasted on their native talents –
or at least never for very long.

He quickly settled down and within a matter of days was writing lively
letters to his mother outlining the school routine (lessons in the morning only),
describing games of trapball and cricket, and recording his pleasure in looking
forward both to her visits and the commencement of bathing in the sea. At
the end of one letter he added a request to Charles Feilding of great significance
and one scarcely comprehensible in a boy of eight years: 'Tell Mamma &
everybody I write to to keep my letters & not burn them.'[4] Most of the
family fulfilled this request throughout his entire life with obvious implications for our understanding of that life and his work.

With a delightful juxtaposition of schoolboy comment and more profound observation, he told his mother on one occasion: 'I have had another v.v.g. in the report . . . send me a plum cake,'[5] and a few days later, 'Bathing goes on very well with me . . . the history of the Jews is very amusing.'[6] On 4 June 1809 he recorded with obvious delight: 'I am very happy here. Mr Hooker praises me very much. He says I have done exercises for a whole month without his correcting a single word which he never did to any other boy before; my lessons are very easy.'[7]

His enthusiastic application to maths was indicated by a note in the already quoted journal (for 14 March 1809): 'Got up early to be ready for Mr Waulthier. He taught me to define circles & triangles & parallel lines & angles & tangents and radii, besides hypotenuses, sectors and secants.' Politics were discussed between mother and son and in April 1810 Henry required a detailed account from Lady Elisabeth of the causes for the riots accompanying the despatch of Sir Francis Burdett to the Tower of London for 'libel on the House of Commons'.*

By the time of his last year at Rottingdean, Lady Elisabeth and Henry were exchanging letters in fluent French, interspersed with Latin and Greek. In a letter dated 7 March 1811 Henry translated a Greek maxim sent to him by his mother and proceeded to give more than a side of Latin with Greek and French by way of conclusion.[8] Lady Elisabeth was delighted: 'Your ready translation of my Greek maxim proves how *beautifully* I must have formed the characters, which I was afraid would have turned out only *Hieroglyphics*. It is quoted by Aristotle in his Rhetoric as an example . . .'[9]

The Reverend Thomas Hooker had no reservations about the young Talbot's future:

[I have] . . . seldom met his equal & never in points of abilities. . . . In addition to the Promise his great powers give earnest of, I have no doubt he will also turn out a most excellent character & a good man, of which, I fully am convinced there is the most happy prospect.[10]

With this encouragement in his ears, the eleven-year-old Talbot set out to Harrow on the Hill.

Harrow School in 1811 was attended by about 200 boys and the individual annual fee was the not inconsiderable sum of approximately £80. The boys

* Burdett was a radical M.P. who long before 1832 was proposing parliamentary reform. The immediate occasion for his committal to the Tower was his denunciation of a House of Commons decision which imprisoned another radical for contempt.

were divided into a number of houses and regulations were relatively relaxed, depending upon a housemaster's attitude. Henry Talbot joined the house of George Butler – headmaster from 1805 to 1829 – who was a brilliant scholar and had been Senior Wrangler (that is first in the mathematical honours list), first Smith's Prizeman and Chancellor's Medallist at Cambridge. The school concentrated on giving a good grounding in writing, mathematics, foreign languages and the classics but Butler, who had considerable talent for the physical sciences, sometimes lectured on these subjects (and including chemistry) to his 'private pupils'.

Talbot was intensely miserable when he first came into residence in July of 1811. On 12 July he wrote a heart-rending letter to his mother:

> I cannot help crying while I write this letter . . . O, I hope Mr Feilding or you will soon come & see me . . . you know not how many many ages seem to me to have been included in one single day! . . . [I hope] you may never be so sorrowful and ennuyé as I am at present.[11]

But within a week or so and after a visit by Charles Feilding – which resolved a problem of incompatibility with those sharing a room with Henry – he had settled down.

A good picture of Talbot's years at Harrow comes from the letters and from the account book which he kept religiously. Through them can be seen the sports and pastimes in which Henry indulged with varying energy and success – marbles, pegtops, rackets, cricket, football, ice skating and chess; his taste in foods and sweets ('fruit and cakes this month 8s. 10d.' and 'mutton chops 4s. 2d.'); his progress to higher things in the later years ('Annals of Philosophy No. 1 – 2s. 6d.'); and a brief excursion into gambling ('pack of cards 6d.' and 'lost at cards 6d.') which was morally balanced by gifts of 6d. or 1s. to a 'poor man' or 'poor woman', as well as by more substantial gifts to his old nurse Betty Vickery.

Talbot fitted well into school life and made friends. Perhaps the closest was Perceval (Jr), a young son of the Tory Prime Minister Spencer Perceval. Another in the early months was Lord Brudenell (son of Lord Cardigan). Although he was only of small-to-average build, Talbot was not afraid to stand out against bullies and he did so when his Welsh cousin Christopher Rice Mansel Talbot ('Kit') came to Harrow in 1814. Kit was 'fathered' generally by Henry who, for example, made sure he had enough to eat.[12]

c

During his time at Harrow two major interests – chemistry and botany, which both fell outside the school curriculum – developed rapidly. Talbot had enjoyed chemistry before going up to the school but it was there that the subject took a serious hold on him, doubtless encouraged (initially at least) by Dr Butler. His account books record numerous chemical purchases, and one of his first letters to Lady Elisabeth once his misery had passed in July 1811 included a long shopping list for equipment and chemicals which had been lost or damaged. He proceeded to enjoy himself immensely. His pleasure was not to continue, however, for in a letter dated 24 May 1812 Henry revealed that something had gone wrong. He referred to a note which Lady Elisabeth had written to Dr Butler about chemistry and went on:

> Cannot you imagine how disagreeable it must be to have a *master* privy to one's *secrets*? Either he will not allow me to amuse myself for fear of my making dangerous experiments or he will be talking to me about it before other boys who plague one to death about it . . .[13]

Lady Elisabeth later explained to her sister Mary Talbot the reason for Henry's 'Chemical misfortunes':

> . . . as he can no longer continue his experiments in Dr Butler's House, he resorts to a good-natured Blacksmith who lets him explode as much as he pleases. He makes 'Pulvis fulminans', and I am quite nervous at the thought of the risks he must run with Nitre [*] and Sulphur and Potash. He has been trying to gild steel with a solution of Nitromuriate of Gold.[†] *This* was the *fatal* experiment which *blew him up* at Dr Butler's as it exploded with the noise of a pistol and attacked the olfactory nerves of the whole Household. Dr B was alarmed and declared the Sun Fire Office would not ensure his house for a single day.[14]

Butler in fact subsequently offered Henry Talbot the use of his chemical books but was adamant that henceforward only the theory of chemistry was to be studied at Harrow School. The boy soon recovered his spirits and his account book shows regular payments to the blacksmith, so presumably the head-master's edict proved to be nothing more than a nuisance.

'Botanizing' was a widely practised pastime of the period and the Talbots and the Fox-Strangways were enthusiasts. Henry caught the enthusiasm. He relished many of the facets of Nature and wrote well about them from his early years:

---

* Potassium nitrate (saltpetre).

† A solution of gold in a mixture of nitric acid and hydrochloric acid.

This place [Harrow] begins to enliven itself at last, the hedges look greenish, and I find some flowers here viz – daisies, giltcups, primroses, sweet scented blue and white violets, and to my great joy, blue bells, and common Arum.[15]

Typically, while deriving enjoyment from botany, Henry Talbot regarded it as a most serious subject for study. He and a friend W. C. (later Sir Walter) Trevelyan prepared an index of the flora of the Harrow area. Talbot seized with alacrity the opportunity to meet experts – for example the eminent Welsh scientist and naturalist Dillwyn,* of whom, wise beyond years, he said: 'There is so much to be learned of such a man. Especially when joined to a very obliging disposition.'[16] Dillwyn in return was obviously impressed with young Talbot. His rapid accumulation of botanical knowledge and his philosophical approach, even at the age of fourteen, indicated his potential calibre.† It was a subject which was to provide Talbot with great enjoyment throughout his entire life – and his contribution to it is evaluated in a later chapter.

It is fascinating to observe Henry Talbot's character developing in the record of his Harrow days. One of the most important traits was a firmness, even a toughness of spirit revealed in his refusal to be bullied, in his preparedness as a young boy of eleven (and younger) to make a coach journey alone from South Wales to London, and in his attitude to inadequate service. The same spirit was revealed in the forcefulness with which he entered into discussion with adults. He argued strongly against his mother's (and the Holland family's) lenient views on Napoleon – he was simply 'mean and cowardly' to Henry – and on another occasion when Lady Elisabeth had asked for details of an exacting coach journey, he replied shortly: 'I must reserve them till we meet, for I have described them so fully to Aunt Mary that I really cannot describe them again.'[17]

---

* Lewis Weston Dillwyn, F.R.S., M.P. (1778–1855). He was the father of John Dillwyn Llewelyn who married Emma Talbot – one of Henry's Welsh cousins – and who was one of the most talented of the early photographic pioneers.

† Talbot wrote to his mother on 16 September 1814 . . . '[botany] is a science which extends pretty far & which by no means consists entirely of nomenclature. It affords excellent exercise to the powers of discrimination, & practices the memory very much. I am sure that I shall find Euclid much easier, after having accustomed myself as I do here, to the attentive examination of plants, in the descriptions of which, every term & expression must be well weighed in the mind, & thoroughly understood. Far from there being no *mind* in it, I think if you . . . ever read Smith's Introduction to Botany, you must confess that there *is* something more to Botany than to know every plant when you see it. Aunt Mary says there is a difference between a philosophical & a *stupid* botanist. The variety of wonderful contrivances which Nature employs for the protection of the flower, & due ripening of the seeds &c. excite one's admiration at every step, & though not so useful, Botany is as engaging as any science I have yet read about.'

He got on well with George Butler but did not hesitate to criticize him – for example in taking more boys into his house at Harrow than he had studies for or for his 'mistaken strictness' which amounted in the twelve-year-old Talbot's view to 'a sort of pleasure in punishing'. When the ladies fussed about his health, he assured them that all was well and doubtless did precisely just as he wanted. (A tactic he was to use many times thereafter.) What might be described as a certain low schoolboy cunning or simply caution was evident on occasion but there also grew a quiet, frequently delightful sense of humour. In one very brief letter, he described a theme he was working on at school: 'It is about frugality – so I shall be frugal of my writing' – and promptly concluded the letter.[18]

His greatest pleasure during these years was undoubtedly to go to Penrice – whence returning to Harrow was 'like leaving the Garden of Eden'. All of his long holidays were spent there and it was scarcely surprising that Jane Harriet, one of his Welsh cousins, should write after his return to school from one holiday: 'We all send our affection and love to our *seeming brother*'[19] and for Lady Elisabeth to threaten to remove his body from the Principality if he did not write more. In the background all this time was Charles Feilding, visiting Henry and writing wise words of guidance whenever they were required. The love which is so important to a child's development existed in another heart beside the maternal and those in Wales.

Talbot's academic performance at Harrow was outstanding. By the time he left at the age of fifteen he had spent over a year in the sixth form and had won at least eight prizes for academic excellence. Family tradition has it that Butler requested Henry be taken away because if he stayed his academic achievements demanded that he be appointed head boy and the headmaster thought this was too heavy a responsibility for a boy of fifteen.

From November 1815 for one year Talbot was tutored – with two other pupils – by the Reverend F. Barnes at Ferrybridge near Castleford in Yorkshire. The experience was not a valuable one. Henry appeared to learn little and did not have much regard for Mr Barnes, although he appreciated his sermons which were 'short, clear and comprehensive' and the fact that he understood some Persian. Talbot also disliked his fellow pupils. However, he indulged in pony riding and shooting, which pleased his stepfather who believed firmly that Henry needed to take more exercise. During his time at Castleford Talbot spent at least six months away from the family – which he regretted – but exchanges of letters with his mother and others continued as a lively substitute for personal contact.

Without doubt the great event in 1816 for Talbot was his first trip abroad. Inevitably he kept a '*giornale*'[20] which revealed an excitement, an eye for detail and powers of expression of a high order – qualities which his travel letters throughout life were never to lose. On Friday 19 April 1816 he wrote in the journal:

> Left Abbeville at half past seven, dined at Beauvais . . . Beauvais appears an exceedingly old town. All the roofs Vandycked, and whitewashed walls intersected with black beams: in the figure of X's and I's so as to resemble somewhat Roman numerals. Arrived at Beaumont sur Oise, good inn. Heard the frogs croaking, but had not any for supper.

In Paris he relished a visit to the opera 'in the Ambassador's box'; he watched a Mlle Garnerin make a balloon ascent and a parachute descent; was fascinated by the Bibliothèque Royale, the Jardin des Plantes, the gardens of the Little Trianon and Malmaison; and was cynically amused by French switches of allegiance between the Royalist and Napoleonic regimes as evidenced in the confused state of street names.

On the journey back to England with Charles Feilding – and less than one year after one of the most famous battles in history – he visited Waterloo:

> . . . A Flemish peasant was our guide, who [had] remained in his cottage during the battle – only in the cellar. Walked all over the field of battle, first to Hougoumont, which is in ruins, the door pierced with musket holes in every part. The musket balls which were lodged in the trees in the greatest abundance have been all carefully cut out for sale, & the trees themselves cut down. The cannon balls have made great holes in the garden walls, & in the fruit trees that grew against them. One shot went through two walls & killed seven men. Saw marks of blood on the wall. Only 25 English were killed in the *garden*, the French lost 600 in endeavouring to enter . . . The sabres, swords, helmets, cuirasses & other more valuable relics of the fray are now become scarce. Fresh arrivals of bullets & buttons from London to be sold on the field, warranted genuine . . . Returned to Brussels and dined again!

The return to Castleford in June 1816 must have been a severe anticlimax and a little later he wrote several long and serious letters to his mother emphasizing that he felt he could gain nothing further from Mr Barnes's instruction and that he could as well continue his studies on his own at home, which, in addition, would be considerably less expensive. His plea was only partly met and in January 1817 he went to study with the Reverend Mr Thomas Kaye Bonney at Normanton in Lincolnshire for the months remaining before he went up to university. Henry Talbot liked and respected Bonney very much and the two remained in contact for many years afterwards.

During this period, the emphasis of his own studies – apart from botany – was on optics and astronomy. He now had a microscope and the fact that he was shortsighted by this time presented no serious problems. Moreover, his self-confidence showed no sign of dimming. On 2 March 1817 he wrote to Lady Elisabeth to get Mr Feilding to compare his calculations of lunar eclipses with those of the Nautical Almanack.[21] His calculations were proved reasonably accurate and on its receipt he wrote further to Lady Elisabeth: 'The Nautical Almanack does not seem to be so correct as it was in Dr Maskelyne's time, for I detected three indubitable errors . . .'[22]

By 1817, the two girls born to Charles Feilding and Lady Elisabeth were nine years and seven years old respectively. Caroline Augusta was somewhat in the mould of her mother while Henrietta Horatia Maria was a born romantic. Between them and their half brother was a deep bond of affection from the very beginning. They vied for his favours and sought to impress him with the fluency of their French and the speed with which they assimilated his teaching on astronomy, botany and a hundred other subjects. Horatia sent verses to her half brother on the occasion of his seventeenth birthday:

O! my little brother dear,
Whether you be far or near,
Still the love between us brings
The fresh stream which ever springs.

Obviously her mother had expressed an opinion on the verses for Horatia added: '*Mamma croit que les lignes sont très mauvaises, néanmoins elle m'a donné permission de vous les envoyer.*'[23]

However, more serious events were in the offing. A few months later Lady Elisabeth expressed a wish that he were going to Oxford. When Henry asked why, she replied – referring to Cambridge's great strength in mathematics:

You seem so mathematically inclined that I ought . . . to send you to Oxford to counteract it, that you may not grow into a rhomboidal shape, walk elliptically, or go off in a tangent – all of which evils are imminent if you go to Cambridge.[24]

But Cambridge – at Trinity College – it was to be.

Lady Elisabeth's misgivings about the 'evils' of mathematics at Cambridge are explained by the fact that the only means of securing a B.A. honours degree, as Talbot planned, was to sit the mathematical tripos. Such was the extent to which mathematics dominated the studies of undergraduates.

The examination for the mathematical tripos lasted for a total of five days in the 1820s. Three days were devoted to the mathematical papers, including the books of Euclid, principles of algebra, plane and spherical trigonometry, conic sections, mechanics, hydrostatics, optics, astronomy, Newton's *Principia* and the principles of 'fluxions' (calculus); one day to logic, moral philosophy and aspects of Christianity; and the fifth day to 'brackets' – when undergraduates could challenge their placing in the list of honours which were based on merit. The examination was held each January in the frequently freezing Senate House and Henry Talbot before his examination in 1821 mused how thereby 'the University in its wisdom has added corporeal to mental fatigue'.[25]

Mathematics was undergoing fundamental changes at this time. In 1666 Newton had revolutionized the subject by the invention of the infinitesimal calculus – a system which then, and in its evolutionary form since, presented a vital instrument for the analysis of, for example, motion. The Newtonian system of *fluxional* calculus was rivalled on the continent of Europe by the *differential* calculus of Leibniz (1646–1716) which led to an intense dispute lasting for many years on the priority of the discovery. The continental methods were rejected by English mathematicians who regarded them as an attempt to defraud the great Newton of the credit for his invention. Newton's followers continued to employ geometrical proofs whenever possible which led to ingenious solutions but required a separate form of demonstration for every class of problem, whereas the system of analysis practised by Leibniz and his followers produced more general processes. The notation (or symbols) of Newton's fluxional calculus was cumbersome and vastly inferior to that of Leibniz's system and the latter was thus better suited for most purposes. European mathematicians – and in particular those in France, Germany, Switzerland and Russia – moved ahead rapidly while in England the misplaced devotion to Newton's genius resulted in the stagnation of new mathematical ideas.

The results of this isolation came to be realized as the first decade of the nineteenth century progressed. Robert Woodhouse, who subsequently was to become the Lucasian Professor of Mathematics at Cambridge University, made the first important move in 1803 by publishing *Principles of Analytical Calcu-*

lation in which he adopted the brilliant tactic of support for the differential notation generally but criticism of some of the methods pursued by individual continental mathematicians. The major assault on the Newtonian system of notation, however, came with the formation at Cambridge of the Analytical Society in 1812 by three undergraduates – George Peacock (1791–1858) who was to spend a lifetime teaching mathematics; Charles Babbage (1792–1871) who became a brilliant scientific experimenter – inventing an analytical machine or *computer* – and who played a prominent role in the later formation of both the Astronomical Society and the British Association for the Advancement of Science; and John F. W. (later Sir John) Herschel (1792–1871), a brilliant son of a brilliant father, who devoted himself mainly to astronomy and chemistry and who was to become one of Talbot's most frequent scientific correspondents and firmest supporters.

The Analytical Society's publication of foreign mathematical texts and open demands that the isolation of English mathematics should be ended gradually had their effect. By the time Henry Talbot took his degree in 1821, the battle to take Britain into Europe mathematically had been won so far as the more progressive and the younger mathematicians were concerned, though the move presented difficulties in adaptation for some. Henry himself could see the advantages of both systems – but it is significant that shortly before sitting the tripos he told Charles Feilding that he had hit upon a 'new & very curious' method in *fluxions* which he intended to develop when he had time.[26]

Henry Talbot's mathematical tutor at Trinity College was John Brown, a man of firm religious beliefs ('a zealous evangelical' according to one view[27]), who was greatly liked and respected for his friendliness, the continual encouragement he extended to his students and his skill as a teacher of mathematics. Talbot himself wrote little about his mathematical studies at Cambridge but fortunately J. M. F. Wright, a near contemporary at Trinity, recorded[28] a sympathetic and somewhat endearing picture of John Brown's teaching style:

The hour of nine having now arrived, we again assembled in the Mathematical-Lecture room. Being seated, Mr B again went over the names, and praised our punctuality, there being not one absentee. After which, he asked, first one & then another, the several definitions of a point, a straight line, a curved line, a triangle, a square, a parallelogram, a pentagon, a circle &c and these questions being answered, with not more than fifty blunders, he came upon your humble servant with, Mr W. what is meant by an axiom?

'An axiom, Sir' (quoth I), 'is a truth so evident, that its terms need only be expressed in language, to be universally understood and admitted'.

'Very good, Sir, although not precisely in the language of Euclid. But what is the first axiom of Euclid, or of geometry, as I may say, the terms being synonymous?'

'Things which are equal to the same, are equal to one another'.

'Very good, Sir! What the second, & what the third?' And so on.

The family was on the Continent for much of the four years Henry was at Cambridge. On several occasions Talbot paid them very brief visits (during one of which he met the great explorer von Humboldt in Paris) but his time, when not at university, was spent mostly on the fashionable 'reading' holidays with friends and a tutor, although he did take a strenuous holiday in the Lake District in 1818 which made him a lover of the area for life.

Talbot's interest in the world of science and discovery – minor and major – continued unabated. He wrote on one occasion in a very critical manner about the 'ludicrous' fad for 'Calleidoscopes' at the University[29] and was much more interested in studies of the effects of iron in a ship's hull and guns upon a compass[30] or on the alleged discovery of perpetual motion.[31]

Whether at home or abroad, Lady Elisabeth was keeping her son informed of political developments. Henry commented unemotionally on the reported level of casualties at the 'massacre of Peterloo' in Manchester,* but Lady Elisabeth's Whig spirits rose in her breast and she denounced the Manchester magistrates (who instructed the military to disperse the gathering) for having 'lit a *flame*' which would spread from 'one end of the Kingdom to the other but [who] seem not at all afraid of a Revolution, tho' the French are all persuaded we are on the eve of one . . .'[32]

The crisis which arose following the recently crowned George IV's attempt in 1820 to free himself of his wife Queen Caroline was another major subject of discussion – and on which Lady Elisabeth could report from the centre of things since she was at that time in London. With that typical family touch for switching subjects abruptly, she wrote to Henry on 4 November 1820:

I find all the world agog about the Queen . . . The House of Lords is still debating. If any Peer brings any news before the bell goes, I will add it . . . Lady Sheffield has just been here & desires me to say she is affronted with you for not dining with her.[33]

Charles Feilding also discussed political matters but his most significant

* In August 1819 a massive rally of workers took place in St Peter's Field, Manchester to listen to the radical Orator Hunt. The crowd was dispersed with the death of eleven people and over 400 wounded. The use of the name 'Peterloo' was intended as a bitter reflection on the casualties suffered.

letters concerned Henry's progress at Cambridge and his approach to life. In August 1818 he gently chided his stepson on not calling on Lord Winchelsea (Feilding's uncle) and went on:

My old dictum is a very good one & I wish you would always remember it. 'La politesse conte peu & rend beaucoup' . . . You are in so many respects exactly what my fondest hopes could wish that I cannot bear to be teazing you about the very few in which you hardly meet my ideas of what you should be but I will not let this letter go without one bit of advice – to watch yourself carefully on the score of self-indulgence. You are a little apt I think to consider too much how any proposal will affect yourself & not enough how other people may be affected by your complying with it. In this world one must give as well as take & if you like (as every one must) that others should sometimes derange themselves to accommodate you, you must pay the price occasionally of deranging yourself to accommodate them. I have said quite enough I am sure to turn your thoughts to the subject & your good sense will do the rest. God bless you.[34]

Lighter relief was provided by the effervescent letters from the rapidly growing girls Caroline and Horatia who were being tutored in music, dancing and languages* and who continued in their friendly rivalry for Henry's approbation: 'Horatie a également des fleurs pour toi, mais je ne crois pas qu'elles soient si rares que les miennes.'[35]

But the serious business was academic achievement. Talbot took a first class in his freshmen's college examination in 1818 (as he did in the following two years) and in 1819 passed from the status of a pensioner to a scholar. He appreciated the much better dinner he obtained in hall at the scholars' table but not the duties of reading grace to the Fellows of the College after dinner and supper and even less so reading lessons in chapel at 7 o'clock on a snowy morning which was 'no joke'.[36] Better things still were to follow in 1820. Talbot sat for and won the Porson University Prize in Greek verse. He wrote with 'pleasure' to give Charles Feilding the good news while Lady Elisabeth predictably congratulated both Henry and herself on his success – 'I hope to make a wreath for my maternal brow'.[37]

Expectations for Henry's performance in his final examination were high from the beginning and Feilding stated on at least one occasion that he believed

---

* About this time, a Frenchwoman, Amélina Petit de Billier, joined the Feildings as governess. Later, after several years' absence in France, she was to accept a position as governess to Henry Talbot's daughters and remain with the family, very much part of it, as companion to Constance and the girls. She died one year before Henry Talbot and was buried in Lacock cemetery.

Her diary is in the Lacock Collection.

his stepson would become Senior Wrangler (that is absolute first) in 1821. Talbot was, however, placed twelfth in the list and it was a measure of what achievements were expected of him that there was a sense of disappointment in the family about the result. If he were disappointed himself, Talbot kept it well hidden for on the back of the list sent to Charles Feilding he commented that he was very well pleased with the place he had secured because he had not liked the examination.[38]

In March 1821 Henry entered for one of the two Chancellor's Classical Medals which were awarded to 'commencing' bachelors of arts who made 'the best appearance in classical learning'. He secured the second medal but there was criticism from his family of his coming second, for on 8 April he wrote to Feilding:

> I am sorry you should think my failure owing to not getting up early and working hard. On the contrary, I never passed a better examination. If you ask then how Ollivant beat me, I tell you honestly I don't know. I think I did the best . . . The examiners did not give the grounds of their decision; they never do . . . I don't quarrel with the examiners, they are very fair and honorable, they decide as they think right; If I thought Ollivant superior to myself, I would be the first to say so, and I would do all in my power to beat him at the fellowship examination, but as it is, I will never try again & have no doubt you will think it best. I have now told you honestly what I think about it; I expected the result & felt much more indifferent about it, than I should once have done . . .
>
> I told you in my last letter that I have been solacing myself with my astronomy. There is nothing like having two or three different pursuits pour se délasser when anything goes wrong . . .[39]

Talbot's explanation of his performance is open and honest and sympathy must be felt for a man who achieved so much and who yet apparently disappointed his family deeply and perhaps himself to some degree. A more reliable assessment of Henry's achievements and attitudes soon after he went down from Cambridge is provided by an unknown person who wrote an evaluation of the young man:

> We have rather a remarkable young man here, a Mr Talbot, a Wiltshire gentleman of independent fortune. He was high in the list of Wranglers at Cambridge, Hallam shewed me his Greek prize exercise which had struck him, a very competent judge, with its extraordinary merit. He is rather *unlicked*, but that don't signify. We have fine gentlemen enough. He is very laborious, not so much I think out of vanity or even ambition as from the mere love of what he is acquiring. He has an innate love of knowledge and rushes towards it as an otter does to a pond. He bids fair to be a distinguished man.[40]

The opinion is shrewd and frank and presents a convincing portrait of the young man by an outsider not subject to the fiercely critical bias of Talbot's loved ones.

For much of the decade of the 1820s Henry Talbot travelled extensively in Europe and there were several years when he was in England for a few weeks only. The Feildings too were absent on the Continent a great deal so that Henry's stepfather was not present to oversee the sound running of the estate. This was, however, in good hands, for in 1820–1 W. Henry Awdry – who had been involved with the conduct of the estate during the young man's minority – was appointed steward. Awdry gave years of excellent and loyal service to Henry Talbot during times of great distress in Lacock. Indeed, although no major decisions were taken without reference to Charles Feilding in the early years or to Henry Talbot thereafter, Awdry's counsel was normally followed and the subsequent absence of riots and disturbances in the area of the village was due in great measure to the compassionate policies he recommended.

Awdry's aim throughout his stewardship – and despite occasional complaints from Talbot about costs – was to keep the hundred or so cottages and other buildings of the estate as well repaired as possible and to consolidate the area of the manor. Thus he advised against the idea of selling any of the properties in the village: better to wait till the occupants in badly deteriorating buildings could be re-housed, then knock them down, sell the materials and rent the gardens to the adjoining properties with a proportionate increase in rent.

> By this Plan, I consider that the present crowded state of the village may be gradually reduced without distressing the inhabitants – the *value* of the Property retained & no inconvenience to Mr Talbot from having other landlords in the village . . .[41]

Similarly he advised against changing any of the houses from a rented to a leasehold occupancy as a means of reducing the heavy annual repair charges, realizing that, in the depressed state of the village, few if any tenants would or could accept responsibility for repairs. He also recommended the sale of property outside Lacock, and purchase of property near by.*

* In addition, Awdry dealt with all the details of building a new village school to mark Henry Talbot's coming of age. The school was completed in 1824.

Prosperity was at a low level for much of the 1820s in Lacock but some years – for example 1822 – were extremely severe. The farmers were in great difficulty and Awdry agreed to their rents being paid in instalments. He and the family's solicitor W. Read King proposed to Talbot that rents should temporarily be reduced by between 5 and 15 per cent. 'I know of no estate,' Read King wrote, 'where the rents are better paid than they are upon yours & it would be so longer than in most cases, for your tenants have never been racked to the fullest extent – nevertheless they cannot pay as they have done.'[42] Awdry's concern for the tenants' situation was again in evidence: he noted that prices for the farmers continued very low and that sales were exceedingly dull so that 'nothing but great patience on the part of landlords can enable them to go on at all'. However, payments were coming in 'and while we can continue to do so in *these* times it will be a great proof of the responsibility of the present tenants'.[43]

Talbot could agree to the rent reductions with a relatively easy mind since, unmarried and with relatively few family responsibilities at this time, he was enjoying his new-found wealth. But his outgoings too were fairly high for the approximate cost of one of his more extensive foreign trips (to Corfu in 1826) was £500. However, the general economic situation remained difficult throughout the decade, and by about 1830 Awdry was having problems in finding new tenants for any farms which became free and was apologizing for the slow manner in which the rents were being paid.

Early in 1824 Talbot was beginning to think about the future at Lacock, and he wrote to Feilding after a meeting at the Abbey with Awdry:

The view from the top of Bowden Hill struck me very much. I was rather disappointed in the Avon, but I have no doubt that in summer it is a very rural stream. The Abbey I think is a fine old pile, the front next [to] the road is unfortunately much the plainest and defaced with *modern* windows *irregularly* placed . . . I don't think that I shall be inclined to renew (Grosset's) lease anymore, but that I should like to talk with you about and the time is long yet.[44]

In 1827 Grosset (whose lease had been renewed in 1821) suddenly announced that because of his wife's deteriorating health he intended to surrender the lease of the Abbey at midsummer and plans were made for a partial re-occupation by Talbot and the Feildings. The news quickly spread and a relative expressed delight at the move – adding the comment, which was entirely predictable with this family, that the highest priority should be attached to the appointment of a gardener. Lady Elisabeth visited the Abbey in November and wrote to Henry: 'The house looked so comfortable. As we walked in we were received by a great fire in the Hall which looked very feudal, as well as the nine servants who lined the steps as we came up & seemed so glad to see us . . .'[45] Once in residence Talbot's mother, in contrast to her feelings about the Abbey in earlier years, became progressively fonder of the building and expressed the view that if she had not to consider the travel and educational interests of her daughters Horatia and Caroline she would enjoy staying there all the year round.

True to the views he expressed on the Abbey's south front in 1824, Talbot ordered a reconstruction to begin in 1828. But when the alterations were partly completed his mother suggested they were too massive, too crude to benefit either the appearance of the Abbey or the comfort of those who were to live there. Her son accepted the advice and the result was the completion in 1831 of the present South Gallery – an alteration met with universal approbation and summed up best by an ecstatic Horatia: 'The Gallery looks so gay . . . the sun comes in again.'[46]

The presence of Lady Elisabeth and the girls attracted a lively social life to the Abbey for by now Caroline and Horatia were eligible young ladies who entered fully into the glittering society of the times. Lady Elisabeth kept a notebook of the musical evenings, soirées and balls which she and the girls attended (including some which they themselves gave) and the list of guests read like a who's who of royalty and the nobility. Horatia wrote breathlessly to her half brother on 29 August 1828: 'I was very much amused at the balls and had more partners than I could dance with.'[47] Lady Elisabeth observed on a later occasion that 'Lady Grey was to have had a soirée but put it off for fear of being crushed by ours,'[48] while a few days later on 23 July 1830 Caroline wrote to Henry:

We are just returned, tired to death, from seeing the King go to prorogue the Parliament, after having sat up & danced yesterday at Devonshire House, the night before at Almacks & the night before that at the Duchess of Bedford's . . .[49]

Horatia perhaps best suggested the sparkling and enjoyable life being led by the girls when she related an incident at a hunt they attended on the way back from a trip to the Midlands:

We saw lots of people we know. Amongst others Lord Wilton, Lord Alvanley, Col. Arden, Mr Ricardo, Lord Graham, Lord Castlereagh, Mr Gilmour and many other distinguished fashionables as the Morning Post wd say. It seemed quite absurd to see all these London faces popping up in the middle of a ploughed field & you may suppose how surprised *they* were at our unexpected appearance.[50]

Henry Talbot attended some of the social occasions both in town and the country with apparent enjoyment, but certain tendencies were already clear – tendencies which were to be accentuated in the years ahead. He could mix easily with people but he increasingly chose to reduce social contact. This was even the case with his family to some degree – going about his own interests and pursuits, holidaying alone and showing every indication of preferring to be alone. In some ways that may be regarded as no more than a normal adjustment on the part of a young man with many developing interests as he grew away from the immediate bosom of a very possessive family. But as he came to identify the subjects of his future researches, he steadily rejected more and more the waste of time inherent in social gatherings and was frequently absent from his family – mother and halfsisters and later wife and daughters – so that he might concentrate with undivided attention and have the appropriate facilities for experimentation. This single-mindedness in no way affected his continuing love for his dear ones. It did result, however, in a limitation upon his willingness to participate actively in affairs in which he had no essential interest. The running of Lacock Abbey and his estate was a prime example of this and was why the support of a capable steward was so important.

Talbot did his duty by his parishioners of Lacock and he viewed their problems with a fair mind and some sympathy. But it is unlikely that he ever did anything more in Lacock than he considered it his absolute duty so to do. He took little if any lead in initiating measures – although there was no doubting his capability when the spirit moved. In February 1830, for example, Lady Elisabeth reported to him Awdry's pleasure – amazement might have been a more appropriate word – at discovering during a meeting at the village that 'you had conducted yourself *in the chair* like an experienced man of business', even if subsequent events were to confirm repeatedly her earlier belief that her son had 'the native distaste' for business *per se* which characterized all her family.[51]

Between 1821 and 1830 there were only perhaps four years when Henry Talbot spent appreciable periods of time in England. He visited France, Switzerland, Italy, Belgium, Austria, several of the German states and made a lengthy botanical trip to Corfu.[52] From the beginning Talbot revealed himself as a consummate writer of travel letters, with a sharp eye for detail, a good-hearted sense of humour, a keen interest in the different customs of his hosts and above all an eye for beauty in nature and man's creations which is not uncommon amongst talented classicists.

His expedition to Corfu in 1826 was undoubtedly one of the major experiences in his life. He came close to the theatre of conflict between the Greeks and the Turks but his mind was on other things:

My first impressions of the island are so various and so novel, everything is so striking, so much of beauty & sublime, that I know not where to begin . . . It amuses me to hear the little children talk Greek and I find I understand a good deal, which is more than I expected. There is an air of improvement so apparent in this colony under the benign influence of British Protection . . . The streets are full of British soldiers, slovenly Greeks and picturesque Albanians . . . I took refuge today from a storm under an olive which had seen several centuries, and close to a hedge, not formed of thorns, but of a singular mixture of weeping willows, scarlet African Geraniums in flower, immense artichokes, that a man might hide in, and tall branching cactuses. Europe jumbled with Africa . . .[53]

The rugged beauty of the region appealed immensely to him and on one occasion, revealing the feeling for composition and subtle lighting effects which was to stand him in good stead when taking photographs more than a decade later, he wrote to his mother:

I wish Claude[*] were here to take a view for me, from the lighthouse of Zante at sunset. I never saw so perfect a view, for generally in real views, something is too much or too little, but with this view the most critical judgment must be contented. The same view looks nothing in the morning when the light falls the wrong way . . .[54]

Talbot showed a considerable interest in painting at this time. On the way back from Corfu, he visited his uncle William Thomas Horner Fox-Strangways† (Lady Elisabeth's half brother) who was Secretary of the British Legation in Florence. Fox-Strangways (who was later to succeed as the fourth

* Claude Lorrain (1600–82) was a French landscape painter who worked and died in Rome. An essential ingredient of his style was an 'all-pervading light'.
† Fox-Strangways (1795–1865) was a career diplomat who was also a considerable botanist and geologist, being elected F.R.S. in 1821 at the age of twenty-six. He was a prolific writer of letters which – besides botany, geology and science generally – were full of politics, gossip and some scandal. He also had a sardonic sense of humour, so if he had been aware of it, he would have relished Caroline Feilding's comment about him: '[Uncle William] . . . who likes flowers better than men, & stones better than flowers.'[55]

Earl of Ilchester) was building up a collection of Italian paintings, many of which he later gave to Christ Church and the Ashmolean Museum at Oxford. His nephew caught the feeling of excitement and between 1826 and 1828 two copies of paintings by Correggio were purchased on Henry's behalf. In June 1826 Fox-Strangways wrote to his sister that 'We shall see a gallery at Lacock & the Cloisters painted in fresco.'[56] In fact there is no evidence that Talbot continued collecting paintings and it may be that the Correggios later passed into Fox-Strangways' collection.

Surprisingly Corfu was the furthest distance Henry Talbot ever went from England, despite repeated invitations from his cousin Kit (who was an inveterate yachtsman and who later had the distinction of owning the first private yacht ever to pass through the new Suez Canal) to join him on an expedition to the Holy Land and up the Nile. Even more surprising, Talbot never made a pilgrimage to the remnants of classical Greece.

The United Kingdom was by no means ignored by Talbot. He travelled widely, and on the first of what was to become many visits to Edinburgh he declared it 'truly picturesque'. Sometimes his experiences did not differ greatly from the present day, for on his first trip to Stonehenge 'the illusion was wholly destroyed by my finding assembled there, five carriages & thirty people, two tents pitched'.[57]

The expeditions abroad were far from mere rounds of pleasure. Talbot applied himself to learning languages and to his researches. His German greatly improved over the period and he commenced Hebrew. His excitement at the decipherment of Egyptian hieroglyphics suggests that he too had been studying the Rosetta Stone. In 1823 Henry wrote excitedly to Charles Feilding and pronounced emphatically that the discoveries of Dr Thomas Young and the Frenchman Jean François Champollion were 'most brilliant & indisputably certain'.[58]

The extent of Talbot's knowledge of hieroglyphics cannot now be established though it may have been considerable. He published no formal papers but in an essay which appeared in the late 1830s he quoted a passage of Champollion's translation from the Egyptian and commented: 'Anyone may satisfy himself that Champollion has correctly translated, as the passage offers no difficulty.'[59] More revealing is a letter dated 16 April 1826 which M. Jules de St Quintin, Curator of the Turin Museum, sent to Charles Feilding:

It is with great pleasure that I must tell you that not for a long time have I met a young man so knowledgeable and so accomplished as M. Talbot. I have been amazed by his

D

great learning and even more by his modesty. He is assured of both my deep esteem and my friendship . . . I can assure you that, apart from M. Champollion, I know no-one so well informed as M. Talbot in the new branch of learning.[60]

At some time Talbot collected a number of hieroglyphic tablets and these are now in the Museum at Lacock.

He continued his mathematical work with energy. At the Cambridge of Talbot's time, the work of the European mathematicians was being studied with enthusiasm but the Newtonian background still exerted its influence and for Talbot the extraction of analysis from geometry and mechanics was only just beginning. This was evident in the nature of the topics which appealed to him on coming down from the university. In his various notebooks – five from the period to 1830 have survived – there are many mathematical topics but the main emphasis was on curve analysis and the theory of numbers. In the 1820s and later he showed an intense care over the logic and validity of every step he took to establish a proof – this was the Newtonian legacy. However, at the same time he was ready – and this was the new Cambridge thinking – to adopt or to invent analytical techniques. Above all he was stimulated by the challenge of existing unsolved problems.

Soon after he came down, he was corresponding with J.-D. Gergonne, the editor of *Annales de Mathématiques Pures et Appliqués* and he continued for a few years as a frequent contributor to the *Annales* either solving or setting problems. One such problem, requiring a curve by means of which cube roots could be found geometrically and angles could be trisected, led to a curve (of the sixth degree in x and y) which went the rounds of the European mathematical journals as 'Talbot's Curve' and a generalized form of it was studied in some detail.[61] It also attracted the attention of the distinguished mathematicians Cayley and Salmon. Other problems solved by Talbot in the *Annales* (some of this mathematics for Gergonne was being done during his stays in Italy in 1822–3) dealt with the summation of certain infinite trigonometric series and with sections of a cone.

As the decade wore on, the contents of Talbot's notebooks contained an increasing proportion of mathematics – largely on the arcs of various curves. Some of this work showed considerable originality and there is no doubt that (though he did not publish) in certain areas Talbot anticipated the work of the brilliant Norwegian mathematician Abel – a subject more appropriately left for consideration in the context of Talbot's mathematical work in the 1830s (see Chapter 3).

Talbot quickly joined a number of scientific societies such as the Royal Institution, the Astronomical Society and the Zoological Society – from then on seeming to make a habit of forgetting to pay his membership dues – but he found it more difficult at first to make the acquaintance of British scientists than was the case with their foreign counterparts. He was a young man in a hurry but the position improved. He was introduced to the famous scientist Sir Humphry Davy; he exchanged the first of many letters with John Herschel whom he approached at first with deference; and via Herschel he made his first contact with David Brewster. He entered into correspondence with Dr Thomas Young who played a leading role in establishing the concept of the *undulatory* nature of light (as distinct from the Newtonian *corpuscular* concept) as well as in deciphering the Egyptian hieroglyphics. Also, he knew Michael Faraday at the Royal Institution well enough to invite John Herschel there to witness an experiment that the two were to carry out jointly.[62] Abroad, he worked for several weeks in 1825 at the Paris Observatory with its director François Arago (whose name was to be prominent in the early history of photography) and he renewed his acquaintance with Alexander von Humboldt. Although there is little written evidence, he clearly had some contact at this time with the brilliant German Josef von Fraunhofer who was involved in the practical design and manufacture of lenses which led in turn to certain fundamental researches into the nature of light. Indeed, through the good offices of his friend the Bavarian Ambassador, Talbot imported a number of lenses, prisms and other optical products from Fraunhofer's workshop – some of which were purchased on behalf of John Herschel while others were borrowed from Talbot by scientists at Cambridge University to use in their lectures on light and optics. When Fraunhofer died in 1826, Henry described it as an 'incalculable loss to science' and lamented that Fraunhofer's method of making flint glass 'will be lost to the world'.[63]

In addition to the emphasis on mathematics, Talbot's notebooks up to 1830 were largely concerned with research in optics (or light) and in astronomy. In Paris with Arago he conducted magnetic experiments, discussed the rival corpuscular–undulatory theories of light and the polarization of light (which was a major factor in the resolution of that controversy), as well as observing the planets and other astronomical objects. He made himself fully and swiftly aware of the work of foreign as well as British scientists – for example the researches into light by the brilliant Frenchman Augustin Fresnel and the chemical investigations of the Swede Berzelius – but he also had an eye for detail proposing possible improvements in the lens system of the camera lucida and in the practical use of the camera obscura. A significant trend of the early notebooks was the *relatively* limited attention paid to chemistry as such. He reported some chemical experiments at the Royal Institution in 1825 and elsewhere discussed atomic weights in the context of gases. But as revealed at least in the notebooks the emphasis on chemical experimentation was not to begin until later.

Judging from those notebooks Henry was not a *systematic* worker at the time. There is no impression of a comprehensive and yet detailed body of research, carefully annotated and cross-referenced to facilitate later work. The lack of such an approach is not to be confused with any lack of application or deep thinking: there are signs of these in plenty. But the character of the entries in the notebooks may be likened to that of a catherine wheel. Talbot's mind worked at high speed and sent reports on experiments, speculations, ideas, questions and comments on a variety of topics flashing out in all directions. The following quotations are characteristic:

Might not the intense cold produced by the evaporation of sulphuret of carbon (carbon sulphide) in a vacuum be applied to the preparation of ice for the table?

Is the blueness of the sky affected by the earth's being covered with snow, or overspread with clouds?

Does not the absolute weight of Bodies increase & diminish according to the position of the Sun and the Moon? Else why the tides . . . ?

Are not falling stars caused by meteoric stones impinging against our atmosphere with immense velocity (100 times that of a cannon ball) thereby ignited & reflected from it: or of falling to earth if they impinge perpendicularly?

The rapid motion of the thundercloud is I think produced by the strong attraction of the electrified surface of the Earth upon it, which continually draws it onwards. The violent gust of wind which precedes the storm is merely the effect of so large a body as a cloud passing thro' the atmosphere, and as the wind is not the *cause* of the cloud's motion, but only its *effect*, it is plain why the direction of the storm does not coincide with that of the wind . . .

Occasionally there was an entry which might be thought scarcely appropriate for the notebooks of a serious 'philosopher' – for example:

Josephus and 51 men took refuge in a cave, but afterwards determined to slay each other. They therefore ranged themselves in a row, and every tenth man was slain till Josephus alone remained. The question is, whereabouts in the row of men had he placed himself? Answer – He was the fourth man in the row.[64]

Perhaps Talbot would have argued that it was an amusing demonstration of the application of mathematics.

But there was one outcome of his work – apart from the mathematical papers earlier in the decade – of very considerable significance. In 1826 the *Edinburgh Journal of Science* edited by David Brewster published an article by Henry Talbot under the title 'Some experiments on coloured flames'.[65] The paper was the first of a number on optics and light which were to follow throughout the 1830s and a description of its scientific context is best included in the later, comprehensive account of Talbot's scientific work in that decade. Its importance here is the extent to which it brought him into contact with the few other experimenters in the area and marked him out as a coming man.

For some years work had been done on a number of interrelated problems in light including the classification of chemical substances by the colour which they generated when burnt, the spectral analysis of such light with a prism and a similar analysis of sunlight.[66] It was Henry Talbot's paper which first outlined the path for future experimentation. He reviewed the characteristic coloured flames of a number of substances (referring where appropriate to the earlier work of Brewster and Herschel) and noted a red line in the spectrum of a lamp burning nitre beyond the spectrum of ordinary candlelight. He speculated that the red ray might be characteristic of potassium salts

... as the yellow ray is of the salts of soda, although, from its feeble illuminating power, it is only to be detected with a prism. If this should be admitted, I would further suggest, that whenever the prism shows a *homogeneous* ray of any colour to exist in a flame, this ray indicates the formation or the presence of a *definite chemical compound* ...

If this opinion should be correct and applicable to the other definite rays, a glance at the prismatic spectrum of a flame may show it to contain substances, which it would otherwise require a laborious chemical analysis to detect.[67]

By indicating the very great potential of spectral analysis in chemistry Talbot inscribed his name permanently in the early history of the science of spectroscopy – where it joined those of Melvill, Wollaston, Fraunhofer, Brewster and Herschel.

Henry Talbot's first book, however, was a somewhat bizarre work, *Legendary Tales in Verse and Prose*, which was published for him in 1830 by

James Ridgway of Piccadilly. In the book Talbot pleasantly recounted some folk stories from Germany, Italy and Denmark. The subject matter was of a predictably romantic nature, but the tales were written with a light touch and were the better for some unexpected endings. Talbot said that he wrote them to amuse himself and hoped they would amuse others. Lady Elisabeth had other opinions. Henry showed her the text before publication and she commented:

They are all very pretty... but to form a volume of them would I fear disappoint expectations so highly raised as they have been about your talents, which have always justly been held to be of a very superior order... If you had published anything *scientific*, *historical* or *political* (which you are so well able to do) then these coming after, would not have signified, but knowing as I do your *sterling* abilities I do not like these tales & poems to be taken in the world for the standard of *what you can do*. If you had made known to the English public the discoveries of Fraunhofer or had taken a critical subject in one of the leading Reviews... it would have placed you where I think you ought to be... I know you have too much *grandeur d'ame* to be annoyed at being put in possession of the truth or at least of what I think so.[68]

Talbot decided to publish notwithstanding – which provided a further demonstration that he was his own master. Besides, his mathematical work, and also his paper on spectroscopy, indicate that he had already published something of considerable value.

Around the middle of 1830 Lady Elisabeth was worrying about her son leading a solitary and idle life[69] and passed on a comment from Kit Talbot that he seemed to have become 'desultory and erratic'.[70] Whatever small truth there may have been in that, if Lady Elisabeth could have known the quantity and quality of the work her son would have produced by the end of the next decade, then even she would have rested content.

3
The Creative Decade

In 1830 Talbot became involved with the affairs of Lacock village under dramatic circumstances as a result of processes of change which had been at work for decades.

From around 1760 onwards the enclosure movement had gathered speed in the English countryside, with the individually tilled small strips of land and common grazing land disappearing and the villager becoming a wage-earning labourer. This fundamental change coincided with the decline of village industries as the Industrial Revolution gathered pace in the north; the great stresses of economic boom and depression as the country fought a lengthy war against France and then had to readjust to peace; and a rapid growth in population.

A system for caring for the poor had existed since Elizabethan times. Basically a village was required to look after its own poor from birth to death and a rate was levied on those able to pay. The problems of the late eighteenth and early nineteenth centuries, however, were too serious and too deep to be coped with by a system devised for Tudor England. In 1795, the magistrates of Speenhamland in Berkshire initiated the system by which the difference between a wage being paid and what it cost to live (defined by the price of the loaf) should be found out of the parish rates. This system became the subject of an intense debate whose nature would seem very familiar today. Some regarded the payments as encouraging sloth; others came to regard the payments as a 'right'; while certain cynical farmers deliberately paid low wages, knowing that they would be made up out of the rates.

The explosion came in 1830. A concerted attempt had been made to cut poor relief and thus to reduce the level of the poor rate. The early and mid-1820s had not been bad years on average but in 1829–30 there was a deterioration and the reduced poor relief cut deep. A background of political unrest at home and revolution abroad provided the setting for an outbreak of rioting, machine-smashing and rick-burning which spread across England's southern counties in the second half of 1830 before being put down by Government action. There was no evidence of any general organization but threatening letters received by farmers and others sometimes concluded with such phrases as 'beware of the fatal dagger' and were signed 'Swing'. Whether any one person of the name of Swing existed or no, he was in due course accorded military rank and the riots identified with the name.

In Wiltshire the threshing machine was the main target in a series of incidents concentrated in a period of just one week in November of 1830. Over the entire course of the unrest from January 1830 to September of 1832, there were in Wiltshire eighteen recorded cases of arson, four 'Swing' letters, twenty riots and assaults, sixty-two robberies, three burglaries and ninety-seven breakings of threshing machines. At the special commission held in Salisbury early in 1831 (others were held in Berkshire, Buckinghamshire, Dorsetshire and Hampshire) 339 cases were heard. Of those involved, over 130 were acquitted, 52 sentenced to death (but only one sentence was carried out) and 152 sentenced to transportation. The uprising was crushed but the problem remained totally unsolved.

Henry Talbot was at Lacock during the period – the rest of the family being in London. Their exchanges of letters provide a vivid account of the imagined and actual happenings of November 1830, complete with colourful exaggerations and a sense of humour reminiscent of letters written during the wartime blitz in Britain. Ever practical, Charles Feilding sent advice on organizing a defence force, and, more to the point, he sent two constables down to support Henry at the Abbey.[1] Lady Elisabeth presented at first hand an account of the great debate between those who felt that concessions should be made to people tried beyond endurance and those who regarded it as fatal – with various opinions in between. Sir Charles Lemon (Lady Elisabeth's brother-in-law and a Cornwall landowner) believed that:

...no power should make him *promise* anything for the *future* whatever he might give them at the moment. Sir C says that all the promises that have been made in different parts of the Kingdom will *impede* the settlement of the question which must be done by an entire *re*-casting of the Poor Laws and laws of settlement, and that *then* labourers must have the power of carrying their labour to the best market, instead of being confined to their parish.[2]

Meantime, another brother-in-law to Lady Elisabeth, James Frampton, a Dorset landowner:

... being it seems the only Gentleman in that neighborhood who had stoutly resisted the rise of wages & lowering of rents, is become a marked man, and as he rides about a great deal it is feared he may be shot at from behind some hedge.[3]

But a sense of humour also existed. Horatia reported that John Fox-Strangways* was most disappointed that there were no adventures at Melbury and that 'he has gone all the way for nothing' while Aunt Harriet (wife of James Frampton) had organized Moreton House into an '*état de siège*'.[4]

Henry Talbot in turn kept the family informed of the situation at Lacock. Significantly, there was no Swing uprising in Lacock itself, though there were many incidents close by. Talbot's presence then – and his previous attitudes – obviously had some effect, as is indicated by a letter from a local magistrate, John Awdry, to him on 20 December 1830: 'We are perfectly quiet to which I have no doubt your kind words and kind acts have greatly contributed.'[5]

Talbot fully supported the various initiatives which were aimed often at both assisting the poor and yet keeping the poor rates within bounds. In December of 1830 he proposed drainage and other improvement works at Nash Hill. In 1833 he invited the roadbuilder Macadam to send a man to instruct the poor in the art of road-making and proposed 'offering a shilling a week extra to the three best workmen, to promote emulation'.[6] This proposal ran into opposition from other interests and Talbot commented: 'I am afraid the farmers will prove averse to *every* scheme of improving the Poor that I can possibly devise.'[7]

His sympathetic approach extended in other directions as well. In April 1831 there was an outbreak of furze burning on Talbot's property and the culprits were convicted and sentenced to one month's hard labour or payment of a £1 fine. 'The chairman gave them to understand it was through your clemency that they were let off so lightly – that had you been rigorous towards them they would in all probability have been transported.'[8]

If the events of 1830 did not touch Lacock itself, the conditions which had

* The Hon. John G. C. Fox-Strangways – half-brother of the third Earl of Ilchester. He was later M.P. for Calne and the County of Dorset.

created the uprisings elsewhere persisted. One method of curbing the inevitable results of population growth in the village – from 1,408 in 1801 to 1,640 in 1831 – was to encourage emigration. In 1832 a party of twenty-one men, women and children set off to a new life in Canada. By then, Henry Talbot had begun his excursion into national politics.

Talbot's short political career presents an intriguing puzzle, both as to why precisely he stood for Parliament in the first place and – having been elected once – why he did not continue. First, however, his political activities from 1831 to 1834 must be set in their context.[9]

In 1830 the Whigs returned to power after many years in the political wilderness and the administration formed by Earl Grey was pledged to an (initially) unspecified degree of parliamentary reform. In the parliamentary system existing before 1832 the counties were under-represented while the opposite was the case with the boroughs. In the latter, the franchise varied greatly between on the one extreme those boroughs where all ratepayers had the vote and on the other the 'rotten' boroughs, the most infamous of which was Old Sarum where two Members of Parliament were returned by seven voters casting their votes in a field. Voting was in public and seats could be bought quite openly.

The Whigs' Reform Bill was introduced into the House of Commons by Lord John Russell on 1 March 1831 and Kit Talbot* sent a graphic account of that occasion to Henry:

Last night will be an ever to be remembered epoch in my life, never was such a state of excitement, such a sudden surprise . . . Never did I contemplate the forced disfranchisement of sixty boroughs, declaring at once their charters nul & void, still less the diminishing the total number of members of Parliament. Glorious Lord John! But the thing can never pass into a law: besides the natural enemies of reform, he has raised up hundreds of additional opponents. It was most amusing as his plan gradually developed itself during the most awful stillness occasionally interrupted by bursts of uncontrollable exultation or deprecation, to see the gradually lengthening visages of the gentlemen on the opposition benches. When he came to the list of to be disfranchised boroughs it was comical to hear

---

* Christopher Rice Mansel Talbot had entered Parliament as a Whig M.P. for Glamorgan in 1830 and, although never holding office, was to continue in politics for many years and ultimately to become Father of the House of Commons. He was elected a Fellow of the Royal Society in 1831 – the same year as his cousin Henry – and had many scientific interests. But unlike his cousin he was also very successful in business affairs. He was a director of the Great Western Railway, a patron of I. K. Brunel, and the principal shareholder in the new docks development at Port Talbot in South Wales – the name being adopted in his honour in 1836. When he died in 1890, Kit Talbot's total estate was valued at nearly £6 million.

the exclamations of each affected individual – 'That dishes me', 'Done by G—', 'I say how do you feel?' &c &c. and now and then a most discontented drawling 'Hear, Hear!' . . . The secret was admirably kept & the surprise to all complete. The alteration of the election law is very obvious and judicious. Of the disfranchisement of the boroughs, I think the question lieth not in a nutshell but 'I for one' am favourable to it.[10]

It was in the cause of this Reform Bill that Henry prepared to fight his first election.

Talbot had grown up in an atmosphere of acute political awareness but his own participation in politics was by no means certain. During a review of the career possibilities open to him in 1823, Charles Feilding expressed the opinion, after consulting political friends, that Henry should not go into Parliament because 'it would be a waste of your abilities'[11] besides the difficulty of obtaining and retaining a seat. In 1830, however, Henry published a political pamphlet 'Thoughts on moderate reform' which – while regrettably no copies have survived – appeared to argue in favour of representation based on numbers. Moreover, Paul Methuen (a friend and neighbour who had shared with Talbot in the experience of the Swing riots) was keen that he should stand. As Sheriff of the County in 1831, and a Whig M.P. himself, Methuen promised to do all that he could (unofficially) to help.

No explicit statements indicate Henry's motivations in standing for Parliament in Chippenham at the election of April 1831. Perhaps he felt he had something to contribute in ensuring that reform and sound policies were adopted, and thereby the avoidance of a revolution in the country. Perhaps Kit Talbot's election in 1830 provided a stimulus. Perhaps he was persuaded to make the attempt – possibly by Lady Elisabeth and others – against his own inclinations.

The franchise in the borough of Chippenham was held by 'freemen' – the freedom being obtained usually by birth, marriage, gift or purchase – and its two seats were controlled by Joseph Neeld as patron. Neeld was a large local landowner who stood for one of the seats himself and who represented the borough from 1830 until 1859 with only one year's break. In addition, Neeld was an anti-reformer. Neeld's brother-in-law Henry George Boldero was standing for the second seat, naturally with the patron's support. A sympathetic local newspaper the *Devizes and Wiltshire Gazette* reported on 28 April:

Out of a population of nearly 4,000, over 129 individuals are entitled to vote, and Mr Neeld has upwards of 60 of what are called free houses; so that he and his brother-in-law calculate, with certainty, upon being returned. Mr Talbot starts on the reforming interest, but it is not expected that the freemen will have the spirit to return him.

The ballot on 30 April was 96 votes for Neeld, 60 for Boldero and 39 for Talbot. Henry's efforts were appreciated by the reformers in Chippenham and he was presented with a silver snuff box.*

Immediately after his defeat Henry Talbot was preparing to stand again at the next election although it is clear that there were some aspects of election-eering that he did not like. His agent, William Wilmot, found it difficult to get his candidate to canvass the electors and – probably on grounds of expense – Talbot was opposed to extensive 'entertainment' of the voters. In addition, the emotions roused and the harsh words passed during the campaign did not commend themselves to the calm, logical brain of Talbot who wrote to Neeld on the matter, being assured in reply that 'I am quite as far removed from any angry feeling arising out of the last election as you can be . . .'[12] That he should raise the matter was tribute both to Henry's character and to his political naivety.

For the next eighteen months Wilmot looked after the Talbot cause in Chippenham with little support from the candidate although members of the family did what they could. However, the next election was to be decided by an electorate in Chippenham which had been increased by about 50 per cent with the passing of the Reform Bill – at long last, in June 1832 – and Henry Boldero had decided to stand down. Neeld expressed a complete lack of interest in the second candidate and so made Talbot's return almost certain even though a third candidate (and a reformer) from outside the borough did contest the election.

Whatever his original intentions, it is possible that Talbot may not have contested the 1832 election if the campaign had been a hard-fought one. Certainly, he scarcely impressed as a convinced and enthusiastic candidate. At mid-year he wrote to his mother: 'I must go on Monday to Chippenham to see some of my friends at their desire, which is a great bore . . .'[13] And shortly before the election in December he commented: 'I hope no Conservative with a long purse will take the field at the last moment. I mean to spend next to nothing, so they may elect me on that principle if they please or not at all.'[14]

Polling took place on 10 December 1832. Beforehand, Talbot had calculated that Neeld would receive around 150 votes, himself 120 and the third candi-

* Which is in the Lacock Museum, as is a copy of a political song composed in his honour.

date (John Mayne) 40 votes. He underestimated his support, for the poll
recorded 139 for Neeld, 133 for himself and 30 for Mayne. For his own part
Henry Talbot must have been concerned with other priorities, for ten days
later he was to be married.

At the time of Caroline Feilding's wedding to Ernest Augustus Edgcumbe
(Lord Valletort) in December 1831, Talbot received a number of suggestions
that he too should be thinking of marrying. In the autumn of the following year
he went alone on a tour into Derbyshire and Yorkshire and spent some time
at Markeaton Hall. Markeaton was the home of the Mundy family into which
a cousin – Harriet Georgiana Frampton, daughter of Lady Elisabeth's sister
Harriet and James Frampton – had married two years previously. At the time
of Talbot's visit the head of the family was Francis Mundy, then M.P. for the
county of Derbyshire.

The purpose behind Henry's visit became clear when he wrote to Charles
Feilding on 7 November 1832:

> ... I am going to be married. The object of my choice is Constance youngest daughter of
> Mr Mundy of Markeaton. [Constance was twenty-one years old at this time.] You none
> of you know her, which I rather regret, chiefly because if you did you could have no doubt
> of the prospect of happiness which this union holds out to me, which until you know her
> must rest upon your opinion of my good judgment. I suppose if I were to tell you what a
> charming person she is you would not believe half of what I should say. Therefore I prefer
> to be silent on the subject, for I could not tell you my own opinion of her without using
> language which might appear to partake of exaggeration ... I did not expect Mr Mundy
> would have given his daughter any fortune, however he says she shall have £6,000.[15]

The family was delighted at Henry's happiness and Lady Elisabeth wrote:

> If I knew Constance I would tell her that as you have ever been the best & tenderest of
> sons you will be to her the best & tenderest of friends and I would congratulate *her* on
> having won such a heart as yours ... If you really have found a person who will *understand*
> the value of your mind, I *must* love her, because she will certainly not be a common
> character ...
> As it is generally considered of some consequence in the eyes of the world the *manner* in
> which a lady is received by her husband's family, I must say that you may depend on my
> expressing myself in the most flattering manner of her *in the world* and saying all that you
> could wish when it comes to be *known*.[16]

Constance's first meeting with Lady Elisabeth and Caroline in London was alarming 'to one of such retiring habits' but they pronounced her gentle, lady-like and extremely pretty. Henry meantime had asked Kit to be a trustee of the marriage settlement but typically had not told him who the girl was nor when the marriage was to take place. Engagement or no, Lady Elisabeth had no intention of allowing her son to forget politics for as soon as she knew the date of the dissolution of Parliament she wrote: 'I lose no time in letting you know that you may avail yourself of it, as instead of being auprés de vos amours you ought to be bestirring yourself at Chippenham.'[17] So Talbot fought his election and then the wedding took place at All Souls, Langham Place in London on 20 December 1832 with the Dean of Chichester officiating. The demands of Talbot's new political life would not allow a leisurely honey-moon tour of the Continent immediately so the couple spent a few days at Lord Lansdowne's villa at Richmond Hill. Henry declared that Constance had 'the disposition of an angel' – and that there were plenty of books that suited them both in Lord Lansdowne's library.[18]

The Parliament which convened on 5 February 1833 contained 149 Tories and the enormous number of 509 reformers of varying shades – one of whom was Henry Talbot. He had a friendly introduction because Kit Talbot, Charles Lemon and other relatives and friends were on hand to welcome the new member. At first it was all very exciting and after two days he commented: 'The Irish members have such fun in them.'[19] Irish measures and the tactics of the Irish members were to occupy such a large and controversial part of the business of the House of Commons that in less than two weeks he had sharply changed his mind and wrote acidly: 'The Library of the House of Commons I intend in future to make my place of refuge from Hibernian oratory.'[20]

The major legislation of the years 1832–4 – apart from Ireland – included the emancipation of slaves, the restructuring of the poor-law system and an act which regulated the employment of children in factories introduced by Lord Ashley (the Earl of Shaftesbury) and Henry Talbot played his part with a will, particularly in initiatives aimed at ameliorating the widespread distress.

Nor did he forget his constituents. He successfully appealed to the Home Secretary, Lord Melbourne, for a sentence of seven years' transportation passed on a man at Wiltshire Assizes to be changed to imprisonment in the United Kingdom and later the Prime Minister Lord Grey agreed to Talbot's request that a young man from the Chippenham area be appointed to a clerk-ship in the customs in London.

Talbot and Constance were separated for much of the first half of 1833 which both found a trial. But the time for their delayed honeymoon tour of Europe finally arrived and they left Dover towards the end of June. They made leisurely progress through France and Switzerland into Italy and it was at Lake Como early in October that by arrangement they met Caroline and her family. The stay at Como was to assume major historical importance for it was there that Talbot's inadequate attempts at sketching inspired subsequent experiments with light-sensitive chemical substances, leading eventually to the discovery of a practical system of negative-positive photography (Chapter 4).

It has been suggested by some writers that Talbot's departure on a six-month wedding tour amounted to a dereliction of his political duty. However, it should be remembered that the House of Commons rose in August 1833 and did not sit again until February of the next year; that attendances always thinned as summer came on; and that the Government was quite content with this situation since it made legislation and parliamentary management all the simpler. Talbot was expressing no more than good sense therefore when he wrote to his mother from Geneva on 4 September: 'Ministers seem to have had it all their own way at last, and not to have wanted any more votes. So I think I was much better in the mountain air last month than I could have been in the House of Commons.'[21]

Talbot returned to the House of Commons in February 1834 refreshed and reasonably enthusiastic.

Yesterday we had a very pretty debate, about five hours long. As it was upon six or seven different subjects one after the other, there was not enough of each of them to be tedious. People spoke short speeches & to the point, the house was in very good humour, and altogether there is great improvement in the style of debate compared with last *year*. How it will be when the majority of members are come to Town, I cannot tell . . .[22]

With all the weight of a few months' experience behind him, he commented a few days later on the Chancellor of the Exchequer's proposals concerning such matters as indemnifying the planters in the West Indies, repealing the tax on houses, poor-law proposals and the abolition of tithes: 'Ld. Althorp's speech was short & much the best I ever heard from him. He has evidently improved in tact & experience.'[23] However, when the Government was defeated on 18 February in a debate on the pensions list Talbot was apparently absent from the House for the vote. No hint as to the reason is contained in his papers but it could be that an interesting experiment at the Royal Institution

had enticed him away. But he was active again in March when he presented
to the House a petition – for the relief of the poor-rates burden – bearing twenty
signatures on behalf of the vicar, churchwardens, overseers and ratepayers of
the parish of Lacock.

Even if they were separated for lengthy periods, the happy relationship
between Constance and Henry – she in one letter daringly wrote: 'I want to
know what room you sleep in, that I may be able to fancy all about you' and
he by return adding a postscript '*je t'envoye mille baisers*'[24] – contrasted remarkably with Talbot's growing exasperation with parliamentary life. The apparently monolithic Whig Government appeared to be breaking up in confusion
as it fought Tories, radicals and the Irish. Possibly the most extreme forms of
disagreement took place between the senior Whigs and ministers themselves.

Talbot did not profess to understand it at all. In the spring of 1834 he wrote
to Charles Feilding:

> For my part I don't comprehend anything about it, nor who can act with who, and
> why the remainder cannot. It is all an enigma to me ... for many months the state of the
> Government has been like a magazine of combustibles to which the hand of a child might
> at any time have applied a match.[25]

Later in the year he told Feilding (who was in Nice) how he wished he could
be there too 'instead of in this land of eternal politics, elections and poor
laws'.[26] Intriguingly, Talbot's critical attitude to the world of politics received
stimulus from those around him. Constance clearly rated papers to the Royal
Society above parliamentary speeches while – much more surprisingly – Lady
Elisabeth urged him to work at his experiments and to publish the results for
'it is a happier line to be distinguished in, in these days, than politics'.[27]

As 1834 moved towards its close and the Tories endeavoured to establish an
effective Government, a general election became a possibility. Before a dissolution was announced, however, Talbot sent a letter to the electors of
Chippenham in which, having outlined his services to them, he concentrated
mainly on the state of the country. He expressed the belief firmly that another
election would be bad because it was likely to foment problems, whereas what
was wanted was 'moderate, temperate and conciliatory measures'.[28] An election was called nevertheless; Talbot did not stand; and on 3 January 1835
Joseph Neeld and Henry Boldero were returned unopposed.

In a letter to a fellow member of the Royal Society Talbot attributed his
decision not to stand to his desire to avoid the expense of a contested election.[29]

But that was only a partial explanation. The key was in his make-up. As has already been pointed out, while he could mix with ease in public if he chose to, he had become increasingly an asocial person. His interests were intellectual ones that were overwhelmingly solitary in nature. As a result, he did not like and increasingly came to detest the contact with the public – and for that matter his colleagues – which was a vital feature of political life. In addition, his logical and coldly rational approach to problems, his willingness to see the other side of an argument and his desire to find an *effective* compromise solution to problems were all out of place in the emotional and power-hungry world of politics. He became completely disillusioned and could not bring himself to support either of the major parties. He maintained an interest in politics but only as a cynically amused observer. His mother – who may have changed even her attitude to politics as the years passed – supported his decision and his devotion to his researches: '. . . it will result in more happiness & fame than ungrateful politics, where after men have strutted their hour, leave but a wreck behind.'[30]

Henry Talbot's scientific and mathematical researches in the decade of the 1830s – which was to be the most intensely creative period of his life – had received the best possible stimulus in March 1831 with his election as a Fellow of the Royal Society. His certificate of recommendation – signed by seven fellows including Michael Faraday, George Peacock and William Whewell as well as Charles Lemon and William Thomas Horner Fox-Strangways – did not specify any particular areas of research as having merited the election but simply that he was worthy of the honour and was likely 'to be a valuable and useful member'. Clearly, however, his published mathematical work in the previous decade and his contributions to optics – one of the most exciting subjects of scientific research at that time – had made his name well known.

The names of David Brewster* and John Herschel did not appear on the certificate but the very warm encouragement they gave Henry Talbot at this time indicates that no significance was to be attached to the fact. A few months after the election Brewster urged him to continue his optical researches as his

---

* Like a number of other prominent researchers, Brewster seemed to find Talbot a valuable source from which to borrow high-quality lenses, prisms and other optical instruments. For his part, Talbot must have received some encouragement and no little amusement from an admission in a letter from Brewster – who was one of the two or three leading researchers of his day in the United Kingdom – that 'I have within the last week had three tremendous explosions . . .'[31]

E

powers 'of original investigation are capable of doing much for science' –
adding, with the touch of an editor looking for good contributions, that 'it
would give me the greatest pleasure to receive occasionally a notice of what
you have done'.[32] Brewster continued in the same vein during Talbot's brief
political career and expressed the view that science should not be neglected
for the 'infinitely less valuable occupation of a political life'.[33] Herschel pressed
Talbot to publish his work as firmly as Brewster had done:

> I have often wondered that being, as I am aware you are, in possession of a number of
> curious & interesting things in optical science and taking on every branch of that subject
> views of no ordinary kind, you should not have embodied them in some more impressive
> & permanent form than you have hitherto thought it worthwhile to do. I am very glad
> therefore that you entertain the idea of communicating some of them to the Royal Society
> in the form of a paper, and I hope when you have fairly begun doing so you will not leave
> off till you have added to our knowledge by a large stock of new facts and to our philosophy
> by a copious disclosure of principles.[34]

Before examining Talbot's researches, it is appropriate to set them briefly in
their context – both as regards the organization of scientific research and the
extent of chemical and physical knowledge of the time. He had received very
little scientific (as distinct from mathematical) instruction at university and was
enabled to conduct his scientific work thereafter only because he was a relatively wealthy man. Both features were typical of the time and were representative of a scientific world far removed from that of today where much
research is funded by Government, industry and other institutions and where
science occupies a prominent position in education from schools to university
and beyond. In the opening decades of the nineteenth century, science was, in
Bernal's words, 'an elegant ornament of society, practised by virtuosi'.[35] It was
to take the entire century for the situation to change to one where science was
a vital factor in everyday life and had fought its way firmly into education and
the professions.

From the 1820s Germany was actively evolving an educational system – at
university and technical school level – with the avowed objective of producing
research scientists, engineers and technicians. Britain had only its learned and
mainly amateur societies – the Royal Society in premier position, with various
specialist societies such as the Linnean Society (founded in 1788) in botany, the
Geological Society (1807), and the Astronomical Society (1820). Fulfilling dual
roles of original research and the popularization of science was the Royal

Institution, founded in London by Count Rumford in 1799 – whose function was broadly performed in the north by the Manchester Literary and Philosophical Society. Many of the prominent names in science were self-taught or when trained at university were highly critical of their experiences there. In England (although not in Scotland*) the likes of Davy, Wollaston, Young, Dalton, Faraday and Joule pursued their researches outside the walls of a university. In some instances – notably that of Faraday – great discoveries were made in circumstances described by one biographer as 'penury'.

There were those in England with very different ideas about the organization and position of science. In 1830, Charles Babbage published his *Decline of the State of Science in England* which was mainly directed against the Royal Society and in the following year he played a leading role in the formation of the British Association for the Advancement of Science. The BAAS was openly intended as an alternative to the Royal Society – as an organization at the *professional* level, directed to raising the status of science and scientists and not infrequently initiating requests for Government support for scientific activities. Its annual meetings, besides providing a valuable opportunity for exchanges of views between scientists, also provided a first-class opportunity for communicating news and views of importance to the general public. For many years the annual presidential address of the BAAS could accurately be regarded as 'the principal public scientific announcement of the year'.[36]

Institutionally however changes were slow to come. The formation of University College, London in 1828 with science as an integral part of the curriculum was a step in the right direction, as was the setting up at mid-century (inspired by the Prince Consort) of a Royal College of Chemistry† – though it had a difficult existence being merged before long with the Royal School of Mines into the Metropolitan School of Science. It was only by the end of the century that significant differences could be seen – changes of attitude on the part of the Royal Society, the existence of new laboratories (the Claren-

* From the latter part of the eighteenth century, the Scottish universities had developed as powerful centres of teaching. As the following century progressed, many of the eminent men of science in Scotland were university professors often serving more than one institution. Scotland certainly did more than England to spread and teach modern scientific knowledge. A Chemical Society was formed in Scotland before that in England and in 1814 it was claimed that Scotland had a greater number of intelligent, practical chemists in proportion to population, than perhaps any other country in the world. Significantly, Talbot in his later years conducted much of his research in university laboratories in Edinburgh.[37]

† Part of the change in attitudes is normally attributed to the visit to Britain in 1842 of Justus von Liebig, the German chemist who played an important role in the organization of scientific education in Germany.

don and the Cavendish) at Oxford and Cambridge respectively, and the formation of new universities at Manchester, Birmingham, Sheffield and elsewhere geared to the application of science to industry. Even then the country lagged far behind the scientific educational research systems of Germany and other Continental countries and in this it can be argued that the Victorians bear some blame for the economic ills which the United Kingdom suffers to this day.[38] But whatever contemporary criticisms of the system there may have been, in a typically English display of paradox individual scientists in this country – whether personally wealthy (like Talbot), supported by a patron or institution, or simply poor – contributed powerfully to the new discoveries in the physical sciences which were to be a feature of the era.

In the eighth decade of the twentieth century the extent of scientific knowledge is vast compared with the boundaries of knowledge at the time of Talbot's most creative period in the 1830s. There were no computers to aid analysis and instrumentation was relatively crude. Laboratories possessed no supplies of gas or electricity for conducting experiments and recording and examining results. Researchers therefore worked in conditions of experimental control (and contamination) which a middle school would consider to be impossible today. Moreover it is evident from the notebooks of the period that experiments sometimes took the form of reasoning 'If I put this with that, I wonder what will happen': the absence of a comprehensive theoretical background made the outcome frequently very problematical not to say hazardous. (This in no way implies criticism of that work – quite the contrary – for our knowledge today is composed of the results of millions of hours of work built upon the preparedness to ask such questions as those above.)

In *physics* the gains in knowledge over the course of the nineteenth century were extensive and dramatic. By the 1820s the Newtonian corpuscular or emission concept of the nature of light had been largely overtaken by the undulatory theory advanced initially by Huygens but which – with major modifications – was associated primarily in Talbot's time with Thomas Young and the Frenchman Fresnel. Diffraction, reflection, absorption and polarization of light were all phenomena attracting much attention in the 1820s and 30s and Talbot's work in microscopy using polarized light was amongst his most important.

Electricity had been a subject of great interest in the eighteenth century but the invention of the electric pile or battery by Alessandro Volta in 1800 provided electric current for the first time. And the later work of Ohm, Oersted,

Ampère and Faraday – who in 1831 discovered electromagnetic induction – led eventually to the world of the electric light, the telephone, electric motors, and household appliances which we know today.

As the century progressed there were new discoveries and insights into the nature of *heat*, James Joule propounding the concept of the so-called mechanical equivalent of heat and Rudolf Clausius evolving the laws of thermodynamics – all basic elements upon which much of present-day science and technology is based. Sometimes theory was in advance of fact, sometimes fact in advance of theory – but steadily gaps in knowledge were lessened and the ability to give an increasingly more comprehensive explanation of interrelated natural phenomena improved.

Some of the above discoveries had direct impact on *chemistry* – for example the voltaic cell or battery immediately provided a tool whereby Humphry Davy and others could investigate chemical substances by decomposing them electrically into their constituent elements. Similarly the growing understanding of the nature of heat was linked with a greater knowledge of the chemical reactions in which it could be produced or which resulted from it. But in many ways chemistry provided the greatest challenge of the century for the number of naturally occurring substances was so vast – even before attention was turned to the synthesis of yet more substances in the laboratory – that bringing them into a meaningful framework of understanding and comparison was an immense undertaking.

In the 1830s this undertaking was only partly under way. Nowhere did Talbot give an outline description of the state of chemistry in this period, but fortunately one was given by the then President of the British Association for the Advancement of Science, Sir Henry Roscoe, in 1877 when he looked back at chemistry forty years before:

In the year 1837 chemistry was a very different science from that existing at the present moment. Priestley, it is true, had discovered oxygen, Lavoisier had placed the phenomena of combustion on their true basis, Davy had decomposed the alkalis, Faraday had liquefied many of the gases, Dalton had enunciated the laws of chemical combination by weight, and Gay Lussac had pointed out that simple volumetric relation governs the combination of the gases. But we then possessed no knowledge of chemical dynamics, we were then altogether unable to explain the meaning of the heat given off in the act of chemical combination. The atomic theory was indeed accepted [in fact this was not generally so] but we were as ignorant of the mode of action of the atoms and as incapable of explaining their mutual relationship as were the ancient Greek philosophers.[39]

Thus it was an exciting, challenging and complex world with many gaps in existing knowledge to which Talbot directed his energies in the 1830s. During these years he prepared more scientific and mathematical papers than in any other comparable period of his life. The scientific papers were mainly concerned with optics – spectral analysis, microscopy using polarized light and crystallography being the most important areas of study – although aspects of chemistry were by no means absent.

The work he carried out on coloured flames in the 1820s has already been outlined. Talbot's notebooks show that he continued his experiments although he did not publish his findings until February 1834 when in a composite article entitled 'Facts relating to optical science' he wrote:

> Lithia and strontia are two bodies characterized by the fine red tint which they communicate to flame. The former of these is very rare, and I was indebted to my friend Mr Faraday for the specimen which I subjected to prismatic analysis. Now it is difficult to distinguish the lithia red from the strontia red by the unassisted eye. But the prism displays between them the most marked distinction that can be imagined. The strontia flame exhibits a great number of red rays well separated from each other by dark intervals, not to mention an orange, and a very definite bright blue ray. The lithia exhibits one single red ray. Hence I hesitate not to say that optical analysis can distinguish the minutest portions of these two substances from each other with as much certainty, if not more, than any other known method.[40]

The hesitant, general approach of his 1826 article was absent but it should be pointed out that here Henry Talbot was not talking about general theory or applications but about two specific examples which he had verified.

Almost two years passed before he returned to the subject[41] in print but then his approach embraced general concepts as well as detailed experiments. In his experiments Talbot deflagrated silver, gold and copper leaf as well as zinc by the action of electricity – the method which had attracted the attention of other workers including Charles Wheatstone. The resulting spectra had all exhibited 'several definite rays' – zinc's, for example, being composed of 'a strong red ray, three blue rays, besides several more of other colours'. Talbot also saw a need for a more general approach:

> It is much to be desired that an extensive course of experiments should be made on the spectra of chemical flames, accompanied with accurate measurements of the relative positions of the bright and dark lines [in the spectra] or *maxima* and *minima* of light which are generally seen in them. The definite rays emitted by certain substances, as, for example,

the yellow rays of the salts of soda [sodium] possess a fixed and invariable character, which is analogous in some measure to the fixed proportion in which all bodies combine, according to the atomic theory. It may be expected, therefore, that optical researches, carefully conducted, may throw some additional light upon chemistry.

Talbot went on to detail the 'exceedingly remarkable' nature of the characteristic flame spectra of salts of copper which contained dark lines which 'resemble in that respect the solar spectrum'. This latter result misled Talbot* but the 'extensive course of experiments' was exactly what was required – and would eventually establish spectrum analysis on a sound footing and as an analytical method of major importance in chemistry and in astronomy. But this did not take place until 1859 as the result of a series of experiments conducted by Gustav Kirchhoff and Robert Bunsen, professors of physics and chemistry respectively at Heidelberg University – who then quickly demonstrated its value by using the method in identifying two new alkali metals caesium and rubidium.

That Talbot himself never proceeded to conduct a programme of experiments – David Brewster did but inconclusively – may have resulted partly from his interest in many other topics and partly from his inability (like all other workers for some years) to see any explanation of the continual presence in flame spectra of the yellow line attributed to sodium when no sodium was *believed* to be present. This problem was eventually solved in the 1850s when William Swan demonstrated 'the almost universal diffusion of the salts of sodium, and the remarkable energy with which they produce yellow light' – i.e. avoidance of contamination was essential.[42] McGucken has pointed out fairly that Talbot can be criticized for inconsistency in talking about *elements* in some cases and chemical *compounds* and *substances* in others[43] – but it is tantalizing to think what might have been the result if Talbot had applied himself to the comprehensive series of experiments that he had correctly identified as being necessary. None the less, the fact remains that his work on spectrum analysis ranks high amongst the small number of early workers – and he was the first to express the concept of chemical spectrum analysis in terms that looked forward to the discoveries of Kirchhoff and Bunsen.

There was one other aspect of spectrum analysis in which Talbot became involved – and this concerned the spectrum of sunlight. Early in the nineteenth

---

* In 1848 John William Draper, Professor of Chemistry at the University of New York, showed the dark lines to be due to the presence of incombustible substances in the flames.[44]

century the English physicist William Wollaston and the young German optical worker Joseph von Fraunhofer had discovered dark lines in the solar spectrum. Fraunhofer devoted considerable attention to them and ever since they have been named after him. He mapped 574 'Fraunhofer lines' – and their cause, like that of the sodium line, remained a puzzle until the Kirchhoff–Bunsen experiments of the late 1850s. The two problems were in a sense linked because the bright yellow-orange line which came to be associated with sodium coincided with one of the most prominent dark lines in the solar spectrum and which Fraunhofer's system identified as dark line D. For some time the dark lines were interpreted as absorption phenomena – the deficient parts of the spectrum having been absorbed, according to this argument, in passing through the atmosphere of the sun and the stars. Brewster favoured this explanation (based on the corpuscular theory) and Herschel too (but based on the wave or undulatory theory of light). In a letter to Herschel, Talbot indicated that the absorption had to be caused by the sun's atmosphere:

> . . . certainly not by the Earth's atmosphere, for then the stars would exhibit the same lines in the spectrum, which are however different for each star. But there is not much likelihood of our being able to determine what gas constitutes the sun's atmosphere, since it has probably a very slight absorptive power & only produces so much effect owing to the immense thickness of it which the light traverses.[45]

Talbot was wrong: the constituents could be found. More than twenty-five years later, Kirchhoff demonstrated practically that there was a direct relationship in the coincidence (when it occurred) between individual bright-line spectra of known elements on earth and the dark lines of the solar spectrum because in effect substances *stopped* the kind of light (and heat) which they themselves were in a condition to radiate – which was the opposite of what Talbot and Herschel believed. Thus, the key to analysis of the constituents of the sun and the stars was delivered.[46]

Whether Talbot's ideas were subsequently demonstrated to be sound or not, his scientific papers – like his mathematical papers – were models of lucidity and always attractively written. In 'Experiments on light',[47] the longest and most detailed paper he had so far (1834) prepared, he presented two main subjects: the polarizing microscope and photometry. Henry Talbot was the first scientist to use the polarizing microscope – i.e. a microscope where the specimen was illuminated by polarized light – and he succinctly summed up its value in a later paper on crystals:

This instrument possesses so great a power of developing the internal structure of transparent bodies, even in their minutest visible particles, that I feel confident the employment of it will lead to many new and interesting results.[48]

In 'Experiments on light' Talbot was intent on passing on his practical knowledge:

As little else is requisite to repeat the experiments which I am about to mention than the possession of a good microscope, I think that in describing them I shall render a service to the numerous class of inquirers into nature, who are desirous of witnessing some of the most brilliant optical phenomena without the embarrassment of having to manage any large or complicated apparatus.

He then described the positioning of the two polarizers in the manner still followed today – one between the sub-stage mirror and the specimen and the other 'between the eyeglass and the eye; and this plate is capable of being turned round in its own plane, so that the light always traverses both [of the polarizers] perpendicularly'.

[It] follows, as indeed is obvious to all who are conversant with this branch of optics, that if the two tourmalines[*] are placed in a similar position, the light freely traverses them both: but if that which is next the eye is turned round 90°, the observer can perceive nothing, except when the light of the sun is used, which causes a small remnant of the light to become visible. Except in this case, however, the field of view is quite dark in this position of the tourmalines, and partially bright in the opposite position. It is only partially, and not entirely bright, because even the best tourmalines have a considerable tinge of brown or green colour, which greatly disturbs and disfigures the colours of all bodies which are viewed through them.

The solution to this problem was already to hand in the form of W. Nicol's 'polarizing eyepiece',[49] which was composed of calcareous spar and which offered perfect whiteness and transparency. The eyepiece was bulkier than tourmalines but, as Talbot indicated, fitting one to the tube of the microscope (and the other beneath the stage) presented no problems.

He first described the use of the microscope with a hair immersed in oil or varnish to prevent diffraction, but quickly passed to crystals:

Seen by common light [they] offer nothing peculiar, but on the darkened field of the microscope they are luminous and splendidly coloured, the colour depending upon the

* Crystalline mineral used as a polarizing plate. It contained a number of chemical elements (including silicon, boron and magnesium) of various colours.

thickness of the crystal, and being the same in all points of its surface, except upon the little inclined plane which forms its extremity. But upon this oblique portion are seen three or four distinct bands of colour parallel to the edge and offering to the eye a visible scale or measure of the rapid diminution of thickness in that part. The observed succession of colours in one experiment [copper sulphate crystals] was the following. Yellow, brown, purple, blue, sky blue, straw yellow, yellow, reddish purple, blue, sea green, green, greenish yellow, pink, green, blueish green, pink.

While emphasizing the scientific value of the instrument in revealing crystal structure, Talbot's sense of wonderment at the world revealed by polarization (particularly when crystallization was observed as it took place on the stage of the microscope) was evident:

[The crystals] rapidly moved onwards, appearing by turns luminous and obscure, and resembling in miniature the coruscations of a firefly. It was impossible to view this without admiring the infinite perfection of nature, that such almost imperceptible atoms should be found to have a regular structure capable of acting upon light in the same manner as the largest masses, and that the element of light itself should obey in such trivial particulars the same laws which regulate its course throughout the universe.

The second half of this article was devoted to practical and theoretical considerations of *photometry* – measuring the intensity of light – which he approached with considerable ingenuity both as regards the measurement of reflecting surfaces and points of emission, and where he applied his mathematics to good effect.

Talbot appeared to be nervous about this first major paper, for a letter from E. W. Brayley (the assistant editor of the *Philosophical Magazine*) sought to reassure him before publication:

Your reputation as an optical enquirer and your known skill in the manipulation of optical researches would of themselves guarantee the propriety of inserting your communication; [but having read the article at Talbot's request]
... I have great pleasure in giving you the assurance you desire, that it shall appear in the Philosophical Magazine and in as short a space of time as is consistent with our present arrangements.[50]

This is an interesting aspect of a character which usually gave little sign of any lack of self-confidence.

David Brewster constantly encouraged his microscopy and in 1837 he dedicated his own *Treatise on the Microscope* to Henry:

In placing your name at the head of this little volume, I express very imperfectly the admiration which I feel for your scientific acquirements, and for the zeal with which you devote your fortune and talents to the noblest purposes to which they can be applied.

A year later the redoubtable Charles Babbage indicated that he would like to add polarizing apparatus to his microscope and turned to Talbot for advice.[51]

Talbot's work with the polarizing microscope had a natural corollary in the study of crystals. The results of his observations figured in a number of papers, and he was still adding to the subject as late as 1847.[52] In July of 1836 a short item in the *Philosophical Magazine* dealt with the colour changes exhibited by iodide of mercury as a result of increasing temperature and, following microscopic examination, Talbot stated with conviction: 'This phenomenon is, I think, the most evident proof which we yet possess of the dependency of colour upon internal molecular arrangement.'[53]

His two most important papers on crystals, however, were delivered to the Royal Society – in May and December of 1836.[54] Both presented detailed findings together with theoretical observations. In the first, Talbot's experiments were concerned solely with the crystals of boracic acid:

The field of view being dark, the little circles become luminous, and we see upon each of them a well-defined and dark cross, dividing the crystal into four equal parts. All these crosses are placed similarly, and are parallel to each other, and their direction remains unaltered when the crystals are turned round in their own plane by revolving the plate of glass upon which they stand. This beautiful appearance can be seen with a moderate magnifying power. I measured the diameter of some of the larger crystals, which I find to be from 1/300 to 1/600 of an inch . . . Each circle has upon it one or more coloured rings arranged concentrically, but the number as well as the colour of these rings is different in different individuals.

He concluded that the crystals probably consisted of spicula diverging from a point 'but which are in the closest possible contact, and in a state of complete mechanical cohesion'. David Brewster had earlier described similar figures as occurring in spheres of glass which had been heated by placing them in hot oil and Talbot reasoned that it was:

. . . not improbable that the circular-polarizing properties of fluids may be owing to the presence of multitudes of particles similar to these [that is, those shown by his polarizing microscope] which they hold in solution.

Talbot dealt with the subject of boracic acid crystals in greater detail in the second paper:

The more energetically any substance acts upon polarized light, the closer and more crowded are the bands and lines of colour which appear upon its crystals. These isochromatic lines, of which there are frequently many alterations, denote lines of equal thickness in the crystal. In the case of boracic acid, when anhydrous or nearly so, these lines are more crowded than in any other crystal that I have yet examined, insomuch that to exhibit them distinctly is as fine a test of the performance of a microscope as to resolve the more difficult lines on the scales of a butterfly's wing, or any other of the known test-objects. And in many cases the microscope only indicates the existence of a still more delicate structure, which, at least in its present stage, it has not power distinctly to exhibit.

He then went on to examine crystals having the power of analysing polarized light in a manner analogous to the tourmalines:

. . for which reason I shall propose for them the name of *Analytic Crystals*. If I am not mistaken, this property has been hitherto confined to the tourmaline and a few other natural minerals; and it has not been known that their effects could be imitated, much less surpassed, by crystals artificially made.

After proposing some theoretical considerations to account for the properties, he looked forward to the possibility that large and permanent artificial crystals might be obtained which would have the advantages and none of the disadvantages of tourmaline.

The Royal Society was impressed with the work on crystals. Although delivered in 1836, 'Further observations on the optical phenomena of crystals' was designated the Bakerian Lecture for 1837. Henry described the announcement to Constance:

While I was drinking tea, the Assistant Secretary of the Royal Society called upon me & informed me that the Council having voted that my paper on crystals which I sent them about a twelve month ago, should be the Bakerian Lecture for the present year, a prize of £4 had thereby become due to me, which he therefore had called for the purpose of paying to me. So I thanked him for his politeness & put the £4 into my new purse and intend to make you a present of them.[55]

He continued with the work and in 'On a new property of nitre' in 1838, he challenged certain general conceptions in the dynamics of crystal formation. In the same year there were a number of references to 'drawings' of crystals

executed by Henry Talbot – some were exhibited at a soirée at Buckingham
Palace by the Royal Duke of Sussex – but it may be assumed that these were
hand sketches of crystal structure as seen by the polarizing microscope as distinct from the photogenic drawings of solar-microscope images, which Talbot
exhibited in the following year after his announcement of the photogenic
drawing process.

Numerous other topics appeared in the papers which – when published in
the *Philosophical Magazine* – frequently took the form of a miscellany or com-
pendium of different subjects.* Besides polarization, Talbot studied such
optical phenomena as interference and diffraction[56] and he returned on several
occasions to the problem of how to generate homogeneous light from artificial
flame. The latter was a critical issue then because it was considered that the
production of a 'pure' homogeneous or monochromatic light would greatly
facilitate the study of light generally, besides solving the microscopist's problem
of achromatic aberration found in early lenses. (In fact later, more critical
examination of homogeneous light showed that it was neither homogeneous
nor monochromatic.)

In one paper he showed an awareness of what we would now term colour
temperature differences in daylight and artificial light, and then proceeded to
propose an arrangement of a spinning mirror and light source which could
make a body in rapid motion appear at rest.[57] In 1835 – significantly well
before his announcement of photogenic drawing in 1839 – he sought to draw
an analogy between the apparently delayed darkening of paper soaked in silver
nitrate when removed from direct daylight and the phenomenon of phosphorescence[58] and – also before the announcement of photogenic drawing – he
conducted lengthy experiments into the effect of *heat* upon silver iodide. Talbot
occasionally moved into other areas of interest and he wrote, for example, on
the manner in which water and heat could affect the colour of substances and
even proposed a method (it must be admitted not very soundly based) for
ascertaining the depth of the ocean.[59]

During much of this period, John Herschel – who was knighted on the

---

* Occasionally Talbot was criticized for this approach, although for the best of motives. In a paper on
optics[56] he included a note on a 'Remarkable property of the iodide of lead' (which crystallized *when
heated*). David Brewster wrote to him: 'Your experiment on the iodide of lead is in the highest degree
beautiful. You do wrong in publishing so important an experiment among others. It should have formed
a separate article in order to attract the attention which it merits . . . It will give me great pleasure to
point out to you some trains of *optical* research in which your powers of observation and mathematical
acquirements would ensure success.'[60]

occasion of Queen Victoria's Coronation in June 1838 – had been away at the
Cape of Good Hope conducting his astronomical observations. But he was
aware of Talbot's work and in 1837 wrote a letter[61] generous in its praise:

I am very glad to perceive by the notices which reach me from time to time of what is
going on in the scientific world in England that you continue to cultivate (and that with
real and brilliant success) those pursuits, both theoretical and experimental, in which,
before I quitted England, you had already done so much to distinguish yourself. I trust you
will feel yourself now too deeply pledged in this career to abandon it and that we may
look upon these things as the earnest of still greater & more important discoveries both in
mathematics and photology.

Published papers indicate only part of Talbot's work; it is the surviving
notebooks of the period which provide experimental detail. Inevitably numerous inconclusive and unsuccessful results were recorded but, with later developments in photo-engraving in mind, it is significant to find in a notebook for
1831–2 a comprehensive series of experiments on the chemical characteristics
of potassium bichromate and, in a subsequent notebook, proposals on etching
techniques involving light and numerous 'galvanic' experiments on the characteristics of different acids and metals as well as on the coating of metals.[62]
Some of his speculations foreshadowed important developments. Thus:

Would it be possible to have a meteorological observatory on the top of a mountain &
to enquire of it the temperature, without visiting it? Perhaps thus, by causing a needle to
move, it might strike a platina wire & immerse it in a mercury cup & thereby call into
action a strong electro-magnet whose force might not only effect other mechanical changes,
but might interrupt the circuit for a time by removing part of the wire from 2 mercury
cups. This wire might then descend of itself, & the time of its descent, or that elapsed before
the circuit was found to be re-established, might be made to depend somehow on the
temperature or on the state of the barometer &c.[63]

This was a crude form of what we would now call telemetry – a subject which
Charles Wheatstone examined in more practical detail in 1844.[64]
    Another possible development in 'automatic' recording was proposed in a
letter to J. W. Lubbock in 1836:

I have a contrivance for registering the height of the tide, which I think would answer
very well on trial. It consists in admitting water thro' a pipe of some length into a reservoir
(to ensure tranquility of surface in the latter) and placing vertically in it a board covered
with white paper on which a chemical composition has been washed, which turns yellow

on contact with water. This will of course mark the highest point to which the water rises, and you are secured from negligence of the attendant, because the register may be read off anytime before the next high water. I have found on trial that this paper is *not* discoloured by the action of a moist atmosphere, but requires the actual contact of water, & when dry again, it does not lose the yellow colour it had acquired, in any degree. Therefore I think it would answer the end proposed . . .[65]

This was an early form of chemical recording paper. (The identity of the chemical is not immediately evident from the notebooks.)

At this time Talbot did not limit his scientific activities to experimentation. On at least one occasion he refereed a scientific paper (by Sir David Brewster) for the Royal Society; in 1836–7 (as well as later in 1842–3) he was elected a Royal Society Council Member along with such distinguished colleagues as George Peacock and G. B. Airy – the Astronomer Royal; he was also sitting on a number of specialist committees including those for mathematics, physics, botany and 'vegetable physiology'.* He was one of the 'persons of the highest scientific eminence' whose support was acknowledged in Taylor's *Scientific Memoirs* published in 1837 – a project that he would have regarded as being of the highest importance since it made available translations of valuable scientific papers by foreign authors. Talbot was only too aware throughout his life that not all scholars had his gift for languages and he not infrequently communicated (and of course attributed) the substance of the results of foreign scientists and other scholars in his own papers. His activity was by no means limited to the national level – for example, in 1834 he donated books to the Chippenham Literary and Scientific Institution and specimens to its Devizes equivalent.

Perhaps the only disappointment in Talbot's scientific writings during the 1830s was the virtual absence of any opinion on the wider issues of science – its objectives and importance. Occasionally, there were brief glimpses. Commenting on the likely choice of the Earl of Northampton as the new President of the Royal Society in 1838 he wrote to his mother:[66] 'There is a sad *dearth* of scientific aristocracy; & in a country, the main springs of whose wealth and commerce are so intimately connected with the improvements of science!' In the same year, after John Herschel returned to England, Henry Talbot told him of a 'fringe' science which had developed in his absence abroad and con-

* He was not uncritical of the Royal Society. In 1847 in a letter to W. R. Grove he condemned its lack of 'vitality and interest' – the quality and delivery of the papers read operating 'rather to drive away the members than to bring a full attendance'. (Royal Institution Collection: 1 October 1847.)

tinued: 'I don't know what to make of it, but I think it ought to be thoroughly examined into. It is unworthy of the dignity of science that such a question should be left in its present half & half condition.'[67]

But the most evocative picture of Talbot the scientist came in 1836. In the summer of that year the annual meeting of the British Association for the Advancement of Science (Talbot was a life member) took place at Bristol. He did not think it a very suitable place for the meeting and decided early on to invite some of the leading scientists attending to stay for a few days around that time at Lacock Abbey – whilst his uncle, Lord Lansdowne, extended a similar invitation from nearby Bowood House. For various reasons Faraday, Lubbock and Peacock could not accept the invitation but in that August of 1836 Henry and Constance entertained David Brewster, William Whewell, Charles Babbage, Charles Wheatstone, P. M. Roget and William Snow Harris (another to be knighted later – for his electrical researches). Brewster wrote to his wife delightedly:

This place is a paradise – a fine old abbey, with the square of cloisters entire, fitted up as a residence, and its walls covered with ivy, and ornamented with the finest evergreens. All are Whigs, and our only stranger today is Tom Moore,[*] a most delightful person, full of life, humour and anecdote.[68]

Constance wrote to Lady Elisabeth about the effect of the visitors – and particularly Sir David Brewster – upon Henry:

You are perfectly right in supposing Sir David Brewster to pass his time pleasantly here. He wants nothing beyond the pleasure of conversing with Henry discussing their respective discoveries & various subjects connected with science. I am quite amazed to find that scarcely a momentary pause occurs in their discourse. Henry seems to possess new life & I feel certain that were he to mix more frequently with his own friends we should never see him droop in the way which now so continually annoys us. I am inclined to think that many of his ailments are nervous – for he certainly does not look ill. I hear from Sir David that he *distinguished* himself at the meeting in a conversation on the Improvement of the Telescope. . . . When I see the effect produced in Henry by Sir D. B's society, I feel most acutely how dull must our ordinary way of life be to a mind like his! And yet he shuts himself up from choice . . .[69]

---

* Thomas Moore, the Irish poet, song writer and biographer of Byron, was no stranger to the Talbot family. He lived in a cottage at near-by Sloperton and had been a frequent and welcome visitor to the Abbey since 1827.

Brewster was to remain Talbot's closest scientific friend throughout his life – but Constance had correctly identified Talbot's growing asocial tendencies which eventually developed to the extent where he found even scientific meetings unbearable and refused to attend them. His paths of scientific research increasingly became solitary ones, interspersed with occasional contacts with scientists for whom he had a high regard. It was this attitude – which steadily developed as the 1830s progressed – that was to make the publicity and controversy surrounding the discovery of photography so distasteful to him.

Henry Talbot's achievements in scientific research in the 1830s were matched cy his mathematical work. It will be recalled that in the previous decade he boncentrated increasingly on the mathematics of the arcs of various curves. His fascination with the subject continued in the 1830s and figured prominently in papers presented to the Royal Society – his interest in the analytical treatment of conic sections merging perfectly with his typical response to the challenge of unsolved or partly solved questions. Mathematics occupied a prominent place in the notebooks of the period – for example, that for 1833–4[70] being taken up almost entirely by integration and representing serious preparation for his papers to the Royal Society in 1834 and for his major work on the integral calculus presented in 1836.

His work was not without setbacks. After presenting his two papers 'On a new property of the arcs of the equilateral hyperbola'[71] and 'On the arcs of certain parabolic curves',[72] Talbot submitted to the Royal Society his 'account of the principles on which this branch of analysis is founded'. It duly came before George Peacock as referee, and he reported:

I have examined Mr Talbot's paper with great care and I am decidedly of opinion that it is not, in its present form, proper to be printed in the Transactions of the Royal Society, for the following reasons.

1. It contains nothing more than a series of examples, which are included as consequences of a more general principle, of which the author says that he is in possession: that principle leads to the assumption of the proper forms, by which the symmetrical equations between the abscissae x and y, or x, y and z, are determined . . . the question may very properly be asked, why is this principle not developed?

2. In the particular conclusions which Mr Talbot has given, there is no determination of the constant . . . without its determination these results admit of no definite geometrical interpretation.

3. There is no determination of the algebraical sign of the abscissae x and y or x, y and

F

z. . . . [this] ambiguity in his results . . . is admitted by Mr Talbot himself, and he gives
no indication of the steps . . . by which this ambiguity may be removed.

Notwithstanding these objections to the publication of Mr Talbot's paper in its present
form, the results contained in it are remarkably curious and are probably connected with
general theorems of great interest and value, the complete development and publication
of which are certainly desirable. It is for this reason that I should recommend that this
paper should be again referred to Mr Talbot, in order that . . . the objections above stated
. . . may be removed.

I have not been able to deduce any of Mr Talbot's results from Abel's theorem, though
they are most probably deducible from it: thus further development of the method
pursued by Mr Talbot in obtaining them would probably settle this question very
easily.[73]

The verdict was delivered to Talbot by J. W. Lubbock in the course of correspondence about the subject of integration in which the mathematical world
was showing renewed interest because of the recent investigations of the young
Norwegian Abel. Lubbock was impressed by Abel's work, and was at first
inclined to see nothing fresh in Talbot's approach.

Talbot took the advice of his mentors and the objections were overcome.
The paper 'Researches in the integral calculus, Part 1' was read before the
Royal Society on 10 March 1836. It was the longest and most important of his
mathematical essays. In October 1835 he had written to William Whewell at
Trinity College:

I am engaged in preparing a mathematical paper for the Royal Society, that I have had
in hand, at intervals, a long time. It is on the Integral Calculus, and offers, in my opinion
at least, a very satisfactory solution of the problem of fixing an algebraic sum of a series
of integrals like $\int \phi(X)\,dx$ where ϕ is *any* function whatever of the *rational* polynomial X. I have reason to suppose that this very much extends the *frontier* of the science
in that direction.[74]

From the time the calculus was invented by Newton and Leibniz the processes
of differentiation and integration had been applied to the geometry of curves,
using the algebraic equations connecting the coordinates by which the curves
are represented on graph paper. *Differentiation* is an operation which obtains
the relation between a small change in a function of a variable and the corresponding small change in the variable itself: it can be applied to any function,

and the result appears as another function. The inverse operation, namely, given a function of x, to find out what was differentiated to produce it, is *integration*, and is not always possible in terms of known functions.

In the particular case of the arc of a curve, although the expression for the arc of a circle is an integral that can be evaluated in terms of known (trigono-metric) functions, that for an arc of an ellipse or hyperbola, for instance, can not. Fagnani, in 1718, had investigated this, followed by Euler and Legendre: they all succeeded in finding a simple expression for the *sum of two such arcs* of an ellipse: but there, up to the 1820s, the matter rested. There was no *general* theory, though Legendre and Gauss were still working at it.

What Talbot did was to invent a new method of obtaining the sum of two, three or more such integrals as algebraic expressions. His method was quite original and different from that of Legendre (and of wider application) and also from that of Abel, which was hailed in 1828 as a breakthrough. Had Talbot completed and published his work in, say, 1825 (when it existed in note form, though he may have thought of it even earlier while still at Cambridge) he would have had the acclaim given to Abel.

Abel's theorem, referred to by Peacock and Lubbock above, was limited in application, although considered novel at the time. His really revolutionary treatment of elliptic integrals, which gained him posthumous fame and which was the foundation of the future theory of elliptic *functions*, taking it away from its geometric connections, was yet to be published.

Probably the best commentary of Talbot's paper is provided in his own words.[75]

In the year 1828 Mr Abel . . . published a very remarkable theorem, which gives the sum of a series of integrals of the form $\int \frac{P\,dx}{\sqrt{R}}$, where P and R are entire functions of x [i.e. polynomials] . . .

Abel's theorem in general furnishes a multitude of solutions for each particular case of the problem: notwithstanding which it is possible to find other solutions which appear not to be comprised in his theorem, nor deducible from it.

On the publication of this theorem the illustrious Legendre . . . devoted a large portion of time to the verification and elucidation of the theorem by numerical examples.

Talbot then gave other classes of integrals for whose solution Abel's theorem 'affords us no assistance' but 'to the solutions of which the following notes will be dedicated'.

Abel's theorem was unknown to me until some years after its publication, and ... these researches were nearly completed before I was acquainted with it. I have, however, made no alteration in them, but have chosen to present the subject in the manner in which it originally occurred to me.

I am not aware that Mr Abel has left any memorial of the successive steps of reasoning by which he arrived at his theorem. Probably they were very different from those which I have employed ...

The first idea of a more extended method occurred to me about fifteen years ago, when pursuing mathematical studies at Cambridge; and it was suggested by an attentive consideration of the process by which Fagnani had rectified the hyperbola ...

Proposing the equation $r + C = S \int \phi x \, . \, dx$ [where $r =$ product xyz ... and S means the sum of such integrals using x, y, z ... in turn] Talbot continued:

This equation I first obtained in the year 1821, but not having leisure at that time to pursue the subject much further, I contented myself with making a note of it ... I afterwards found it to be the key of the whole method. In the year 1825 I resumed this investigation ... I here give the results of some of these early trials, just as I find them in the original papers ...[76]

I now perceived that the hypothesis upon which my method was grounded, viz. that $n - 1$ symmetrical equations existed between n variables, was the same thing as to suppose that these variables were the roots of an equation of n dimensions, *one of whose coefficients at least was variable*, the others being either constants, or functions of the variable one. This consideration introduced a great degree of clearness and simplicity into the subject, besides facilitating ... the progress of research.

That was the breakaway from routine methods: but it implied a further necessity:

... the inverse problem still remains. *Given the function $\phi \, x$, or the integral $\int \phi \, . \, dx$, to find the equation*

$$x^n - px^{n-1} + \ldots \ldots \pm r = 0,$$

of which $x, y, z, \ldots$ must be the roots, in order that $S \int \phi x \, . \, dx$ may have an algebraic sum?

This is evidently the most important part of the subject, for in applying the method to practice the form of the function ϕx is given beforehand ...

Of Example 1, $\int \dfrac{dx}{\sqrt{1 - x^3}}$, Talbot said in his paper:

This is Mr Lubbock's first example in his paper on Abel's theorem in the Phiolsophical Magazine [vol. vi, p. 118] . . . For the sake of comparison I will take this as the first example of my method . . . ,

proceeding to obtain Lubbock's results by what was undoubtedly a much simpler and clearer method than Lubbock's adaptation of Abel. (The result of both methods was

$$\int \frac{dx}{\sqrt{1-x^3}} + \int \frac{dy}{\sqrt{1-y^3}} = \text{const.}$$

if x and y satisfy the equation $xy - (x+y) = 2$.) He went on to show that the sum of three integrals of the form $\int \frac{dx}{\sqrt{1-x^3}}$ was constant, provided that $xy+xz+yz = 0$, and $xyz = 1$.

The second point of Peacock's criticism can now be seen – no determination of the constant and consequently no geometric interpretation: the integrals applied in this way, have meaning only by becoming definite integrals, between assigned limits of the variable. Talbot's own notation shows how he overcame the difficulty. Representing the three integrals by $\int_x$, $\int_y$, $\int_z$, he proved $\int_x + \int_y + \int_z = \text{constant}$, subject to the relations between x, y and z. He next took three other values of the variables, x', y' and z', and then $\int_{x'} + \int_{y'} + \int_{z'} = \text{the same constant}$, if x', y' and z' satisfy the same conditions.

By subtraction, $(\int_x - \int_{x'}) + (\int_y - \int_{y'}) + (\int_z - \int_{z'}) = 0$, and $\int_x - \int_{x'}$ represented the length of an arc between two points whose abscissae were x and x'. Thus Talbot proved his theorem – that subject to certain conditions the (algebraic) sum of three arcs was zero. The task of finding numerical values of x, y, z and x', y', z' to satisfy the required relations involved, and of checking by substitution in the equivalent infinite series, demanded much calculation, and Talbot hoped that agreement to five places of decimals would 'be considered to be a sufficient trial of its accuracy'.

After a number of examples, and the numerical verification, he added a note:

The integrals comprised in the formula $\int \frac{P\,dx}{\sqrt{R}}$ have been called ultra-elliptic by

Legendre. I think I have sufficiently shown that no line of distinction can be drawn between them and integrals in general: all of which, that are functions of a given polynomial, possess the property which was supposed to characterize the ultra-elliptic class.

Part 2 of the Researches followed in November of the same year.[77] But before its publication an almost converted George Peacock wrote his report:

. . . it is well worthy of being printed in our Transactions. This memoir is entirely occupied with examples illustrating the general theorem contained in his former memoir and many of them are of great interest and novelty. After showing its application to some well-known and some new and remarkable properties of circular arcs, he proceeds to apply it to arcs of the parabola, ellipse and hyperbola, establishing by means of it not merely most of those theorems . . . which have been known previously, but likewise many others which are quite new; the facility with which these conclusions follow from his theorem is the best proof of its very comprehensive character: it ought to be observed, however, that these conclusions do not follow directly from it, but require the aid of assumptions, which are remarkable in many cases for their ingenuity. It is unquestionably a defect of this and the preceding memoir that the principle of those assumptions is not sufficiently laid down. The last example given in this memoir, in which it is shown that three hyperbolic arcs can be formed whose algebraic sum is equal to zero, gives a very remarkable and unexpected conclusion: it requires however further development.[78]

Peacock also wrote in August 1836 to the Assistant General Secretary of the British Association for the Advancement of Science suggesting that Talbot should be invited to give some comments on his researches at the Bristol meeting for 'his results are very curious & in some respects more general than those of Abel'.[79]

The 'last example', to which Peacock's report referred, was the same theorem as that which Talbot had demonstrated in 1834 to the Royal Society in the *Proceedings*, and again in Part 1. In Part 1 he had said of it – and the comment is characteristic –

When I arrived at this result, I immediately perceived that (provided there were no error in the reasoning, of which I at first entertained some doubts) it was an entirely new and undiscovered property of the hyperbola.

His final note – in Part 2 – again referring to this last property, was:

This appears to me to show the possibility of finding three arcs such that (neglecting their signs) the sum of two of them shall be equal to the third (though not superposable in any part). I believe that it has been hitherto held that this equality is impossible in the ellipse and hyperbola, without the addition of *some algebraic quantity*.

The Royal Society had no doubts as to the value of his contribution and awarded a Royal Medal to Talbot in 1838 for his researches on the integral calculus.* He described how he learned of the award in a typically amusing and slightly self-deprecatory letter to his wife:

Yesterday when I went to attend the meeting of the Royal Society I was rather late and found them all seated. The Assistant Secretary came up & begged me to go and sit upon the bench nearest to the Chairman. I asked him, why so? and he said, because I was to receive the Royal Gold Medal. I told him I knew nothing about it & considered that he must be mistaken, upon which we adjourned to the library & examined the proceedings of the Council for the last week or two, but could make out nothing. In this rather singular dilemma, I thought it best to send him to make private enquiry of the Secretary what was the truth of the matter, and he came back and said that it was the fact that the Council had awarded me the Medal for my mathematical papers published in their Transactions but that the award having been made only *yesterday* they had not been able to apprize me of it. A medal was also awarded to Dr Faraday for experiments on electricity. Dr Roget [The Society's Secretary and the author of *Roget's Thesaurus*] read the report of the Council, eulogising these researches and investigations; and then Mr Baily the Chairman made us a short speech & informed us that it having been necessary to cut a new die with the head of Her Majesty, which was not yet finished, of course the medals were not yet struck; and consequently he could only inform us that we were entitled to them & should receive them at a future time . . .[80]

After 1837 Talbot gave no more mathematical papers to learned societies for twenty years. He did, however, maintain some interest in mathematics. In 1843 he wrote to Herschel:

Talking of comets, in my more mathematical days I once found out the following simple theorem. If the passage of a comet thro' *both* its nodes is observed, these 2 observations suffice to determine the orbit rigorously & by a very simple geometrical construction. Except the *inclination*, which remains indeterminate . . . I had afterwards reason to believe that my theorem was not altogether new, but I have since lost the memoranda I made on that point. The orbit is assumed parabolic.[81]

The earliest surviving notebooks contain much about the motion of comets, but not, it seems, the theorem in question.

* Two Royal Medals were awarded by the Queen annually on the recommendation of the Council of the Royal Society. At that time one was awarded for a 'most important contribution' in the physical sciences and one in the biological sciences.

Correspondence between Herschel and Talbot in 1844 showed them still discussing what were now called Abelian integrals. Herschel referred to his own work on transcendents:

In my specific applications of the principle, only *explicit* functions . . . are used. You, by extending your views *most happily* to *implicit* functions . . . tapped a fresh spring out of which have welled forth some very sparkling & delicious theorems. There yet remains another rock to be struck . . . I regret my disuse of mathematics & fifty other reasons . . . prevent my going to work at it.[82]

Talbot matched Herschel's imagery:

At every step you take, you start coveys of beautiful theorems (excuse a September metaphor) which hardly by any other means can be got hold of, else Legendre and others would certainly have found them.[83]

They were also discussing plane sections of an oblique cone, a fairly elementary property. Herschel, at the second attempt, got the correct analytical picture of the sections but Talbot was not satisfied that his own original doubts were resolved.

I take the circular section which you have obtained, and consider it to be the base of the cone, and now how do you show that any difference exists between this cone and a common oblique cone, having [the] same base and vertex? They must be identical. But then, it may be said, this is self-evident and could not escape the penetration of a geometer like M. Chasles. So that I am fairly at a loss what to think of it.[84]

Not for the first time Talbot was reluctantly confident that he had found a flaw in the reasoning of an accepted authority.

Politics, marriage, science and mathematics – but Talbot was still not finished with the decade. In July 1838 he published the first volume of *Hermes – Classical and Antiquarian Researches* and in October 1839 a second volume in the same series. In between – in April 1839 – he published *The Antiquity of the Book of Genesis Illustrated by Some New Arguments*. All three comprised essays on etymological subjects – sometimes in support of generalized theories – and occasionally on topics of literary criticism from the classics.

Talbot described his intention in publishing the two *Hermes* volumes – each was a little under one hundred pages long – in the preface to No. 1. The antiquities of Greece, Italy and Egypt together with the ancient mythology of the Etruscans were the subjects, and he had set out

... to submit to the judgment of those who take an interest in similar enquiries, the series of short essays upon points of classical antiquity, with respect to which I have arrived at conclusions different from those which are generally entertained, or which I hope to present in a new light, not unworthy of the attention of the learned reader.

He had decided to present the researches in the form of a miscellany because researches into remote antiquity 'naturally lead to hypothesis and speculation' and an attempt to 'advocate any particular system' ran the risk of being rejected *in toto* whatever the merits of individual points whereas in a miscellany the 'judicious critic' was more likely to judge each point or essay on its own merits. A selection of the essay titles indicates the scope – 'On the names of the ancient Roman months'; 'Was Homer acquainted with the art of writing?'; 'On the original meaning of the words drama, comedy, and poetry'; 'Observations on Etruscan antiquities'; 'On the great antiquity of the Latin language'; 'On the fable of the Danaïdes'; 'On the word neophyte'; 'Explanation of a passage in Callimachus';* and 'Corrections of a passage in Fronto'.*

The extent of Talbot's classical knowledge needs no emphasis and the *Literary Gazette* enthusiastically welcomed the volumes. In a composite review of *Hermes* No. 2 and *The Antiquity of the Book of Genesis*, its reviewer wrote:

When the First Number of *Hermes* appeared, we had great pleasure in pointing out some of the very curious results at which the author had arrived, and paying the compliments due to his extensive critical research, ingenious philosophical conjectures and abundant references to ancient writers (some of them seldom referred to), in support of the various interesting hypotheses which he had undertaken to maintain. Both the publications above indicated merit similar praise; and even where they fail to bring perfect conviction, they are sustained by so many remarkable illustrations, drawn from obscure, remote and difficult authorities, as well as from more familiar classics, that it is impossible to peruse them without feeling, with great satisfaction, that we are receiving immediate instruction, and being led at the same time, to further reflection and investigation, which will reward our thoughts and repay our labour.[85]

For his part Talbot's old headmaster at Harrow, George Butler, found *Hermes* No. 1 'a very learned & most ingenious production, and I am happy to see

* Callimachus was a major Greek poet of the third century B.C. Fronto was a writer in Rome during the second century A.D.

that your powerful mind finds leisure for such profound researches. In truth
I am quite astonished at the wide range of learning, the multum in parvo,
compressed within the narrow limits of 95 pages.'[86]

Viewed against the standards of the time in England, the volumes had much
to commend them. As the *Literary Gazette* indicated, the learning was deep and
the inevitably speculative etymology stimulating even where it could be
argued that it was wrong. As in his mathematics, Talbot demonstrated, where
appropriate, a refreshing scepticism about the judgements of classical authorities. His treatment was lively – his wry sense of humour being occasionally
displayed – and he could overcome a problem or a lack of evidence by a fine
sense of what a context *required* for a solution. Hence some of his proposals
and theories would be supported by modern classical scholars and etymol-
ogists.

What the volumes lacked, however, was a knowledge or full awareness of
the philological framework which was being evolved in Talbot's time on the
Continent of Europe. Philology demanded a knowledge of the origins and
interrelationships of different languages – and the study had commenced as
early as the British occupation of India through contact with Sanskrit. In 1786
Sir William Jones had proposed a relationship between the classical languages
and Sanskrit from 'a common source which perhaps no longer exists'. In the
following century the Dane Rasmus Rask and German scholars such as Jakob
Grimm pursued researches into phonetic changes between languages and
evolved 'sound laws' which eventually led to a philological structure in which
all of the languages featuring in Talbot's researches were established as having
stemmed from an original Indo-European parent language dating to perhaps
3000 B.C. The Napoleonic Wars cut Britain off from knowledge of this work
during the very early nineteenth century – but the first detailed grammar of
the Indo-European languages (Franz Bopp's *Analytical Comparison of the
Sanskrit, Greek, Latin and Teutonic*) appeared in translation in England in 1820
and – as a German reader – Talbot ought to have been aware of Bopp's comparative grammar which was first published in 1833. To be fair to him, it must
be stressed that it was only in the latter half of the nineteenth century that
phonetic changes between languages really came to be understood and scholars
were able to explain the apparent exceptions to earlier rules.

None the less, unawareness of the relationships which were already being
elaborated by scholars in Europe led Talbot to make comments and claims
which were not valid – for example, he referred in one essay[87] to 'the immense

multitude of Teutonic roots in the Latin language' not realizing that both inherited common elements from the Indo-European parent language. Similarly, he endeavoured to make identifications between Greek and Hebrew[88] which were not valid since the two languages are not related.

Thus despite Talbot's talented and individual approach in the two volumes of *Hermes*, he did not contribute anything of lasting value to etymological and philological studies. The volumes remain as enjoyable, lively and sometimes inspired products of a brilliant Victorian mind which – surprisingly in view of Talbot's cosmopolitan approach to learning and his later obvious awareness of European researches in, for example, Assyriology and related matters – were outside the main stream of philological scholarship on the Continent.

The probable reason for this was that Talbot's approach was that of the dilettante – he was working in so many different areas that he could not or would not devote the time to a subject that demanded the dedication of the professional. This criticism was raised by Thomas Babington Macaulay* when he wrote to Talbot on the publication of *Hermes* No. 1:

> I am truly glad to see such promise of great services to literature as your *Hermes* exhibits. I wish that you would undertake some extensive work. Give us a translation of Herodotus – not like Beloc's wretched performance but in the style of our old English chronicles with all the poetical naivete of the original: and fill the notes as you well know how, with curious information and ingenious speculations.[89]

It was not the first time that a proposal that Talbot should undertake a major work had been made, but it was not to be.

The two volumes of *Hermes* had been published by Longman at Henry Talbot's expense. Some 250 of No. 1 and 200 of No. 2 were printed but sales were not high – only 73 and 40 respectively. Many were given by Talbot to friends and scholars and the remainder were returned eventually by the publishers to Lacock Abbey.

The observations concerning the volumes of *Hermes* may be applied equally to *The Antiquity of the Book of Genesis*. In this collection of essays Talbot regarded as accepted fact that there were allusions to Bible narratives in the histories and mythologies of other nations but proposed to show that

---

* This was shortly before the man who was to become famous for his *History of England* entered Lord Melbourne's Second Government as Secretary of War. He was briefly M.P. for Calne in Wiltshire (a seat controlled by Lord Lansdowne) and it may have been as a result of that connection that Talbot and Macaulay first met.

... there remained a memory in heathen lands, of some mysterious Book having been known to their ancestors, though lost long since, and the greater part of its content forgotten. But that, nevertheless, a recollection had been preserved of the *subject* of the Book. *That it related to the Creation.*[90]

Erudite, lively and ingenious – the essays are of lasting value only in that they reveal early Victorian attitudes and interests: they might indeed be referred to as a 'curiosity'. Talbot had to rely almost exclusively on literary sources and his philological knowledge was patchy, as we have seen. Thus his conclusions were too direct and simplistic: later research has shown the compilation of Genesis to have been an extremely complex matter, more so than Talbot could have known. Moreover, wishful thinking seemed to get the better of him and few readers can have been convinced by his argument that 'the beautiful poetical fable of Pandora must have been borrowed by some very ancient Greek poet or moralist from the biblical narrative of the temptation of Eve',[91] any more than it could be argued convincingly that any ancient peoples (like the Phrygians) believing in a 'universal mother' must have conceived the belief originally from knowledge of the story of Eve.[92] The consolation for Talbot in any modern evaluation of the subject is that many of the topics are still debated fiercely.

The Antiquity of the Book of Genesis sold better than the volumes of *Hermes* – almost ninety out of a print order of 200 – and etymology (particularly in the area of the classics) continued to fascinate him. As late as January 1840 he was planning a third volume of *Hermes* – though as far as the work had progressed it was 'extremely dull'[93] – but his researches subsequently took another direction. Talbot may not have been able to devote sufficient time (or have had the comprehensive knowledge) to make his etymological studies authoritative but no less than twelve surviving notebooks compiled in the 1830s, as well as others compiled later, are an indication of his energy and application in the midst of distractions from many quarters.

Three daughters were born to Henry and Constance Talbot in the decade – Ela Theresa on 25 April 1835; Rosamond Constance on 16 March 1837; and Matilda Caroline on 25 February 1839. Constance was very ill after Ela's birth but fortunately recovered and the other two births were accompanied by no such worries. The family was delighted at the arrival of the babies as most families are, Caroline describing Ela to Lady Elisabeth for example as having 'fine large dark blue eyes, black eyelashes and dark eyebrows . . . a nice fat strong-looking Baby'.[94] Henry, whenever he was away on his travels or in London researching, never forgot their birthdays. He delighted to record their progress in letters to more distant relatives, permitting himself the hope on Ela's birth that 'she means to be very intelligent' and confiding to Horatia when the children began to talk that '[Ela] has got hold of a picture of Mary Queen of Squats [Scots]. I must endeavour to correct the pronunciation, for among all the faults imputed to Mary, I never heard that she deserved that reproach.'[95]

For much of this period Constance and Henry were on their own for Caroline was of course already married and living away from the Abbey and Lady Elisabeth, Charles Feilding and Horatia spent some years on the Continent, mainly at Nice. This enabled Constance to learn the responsibilities of the lady of the house (and of the Manor) without undue stress from the presence of in-laws whom she obviously found somewhat daunting initially. She had to learn how to organize housekeeping, to receive occasional large parties of guests and in Henry's frequent absences to be self-reliant generally – even when a sudden invitation arrived to visit the nobility ('I am summoning all my courage for Lansdowne House this evening as I perceive I shall be obliged to go alone . . .').[96]

She learned fast and as time passed it was obvious that she organized well and was respected by the servants – the respect being returned in a practical manner such as providing medical care for members of the staff who had shown themselves to be devotedly attached to the children. The respect and appreciation came not only from the servants, for after one visit the poet the Revd W. L. Bowles (a frequent visitor to Lacock Abbey as well as to the literary circle at Bowood House) dedicated some verses to her. She stood up firmly to Henry on the few occasions when she thought he was being unjust or failing in any way but the very great love she bore him and the extent to which she missed him was evident even allowing for the somewhat decorous expression of feelings permitted in the letters of the time. 'Adieu, it would do me good to embrace you sometimes – for I miss you very much.' And again: 'I hope when we meet again at home you will take up your abode somewhat nearer to me – would it not be a good opportunity for making an alteration? That is, if you can tear yourself away from the comforts of the confessional.'[97] (The confessional is believed to be the name that was given to a small room off Talbot's study: evidently he often slept there when working at the Abbey.)

Pleasure at the birth of children to Constance and Henry was marred in 1837 by the death of Charles Feilding. He had been ill for some years with severe gout but had borne the affliction bravely. He continued to follow Henry's activities with the fondness of a father and not long before he died insisted on trying to pay back to his stepson a loan of £500 which the latter had made not long after he came of age and which he now refused to accept:

> I only wish I had a larger sum of disposable money at present, for nothing in the world would give me so much pleasure as now that your expenses are increasing, being able to add to your comfort and happiness, who have in so many ways contributed to mine.[98]

Feilding died on 2 September 1837 in London. He had expressed the wish to be buried in a coffin made from the timbers of a ship of the Royal Navy and Henry saw that this was done. Constance (of whom Feilding had written in his will 'it is impossible to know and not to love') felt deeply for Lady Elisabeth and wrote to her husband:

> Dearest Henry – I hope there are yet brighter days in reserve for us, although the sky seems at present overcast . . . I will do my best & if any efforts of mine can avail in the slightest degree to minister comfort either to dear Lady Elisabeth or Horatia I shall feel abundantly satisfied.[99]

Lady Elisabeth in fact remained in London for some time but she appreciated Constance's attitude. On 6 October she wrote her a fond and affectionate letter expressing both the love of her late husband and herself for Constance – and returning to an earlier theme as regards Henry:

> . . . often has he [Feilding] lamented to me in private, that with Henry's extraordinary and super eminent understanding he did not make to himself such a celebrity as he ought and *easily* could, with only a little more perseverance in any one of the many things in which he excels. He certainly loved him like a son and *much more* than I believe Henry ever knew – or imagined.[100]

Lady Elisabeth's long absence abroad had made her pine for the Abbey and when she eventually returned there, she set to work with energy in the garden. Transplanting young oaks was one task: 'I hope you will come and see my Herculean labours, certainly if I had lived in the time of the Ptolemys I should have built a Pyramid.'[101] Her son – deep in his researches – came in for inevitable criticism for not acting decisively and quickly on estate matters. 'You ought to have been an antidiluvian, you take one year to think, another to consider, another to project, another to order...'[102] But there was one thing about Lacock Abbey worrying her far more – and that was Henry's long-standing threat to leave it.

In 1835 he had pronounced himself unsuited for the life of a country gentleman. Lady Elisabeth regarded this as 'alarming' and hoped that it did not include the Abbey: 'I hope for many years of comfort with you enclosed in those cloistered walls, which is the haven in which I would be, and being quite determined to pass my old age there, if you are willing.'[103] Talbot replied that he had no intention of taking any action for several years and had no wish to deprive his mother of staying at the Abbey but that his will to live somewhere else kept increasing:

It is a residence not well suited to me; I like high and dry, rather than low and damp . . . what I should like would be, could I afford it, to live somewhere else & visit Lacock now and then, in the summer.[104]

But Talbot was true to his word and though there was no indication that he had changed his mind, the decade closed with the Abbey still firmly in the family's possession.*

With his numerous researches Henry Talbot was hard pressed to devote much time to the affairs of the estate and the village. Fortunately severely bad times were only encountered in 1837–8 and then W. H. Awdry and his son West (who was assisting his father) continued to handle the inevitable problems sympathetically and well. W. H. Awdry was now ailing after endeavouring to cope for some time with the positions of both bailiff and steward – not too successfully at his age – and he eventually stepped down entirely in 1840.

Talbot's travels continued but in the last years of the decade they were limited to England and Wales. He continued to show his unerring touch as a writer of travel letters. In Malvern in 1838 (where he was holidaying with Constance) he wrote to Lady Elisabeth of the marvellous view – 'One of the most conspicuous objects however being a certain chimney about fifteen miles distant, certainly the tallest in creation as far as my researches on that subject; thus are manufacturers invading the domain of the picturesque.'[105] A few days later he

* Subsequently, Talbot made Lacock Abbey the most photographed building in the early history of photography. None the less in 1841 he wrote to Herschel: 'I must now really transport my apparatus to some locality where picturesque objects are to be met with, such as a Cathedral, or a Seaport Town, for my own neighbourhood is not particularly suited to the artist, and offers no great variety of subjects'.[106]

summarily dismissed the Royal Hotel at Manchester – 'where a waiter thinks
he confers a favor on you if he makes you an answer'.[107]

Thomas Moore recognized Talbot's talent, for a few weeks earlier he had
written to Lady Elisabeth from his cottage at Sloperton:

> Tell Talbot if he will undertake a railroad journey over England (at least where there
> are railroads, for I am not unreasonable) and write me such clever letters at every stopping
> place, I'll ensure him a good round sum for the copyright of his Epistles.[108]

But Henry Talbot was turning his thoughts in a different direction. When his
third daughter Matilda was born in February of 1839, one of his cousins
suggested that she should be given the name *Photogena*. It was a significant
indication of the prominence that photography would occupy in the life of
Henry Talbot and his family for years thereafter.

I. *A Daguerreotype of Talbot made by Antoine Claudet about 1845. (This reproduction has been reversed laterally to correct the mirror image of the original Daguerreotype.)*

9. *Sir John Herschel, photographed by Richard Wheeler Thomas*

10. *Rear Admiral Charles Feilding – from an original water colour*

11. *William Thomas Horner Fox-Strangways, Henry Talbot's uncle and frequent correspondent, who became the 4th Earl of Ilchester*

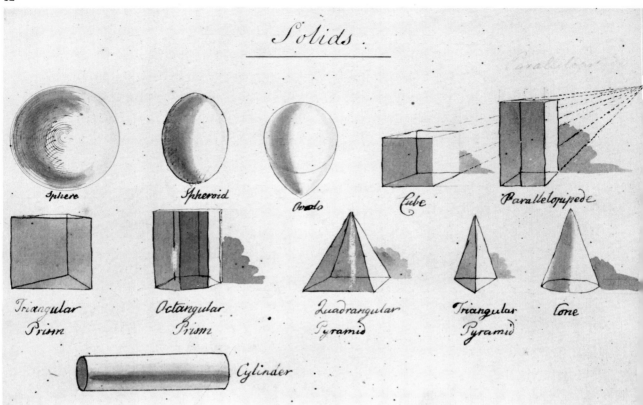

Solids.

Sphere — Spheroid — Ovato — Cube — Parallelopipede

Triangular Prism — Octangular Prism — Quadrangular Pyramid — Triangular Pyramid — Cone

Cylinder

12. *An early entry in Henry Talbot's mathematical and astronomical sketch-book, which he began at the age of nine*

13. *The heavy burden of the poor rate was a continual source of complaint amongst those who had to pay it. Accordingly, village officers administering the system were at pains to account in detail for the money given to the poor – as is demonstrated by this Lacock poster for 1835*

PARISH OF LACOCK.

The Fifth Month's Expenditure for the Year 1835.

MONTHLY PAY.

	£	s	d
Angel Nathaniel, (shirt 2s. 2d.)	0	12	2
Barton Mary, widow	0	4	0
Brinkworth John,	0	18	0
Baker's family, *Bradford*	0	8	0
Barnes William, *Chippenham*	0	16	0
Bond Jane, *Calne*	0	8	0
Barnes Geo. jun. (bread 3s. 6d.)	1	8	6
Barnes Robert,	0	9	0
Barnes J., sen. *Notton*	0	15	0
Barnes Mary, widow	0	6	0
Barnes George, sen.	0	9	0
Barnes J., jun. cripple	0	9	0
Brinkworth Mary, sen.	0	10	0
Brinkworth Ann, sen.	0	12	0
Brinkworth Kezia,	0	3	0
* Brinkworth P. shoemaker, (bread 1s. 8d.)	0	7	9
Brinkworth Susan, widow	0	9	0
Bond George,	0	18	0
Bond Maria,	0	10	0
Beasant Widow, *Chippenham*	0	9	0
Bailey William,	0	10	0
Button Sus., (bread 3s. 6d.)	0	19	6
Banks Robt., blind, (do. 3s. 6d.)	0	16	6
Bath Widow	1	12	0
Banks Ann, widow	0	12	0
Bridgeman's fam., *Chippenham*	1	4	0
Bruton Wm. *Bradford*, weaver	0	2	0
Brinkworth Jas. (shirt 2s. 2d.)	0	6	2
Caines Betty, widow	0	8	0
* Crew John, labourer	0	4	0
Crew Arthur,	0	10	0
Croker James, (bread 3s. 6d.)	0	18	6
Church Elizabeth,	1	0	0
Cullermer Sarah,	0	9	0
Crew Robert,	0	10	0
Crew James, pension	0	14	0
Clark Jane, *Corsham*	0	8	0
Cott Mary, wid. *Bath*,	1	2	0
Dummer George,	0	12	0
Drew Ann,	0	10	0
Drew Sarah, widow	0	4	0
Dummer Sus. *Holt*	0	8	0
Escott Ann,	0	9	0
Escott William,	0	8	0
End John,	0	10	0
Elms Robert, (shoes 1s.)	0	5	0
Ford widow, *Limpley Stoke*	0	10	0
Flower James	0	10	0
Freame H. *Nunny*, 24 weeks, and 1s. extra	3	1	0
Gibbons Sarah,	0	9	0
Goodman John	0	4	0
Hunt Jane, *Melksham Forest*	0	9	0
Hudd Thomas, *Wick Lane*	0	18	0
Hudd Betty	0	4	0
* Hudd George, tanner	0	4	0
Hudd James, *Wick Lane*	1	0	0
Heath Hannah, widow	0	6	0
Heath Ann, widow	0	8	0
Heath Lovey,	0	10	0
Hood Mary, widow, *Calne*	0	4	0
* Hood Daniel, labourer	0	4	0
Hillier Daniel,	0	18	0
Humphreys Anthony,	0	18	0
Hunt Charles, sen.	0	6	0
Hunt Ambrose,	0	10	0
* Hancock W. (for sick wife) lab.	0	4	6
Carried up	£39	0	7

	£	s	d
Brought up	39	0	7
Harper James,	0	12	0
Hayward Betty, *Pickwick*	0	9	0
Harring Robert, *Trowbridge*	0	14	0
Hambleton Mary, for nursing James Croker's child	0	6	0
Hudd Sarah	0	16	0
Jenkins Betty,	0	9	0
Jones Mary,	0	8	0
Mathews Grace, widow	0	10	6
Mathews Sarah, sen.	0	10	0
* Mitchell D. (bread 1s. 9d.) lab.	0	2	3
Newman's family, *Chippenham*	0	10	0
Oliffe Sarah,	0	9	0
Parsons Sarah, wid. *Yarnbrook*	0	6	0
* Pegler James, (bread 1s. 9d.)	0	6	3
Pullen Joseph	0	14	0
Pearce William	1	0	0
* Powney John, (bread 1s. 9d.)	0	6	3
* Paradise William, *Beckington*	0	11	0
Paradise Elizabeth. *Martick*, 62 weeks	4	3	0
Robins Betty,	0	10	0
Robins Widow, *Chittoee*	0	10	0
Reynolds Jane,	0	6	0
Robins Thomas	0	4	0
Stevenson Jane,	0	8	0
* Stevens William, labourer	0	4	0
Stevens Robert,	0	18	0
* Spackman Joseph, labourer	0	4	0
Shewring Robert,	0	18	0
* Sadd James, tanner	0	4	0
Self Hannah,	0	9	0
* Smith John, labourer	0	4	0
Tadd Isaac,	1	0	0
* Tadd Jerry, labourer	0	4	0
* Taylor George, labourer	0	4	0
Tuff Roger	0	12	0
Tanner Rachael,	0	9	0
Tanner William, *Chippenham*	0	10	0
Tugwell Priscilla, *Calne*	0	10	0
Townsend Eliz. *Trowbridge*, 18 weeks and 6d. extra	1	7	6
* Webb Samuel, labourer	0	4	0
White Elizabeth,	0	6	0
* Wheeler J. *Chippenham* cobbler	0	4	0
	£62	12	4

BASTARD PAY.

	£	s	d
Banks Elizabeth	0	5	0
Harring Eliza,	0	5	0
Hiscock Sarah,	0	8	0
Jenkins Jane,	0	6	0
Morse Edith, *South St. Cerney*, 12 weeks	0	12	6
Reynolds Sarah	0	5	0
Self Eleanor,	0	4	0
	£2	5	6

OTHER PARISHES.

	£	s	d
W. Weston, for Parish of Baydon	0	5	0
Widow Mathews, for Parish of Weston	0	12	0
William Dunkerton, for Parish of Warminster	0	18	0
	£1	15	0

EXTRA PAY.

	£	s	d
James Crew's wife, lying-in	0	5	0
Charles Tadd's wife, ditto	0	2	0
William Hudd, *Notton*, (child dead)	0	3	6
Thomas Hudd, absconded with £1 obtained under false pretences	1	0	0
James Giddings, (child ill)	0	1	0
George Caines (bread 5s. 3d.)	0	2	0
James Jenkins, gratuity of Select Vestry, for good character	0	10	0
Mary Ann Elms, gone to service	0	10	0
Jas. Taylor 3d.—Ann Hiscock 3d.	0	0	6
Shroud for Bridgett Harring, as per bill*	0	5	0
Publishing Poors' Rate in Church	0	1	0
Postage of Letters, and Paper	0	2	4
Harness for G. Paradise, as per bill	1	4	0
Harness for Jas. Taylor, as per bill	1	4	0
One year's Interest on £60 advanced for purposes of Emigration, due May the 12th	2	14	0
Summonses, Justice Meeting Expences, &c.	0	13	0
Mr. Aberdeen 33 gallons of bread, at 10d. per gallon, as per bill	1	7	6
Mrs. Barton 67½ gallons of bread, at 10d. per gallon, as per bill	2	16	3
Mr. Howell for coffins, as per bill	1	10	6
County Rate	21	8	0
	£35	19	7

*Shrouds are now made in the Asylum at 1s. each.

Total Expenditure of Fifth Month.

	£	s	d
Monthly Pay	62	12	4
Bastard Pay	2	5	6
Other Parishes	1	15	0
Extra Pay	35	19	7
	£102	12	5

Names and Description of Paupers in the Asylum.

Names.	Age.	Description.
Maria White	34	Illegitimate; extremely deaf, and defective in speech.
Caroline White	13	Children of the above, all illegitimate, and by different fathers. Entered the Asylum with 4—one since dead.
Isaac White	8	
Wilmot White	4	
Caroline Elms	11	Sisters—taken from their mother, Betty Elms, on account of her bad conduct towards them. Another Sister, Mary Ann, has been put out to service, and is doing well.
Emma Elms	9	
Henry Prosser	11	Brothers—mother dead—deserted by father soon after their mother's death.
John Prosser	8	
James Escott	44	One family—the man sick—woman ditto and subject to fits.
Hester Escott	27	
Eliza Escott	5	
John Fry	15	Orphan—son of Samuel Fry.
William Prosser	18	Sick.
Mary Humphreys	45	An Idiot (commonly known as Crazy Poll.)
Catherine Drew	50	Deserted by her husband 9 years.
James Drew	4	Child of the above !
James Hiscock	13	Illegitimate—father Geo. Barnes.

30 other persons have been admitted into the Asylum from its first opening in August, 1834, but have left it of their own will, or have been discharged.

Those Names which have BREAD standing against them, have received Bread to that amount, in addition to the Money in the Column.

Those Marked thus (*) are able-bodied.

THOMAS SHEARN, *Assistant Overseer.*

PRINTED BY J. NOYES, BOOKSELLER, BINDER, &c. CHIPPENHAM.

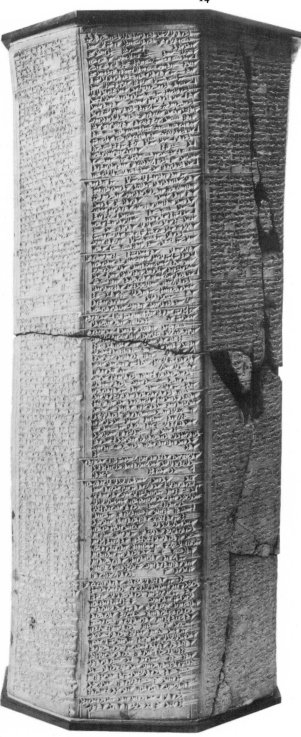

14. *A cylinder dating from the reign of the Assyrian king Tiglath-Pileser I. Talbot proposed that translations of the inscription by different scholars working separately would demonstrate the degree of success achieved in the decipherment of cuneiform*

15. *For a brief period, Henry Talbot and Charles Wheatstone cooperated on research into electric motors. This electrolytic engine – built in 1840/1 – was one result of their joint efforts*

16. *Henry Talbot's solar microscope*

15

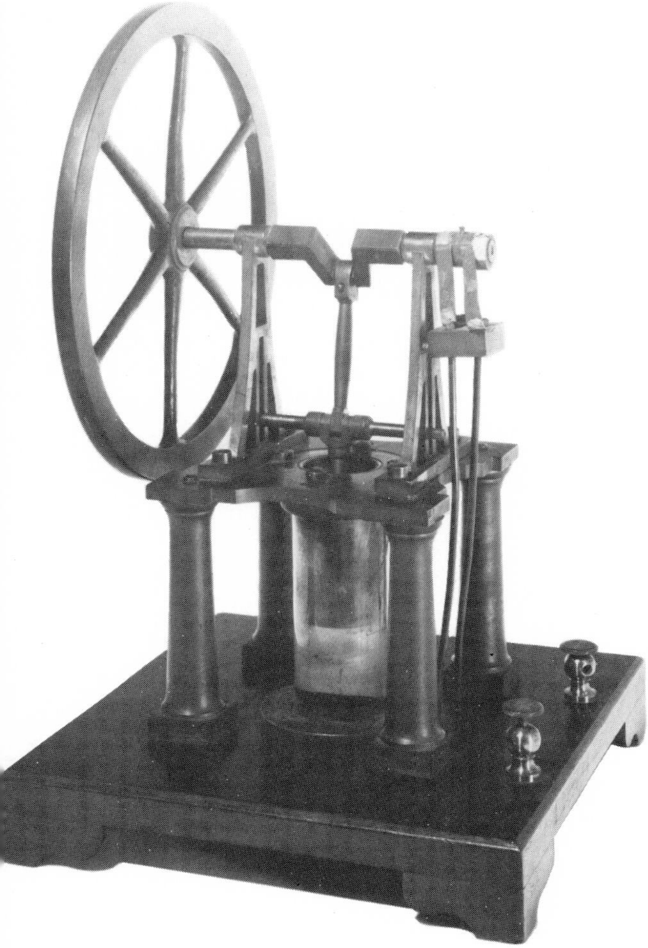

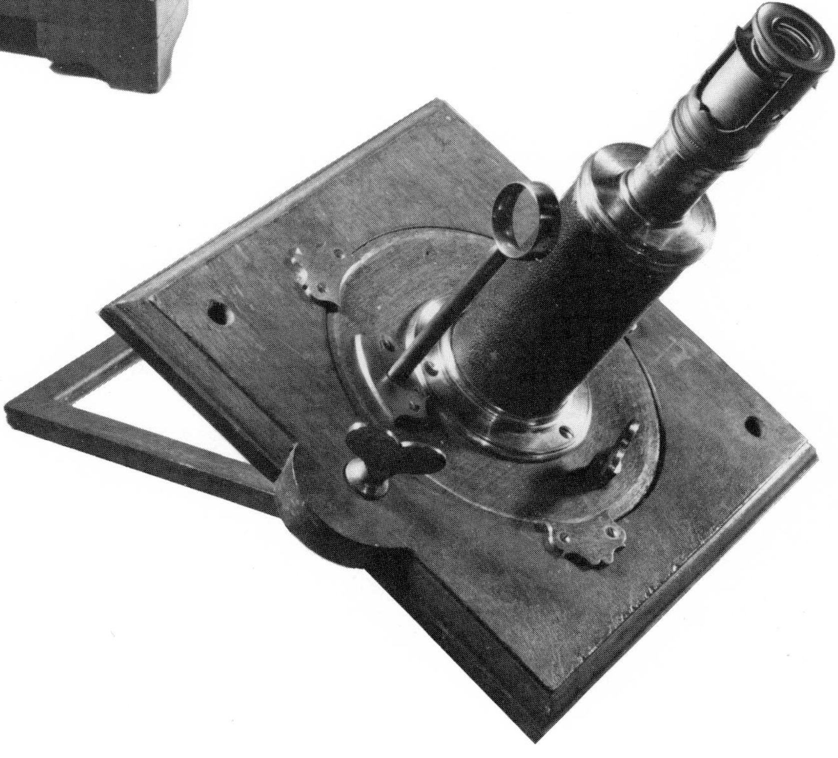

16

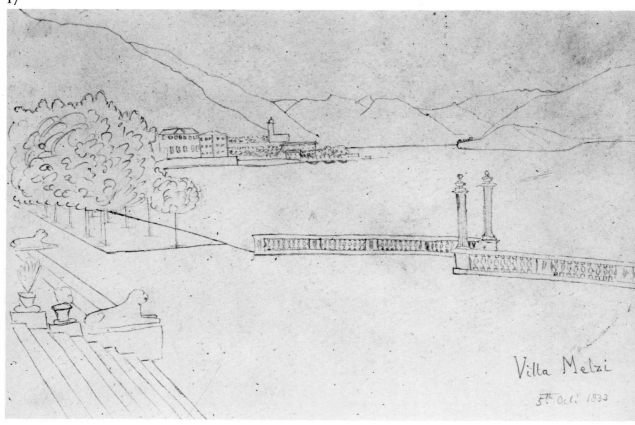

17

Villa Melzi

5ᵗʰ Oct. 1833

17. *It was Talbot's disappointment with sketches like this, made in Italy in 1833, which led to his photographic experiments*

18. *Three of the very small cameras used by Talbot in the period 1835-9*

19. *Three of his relatively early, but larger, cameras. In the centre camera, field curvature of the lens required the sensitized paper to be curved and the image was also circular. For photography of tall objects, the camera at left could be tilted, being held in place by a ratchet. The 'bung hole' at the front of each of the cameras was probably used to check the initial focus*

magnet   magnet

Piston is attached to the piece A. Elastic substances are not
necessary to enable the piston to recover its former position,
as the magnets are to act alternately.

In the Photogenic or Sciagraphic process, if the paper
is transparent, the first drawing may serve as an
object, to produce a second drawing, in which the
lights and shadows would be reversed. If an
object, as a flower, be strongly illuminated, or
its image formed by a camera obscura, perhaps
a drawing might be effected of it, in which case not
its outline merely would be obtained, but other
details of it. For this purpose concentrated solar
rays might be thrown on it: but best employ only
violet light because we want chemical rays
and not heating rays lest the flower should be
scorched by their intensity. My large concave
mirror might be covered with plate glass washed over
with blue gum or resin. Perhaps ammonia &
copper might be made to unite with water and
gum, so as to remain transparent when dry:
if not, it might be used in a viscid state
pressed between 2 plates of glass — At any rate
the rays might be intercepted by a small blue
glass nearer the focus.

'Tis the last rose of summer

Left blooming alone;

All her lovely companions

Are faded and gone;

Collodion process on paper

Dec. 2. 1854   *H.F.T.*

20. Notebook entry for 28 February 1835:
Talbot describes the negative – positive principle
of photography

21. A negative of lines composed of individual
letters cut out and placed on a ground and then
copied with the camera. The concept was
included in Talbot's photographic patent of
1843

22. That collodion could be used on paper
as well as glass was an important element in
Talbot's defence of his 1841 patent at the Talbot
v. Laroche trial of December 1854. This example
of a collodion paper negative was prepared as
evidence and bears Talbot's own handwriting

23. *A view of Talbot's Reading establishment, formed by joining two Calotype originals. The activities shown include a portrait session, the photography of works of art and the 'printing out' of paper positives by the action of light. Nicolaas Henneman is third from the right. It is surmised that some of the members of the staff appearing in one of the pictures moved to different poses in the other. The two original Calotypes were taken possibly in 1846/7*

Windsor Castle
May 6th

Admit Mrs Talbot to walk
in The Slopes to make Drawings

Errolls

a Ld Steward.

24.   *Signed authority from the Lord Steward for Talbot to take*
photographs in the grounds of the royal residence at Windsor in 1841

4
Photogenic Drawing

Some time in the second or third week of January 1839, Henry Talbot received the startling news that Louis Jacques Mandé Daguerre – joint founder of the Diorama, a theatre of optical illusions in Paris – had discovered a means of permanently recording the images from nature secured in a camera obscura not by the subjective medium of the artist's pen or brush but by the action of light on a prepared plate. Daguerre in fact had been working on his process for some years and in 1838 had reached the stage where financial support for its further development was being openly canvassed. Not a word of this reached Talbot – which was surprising in view of his frequent visits to Paris and his many contacts with French men of science – but the cause may have been his concentration in the second half of the 1830s first on his papers on integral calculus and then on the publication of the two volumes of *Hermes* and that of *Genesis*. Had he heard any news of Daguerre's work it is certain that he would have prepared a major paper for submission to the Royal Society as a matter of some urgency for he, too, had been researching on the effects of light on chemical preparations used both in the camera obscura and outside it. These researches, which had been extremely intermittent in the face of the demands of other work, had reached a stage worthy of scientific notice even if they were not as perfect as he would have wished. Now somebody else had made an announcement first.

The *Gazette de France* carried news of Daguerre's discovery in its issue of 6 January and on the following day François Arago – a secretary of the Académie des Sciences, director of the Paris Observatory, a member of the Chamber of Deputies and as such one of the most powerful figures in French

G

science – made a formal announcement to the Académie. While relatively little practical detail was revealed in these early announcements (this was not to come until August) it was clear that Daguerre worked with polished metal plates whereas Talbot's system was based on sensitized paper. He may not have realized this initially – although the *Literary Gazette* of 12 January and the *Athenaeum* of 26 January both referred to metal being used in Daguerre's process[1] – or perhaps with a cynical disbelief in the accuracy of the press and having been pushed into action finally he may have decided that there was nothing to lose by pursuing all means open to him of establishing an independent claim of discovery.

The first step was an exhibition of what Talbot already termed his *photogenic drawings** at the regular meeting of the Royal Institution on 25 January. At the conclusion of a lecture on the polarization of light, Michael Faraday drew the audience's attention to the examples of Talbot's work in the library, and observed, according to the *Literary Gazette* account that:

> The principal object of the exhibition of the photogenic drawings, on this occasion, was meant (as was understood) to establish a date, in order, that should M. Daguerre's discovery be made public previously to the reading, before the Royal Society, of Mr Talbot's paper detailing his process, no charge of imitation could be brought against Mr Talbot, in case of identity of process. And that each discovery should be thus proved to be original.[2]

The pictures included views of Lacock Abbey taken in 1835 by the camera obscura, representations of flowers, leaves, lace and engravings which had been pressed into contact with Talbot's sensitized paper which was then exposed to daylight, as well as specimens obtained with the solar microscope.†[3]

An initial exposure in Talbot's system produced what was to become known a little later (and ever since) as a *negative* but the *Literary Gazette*'s account of the Royal Institution evening indicated that the photogenic drawings included some of engravings in the form that was to become known as *positive* – the result, it said, of 'a singularly ingenious' method in which the reversed impression was copied again so that the 'lights and shades' were correct.[4] Shortly

---

* The *Literary Gazette* in its issue of 2 February was not slow to compare this example of nomenclature adopted by 'our unpretending countryman' with that of Daguerre whose discovery was to be called the *Dagueroscope* according to the magazine.[5]

† An early microscope unit which was normally fitted in a wall so as to collect sunlight and project it through a specimen into a darkened room where the enlarged image of the specimen appeared on a suitable surface. It was often used for demonstrations to groups of people. A Talbot solar microscope is displayed at the Science Museum.

afterwards the *Athenaeum* – which was to become a firm advocate of the superiority of the quality of the Daguerreotype – perceptively noted in a balanced and brief review of the two, then little known systems that there could be no question as to the superior convenience of a system that was based on paper as opposed to metal.[6]

Talbot's second move was to send a letter in French to Arago and the distinguished, veteran physicist Jean–Baptiste Biot (also a secretary of the Académie) to establish formally the priority of his discovery of photogenic drawing. Dated 29 January, the letter read in translation:

Gentlemen: In a few days I shall have the honour of sending to the Academy of Sciences a formal claim of priority for two principal features of the discovery announced by M. Daguerre:

(1) The fixing [Talbot may well have meant 'obtaining'] of images in the *camera obscura*;

(2) The subsequent preservation of these images so that they are able to withstand sunlight.

Extremely busy at the moment with a paper on the subject, which will be given to the Royal Society the day after tomorrow, I must limit myself to begging you to accept the expression of my deep respect. H. F. Talbot, Member of the Royal Society of London.[7]

Since Henry Talbot had little information on the nature and evolution of Daguerre's discovery the claim of priority was speculative and he would have been better advised to concentrate on sending details of his own discoveries so that matters of priority could have been resolved later. Arago received the letter with cool correctness (Talbot, he said, was a 'talented English physicist') but in sketching the background for fellow members of the Académie declared that Daguerre had not 'announced a discovery' but had shown the results to the world. This was not strictly accurate. Biot – much less of a nationalist than Arago and a man of tolerance as well as good humour – explained that M. Talbot did not have full knowledge of the circumstances and read out a letter (dated 31 January) which he had sent to Talbot in which he explained amongst other things that Daguerre had been working on his process for more than fourteen years. This letter – which Biot closed with a reference to 'the esteem I have for your previous work in optics as well as the consideration you have been kind enough to shew me'[8] – was the beginning of a frequent and friendly correspondence between Biot and Henry Talbot which was of value to both men, spreading as it did over much wider scientific matters than photography

alone. Certainly Talbot accepted Biot's statement without reservation and in any case the later realization of the very different character of the inventions rendered the claims of priority less than academic.* Biot's primary interest was scientific enlightenment in the widest of senses and he frankly stated in a subsequent letter:[9]

Far from regretting that M. Daguerre's exhibition decided you to publish your results now, which you might have preferred to conserve with the object of further improvement, we are naturally pleased purely from the scientific point of view since we shall probably have this subject treated from different points of view and by different means.

Henry Talbot's third step after the announcement of Daguerre's discovery was formal communication to the Royal Society. The first part of this was a paper read for him to a meeting of the Society on 31 January 1839. 'Some account of the art of photogenic drawing' – subtitled 'Or the process by which natural objects may be made to delineate themselves without the aid of the artist's pencil' – was a largely descriptive, as distinct from analytical, account of his researches. Talbot sketched the historical background to his application of 'the very curious property which has long been known to chemists to be possessed by the nitrate of silver; namely its discoloration when exposed to the violet rays of light'. He properly underlined the problem of *fixing* – he used the term which is still employed – or preserving the effects of light on chemically sensitive paper which had defeated previous researchers but which he had overcome. (In fact, the fading of photographs was to continue to be a problem for years and still is when incorrect processing procedures are followed.) This fixing of the 'fleeting and momentary' shadow he described as:

... a new proof of the value of the inductive methods of modern science, which by noticing the occurrence of unusual circumstances (which accident perhaps first manifests in some small degree), and by following them up with experiments, and varying the conditions of these until the true law of nature which they express is apprehended, conducts us at length to consequences altogether unexpected, remote from usual experience, and contrary to almost universal belief.

By placing objects – flowers, leaves, paintings on glass, engravings – in contact with the sensitized paper, copies could be obtained; the process could be

---

* Lady Elisabeth Feilding left her son in no doubt about her views on his tardiness in publishing: 'I shall be very glad if M. Daguerre's invention is proved to be very different from yours. But as you have **known** it *five years* à quoi bon concealing it till you could by possibility have a competitor? If you would only have made it known *one* year ago, it could never have been disputed, or doubted . . .'[10]

applied to making silhouette portraits and recording solar microscope specimens;* and the camera obscura could be used in the 'most curious application'
of the new art – obtaining images of architecture, landscapes and 'external
Nature'. Talbot indicated exposures in the last application ranging downwards
from several hours to thirty minutes so his exclusion of portraiture from life
was understandable, though some time afterwards he wrote that while he had
not yet accomplished what was perhaps this 'most important application of
which the new art is susceptible'[11] he saw no reason to doubt the practicability.
Towards the end of the paper (and in the context of copying engravings) he
described in matter-of-fact terms the technique with which his name will ever
be associated – the making of a *positive* image from the initial *negative* image:

... if the picture so obtained is first *preserved* so as to bear sunshine, it may be afterwards
itself employed as an object to be copied; and by means of this second process the lights and
shadows are brought back to their original disposition. In this way we have indeed to
contend with the imperfections arising from two processes instead of one; but I believe
this will be found merely a difficulty of manipulation.

Virtually every other experimenter before – and many immediately afterwards – regarded an initial positive image as the ideal but Talbot both solved
the problem of converting the negative image to the more natural form of the
positive and moreover recognized from the beginning the great value this
possessed for the multiplication of copies.[12]

Interest in the paper was considerable and the two weekly magazines the
Literary Gazette and the *Athenaeum* requested advance copies of the paper for
publication. This presented Talbot with a problem since the Royal Society
ruling was that no paper would be published in the prestigious *Philosophical
Transactions* if it had been published elsewhere first. Through the good offices
of Sir John Herschel,[13] however, a compromise was reached: the covering of
the paper in the two magazines could proceed, with an abstract appearing in
the Society's *Proceedings* immediately and with a detailed account to follow in
the *Transactions*. This last did not take place but Talbot must have been pleased
with the response. His own attractive and popular version of the paper appeared
in the *Literary Gazette* of 2 February[14] (in this he likened the impact of the
process on the uninitiated to something resulting from 'the Genius of Aladdin's
Lamp' and with some modesty wrote: 'I do not profess to have perfected an

* In fact, Talbot indicated clearly in the paper that it was his success in obtaining solar-microscope
images which inspired him to attempt to secure images from 'external nature' in the camera obscura.

Art, but to have *commenced* one . . . it will be for more skilful hands than mine to rear the superstructure') while the *Athenaeum* of 9 February carried the paper in full. The *Philosophical Magazine* also published the account in full and for good measure Talbot had it printed privately in February 1839, this constituting the first ever publication to be devoted exclusively to photography. He was also careful to send a copy to Biot in Paris.

It was inevitable that scientists and others interested in the new discovery would press Talbot for further details of the actual method and he obliged with a letter to the Royal Society which was read on 21 February – Biot communicating the detail to the Académie in Paris on 25 February. Talbot described the selection of superfine writing paper which was initially dipped in a weak solution of common salt (sodium chloride), wiped dry, and then spread with a solution of nitrate of silver (diluted in water in the ratio of about 6 or 8 to 1) on one side, subsequently being dried once again. Talbot warned against using too much salt which reduced the sensitivity. This paper was suitable for 'all ordinary photogenic purposes' such as recording the images of leaves and flowers, but further treatment by alternate washings with salt and silver nitrate rendered the paper adequate for use in the camera obscura. Talbot emphasized that the results obtained in the camera depended greatly on 'small and accidental variations in the proportions employed' and that his own method was to produce a number of differently sensitized test papers approaching as close as possible to a condition just short of that in which the silver chloride 'is disposed to darken of itself, without any exposure to light'. Two fixing solutions were recommended – a solution of iodide of potassium which formed an iodide of silver in the picture (and which Talbot incorrectly believed was absolutely unalterable by the subsequent action of sunlight) or – and this was his usual method – a strong solution of salt which thus, he said, had the singular property of both giving sensitivity to the photogenic paper and being capable of destroying it. The pictures were then to be washed and dried, those treated with salt having a pale lilac tint and those with potassium iodide a 'very pale primrose yellow'.[15]

Talbot indicated that research by others (particularly directed to increasing the sensitivity of the paper) would be welcome and that he intended to continue his work in this direction. Indeed, just four weeks later he announced that paper prepared with potassium bromide and silver nitrate was sensitive 'to the light of the clouds, and even to the feeblest daylight'.[16] Though important for the future, the practical effect of the introduction of bromides in sensitized paper at the time was overestimated by Talbot. In these early days of photography there were innumerable problems and apparent inconsistencies and it would be years before many of them were understood and overcome.

But the first major steps at least had been taken in France and England and it is appropriate to place them briefly in the context of the work which had preceded them. Clearly in the case of images 'from Nature' two elements were necessary – an optical instrument which formed an image and a means of permanently recording that image. In the initial stages and until greater sophistication was required (for example, in curtailing the length of exposures so that portraits could be taken) the first element was available to the early experimenters in the camera obscura. That a small hole in one wall of an otherwise dark room created an inverted image of the world outside on the facing wall may have been known to Chinese scholars some centuries B.C. and in the second half of the fifteenth century the effect in the darkened room (or camera obscura as it came to be called) was well known to Leonardo da Vinci. By the seventeenth century, portable boxes with screens of ground glass to receive the image were in common use as an aid to drawing and the typical camera obscura of Henry Talbot's day had a lens at one end and a mirror set at an angle of 45 degrees at the other which reflected the image on to a ground glass screen at the top of the box where its clarity was protected from ambient light by a viewing hood. The artist used the camera either as a selective guide to a scene as he painted or to take a tracing as a later aid to memory. This, then, was an adequate basic instrument for Daguerre and Talbot – and for those who preceded them. The major problem, however, was the means of retaining the image produced by the instrument.

Again from early times, it had been known that certain substances darkened under the influence of light and that others faded. In 1727 J. H. Schulze – a German professor of anatomy – demonstrated convincingly that silver salts darkened through the action of light alone (and no other medium) and using a liquid mixture of chalk and silver nitrate together with stencils on the outside of a glass container in which the mixture was placed, was able to obtain darkened images on exposure to light. The Swedish chemist C. W. Scheele in the last quarter of the eighteenth century showed that the darkening of silver salts on exposure to light was caused by the formation of metallic silver and that the violet (shorter) wavelengths of the visible spectrum had a more rapid darkening effect on silver chloride than other wavelengths. Schulze's and Scheele's experiments were not directed towards photography nor were those of the Swiss librarian Jean Senebier who in the early 1780s extended Scheele's work to establish the varying speeds at which silver chloride was darkened by different wavelengths of the spectrum. By the end of the eighteenth century these experiments were well known in scientific circles and at that time the research was taken in a more recognizably photographic direction by Thomas Wedgwood, son of the famous potter Josiah, and the distinguished chemist Humphry Davy.

An account of Wedgwood's experiments, together with a commentary by Davy, appeared in the *Journals of the Royal Institution* (which Davy edited) of 22 June 1802. White paper or white leather, moistened with a solution of nitrate of silver and exposed to light behind paintings on glass or profiles of figures, darkened differentially according to the tone of the original – and where most light was transmitted, the colour of the nitrate became deepest. But the fixing of the images defeated both Wedgwood and (more significantly) Davy as well. Davy did find silver chloride more sensitive than silver nitrate and obtained some solar microscope views. In addition, he wrote:

> The images formed by means of a camera obscura, have been found to be too faint to produce, in any moderate time, an effect upon the nitrate of silver. To copy these images, was the first object of Mr Wedgwood, in his researches on the subject, and for this purpose he first used the nitrate of silver ... but all his numerous experiments as to their primary end proved unsuccessful.

The upper-middle-class French inventor and amateur scientist Joseph Nicéphore Niépce advanced on Wedgwood when in 1816 he obtained a negative image on silver chloride coated paper in the camera obscura – but he too was unable to fix it. His fame was to be won in a different direction. For years he had had a major interest in lithography and he strove to discover a method of producing printing plates by the direct action of light. By mid-1822, using a metal plate coated with a thin layer of bitumen of Judea (a form of asphalt), he had succeeded in making permanent images from engravings which had been made translucent and exposed to light in contact with the plates. The surface of the bitumen under clear areas of the engraving was hardened while that under lines remained soluble and was removed by washing with lavender oil and spirit. Niépce's system of 'heliography' was later successfully adapted and applied to printing by his cousin (see Chapter 9). In 1827, however, Niépce used a pewter plate sensitized with bitumen to obtain an image in a camera – and this result of an eight-hour exposure showing part of Niépce's house at Saint-Loup-de-Varennes constitutes the world's oldest surviving photograph. For direct photography the system was clearly impracticable as it stood and Niépce continued with his researches. In 1829 he entered into an agreement with Daguerre – who had been conducting his own individual research for some time – but in 1833 Niépce died. Daguerre continued with the work which he brought to a successful culmination in 1837 and this was the system that was announced to the world in the first week of January 1839.

A copper plate was coated with silver and highly polished. It was then exposed to iodine fumes which resulted in the formation of silver iodide. The plate was placed in the camera, the exposure made, and the surface exposed subsequently to the fumes from heated mercury. The mercury vapour formed an amalgam where the action of light had caused specks of metallic silver to appear in the layer of silver iodide – this was whitish in colour and formed the highlights. The polished silver surface, from which the unused silver iodide was removed subsequently, was viewed so as to reflect a dark ground and thereby represented the shadow areas. Though the appearance of the picture varied with the conditions in which it was viewed, it was essentially a unique positive which was reversed right to left, as in a mirror.

Talbot, as we have seen, pursued a different path which was basically that of Wedgwood and Davy. The introduction to *The Pencil of Nature* published in 1844, his 31 January 1839 paper to the Royal Society and his scientific notebook M* (December 1834–September 1835) contain sufficient information to construct an outline account of the course of his work. It was fortunate that he knew nothing of Wedgwood's and Davy's failure to fix images until *after* he had discovered the effect of working with salt or potassium iodide for on his own admission[12] the failure of a man of Davy's standing to solve the problem might have led to his giving up the attempt as hopeless.

The initial spur to Talbot's researches is now well known. During his delayed honeymoon tour of Europe with Constance in 1833 he became disillusioned with his attempts to sketch the scene at Lake Como in Italy with the aid of a camera lucida† which in his hands 'only left traces on the paper

* Regrettably, notebook L which covered most of 1834 has not been traced.
† Invented by William Wollaston in 1807, the camera lucida comprised essentially a four-sided prism which was used by artists and others as an aid in drawing the correct perspective of objects and views. The prism was held or positioned over the drawing surface and presented a reflected image of the view which could be sketched by the artist without the need for continual head movements to study the actual scene.

melancholy to behold'.[17] (Some of these sketches dated October 1833 are in the collections of the Royal Photographic Society and the Science Museum.) He considered turning to the camera obscura but remembered the difficulties he had encountered when he had used it in Italy during earlier visits in 1823 and 1824:

And this led me to reflect on the inimitable beauty of the pictures of nature's painting which the glass lens of the Camera throws upon the paper in its focus – fairy pictures, creations of a moment, and destined as rapidly to fade away. It was during these thoughts that the idea occurred to me . . . how charming it would be if it were possible to cause these natural images to imprint themselves durably, and remain fixed upon the paper![17]

Following his return to England, Talbot began experiments in 1834* to turn the hope into reality. Working initially with objects and not a camera obscura he experienced disappointing results with silver nitrate and silver chloride used separately on paper – and with solutions of salt and silver nitrate applied to the paper so that silver chloride was formed thereon. Chemical theory offered little or no help – it was behind chemical practice rather than ahead of it – and it was Talbot's power of observation which provided the breakthrough:

On some occasions certain portions of the paper were observed to blacken in the sunshine much more rapidly than the rest. These more sensitive portions were generally situated near the edges or confines of the part that had been washed over with the brush.

After much consideration as to the cause of this appearance, I conjectured that these bordering areas might have absorbed a lesser quantity of salt, and that, for some reason or other, this had made them more sensitive to the light. This idea was easily put to the test of experiment. A sheet of paper was moistened with a much weaker solution of salt than usual, and when dry, it was washed with nitrate of silver. This paper, when exposed to the sunshine, immediately manifested a far greater degree of sensitiveness than I had witnessed

---

* In the Lacock Collection is an undated draft[18] in Talbot's hand which appears to be the text of an announcement or of a title page. It reads:

'preparing for publication the method of
Photogenic Drawing
or
Nature Painted by Herself
invented in the year 1833 and since perfected by
H. F. Talbot Esq. FRS
including
the Art of fixing the images formed by a Camera Obscura
and by a Solar Microscope, upon prepared paper'.

The reference to 1833 is intriguing but must be regarded as an error on Talbot's part.

before, the whole of its surface turning black uniformly and rapidly: establishing at once and beyond all question the important fact, that a lesser quantity of salt produced a greater effect. And, as this circumstance was unexpected, it afforded a simple explanation of the cause why previous inquirers had missed this important result, in their experiments on chloride of silver, namely, because they had always operated with wrong proportions of salt and silver, using plenty of salt in order to produce a perfect chloride, whereas what was required (it was now manifest) was, to have a deficiency of salt, in order to produce an imperfect chloride, or (perhaps it should be called) a *subchloride* of silver.[17]

Talbot also saw the reverse facet – that since an *excess* of salt reduced sensitivity to light then it might be used as a means of fixing the images obtained by employing the 'deficiency of salt'.

The discovery of the more sensitive paper was made in the spring of 1834 and the use of potassium iodide as a fixative probably came in the autumn of that year. It is not clear when Henry Talbot commenced using salt as a fixative but it may not have been before 8 February 1835 when he entered a note on the use of both salt and 'iodine' in that capacity in his notebook.[19] The new paper was more than adequate to obtain impressions of leaves and other objects but exposures of hours in a camera obscura failed to record more than the outline of the roof and chimneys of Lacock Abbey against the sky. Success there did not come until 1835 when Talbot found that he gained extra 'speed' in his sensitive paper by preparing it with repeated and alternate washes of salt and silver and exposing it in a moist state in the camera.[17]

When he used this paper in the 'brilliant summer' of 1835 in a camera obscura which he made out of a large box, the exposures were still long – 'an hour or two' – but 'a very distinct representation of the building' was obtained.[20] Talbot found that by employing very much smaller cameras (they were simple wooden boxes forming a cube between 2 and 3 inches on a side) and lenses of shorter focal length (2 inches) the exposures were shorter out of doors – ten minutes according to the introduction to *The Pencil of Nature* and up to half an hour according to the 31 January paper to the Royal Society.*

Although the actual image area depended on the lens employed in each camera, the maximum negative size yielded by the smallest of the cameras was

---

* A number of the earliest cameras are in the collections of the Science Museum and the Royal Photographic Society, London. There is a strong local tradition that the very small cameras were made by the Lacock carpenter Joseph Foden. No conclusive evidence of this fact has been traced but since Talbot stated in the Royal Society paper that 'I had several small boxes made' (as distinct from the first, larger camera obscura which he himself constructed) it seems possible that he would have turned to a local craftsman. From 1839 onwards his cameras were purchased from London instrument makers.

about two inches square. Talbot described them as 'very perfect but extremely small pictures; such as without great stretch of imagination might be supposed to be the work of some Lilliputian artist'.[21] He used a number of the small cameras around and in Lacock Abbey during that summer and mistakenly thought that the Abbey was the first building 'to have drawn its own picture'. (The house of Nicéphore Niépce had already accomplished the feat.) However from this period of experimentation dates the earliest, authenticated surviving negative in the world which is now at the Science Museum in London: it is of one of the oriel windows in the South Gallery of the Abbey viewed from within. The lilac tone of the negative indicates that it was probably fixed with salt. On it Talbot wrote: 'Latticed Window (with the Camera Obscura) August 1835. When first made, the squares of glass, about 200 in number,* could be counted with help of a lens.' This negative antedates the earliest surviving Daguerreotype by two years.[22] In his paper to the Royal Society Talbot indicated that it was about this time, too, that he obtained images from the solar microscope with a $17\times$ magnification but there is some confusion on this point for later he indicated[23] that he first obtained images from a solar microscope around the time of the announcement of photogenic drawing early in 1839.†

It is not known when Talbot made his first 'transfers' or 'copies' – these were the words he used most frequently during this early period of photographic experimentation to describe what we now call positive prints – but the concept appeared in a notebook entry on 28 February 1835: 'In the Photogenic or Sciagraphic (Greek: *skia* – a shadow) process, if the paper is transparent, the first drawing may serve as an object, to produce a second drawing, in which the lights and shadows would be reversed.'[19] We do know, however, that with such small camera negatives initially and since all printing of positives was by contact and not enlargement, the first positives were almost certainly contact copies of objects or engravings. Talbot's perceptive and immensely significant notebook entry was followed by another practical idea which five or more years later was to become a popular technique in the glass-house portrait studios to protect sitters from the glare and heat of sunlight:

* There are in fact well over 500!

† The detailed information in his Royal Society paper of 31 January 1839 appears to show clearly that he obtained the first solar-microscope images in 1835. Solar-microscope images were included in the 25 January 1839 display at the Royal Institution and it was most unlikely that he could have *prepared* them at that season.

If an object, as a flower, be strongly illuminated & its image formed by a camera obscura, perhaps a [photogenic] drawing might be effected of it, in which case not its outline merely would be obtained, but other details of it. For this purpose concentrated solar rays might be thrown on it: but best employ *only violet* light because we want *chemical* rays and not *heating* rays lest the flower should be scorched by their intensity. My large concave mirror might be covered with plate glass washed over with blue gum or resin . . . At any rate the blue rays might be intercepted by a *small* blue glass mirror nearer the focus.[19]

Some historians of photography have been critical of the limited results achieved by Talbot in the period between early 1834 and January 1839, even though during that time he laid the basis of the negative–positive system of photography which we still use. A study of the available documents, however, suggests that his experiments were limited to two very brief periods in 1834 and 1835 and that the three years 1836, 1837, 1838 were entirely devoid of such experiments save for a primarily optical experiment at the end of 1838 on the effect of particles of iodine on silver.[24] In addition, the exhibits at the Royal Institution on 25 January all dated almost certainly from 1835.[25] The only fair criticism or – rather – regret in retrospect is that Talbot, despite the many other demands on his time and attention, did not pursue his photographic experiments with greater application and awareness of their potential importance. He himself was to regret his tardiness in publishing details of the experiments but this was for the praiseworthy reason that he considered he had made insufficient progress – 'However curious the results which I had met with, yet I felt convinced that much more important things must remain behind, and that the clue was still wanting to this labyrinth of facts.'[17]

The extent to which Talbot communicated information about his photographic work to his scientific colleagues prior to 1839 constitutes something of a puzzle. His family, of course, was fully aware of it. In a letter dated 12 December 1834 there occurred the earliest surviving reference to the work when Constance Talbot's sister Laura Mundy wrote from Markeaton:

Thank you very much for sending me such beautiful shadows. The little drawing I think quite lovely . . . I had no idea the art could be *carried* to such perfection. I had grieved over the gradual disappearance of those you gave me in the summer & am delighted to have these to supply their place in my book.[26]

In September 1835, Constance wrote about rowing by moonlight during her holiday at Cowes:

The colouring reminded me a good deal of some of your shadows, especially of the moonlight scene at Venice. [Presumably a copy of an engraving.] I wish you could have taken the outline of the castle & fine elms behind just as I saw them but I think you told me you could not produce the desired effect by any light except that of the sun. Shall you take any of your mousetraps[*] with you into Wales? It would be charming for you to bring home some views.[27]

It also seemed that examples of Talbot's work were shown to visitors for in September of 1837 Constance informed her husband that during the visit of one party to the Abbey, 'No desire was expressed to see the Photogenic Drawings, so that I was not called upon to do the honours for them.'[28]

But did Talbot attempt to keep knowledge of his researches from his scientific colleagues – until they had reached a stage more worthy, in his view, of their attention? During the scientific gathering at Lacock Abbey in August 1836 (page 80) Constance wrote to Lady Elisabeth that: '[Henry] almost promised to go next week to Leamington & take a picture of Warwick Castle with Sir David (Brewster) . . .'[29] On the other hand, Brewster made no mention of the experiments in letters to his daughter at this time and, even if he had been asked not to by Talbot, he surely would have indicated that he had first-hand knowledge of Talbot's researches prior to the January 1839 announcement when he subsequently wrote on photography in later years. Would not Wheatstone and Babbage, too, have indicated the same fact at some time – and apparently have been somewhat less surprised when the 1839 announcement was made? Further, would it not have been natural for Talbot to have mentioned in his first Royal Society paper showing some of his early work to fellow scientists *prior* to 1839 if this had in fact been the case? We may therefore speculate that Constance's comment meant that Talbot discussed with her the possibility of a photographic excursion in 1836, and that he did not reveal the nature of his researches to the scientifically knowledgeable until his hand was forced by Daguerre in 1839. This would have been consistent with his opinion of the inconclusive nature of the work and his cautious inclinations.

It has been indicated already that empirical results in the chemistry of photography had run ahead of theory and Talbot admitted this frankly early in 1839 when he wrote: '. . . as to the theory, I confess that I cannot as yet understand the reason why the paper prepared in one way should be so much

* A reference to Talbot's small cameras. This is the only such reference that has been traced and neither Constance nor certainly Talbot himself ever used it in any other letters. The impression that has been created subsequently that the expression 'mousetraps' was in frequent use is therefore inaccurate.

more sensitive than in another'.[30] The same lack of theoretical understanding attended the fixing process he had adopted:

But upon what chemical reasons does the process depend, or why should it be at all possible, to obtain fixation in this manner? Nothing that is said in chemical works concerning chloride of silver has any bearing on the subject, nor do they even mention its insensible state.[31]

We now know that the greater sensitivity of Talbot's paper compared to that of the early experimenters resulted from silver ions being in excess (this was his 'subchloride') – extremely small, brown coloured specks of silver appearing by the direct action of light upon the paper. In this light-engendered chemical reaction, the chloride ions released from the silver chloride would have recombined with the silver unless they had been absorbed elsewhere and fortunately this was accomplished by the constituents of Talbot's paper base and the materials used to size it. English papers of this period were sized with gelatin (which has been a major element in photography ever since) whereas Continental papers were not. Hence it has been argued persuasively that if Daguerre had concentrated on a paper instead of a metal support during his experiments he might well have given up in despair. It should be emphasized for those used to the modern techniques of developing an image with a chemical solution that no such development was involved in photogenic drawing – nor in the printing out of positive copies from negatives for many years thereafter: the image appeared entirely as the result of the 'print out' action of light.

As to *fixing*, Talbot at this time did not in fact fix his images as it is understood today. He *stabilized* them. The use of the subsequent wash of strong sodium chloride reduced the sensitivity to light of the crystals of silver salts in the paper by providing excess chloride ions to be absorbed. With potassium iodide, iodide ions accomplished the same relative desensitizing action as the chloride ions, the silver salts in the image being converted to the relatively insensitive silver iodide.[32] Under optimum conditions both forms of stabilizers (as they should be called) achieved good results and the process was still in use in the middle of the twentieth century in some document-copying processes. None the less, Talbot's hopes of permanence were not fulfilled. All silver salts when they are not removed are sensitive to light to some degree and he could not but be aware of the unreliable and unpredictable results he obtained particularly with the tendency of potassium iodide subjects to bleach on further exposure to light.[33] There was already to hand a generally more effective means of rendering an image insensitive to the further action of light – but that too had its problems.

On 25 January 1839 Talbot wrote to the recently knighted Sir John Herschel that he would be 'most happy' to show him specimens of the 'curious process' which he had discovered.[34] It was arranged that Henry would call on Sir John at his home in Slough on 1 February – and in a letter sent on 30 January Herschel broached the subject of preserving the images and suggested the use of hyposulphite of soda, which would 'wash away all the chloride which had escaped the action of light & leave the reduced silver black as before. Thus there is nothing further left for the light to act on . . .'[35] Hyposulphite of soda had been discovered by François Chaussier in 1799, but it was Herschel who discovered its property of dissolving silver halides in 1819. (Hyposulphurous acid from which the salt was derived was subsequently renamed thiosulphuric acid, and the salt therefore sodium thiosulphate, but to photographers it has been 'hypo' ever since.) Herchel's findings had been published in the *Edinburgh Philosophical Journal*[36] and at least one other publication but Talbot appeared to have missed them.

Since learning of the announcement of Daguerre's discovery on 22 January (and of Talbot's a few days later) Herschel had conducted a series of brilliant and intensive experiments so that when Henry Talbot arrived on the first day of February, he was shown an engraving and an image (of Herschel's telescope) obtained in the camera on paper sensitized with silver carbonate and fixed with hypo. According to Sir John's notebook, he explained these processes to Talbot but the latter, while showing specimens of the results he had obtained, 'did not explain his process of what he calls "fixing" '. They then proceeded to test the efficiency of hypo on an unfixed specimen brought by Talbot.[37] It is difficult to explain Henry Talbot's reluctance to talk frankly to Herschel whom he had known and respected greatly for years. Possibly it resulted from his desire still to withhold the details of his process until he had brought it to greater perfection, possibly David Brewster even at this early stage already may have advised him to keep the details secret – advice that was certainly contained in his letter to Talbot of just three days later.[38] Whatever the reason, it was not until 19 February that Talbot sent details of his method of fixing to Herschel. Some photographic historians have criticized Henry Talbot severely for obstinately refusing to adopt hypo until later – one suggestion being that it was because it was another man's idea – even though in almost the same breath Talbot is criticized for rushing with indecent haste to appropriate other men's ideas and patent them – but a detailed study of the documents reveals a different story.*

Initially Talbot was enthusiastic about the use of hypo – identifying Davy's lack of knowledge of the 'ingenious recipe' as a possible reason why he failed – and asked if Herschel was planning to publish any account of his method since they could then either make a joint or separate presentation to the Royal Society.[39] Herschel replied that he had no objections to Talbot publicizing the use of hypo whether privately or publicly[40] but subsequently Talbot had second thoughts about publishing the details of their processes since he considered this might enable the French and others to publish some results employing the new methods before Herschel and he were ready to do so.[41] It was this thought to which Herschel replied on 12 February:[42] 'I shall mention no further the process of washing out with the Hyposulphite if you disapprove of it . . .' and which historians have interpreted incorrectly to mean that Talbot was opposed to the use of hypo – whereas he was in fact only suggesting that there were reasons why it should not be *publicized*.[43] In the same letter Herschel looked forward to receiving details of Talbot's method of fixing which, as we have seen, the latter communicated on 19 February – two days before he revealed details of the entire process to the Royal Society. Within some ten days Talbot – apparently even more enthusiastic at this stage about the value of hypo and having become less worried about the activities of others – requested Herschel's permission[44] to communicate information about hypo to Jean-Baptiste Biot for transmission to the Academy of Sciences in Paris, together with details of the action of potassium ferrocyanate which Herschel had wrongly supposed from his own experiments prior to 19 February to be Talbot's chosen fixing agent. Herschel was in favour and Biot read extracts of Talbot's letter to the Academy on 4 March, referring to the action of sodium chloride, potassium iodide, potassium ferrocyanate and finally of

---

* While allowance must be made for the very limited number of photographs produced by Sir John Herschel, a fact that should be borne in mind in this context is that whereas Talbot's 1835 negative of the oriel window at Lacock Abbey still survives – and of course many subjects of a later date – all of Herschel's originals have faded to the extent of scarcely being visible.

Further, photographic historians have compared the speed with which Daguerre adopted the use of hypo as a fixative with Talbot's approach and imply criticism of the latter. It must be emphasized that hypo used on a metal plate results in few, if any, problems compared with those encountered with its use on paper, where there are complex reactions *within* the medium of the paper.

H

hyposulphite of soda which was worth all the others combined – 'This method of preserving the drawings differs essentially from the three others in that the silver salt is not *fixed* or *rendered insensitive* in the white (i.e. unexposed) parts of the drawing, but is completely removed.'[45]

Thus, this far Talbot – far from refusing to adopt the use of hypo – had become an advocate. But hypo had to be used in a very careful manner to be effective and not to have adverse side effects on images – and its detailed action was little understood whether by Herschel or anybody else. On 21 March Talbot sent a specimen of his work to Herschel but admitted it was 'a poor specimen, the hyposulphite having failed somehow to do its duty'.[46] A few weeks later Talbot returned to the subject:

I have discontinued lately the use of hyposulphite as a fixer in consequence of having spoiled some pictures with it, without being able exactly to ascertain why. But I think it arises from something in the paper, since others made at the same time were properly fixed. Probably a few experiments directly made for the purpose would show the cause of failure and the way to avoid it in future.[47]

Talbot's problems resulted in part from not washing the paper adequately after use of hypo[48] but Herschel too had encountered problems. In his notebook on 25 March he wrote: 'Talbot's sensitive paper will not fix well. It is too full of silver for the hyposulphite of soda.'[49] Though Herschel went on to suggest that hyposulphite of ammonia was more effective he returned to the subject in his notebook on 19 April.[50] He noted the problems encountered in fixing with 'much used' hypo and also with salt and determined to try copious washings with water where soluble silver compounds were involved. Not until 14 June did he satisfy himself – the paper was to be washed before fixing, fixed using very strong hypo and then the paper was to be given thorough washings of water. 'If the *least* hyposulphite of silver be left it undergoes spontaneous decomposition and turns a *filthy* brown in the whole substance of the paper. The thicker the paper the more thoroughly it must be sponged.'[51] Later, Sir John identified difficulties of another kind – for example, that the hyposulphites were not readily procured in the shops. They were also expensive.[52]

None the less, this was substantial progress and a clinical attention to John Herschel's recommendations would have prevented many of the failures that occurred for many years thereafter. But there was a continuing problem which Herschel could do nothing about and which Talbot isolated in a letter to him on 7 December 1839: 'I am rather surprised that you find the hyposulphite never fails. I find that unless it is strong it does not fix the *lights* quite white . . . and if it *is* strong, it is apt to destroy the more delicate shadows.'[53] Talbot had discovered that hypo reduced the density of silver print-out images which was a very serious matter when the images were produced after lengthy exposure in a camera or printing frame – and was an incontrovertible fact encountered by users of print-out process systems in the twentieth cnetury. This was why his initial enthusiasm waned and he did not wholeheartedly adopt hypo until – in the case of negatives – sometime after the discovery of a development process that yielded images which were usually stronger in density and produced far more quickly. And even then there continued to be some problems.*

Sir John Herschel was a brilliant scientist who researched widely and deeply in photographic science for an all too brief period from 1839 to 1844. Many of his findings were gathered together in a powerful paper which was presented to the Royal Society on 20 February 1840[54] and which ranged over optics, photo-chemistry, the recording of natural colours and other subjects with profound insight and skill. Talbot and he differed in character – Herschel tending to be outward-going and generous intellectually whereas Henry Talbot was more inward-looking and cautious in communicating information – but both had the highest admiration for the other and their liaison continued amicably for many years. For some reason, however, the attempt has been made to denigrate Talbot's attitudes and achievements in the context of his relationship with Herschel. Thus the matter of days early in 1839 in which John Herschel with admitted brilliance managed to secure his first images is compared unfavourably with the years taken by Talbot (and for that matter Daguerre): this point has already been answered elsewhere. Moreover, the point can be made fairly that Herschel stated in February 1840 that Talbot's paper far surpassed in sensitivity any that he himself had produced of a manageable kind, and that for all ordinary purposes he had 'ended in adopting his process of preparation'.[55]

In addition, the decision by John Herschel to withdraw from further notice a paper 'On the art of photography' read on 14 March 1839 and published in brief in the *Proceedings* of the Royal Society[56] has been construed as indicating

---

* In his 1843 photographic patent Talbot recommended a system of overexposing positive prints so that the shadows were 'too black', followed by bleaching with potassium iodide and then fixing with hypo. This was almost certainly intended as a counter to the print-out density loss resulting from the use of hypo with normal exposures.

explicitly or implicitly that he did not wish to appear to be taking any of Talbot's distinction as an inventor from him nor disagreeing over the use of hyposulphite of soda. It is true that Herschel perhaps with typical generosity paid tribute to Henry Talbot's 'just and long-antecedent claims' in his paper to the Royal Society in February 1840 but the alleged reason why the paper was withdrawn seems unlikely. In the first place, Talbot had already announced his process and its details on 31 January and 21 February so Herschel could not possibly be accused of interfering with his priority; secondly, if Herschel had been worried on that score why deliver the paper at all at that time; and thirdly – as we have seen – Talbot was not opposed to the use of hyposulphite. Hypo, however, may constitute the reason why Herschel's paper was withdrawn. Herschel's notebooks show that he began encountering difficulties in the use of hypo with Talbot's paper by 25 March (if not before) and the problems were not resolved fully to his satisfaction till the following June. What was more natural, therefore, than that a scientist of Herschel's standing would wish to solve the unexpected problems before presenting his full proposals to the Royal Society – which he did in his 1840 paper?[57]

There are other claims – for example that in a letter dated 12 February 1839,[58] Herschel suggested cooperation ('. . . in studying those processes each may hit on something useful on different lines, and on comparing notes a process may arise better than either would have devised separately . . .') which Talbot, arrogantly it is implied, rejected. In fact, both were to a considerable extent lone workers by nature but the correspondence between them which is now preserved in the Royal Society Library and the Science Museum in London indicates that they did indeed 'compare notes' on many subjects for some time thereafter.* Additional points could be raised and answered but it would become tedious. Here were two men who admired each other's work, who corresponded for years from the 1820s onwards and between whom never an angry word appeared to have passed. It is only subsequently that an attempt has been made to decry the achievements of one by comparing them with the other's – in almost every instance on the basis of dubious or inaccurate facts, or fallacious arguments. Sir John Herschel doubtless would have been amazed and appalled.

---

* Talbot did *not*, however, tell Herschel of his discovery of the Calotype process until after his patent had been registered. Intriguingly, he gave advance news of the discovery to both Sir David Brewster and Jean-Baptiste Biot – to the former in October 1840 and to the latter in January 1841. The patent was taken out on 8 February 1841.[59]

Sir John Herschel had a significant effect elsewhere in photography – in the nomenclature of the discovery. From the beginning he was an ardent advocate of 'photography' (Greek: *phos* – light and *graphein* – to write) and specifically recommended its adoption instead of photogenic drawing (Greek: *genesis* – source) to Henry Talbot in a letter dated 28 February 1839.[60] He had already used the term 'photographic' in a letter to Talbot on 10 February[61] and Henry himself first used the noun 'photograph' in a notebook entry dated 27 February.[62] While there is no doubt that Sir John Herschel was the earliest, most consistent user of the term which is still with us today, his was not the earliest recorded usage – this honour falls to Charles Wheatstone who in a letter to Talbot dated 2 February 1839 concerning the action of light on various substances included the adjective 'photographic'.[63] Within a very short period it was being used extensively: Brewster was employing it at least as early as 14 March and, amongst the non-scientific, the matronly Lady Elisabeth adopted and used it interchangeably with 'photogenic drawing'. Her son did similarly, showing some loyalty to his own term which was sensible on the grounds that both the Daguerreotype and photogenic drawing were examples of photography and needed to be differentiated. Herschel's use of 'photography' in print in his paper to the Royal Society on 14 March 1839 was believed to be the first public employment of the word but in 1932 Professor Erich Stenger found it in an article about Talbot's invention by Johann von Maedler of Berlin published in the *Vossische Zeitung* of 25 February 1839.*[64]

But to Herschel undoubtedly falls the distinction of the first systematic use of the terms 'negative' and 'positive' – which he defined in his paper to the Royal Society of February 1840.[54] To Talbot himself may be attributed the first continuous usage of another word still employed today – the 'fixing' of the photographic image – though he used it interchangeably by way of explanation with the word 'preserve'. In those early years there was sometimes a confusing mixture of generic terms with those of different systems – thus in September 1839 Talbot was sent a copy by the publishers of a translation by Dr J. S. Memes of Daguerre's Manual which appeared in England under the title *History and Practice of Photogenic Drawing*,[65] while as late as the time of the Great Exhibition in 1851 Brewster and Talbot were exchanging condolences about the use of the term 'Daguerreotype sur papier'.[66]

* The various claims depend on the definition of 'public employment'. Thus L. Desmarést used the word 'photographique' on the cover of a sealed paper deposited with the Academy of Sciences in Paris on 12 February 1839.

Once Talbot had announced the details of photogenic drawing the enterprising endeavoured to turn it to money making and the ingenious to practical use. Within a month of Talbot releasing the chemical basis of this system, J. T. Cooper – a chemist at the Royal Institution – was advertising photogenic drawing paper for sale, and in April Ackermann (the Strand printsellers), a photogenic drawing box with the necessary materials to produce copies of objects – price 21s. complete with packets of paper available separately for 2s.[67] At the end of April, Mary Talbot wrote to her cousin from Wales: 'I saw some very good paper [prepared] from Clifton. Mr West of the Observatory makes it for sale – he also sells somethings ready done.'[68]

Equally as swift, though in a practical application of Talbot's discovery, was T. B. Jordan who on 21 March 1839 showed the Committee of the Royal Cornwall Polytechnic Society* examples of photogenic drawing paper used to record barometric pressures on a forty-eight-hour scale – the mercury column occluding light entering a window and thus resulting in a varying area of darkening of the paper which was fixed to a revolving drum.[69] Photogenic drawing was applied equally early to the woodcut system of printed illustration (Chapter 9).

Talbot himself was involved in one possible application which was over-optimistic in 1839 but which was of important potential value. Toward the end of the year James Charles Ross took the ships *Erebus* and *Terror* toward Antarctica in what was to become one of the most famous sagas of exploration of that continent. A member of the committee who knew Talbot suggested that the expedition take out several cameras to make photogenic drawings and reported that Captain Ross had agreed.[70] Talbot offered to give instruction to Robert McCormick, a surgeon and naturalist, and to Joseph Hooker, who was assistant surgeon (and later to achieve fame as a botanist). On 31 July McCormick wrote from *Erebus* at Chatham to Henry:

. . . we shall be most happy to avail ourselves of your friendly aid, in an art which promises to be of incalculable value in delineating the various objects of Natural History, which we may meet with during our voyage to the Antarctic Regions; more particularly, in obtaining faithful representations of those evanescent forms inhabiting the ocean . . .[71]

The evidence is inconclusive as to whether Talbot did meet McCormick or whether the expedition took any camera obscuras and photogenic drawing

* Sir Charles Lemon, Henry Talbot's uncle by marriage, was President of this Society from 1833 to his death in 1868.

paper. Certainly no images survived and it is difficult to imagine how photogenic drawing could have been applied at this stage of its development in the manner proposed – particularly in conditions which have continued to test photographers' skill and endurance to the present day.

The period from January 1839 to 1841, when Talbot introduced the Calotype system and the speed of the Daguerreotype plates was greatly increased by other researchers, has tended to receive little attention from historians but it holds much interest – particularly in what it reveals about Talbot's character. Once the initial announcements were out of the way, he endeavoured to promote interest in the new 'art'. Photogenic drawings (together with work by both Sir John Herschel and Niépce – the latter dating from the 1820s) were displayed at the first soirée held by the new president of the Royal Society, the Marquis of Northampton, in March[72] and Talbot spoke on aspects of his own work and of Daguerre's discovery at the meeting of the British Association for the Advancement of Science in Birmingham in August.[73] The biggest exhibition of his work to date took place there – a total of ninety-three specimens comprising negative copies of botanical specimens, positive copies of engravings and solar microscope views together with positive prints and a negative of Lacock Abbey made in the camera. Lady Elisabeth delighted in the attention being devoted to her son's invention and distributed examples amongst her many distinguished friends who appeared to be a demanding clientele. ('People pillage me dreadfully.'[74]) In April photogenic drawings – the first of a large number of examples of Talbot's work to be presented over the years – were given to Queen Victoria and were 'met with universal admiration from a large party'.[75] Later Lady Elisabeth organized the despatch of some of the drawings to Metternich, the Austrian leader, who showed great interest in both Talbot's and Daguerre's work.[76]

Constance Talbot was certainly the world's first female photographer and photographic processor:

I have been trying to get a few Abbies done for you but the Sun has not been steadily bright & what was more adverse, no paper had been made. The 2 frames containing the Tower and South Front [of Lacock Abbey] are now at work but will not be done in time for the Basket [up to London]. Besides the fixing has failed of two others which I made this morning myself. So there is no use in sending them . . .[77]

And again:

I have been labouring hard at the photographs without much success for though some of the pictures were pretty good I spoilt them afterwards with the iodine. I ought to have begun my study of the art while *you* were at hand to assist me in my difficulties. As it is however I shall have gained experience by my unsuccessful attempts & therefore not wholly wasted my time & strength. I set the camera today to take my favorite view near the Cauldron [still to be seen at Lacock Abbey although *inside* the building] but I believe I failed in getting the right focus, for the outline is sadly indistinct, though the general idea is perfect in its resemblance. Yesterday & Saturday were not bright enough for the camera & Sunday was only bright during the hours of church & preceding ones when I was not ready for work.[78]

Reports from Wales indicated that Henry's cousin Emma and her husband John Dillwyn Llewelyn were taking up photogenic drawing with enthusiasm[79] and they were later to cooperate in creating some of the best Calotypes of the 1840s. So too was Kit Talbot's friend the Revd Calvert Richard Jones who was reported to be 'wild' about Talbot's discovery.[80] Henry did his best to help everybody who wrote to him about the best method of proceeding whether members of the family or complete strangers – and he sent a delightful reply to queries from his cousin Charlotte Traherne:

As you are experimentalizing, I daresay you have already found out in using nitrate of silver it is best to operate with gloves on, as that substance stains most unmercifully & lasts, not eternally indeed, but sometimes for a fortnight or two. In my communication to the Royal Society I did not mention this, because it was 'beneath the dignity of science' but I hope you will be cautious with it . . .

If you intend making use of the *camera*, you must first acquire the art of making the *most* sensitive paper by repeated trials; and then I advise *not* using at first a regular instrument bought at an opticians, but a large lens of short focus, such as a very strong reading glass or magnifier, & fixing it in a board & the paper upon another, exactly in the focus & excluding all extraneous light. The best object to begin with is a window and its bars, placing the instrument in the interior of the room. If you don't succeed tell me & I will see if I can help you further. The lens must be as large as possible *compared with its focal length*; if it makes a good *burning glass*, it will answer.[81]

The witty Thomas Moore was not to be denied in the excitement and wrote after a visit to Lacock Abbey that: '. . . both Talbot and his collaborateur, the Sun, were in high force & splendour, and I promised to write something about their joint doings, if I could but get paper sensitive enough for the purpose'.[82]

Yet there was no doubt of the Daguerreotype's superiority at this time – yielding as it did under optimum conditions superbly detailed positive views (though reversed right to left) from the camera on plates which could be as large as 8½ inches × 6½ inches while initially Talbot could only offer his small cameras yielding an even smaller negative which in those days, long before projection enlarging, were of limited value. Contact photogenic drawings of objects, which could be on much larger sizes of paper, were intriguing and so too were solar-microscope views (involving as they did their own inherent enlarging system) but the major interest and potential lay in views obtained in the camera. In May, Herschel – together with two other scientists, Sir John Robison and James Forbes – travelled to Paris to see Daguerre's pictures and they were amazed by the quality. Herschel wrote to Talbot:

> It is hardly saying too much to call them miraculous. Certainly they surpass anything I could have conceived as within the bounds of reasonable expectation. The most elaborate engraving falls far short of the richness & delicacy of execution. Every gradation of light & shade is given with a softness and fidelity which sets all paintings at an immeasurable distance . . . The beautiful effect of river scenes *in rain* must be seen to be appreciated . . . In short if you have a few days at your disposition I cannot counsel you better than to *come & see*.[83]

(In fact Talbot did not go at that time despite pressing invitations from Jean-Baptiste Biot also.) The *Athenaeum* published John Robison's enthusiastic praise for the Daguerreotype and stated forthrightly: '. . . all comparison between photogenic drawings and the works of M. Daguerre is quite ridiculous.'[84]

Talbot was fully appreciative of Daguerre's achievement. At the August British Association meeting he described Daguerre's method of 'bringing out' the image on the plate by mercury vapour as 'remarkable'[73] – and, when displays of Daguerreotypes executed by the inventor himself were staged later at the Adelaide Gallery in London, following his own visit he urged Constance to attend. This she did declaring herself 'delighted' with some of them.[85] He purchased all the equipment necessary to produce Daguerreotypes (much of which is now at the Royal Scottish Museum in Edinburgh) but it is not clear whether in fact he was able to find enough time to use it.* Later, in the introduction to *The Pencil of Nature*, he described the Daguerreotype as a 'splendid' and 'great' discovery and praised its 'beauty'.

The attitude of François Arago was another thing entirely. Arago, a politician as well as a distinguished scientist, was fiercely nationalistic and he

---

* Harold White has pointed out that the dark slides of Talbot's Daguerreotype cameras were mostly adapted to use *paper negatives*.

identified himself personally with the successful promotion of the Daguerreotype. When, in the absence of Daguerre, Arago finally revealed details of the
system in Paris on 19 August, he did not mention Talbot's discovery in the
historical outline that he gave. The *Literary Gazette*, commenting on a previous
Arago speech in its issue of 20 July, reported that he 'alluded to the importance
of the [Daguerreotype] discovery, which he contended was proved by the
avidity with which the subject has been taken up by other nations, and the
trifling pretexts they had seized to establish their priority of invention'. The
magazine added as a footnote: 'M. Arago is always sufficiently national, and
partial to the claims of his own country and countrymen. In this instance he is
evidently unjust to the claims of others; and even more French than usual.'[86]

Arago appears to have made various comments from time to time to which
Talbot – usually a very reserved man in expressing his own feelings – took
exception:

> There can be no doubt of the great injustice of M. Arago. He does not seem to recollect
> that candour would be as great an ornament to his character as scientific eminence, and that
> the want of it, when conspicuous & evident to the whole scientific world, must result in
> injury to his own reputation . . . M. Biot on the contrary is very friendly in all his com-
> munication to me.

Talbot's sense of humour reappeared, however, when he added that there had
reportedly been some problems with Daguerreotype plates produced in
England and that 'if M. Arago knew this, he would say that it was a new
proof that the invention was "vraiment Française" since the Art itself evinced
antipathy to England'.[87] Biot – who had no time for national controversies –
put the Arago matter into a friendly perspective when he wrote to Talbot in
November 1839: 'Scientists sometimes gossip like old women but, unfortunately, their gossip spreads over Europe instead of being confined to the
home.'[88]

Talbot realized all too clearly the considerable degree of improvement that
was required before photogenic drawing could meet the quality and advantages of the Daguerreotype. It may be that this was why he did not attempt
to patent the system despite the advice of Sir David Brewster who wrote on
4 February:

> I hope you mean to pursue the subject and endeavour to perfect the process. You ought
> to keep it perfectly secret till you find you cannot advance further in the matter and then

it would be advisable to secure your right by a Patent. Altho' you do not require to deal with the matter commercially yet a Patent would give a more fixed character to your priority as an inventor and I do not see why a gentleman with an independent fortune should scruple to accept of any benefit that he has deserved from his own genius. A Patent too would have the effect of stimulating yourself, and any active chemist whom you might associate as a fellow labourer, to bring the Art to perfection.[38]

His decision not to patent paved the way for publicizing details to the Royal Society on 21 February which, Talbot told Herschel, 'will then be free to all the world to adopt or to find out better ones for themselves'.*[89]

Better camera equipment was one means of improving photogenic drawings (and in securing bigger negatives) and for several years from February 1839 Talbot purchased a series of cameras. Most of them came from the London instrument maker Andrew Ross and those delivered in 1839 included a camera obscura with a $2\frac{1}{2}$-inch achromatic lens costing £7 15s. 0d.; a solar microscope camera at £4 5s. 0d.; two camera obscuras at £2; and one experimental camera with four large lenses at £4 0s. 0d. Ross supplied seven cameras in 1840–1, a 'portrait camera' costing £7 2s. 0d. in 1842 and the London instrument makers Watkins & Hill another camera with ancillary equipment in 1844.†[90] Lady Elisabeth was so keen to see Talbot's work progress that it seems likely that she paid for at least some of these purchases, the high cost of which may be compared with a typical servant's wage at the time averaging between £10 and £20 per year.

The extent to which Talbot in 1839 was producing positives from negatives exposed in a camera is not known but as late as 27 April of that year he wrote to Herschel: 'I have found that the camera pictures transfer very well & the resulting effect is altogether "Rembrandtish" '[91] – which suggests that the operation was still comparatively new with camera subjects. The following June the Literary Gazette felt it necessary to apologize to its readers in not announcing several weeks before 'that Mr Talbot had succeeded in getting the

---

* Daguerre received a pension of 6,000 francs (£240) a year from the French Government for his invention on the grounds that the invention could not be patented and that France should adopt it and 'generously donate it to the entire world'. In August 1839, however, Daguerre patented his system in England, Wales and the Colonies through Miles Berry, a patent agent. It was the only patent that he took out anywhere in the world and aroused much ill feeling since it was regarded as being contrary to the announcements made by Arago, the French minister of the interior Duchatel and others when arguing in favour of the pension. (The Daguerre patent was sold to Richard Beard for £800 in June 1841.)

† Talbot also purchased some cameras from France. (For example, see Notebook P, entry probably to be dated to 23 June 1840.)

lights and shades of his photogenic copies in the natural order. We have several specimens in our possession, which are perfectly accurate and quite useful'.[92]

The large cameras were one factor in improving the situation. But the sensitivity and reliability of the prepared paper were the crucial factors. Talbot was not without encouragement from others. Biot constantly underlined the value of paper photography and, following his May letter praising the Daguerreotype, Herschel wrote that while he was not disposed to change that view, he was of the opinion that 'the processes which have *paper* for their field of display should be perfected, as I do not see how else the multiplication of copies can take place, a branch of the photographic art which Daguerre's processes do not by his own account admit of'.[93] Talbot too was convinced: in April he referred to the 'English method' of the negative/positive system which: '... by the method of retransferring ... by a fortunate and beautiful circumstance rectifies both the errors in the first picture *at once*; viz, the inversion of right for left & that of light for shade.'[91] In December he was just as sure:

> I am convinced we are only on the threshold of what may be done. Although the perfection of the French method of photography cannot be surpassed in some respects, yet in others the English is decidedly superior. For instance in the capability of multiplication of copies & therefore of publishing a work with photographic plates.[94]

What he had to do was to secure a dramatic improvement in the chemistry of his system. And this he proceeded to do.

Fortunately Talbot's notebooks for 1839–43 have survived so that the course of his research can be followed. The entries for 1839 and much of 1840 are extensive and show he ranged widely in his attempt to improve photogenic drawing – both in its chemistry and in procedures generally. Thus he examined the sensitivity of papers prepared with ammonia and silver nitrate, the use of gelatin to increase 'speed' and the advantages of making the negative transparent for contact printing, as well as the continuing problem of fixation. He studied different lens systems and – with an eye to the lack of sensitivity of both paper and plates to *red* light – anticipated later applications of the phenomenon when he proposed a 'camera obscura with red glass window', though in his case it was 'to see how the work progresses'. Later he indicated another application of potentially great significance: 'Telescopic photographs wd be useful for taking objects w'ch cannot be conveniently approached.'[95]

Talbot's thoughts were not only concerned with the detailed, practical problems. At a more theoretical level he exchanged views with Jean-Baptiste Biot* and John Herschel about the wider issues of radiation and the formation of colours. Biot sent reports of the researches he was conducting with another French physicist Edmond Becquerel, and their realization that much more than light was involved was summed up well when Biot wrote in the *Journal des Savants*:

> The elements of general radiation that can thus be identified and analysed are the agents which excite – perhaps even which determine – an infinite number of reactions of living organisms, and the very impressions which they experience. For example: the sensation of light, of heat, superficial secretion, and absorption, probably still many other functions that we know nothing about, because we lack the physical means of studying or making them manifest. Who knows if radiation of all kinds – igneous, celestial, terrestrial – are of the same nature, or if they have specific properties which influence inorganic and organic bodies differently?[96]

Herschel directed his attention in particular to the formation of colours in silver salts and by the medium of vegetable extracts (Robert Hunt too investigated the formation of colours certainly on paper and possibly on sensitized plates) being optimistic enough to hope that the results obtained offered 'very fair promise of solving the problem of coloured photographs'.[97] Talbot remained sceptical – 'I should be much surprised if it were found possible to represent the prismatic tints vigorously, because I see no connection between the colour of the ray dependent upon the length of the undulation & the colour of the photograph, dependent upon it is very difficult to say what.'†[98] Talbot occasionally allowed himself flights of fancy but even then did not allow himself to go too far from the problem to hand:

---

* Biot found Talbot very different from Daguerre in this direction. He wrote to the Englishman in March 1840: 'It is very unfortunate for Science to see a man [Daguerre] with such ability always considering the results from the artistic point of view and never at all from the higher purpose of contributing to the progress of discovery in general. But I have given up preaching to him on the point'.[99]

† In 'Some account of the art of photogenic drawing' Talbot recorded 'indications of colour' in the paper when copying designs drawn on glass – but he never gave much attention to this issue subsequently. Obtaining a representation of colours in silver sensitized *plates* may have resulted from the interference phenomena on which the Lippmann process was based at the end of the nineteenth century, but it is very difficult to explain how Herschel's crude representation of colours from silver salts on paper (which he could not fix) was secured. Colloidal silver itself can be coloured and it may be that Herschel and other workers secured some colour due to the increase in the size of colloidal silver particles with increasing exposure.[100]

Whenever there comes a very bright day, it is as if nature supplied an infinite designing power, of which it is only possible to use an infinitesimal part. It is really wonderful to consider that every portion of the whole solar flood of light should be endowed with so many complicated properties, which in the vast majority of instances must remain latent, since most of the rays pass away into space, without meeting with any object.[101]

But using some of them much more effectively was the very point.

The spring of 1840 was a delightful one – the weather being 'the finest and most settled since the birth of photography'[101] – and Talbot took the opportunity to expand his picture-taking activities. There was no breakthrough at this stage and it must be assumed that the improved results he obtained stemmed from improved procedures, better cameras and also the possible adoption at this time of a particular make of paper – J. Whatman Turkey Mill.* Already in March 1840 Biot had presented 'forty photographic images' of both copies and camera views to the Academy in Paris which was impressed. In May, the *Literary Gazette* reported that it had examined an album of photogenic drawings which were due to be exhibited at the Graphic Society and was unstinted in its praise. There was an immense variety of subjects it said – 'every matter, from a botanical specimen to a fine landscape, from an ancient record to an ancient abbey' – which were given 'with a fidelity that is altogether wonderful'.[102]

Herschel was as enthusiastic when he received examples of the work: early in May, he declared Talbot's art to be the equal of Daguerre's in many respects and that in a year or two he would beat it. On 19 June he wrote thanking Talbot for 'the very, very beautiful photographs. It is quite delightful to see the art proceed under your hands in this way. Had you suddenly a twelve month ago been shown them, how you *would* have jumped & clapped hands (i.e. if you ever do such a thing)'.[103] Charles Babbage welcomed the prints which doubtless added to the prestige of his parties and Lady Elisabeth shrewdly urged her son to do more landscapes and 'other things *from nature*'.[104] His half-sister Caroline (now a Lady of the Bedchamber to Queen Victoria) showed an album to the Queen and Prince Albert who 'admired the great progress' made, the Prince thinking that Talbot's discovery would be of great consequence to

* See Notebook P, entry for 7 May 1840. This paper, produced at Hollingsworth's Mill at Maidstone, Kent was used extensively by Talbot and his employees in subsequent years. It had good wet strength, a smooth surface and generally uniform texture although variations were encountered when used for such a critically demanding process as photography. Another suitable paper came from R. Turner's Chafford Mill.

the arts. In communicating this (and the fact that Caroline promised the Queen that 'her brother would be proud to do some on purpose for her Majesty, to which she responded she would like it very much . . .') Lady Elisabeth raised a practical aspect of the work when she asked Talbot from Lacock Abbey: 'What is to be done with all those photographs you left in frames in the drawing rooms?'[105]

During the summer Talbot did not consider much progress had been made – his enforced duty as Sheriff of Wiltshire was partly responsible though he continued also with his many other researches – and early in September he told Herschel that he had not been able to give more than 'desultory and divided attention to photography' and that the art remained 'in status quo'. He identified the twin needs as a more sensitive paper and an improved lens incorporating a large aperture.[99] (This would admit more light and thus speed the picture-taking process.) Within just a few days of writing that letter, however, he made the major breakthrough to increased sensitivity with a discovery which in its essence is the system still used to this day.

5
The Calotype

As far back as the spring of 1834 *gallic acid** had been among the chemicals secured by Talbot for his chemical experiments, though in the absence of his 1834 notebook and on the evidence of his later comments there is no indication that he learned anything of significance about its properties in the photographic process.[1] In February 1839 Herschel noted in a letter to Talbot[2] that he had 'most hopes of the Gallate of Silver which is affected by light very differently from its other salts' – a reference he repeated in his Royal Society paper in February 1840 though he did not actively pursue the idea. Another early worker the Revd J. B. Reade also used gallic acid and Talbot noted this fact specifically in his scientific notebook on 5 April 1839.[3] Earlier he had written to J. W. Lubbock:[4]

I recommend to you to try the sensibility of paper washed first with the nitrate of silver & then with gallic acid the latter to be pure. I have not tried it yet, but it has been mentioned to me both by Herschel & another experimenter [Reade presumably] so that I think it must be among the best recipes yet found out.

Talbot purchased some crystallized gallic acid on 30 March 1839[5] and on 5 April commenced experiments with it in solutions with silver nitrate, ammonia and potash.[6] On 13 April he noted that: 'Bromine paper is greatly

* Gallic acid was 'obtained from Gall nuts, which are peculiar excrescences formed upon the branches and roots of the *Quercus infectoria* by the puncture of a species of insect. The best kind is imported from Turkey and sold in commerce as Aleppo galls. Gall nuts do not contain Gallic Acid ready formed but an analogous chemical principle termed Tannic Acid . . . Gallic Acid is produced by the *decomposition and oxidation* of Tannic Acid when powdered galls are exposed for a long time in a moist state to the action of air.'[7]

increased in sensibility by washing it with saturated solut'n of Gallic Acid.' He conducted fixing experiments and proposed to call bromine paper washed with gallic acid 'Gallic paper'. There was then a lengthy gap when he turned to other substances but he again experimented with gallic acid on 30 January and 23 March 1840 – on the latter date washing paper with weak acid, followed by gallic acid and nitrate of silver, which was close to the eventual procedure which would constitute the breakthrough. At this time he was endeavouring to find out whether sensitive paper could be 'excited without being darkened' (that is before exposure in the camera) and wondered if the presence of hydrogen gas or exposure to certain parts of the spectrum would achieve this result. 'In such case, an image thrown on it in ye usual way wd perhaps be more readily impressed.'

Once again there was a pause in experiments with gallic acid but he recommenced them on 20 September and the next day discovered that an 'exciting liquid' composed of silver nitrate, acetic acid and gallic acid increased the sensitivity of bromine paper but 'much more that of yellow or iodine paper'. But there was still more to it and Talbot's notebook communicates the stages of discovery, although with no apparent tone of excitement:

September 23: The same exciting liquid was diluted with an equal bulk of water, and some very remarkable effects were obtained. Half a minute suffices for the camera, the paper when removed is often perfectly blank but when kept in the dark the picture begins to appear spontaneously, and keeps improving for several minutes, after which it should be washed and fixed with iod. pot.

. . . A camera picture made yesterday in 2' [minutes] & which was faint the spontaneous action having been stopped by fixing it with iodine, was washed with the exciting liquid & revived, or rather, the spontaneous action recommenced as if it had not been interrupted . . .

. . . Yellow iod. paper washed with E (the exciting liquid above mentioned) and washed out with water, remains very sensitive, and as it appears to keep well for a day or two, may make a useful sort of photoᵉ·, paper for common purposes, or transfers &c.

September 24: . . . I find 8 seconds enough for a strong impression of the outline of the house in cloudy weather. Also the lighter tiles on the roof are very plainly depicted. If the impression is not strong enough, I find it may be strengthened by immersion in iod. pot. and then more of the G. wash. [Talbot dropped use of the term 'E' for exciting liquid and used 'G'.] In 3 minutes a singular picture was obtained, the sky deep fiery red especially by transmitted light, against which the roof almost white contrasted as if covered with snow.

I

September 26: . . . This washed G paper wd evidently be very useful in the Camera because it would *keep* a certain time, & perhaps need not be *brought out* the same day that it was used . . .

October 1: Washed G paper keeps several days and is then very sensitive when exposed at the window and brought out with G and spont. Doubtful whether it can be used in the camera.

October 2: . . . I find that it can. And some hours may be allowed to elapse before it is *brought out* . . .

Talbot thus found that using the new method of sensitizing paper, a 'latent picture' (he used the term on 23 September in discussing the revival of 'old' images by subsequent development) was created after exposures much shorter than those hitherto made and that the picture could subsequently be made to appear. The first part of the discovery was that (23 September) when the prepared paper was exposed *wet*, the image spontaneously developed subsequently because – provided there was sufficient moisture – the developing agents would diffuse through the paper without anything further being required. Then he found (24 September) that such a picture if it was not sufficiently strong could be further 'brought out' using the developer – and, finally, that when the sensitized paper was used dry (1–2 October) the latent image could be developed afterwards by washing in the solution of gallo-nitrate of silver which had been used initially to sensitize the iodized paper.

Although it was only with the evolution of electron microscopes that the precise manner in which the chemistry of latent-image formation and development took place was discovered, this is what was happening. In the printing-out of images, as in photogenic drawing, the action of light alone gradually converted some of the sensitive silver halides (that is bromides, iodides and chlorides) into very small specks of metallic silver and it was these – in an almost grainless structure since they were so small – which formed the image. All that was required then was to render the remaining silver salts insensitive to light or to remove them. In Talbot's new system, the initial short exposure resulted in particles of silver (completely invisible save under high magnification) being released in or on the halide crystals in the parts of the sensitized paper affected by light. The 'exciting liquid' or developer containing soluble silver salts and a mild reducing agent (gallic acid) acted as a plating solution which deposited metallic silver on to the invisibly small silver specks until they were collectively large enough to form a visible image. The acetic acid acted as a restraining influence to prevent unexposed silver halide crystals being reduced to metallic silver by the action of the gallic acid. This process is now known as *physical development*: it was replaced in the early 1860s (with the advent of new sensitized emulsions) by *chemical development* with alkaline solutions – in which the silver used to build up the visible image came not from the developing liquid but from the halide crystals themselves. None the less, Talbot's was that first quantum jump which eventually was to make negative-positive photography a recording tool of fundamental importance in the arts and sciences.

In the early days of October 1840, Talbot took a series of photographs with what even for him must have been a sense of excitement and some of these images still survive. A pale lilac-coloured positive of Constance Talbot in the Lacock Collection may be dated tentatively to 6 or 8 October according to her husband's list of exposures and this would make it the oldest surviving photographic portrait on paper in the world. Another portrait of Constance Talbot in the Royal Photographic Society Collection may be dated to 10 October. By today's standards the exposures were still relatively long – 5 minutes in the case of those taken on 6 October and 8 October when Talbot did not have the benefit of sunlight – but when he did the exposure could be reduced to 30 seconds. Another very early example of the new method of photography was the image of a coach and attendant (the latter dressed in the resplendent uniform doubtless required during the time of Talbot's official duties as High Sheriff of Wiltshire) which was exposed in 3 minutes on 14 October. Negatives and prints made at this time indicate Talbot was using a variety of cameras yielding images from approximately $8\frac{1}{2}$ inches $\times$ $6\frac{1}{2}$ inches down to approximately 3 inches $\times$ $3\frac{1}{2}$ inches in size.*

Talbot gave the name *Calotype* (Greek: *kalos* – beautiful) to the new system – a word which first appeared in one of his scientific notebooks as early as 30 January 1840.[8] In October and November David Brewster urged him not to be in a hurry to publish details and it is evident that, while announcing to his Scottish colleague that he had made significant progress, Talbot did not at that time reveal details. He communicated similarly with Biot in January of 1841.[9] This time – unlike his attitude to photogenic drawing – Talbot had

* One of the first applied uses of Talbot's new system was in forwarding Charles Wheatstone's experiments in stereoscopy. In December 1840 Wheatstone considered the pairs of prints sent by Talbot to show considerable potential for stereo viewing, but noted that the angle of separation chosen ($47\frac{1}{2}°$) was too large and that the pictures must not be taken when the shadows were falling differently.[10]

decided to take out a patent and this was dated 8 February 1841. To Herschel on 17 March 1841 he wrote: 'I have taken a patent for the calotype, but nevertheless intend that the use of it shall be entirely free to the scientific world ... There appears to me to be no end to the prospect of scientific research which photography has opened out.'[11] Herschel replied: 'You are quite right in patenting the calotype. With the liberal interpretation you propose in exercising the patent right no one can complain. And I must say I never heard of a more promising subject for a *lucrative* patent of which I heartily give you joy ...'[12] Brewster also welcomed the news of the patent, adding with doubtful logic but undoubted hope: 'To extend it to Scotland wd be impracticable.'[13] (Talbot never did patent the Calotype there.)

The announcement of the new system, like that of photogenic drawing, was directed to both popular and scientific audiences. On 5 February – three days before the patent was secured – Talbot wrote to the editor of the *Literary Gazette* for publication that he had discovered a new, far more sensitive process (his estimates of exposures were between 8 seconds and 5 minutes in the shade), that objects were rendered with increased sharpness and distinctness,* and that there were important implications for travel photography and portrait taking. In another letter to the editor fourteen days later, Talbot – without going into details of the process which were, he said, reserved for announcement to the Royal Society – related the concept of the latent image and the manner in which it had been discovered. Here the exposures were indicated as being from a quarter of a minute upwards and the 'bringing out' period extending from 1 to 5 or 10 minutes, according to the strength of the initial exposure. He referred to the power of the Calotype technique to *revive* images and also to one aspect of the process with which photographers to this day would agree: 'I know few things in the range of science more surprising than the gradual appearance of the picture on the blank sheet, especially the first time the experiment is witnessed.'[14]

Talbot's paper to the Royal Society 'An account of some recent improvements in photography' was read on 10 June. (Biot had conveyed the substance to the Academy in Paris three days before.) In it he gave extensive detail based mainly on the patent specification:

---

* Usually, a print-out image would be of lower contrast than a developed image – therefore the latter would appear to have greater sharpness. There would also be less 'image spread' with the developed paper. In addition, apparent sharpness would have benefited from the shorter exposure (and therefore more limited camera movement) when using the Calotype.

Preparation of the paper – Take a sheet of the best writing paper, having a smooth surface, and a close and even texture . . . Dissolve 100 grains of crystallised nitrate of silver in 6 ounces of distilled water. Wash the paper with this solution, with a soft brush, on one side, and put a mark on that side whereby to know it again . . . When dry, or nearly so, dip it into a solution of iodide of potassium containing 500 grains of that salt dissolved in one pint of water . . . All this is best done in the evening by candlelight. The paper so far prepared the author calls *iodized paper*, because it has a uniform pale yellow coating of iodide of silver. It is scarcely sensitive to light, but, nevertheless, it ought to be kept in a portfolio or a drawer, until wanted for use. It may be kept for any length of time without spoiling or undergoing any change, if protected from the light. This is the first part of the preparation of Calotype paper, and may be performed at any time. The remaining part is best deferred until shortly before the paper is wanted for use. When that time has arrived, take a sheet of the *iodized paper* and wash it with a liquid prepared in the following manner:

Dissolve 100 grains of crystallized nitrate of silver in two ounces of distilled water; add to this solution one-sixth of its volume of strong acetic acid. Let this mixture be called A.

Make a saturated solution of crystallized gallic acid in cold distilled water. The quantity dissolved is very small. Call this solution B.

When a sheet of paper is wanted for use, mix together the liquids A and B in equal volumes, but only mix a small quantity of them at a time, because the mixture does not keep long without spoiling. I shall call this mixture the *Gallo-nitrate of silver*.

Then take a sheet of *iodized paper* and wash it over with this *Gallo-nitrate of silver*, with a soft brush, taking care to wash it on the side which has been previously marked. This operation should be performed by candlelight. Let the paper rest half a minute, then dip it into water. Then dry it lightly with blotting paper, and finally dry it cautiously at a fire, holding it at a considerable distance therefrom. When dry, the paper is fit for use . . . it should be used in a few hours after it has been prepared. If it is used immediately, the last drying may be dispensed with, and the paper may be used moist . . .

The method of causing the impression to become visible is extremely simple. It consists in washing the paper once more with the *Gallo-nitrate of silver*, prepared in the way before described, and then warming it gently before the fire. In a few seconds the part of the paper upon which the light has acted begins to darken, and finally grows entirely black, while the other part of the paper retains its whiteness. Even a weaker impression than this may be *brought out* by repeating the wash of gallo-nitrate of silver, and again warming the paper. On the other hand, the stronger impression does not require the warming of the paper, for a wash of the gallo-nitrate suffices to make it visible, without heat, in the course of a minute or two . . .

The fixing process. – To fix the picture, it should be first washed with water, then lightly dried with blotting paper, and then washed with a solution of *bromide of potassium*, containing 100 grains of that salt dissolved in 8 or 10 ounces of water. After a minute or two it should be again dipped in water and then finally dried. The picture is in this manner very strongly fixed, and with this great advantage, that it remains transparent, and that, therefore, there is no difficulty in obtaining a copy from it. The Calotype is a *negative* one, in which the lights of nature are represented by shades; but the copies are *positive*, having the lights conformable to nature. They also represent the objects in their natural position with respect to right and left. The copies may be made upon Calotype paper in a very short time, the invisible impressions being *brought out* in the way already described. But the author prefers to make the copies upon photographic paper prepared in the way which he originally described in a memoir read to the Royal Society in February 1839, and which is made by washing the best writing paper, *first* with a weak solution of common salt, and *next* with a solution of nitrate of silver. Although it takes a much longer time to obtain a copy upon this paper, yet when obtained, the tints appear more harmonious and pleasing to the eye; it requires in general from 3 minutes to 30 minutes of sunshine, according to circumstances, to obtain a good copy on this sort of photographic paper . . .[15]

The reactions to the new process were overwhelmingly favourable – both from the scientifically knowledgeable and those less so. Herschel greeted the news with generous delight: '. . . this is really magical. Surely you deal with the naughty one' – and judged the portraits sent to him 'much superior in effect to the Daguerreotype'.[16] Brewster was amazed by the Calotype's sharpness after light had passed through and been dispersed by *writing paper*[17], while Charles Lemon identified improvements in both chemistry and optics which had 'got rid of the indistinctness which used to prevail near the margin of the picture'.[18] Robert Hunt, already at work on his *Popular Treatise*, wrote thanking Talbot for 'those very beautiful specimens of your new process which indeed promises to realize many of my dreams'.[19] From home and abroad came requests for examples of the new process which Talbot strove to fulfil with good heart. Some were from scientists and others who had been experimenting themselves – many too were from members of the family. All delighted in the progress – cousin Mary in Wales in a typically quiet manner praising the specimens sent to her as 'beautifully clear and distinct'[20] and George Butler singing his former pupil's praises as a 'most admired magician' for working 'a mass of wonders . . .'[21] Talbot's cousin Shelburne – son of Lord Lansdowne – requested some Calotypes prior to his departure for the Continent, something which Lady Elisabeth told Constance he had never done before because 'he wishes now to be *considered* on the Continent as the cousin of the inventor. They make ten times more fuss about it abroad than they do here . . .'[22] She also reported – as in 1839 – that visitors to Lacock Abbey were expecting to receive specimens of the new art and that after Lady Lansdowne had departed recently with much booty 'it is proper this sort of *shoplifting* or swindling should be made known to the owner'!

It was Constance who once again assisted her husband with the production of prints during the spring and summer days of 1841. Talbot was frequently absent from Lacock about his other work – from 1840 to 1842 he was experimenting and taking out patents in motive power and metal-coating techniques – and his wife set to work with good heart, despite the fact that she was again pregnant. Two of the servants at the Abbey – Henneman and Porter – afforded some help and Constance expressed the views of the world's first female photographic processor to her husband in a forthright manner:

You must really invent some other fixing process or some new fixing liquid . . . The *paper* in the press is not keeping well. I observed it to be a good deal discoloured when I went this morning to take out a bit for the Queen . . . Why did you *fold* your picture? You observe the line has copied itself.[23]

This last was an extraordinary habit of Talbot's. After producing negatives with what must have been considerable effort, he carelessly folded them to post back to Lacock Abbey and Constance complained about the habit on a number of occasions.

This early period also saw the introduction of techniques which were to be widely adopted later – for example in June 1841 Talbot wrote to Constance requiring that Henneman iron negatives prior to printing, adding that 'one or two of the portraits are so *thick* that [Henneman] had better *wax* them. He knows how to do it.'[24] Waxing and ironing were methods of making negatives more translucent, thus increasing the detail in the positive copy and shortening the exposure time to the sun in the printing frame. In his absences from home Talbot may have sent the negatives to Lacock for printing partly for convenience, but the actinic quality of the London atmosphere also played some part – Henry observing on one occasion that the London atmosphere prevented a good result 'even when fog is hardly visible to the eye'.[24] The need for a regular photographic assistant was suggested by members of the family on several occasions at this time but Talbot rejected the idea because he felt that there was not sufficient work.

Another suggestion by Talbot's scientific friends and family also found little favour with him but this one did win the day. Toward the end of 1840 Lady Elisabeth began using the name *Talbotype* instead of *Calotype*[25] – and as soon as the new process was made known to him John Herschel too pronounced that all the rest of the world would assign to it the name of Talbotype.[26] David Brewster concurred (partly to prevent having to explain the derivation of the word Calotype) and told Talbot 'you must put up with the affront the best way you can'.[27] It was Brewster who first publicized the name – at a meeting of the Literary and Philosophical Society of St Andrews on 1 November 1841. Although *Talbotype* was used extensively during the subsequent period when the system was being promoted to the public – first by Antoine Claudet as a licensee of Talbot's and then by the Talbot establishments in Reading and London – he personally used the term rarely, preferring the original name of Calotype. It reveals something of his character.

On several occasions from January 1839 onwards Henry Talbot stressed that it was for others to take the new discoveries further. In fact he did not stop his own researches – and at least until the end of 1843 devoted much time to discovering improvements in the Calotype process. The last surviving scientific notebook took the story up to April 1843,[28] and then he seemed to stop keeping formal notebooks of his experiments for batches of notes are found amongst his letters. These reveal that Talbot was intent on perfecting an entire system – from preparation of sensitized negative paper to the fixation of the final positive print. He was not the kind of person who made a discovery and left others to perfect it – whatever he may have said otherwise from time to time. Thus he tried to increase the speed of the Calotype even further, to solve the fixing problems in both negatives (now produced by development) and positives (still printed out by the action of light) and to increase the translucency of the negative to aid printing. He experimented extensively with the preparation of copy paper to make positives from superimposed negatives by means of development (thereby greatly reducing the length of the exposure required in the sun) but he never adopted the technique, probably for the reasons mentioned in his June 1841 paper to the Royal Society – the harshness of the dark tones in the *developed* image compared with the softer, 'more harmonious' hues of a printed-out image. But the patent which he took out in 1843[29] for a series of improvements – both major and minor – revealed his application.

By that time Talbot was satisfied with the value of hypo as a fixing agent given proper management – but he went one stage further and discovered that very hot hypo would discharge the residual, undeveloped silver iodide in the negative image (which gave it a typical yellow colour) thereby making it whiter and more transparent and therefore easier to print from. He considered that warming Calotype paper prior to exposure made it more sensitive and that preparing the paper by washing iodized paper with gallic acid first and *then* with silver nitrate prior to use (not with gallic acid and nitrate of silver *together* at the same time) was advantageous because the mixture of gallo-nitrate of silver 'decomposed' quickly. An adjustment in the proportions of gallic acid to silver nitrate gave better results if the paper was to be used dry and he made a suggestion that the contrast of prints could be softened by waxing them and then backing them with white or coloured papers. The deliberate overexposure of a positive copy from a negative, followed by bleaching treatment with potassium iodide, has already been mentioned. Another Talbot proposal was the photocopying of pages of print built up specially from existing type. His last proposal in the patent of 1843 was for a system of mass-producing prints for publication so that they were as similar as possible, having the quality of permanency as well as being agreeable to the eye.

Thus Talbot continued to work at his process and in 1842 his discovery was recognized when the Royal Society awarded him its biennial Rumford Medal (whose previous recipients included Davy, Brewster, Fresnel and Biot and which Faraday was to receive in 1846) for 'many important discoveries made in photography'. Typically Henry Talbot was not at the Royal Society meeting to receive the medal and the £70 which accompanied it, nor to hear the council of the Society declare the highest respect which was entertained for the value of his discoveries. But even he must have felt some pleasure at that moment.

But what of the Daguerreotype? Despite its advantages over photogenic drawing initially it too was far too slow to make the taking of portraits a feasible proposition. John Frederick Goddard – working for Richard Beard who in June 1841 purchased the Daguerreotype patent covering England, Wales and the Colonies from Miles Berry – succeeded in increasing the speed of the plates by sensitizing them with fumes of bromine as well as iodine, while Antoine Claudet announced to the Royal Society on the very same day that Talbot's paper on the Calotype was presented that he too had secured significant gains in sensitivity by exposing the metal plates to chlorine fumes as well as those of iodine. As usual the estimates of exposure times varied immensely and optimistically – from 3 seconds to 5 minutes – but commercial Daguerreotype portraiture was now possible particularly after Joseph Max Petzval had designed an f3.6 lens which was far faster than any which had been used hitherto.* Beard opened a public studio on the roof of the Royal Poly-

---

* Talbot thought that his 'portraits from life' in October 1840 antedated the first Daguerreotype portraits (letter to *The Index* published 20 January 1849). This seems not strictly to have been the case.

technic Institution in London in March 1841 and Claudet followed suit at the Adelaide Gallery in June.* Other studios in the provinces followed. The early Daguerreotype portraits executed for sale were far from perfect – but they improved greatly in a very short time and being photographed caught on amongst the members of the public who could afford it. Henry Talbot decided to explore the portrait-taking capability of the Calotype too.

Henry Collen was the first professional Calotypist – his agreement with Talbot commencing in August 1841. Collen was a miniaturist and a member of the Royal Academy who had for some time been a drawing master to Princess Victoria before she ascended the throne. His work was regarded by a contemporary opinion as 'uneven'[30] but he realized as quickly as any of his professional colleagues that it was the miniaturist who suffered the greatest danger from the new art of portrait photography. Those of his photographic portraits which survive had been retouched (some extensively) and showed competence rather than any high degree of skill. However, it must be remembered that Collen was the first person called upon to wrestle with the difficulties of the Calotype process professionally and his place in the history of negative–positive photography is therefore secure.

The business relationship between Talbot and Collen lasted from the middle of 1841 until at least 1844[31] and inevitably was subjected to the strains of an entirely new experience in both the technology and commercial exploitation of a new invention. Collen's studio was a glass-covered yard at the back of 29 Somerset Street (near Portman Square) in London and he learnt the technical skills as he went along. It is difficult to establish how much help Talbot, who was highly involved with his own numerous other activities, gave Collen but it may not have been much for in August of 1842 Collen wrote to Talbot:

I scarcely ever have a portrait fail, except when caused by a sitter, but this point of success is the result of laborious application and I have lost a great deal of time for want of sufficient explanation of both theory & practice; photography being entirely a new subject to me until I commenced with [the] calotype . . .[32]

* Both Claudet and the Beard studio took Daguerreotype portraits of Talbot which still survive (Frontispiece and Plate 1).

Beaumont Newhall indicates that Daguerreotype portraits ('probably . . . corpse like images . . .') were obtained in France and the U.S. during 1839 and Gernsheim that Beard and Goddard were experimenting with Daguerreotype portraits 'during the summer and autumn of 1840'. None of the Daguerreotype portraits, however, appears to have been larger than just a few inches square.[33]

Collen does not seem to have been an efficient 'manipulator' but if his comment was substantially true it was extremely shortsighted of Henry Talbot not to pass on all he knew at that time. Collen also had difficulties with his equipment. Andrew Ross, the London instrument maker, had been commissioned by Collen to produce a faster lens for portraiture. The lens – which is now in the Science Museum[34] – was only slightly less fast (maximum aperture of about f4) than the Petzval lens increasingly being used at this time in Daguerreotype studios. It seems that Ross may not have delivered the lens until after August 1842 and Collen was at one time thinking of turning to German manufacturers for a solution.[32] Hence the contemporary praises extended to Collen's efforts[35] prior to 1842 were won under conditions of great difficulty.

The contractual arrangements between Collen and Talbot were a source of some disagreement, particularly when Talbot entered into discussions with Richard Beard in 1841–2 for the latter to act as his licence agent. After an amicable discussion of the possibilities, Beard decided that Talbot's proposals were not attractive enough financially[36] and there did not appear to have been any subsequent attempt on Talbot's part to operate the licence through an agent. In retrospect this is to be regretted as the Calotype was never promoted commercially with the aggression that a Beard would have demonstrated – and certainly was pursuing in his promotion of the Daguerreotype. Talbot and Collen discussed various ways of promoting the Calotype but with no great drive or skill and both were dissatisfied with the outcome. Various modifications were introduced into their agreement and it should be stressed that, in his negotiations with Beard, Talbot insisted on the safeguarding of Collen's position as first licensee.

Compared with the great popularity attributed to the Daguerreotype studios, Collen's business was at a very low level. While no copy of the initial licence agreement has been traced, it can be assumed that the major financial stipulation was the payment to Talbot of 30 per cent. (later 25 per cent.) of Collen's takings. In the period between 16 August 1841 and 24 June 1842 Collen took 209 portraits (at £1 1s. each) and made 57 copies (at 5s. each). This produced an income for Talbot of £70 2s. 0d.[37] Business thereafter may well have slowed even further for in May of 1844 Collen wrote: 'I am doing really next to nothing with the Calotype and have not the means of making a positive impression on the public by advertising which I am fully aware is the only mode by which a business can be made of the art . . .'[38] Evidence of Collen's total business over the three years to August 1844 is not complete but in

1854[39] he estimated that the *total* dues paid to Talbot during the period amounted to under £120. Other information suggests that this may have been an understatement[40] but the amount was certainly unlikely to have been more than £200. On this basis, we may estimate a total turnover in Collen's business of no more than perhaps £700 – representing possibly 650 portrait sessions together with a small number of commissions for copies. That represented an average over the three years of only 4 to 5 sessions per week which was completely uneconomic and a disappointing performance. But Collen's and Talbot's relationship survived all the problems well for when the latter was beset with patent litigation in 1854 Collen wrote to Henry 'wishing you may yet be successful in the establishment of your right'.*[39]

During these early years of the Calotype patent considerable interest was shown by potential professional licensees but few contacts progressed beyond the preliminary stage and this was probably due mainly to Talbot himself. That he was engaged in numerous other activities and was also out of the country for considerable periods of time were undoubted facts but he should have placed the exploitation of the licence in capable hands and hands which he could trust. Thus in 1843 a prospective licensee from Birmingham had to follow up an initial enquiry because he had received no reply, and another enquirer was completely confused as to the exploitation of the Calotype in the London area. It was possible, too, that the failure to attract more active licensees from those with whom Talbot did correspond resulted from his desultory approach to commercial negotiations. During 1842 the Scottish Daguerreotypist H. W. Treffr(a)y expressed keen interest in a London licence and Robert Hunt was also seriously considering the professional exploitation of the Calotype in the provinces. Neither possibility came to anything however. But Talbot did get as far as outlining proposals for professional licences in 1842 and these went into considerable detail.[41] A portraiture only non-exclusive licence for London was 200 guineas (presumably a once-and-for-all payment). Outside of London an exclusive licence for a town of 10,000 inhabitants and its surrounding district for the life of the patent (nearly thirteen years) was £100 down or £10 down and 30 per cent of the proceeds (with a

* Collen assisted Wheatstone's stereoscopic experiments by making a stereo portrait of Charles Babbage in 1841.[42] He continued to take an interest in photography until his death in 1879. In the *British Journal of Photography* on 27 October 1865 (p. 547) he proposed a tri-chromatic system of photography based on materials sensitive to red, blue and yellow light. (It should have been red, blue and *green* – and in proposing yellow Collen was following the erroneous theory proposed by David Brewster some years before.)

minimum of 100 portraits a year) or a down payment of £50 for a period of three years. There were proportionately higher charges for areas with larger populations and selling prices were to be fixed at between 10s. 6d. and £1 1s. for portraits and 5s. for further copies. A non-exclusive non-portrait licence for anywhere in England and Wales was £20 down and 30 per cent of proceeds on sales. The terms were by no means unfair but the Calotype portrait never caught up with the popularity of the more glamorously packaged and promoted Daguerreotype despite the capability of the process to give the portraitist a far greater potential for artistic expression. It is difficult to estimate precisely how far this resulted from Talbot's own inadequacies as a businessman and how far from some admitted deficiencies of the Calotype – for example the problem of image fading – but when Antoine Claudet entered into a licence agreement with Henry Talbot in 1844, the latter may have had hopes of a significant breakthrough particularly as by this time he had opened his own establishment at Reading.

Antoine François Jean Claudet was born in Lyons in 1797 but came to England in 1829, where with an English partner, he established a glass business. As soon as the Daguerreotype was announced, he took instruction from Daguerre personally and proceeded to improve the system and open a Daguerreotype portrait studio. Besides producing some of the most artistically satisfying Daguerreotypes, Claudet was a scientist – mathematician, chemist and physicist – and as such it was natural that Talbot would have more in common with him and moreover seek to persuade him to practise the Calotype. Discussion of the possibility and of a formal agreement extended from the autumn of 1842 to the summer of 1844,[43] a major stumbling block being Talbot's initial desire to be free to grant other licences in London if Claudet's payments to him fell beneath a minimum figure of £400 in one year. Claudet however realized it would take some time to develop the system both technically and commercially and held out for an exclusive licence. With the ending of Collen's licence this became possible and the two scientists settled in July–August 1844.

Claudet received instruction in the Calotype process from Talbot's assistant Henneman and then proceeded to promote the Calotype business (rather, Talbotype, for Claudet was the first to use the name in advertisements). He did so with energy and Lady Elisabeth noted approvingly: 'Claudet I see advertises the Talbotype Portraits almost every day in The Times.' She had a high regard for the Frenchman and elsewhere expressed the view that 'Claudet having the stimulus of his own interest will spread your Fame by his success.'[44] Claudet was a talented photographer. In him was a happy union of the scientist and artist which made him an admirable source for evaluating both the strengths and weaknesses of the Talbotype with objectivity and a knowledge of its chief rival.

> Until we have a paper with a surface as uniform and perfect as a silver plate I say that the Daguerreotype gives images more delicate, finer and of greater perfection than the Talbotype. Until we can operate with the Talbotype in several seconds and as rapidly as with the Daguerreotype so that one can get more pleasing poses, then I say that the advantage is on the side of the Daguerreotype. But I also say that the Talbotype has [a] beauty which the other has not, that the impressions are more portable and circulate more easily, that it is possible to send them through the post, stick them in albums etc, and finally one can obtain an unlimited number of copies.[45]

Claudet geared his studio for the quantity production of portrait Calotypes – by November 1844 he had the facilities to produce 40 negatives a day – but his payments to Talbot revealed a lack of success despite all his energetic application. In the six months to December 1844, only 23 portraits were commissioned with prices varying from £2 2s. to 10s. 6d. with 19 copies ordered: this yielded Talbot a 25 per cent share of £7 0s. 10d.[46] which he promptly passed to his wife Constance 'to buy something pretty with'. In the six months between March and September 1845 business was even worse – 17 portraits only. At mid-year Claudet wrote to Talbot that he was sorry to communicate such poor results, which did not even cover the cost of an assistant.[47] He suggested that they consider jointly methods of improving the situation but it could not have been long thereafter that Claudet once again devoted himself exclusively to his Daguerreotype business. The relationship between the two men had always been based upon a strong mutual admiration and this happy relationship continued thereafter. When in 1853, for example, Claudet decorated his new studio in Regent Street with painted portraits of the inventors of photography Henry Talbot was in pride of place together with Daguerre.

Infinitely greater success was enjoyed with the Calotype as a medium for portraiture in Scotland. The system was not patented there but it was only practised professionally at first by Robert Adamson and then by Adamson in partnership with the artist David Octavius Hill. That partnership resulted in some of the most impressive examples of the artistry that could be created with the Calotype – many of which fortunately still survive in a number of albums, including those in Scotland and in that collection of Adamson and Hill secured for the National Portrait Gallery in 1973.[48]

The Calotype was introduced to Scotland by David Brewster – at the time principal of the United Colleges of San Salvador and St Leonard of the University of St Andrews – whom Talbot told of his discovery shortly after it had been made. A medical practitioner Dr John Adamson – who was a curator of the college library and who also lectured on chemistry and natural history elsewhere in St Andrews – was the keenest student of the new art in Brewster's close circle of acquaintances. Much of 1841 was taken with an exchange of letters between Brewster and Talbot – Brewster recounting the problems encountered by his colleagues in mastering the process and Talbot sending examples of his own work by way of encouragement. In October 1841, Brewster pronounced that St Andrews was 'the headquarters (always excepting Lacock Abbey) of the Talbotype' and the claim was reasonably justified for by the following spring he could add that 'Dr Adamson is much pleased that you think so well of his pictures, and is going on with double energy.'[49]

In the summer of 1842 John Adamson's brother Robert – who originally intended to become an engineer but was prevented from doing so by indifferent health – decided after tuition from his brother to practise the Calotype professionally in Edinburgh and the album of their joint work which John sent to Talbot in November[50] 'in testimony of the great pleasure we have derived from your discovery' (and which is in the Lacock Collection) augured well for the future. Robert Adamson began professional operations in May 1843 and as he set out for Edinburgh Brewster wrote to Talbot:

He has made brilliant progress, and done some of the very finest things both in Portrait and Landscape. His risk & outlay are considerable; & he is therefore anxious to make a good beginning. For this purpose he is desirous that you will allow him to state that he practises the art with your concurrence and countenance.[51]

Although Talbot's letters to Scotland have not survived it may be assumed that he was only too willing to encourage the Scottish initiative and by July Brewster could record that Adamson was established in Edinburgh 'with crowds every day at his studio'.[52]

It was in the summer of 1843 that David Hill became involved in photography. Some time before, a group of ministers had broken away from the Church of Scotland and resolved to form a Free Church. The formal breach took place at the General Assembly of the Church of Scotland on 18 May 1843 and Hill – a lithographer, book illustrator, painter and secretary of the Royal Scottish Academy – who was reportedly present on the occasion, decided to paint the scene.* Brewster, who supported the Free Church, suggested to Hill that photography was the means of securing the 'likenesses of all the principal characters before they dispersed to their respective homes. He was at first incredulous, but went to Mr Adamson and arranged with him the preliminaries for getting all the necessary portraits.' The two men must have struck up a first-class relationship from the beginning, for they agreed to establish a partnership and Brewster delightedly told Talbot that they proposed 'to apply the Calotype to many other general purposes of a very popular kind, & especially to the execution of large pictures representing different bodies of classes of individuals. I think you will find that we have, in Scotland, found out the value of your invention not before yourself but before those to whom you have given the privilege of using it.'[52]

Brewster spoke no more than the truth. Although Hill's completion of his painting was to take twenty-one years, between 1843 and the autumn of 1847 when Robert Adamson became seriously ill (he died in 1848) the two men produced something like 2,500 Calotype pictures. These were created not only at their studio in Rock House, Calton Hill Stairs in Edinburgh but in many locations around as well as across the border in Durham and York. At the height of their fame albums were sold for as much as forty guineas and the deliberate attempt they made to re-create the power of a Rembrandt impression with a modern technique was so successful that examples of Adamson's and Hill's work – with its masterly combination of artistry and technical skill – are today amongst the most sought-after specimens in the history of photography. Brewster gave an indication of the variety of their work when in 1843 he wrote to Talbot:

I wish I could send you some of the fine Calotypes of ancient churchyard monuments, as well as modern ones taken by Mr Adamson and also specimens of the fine groups of Picturesque personages which Mr Hill and he have arranged and photographed. Those of the fishermen and women of Newhaven are singularly excellent. They have been so overwhelmed with work that they have not been able to send me a collection which they have promised . . .[53]

* He later changed his mind and painted the signing of the Act of Separation by 450 clergymen which took place on 23 May.

The direct contact between Talbot and Adamson and Hill was very limited. In 1844 the British Association for the Advancement of Science met at York and the two Scotsmen sought Talbot's permission to come south of the border to photograph some of the famous scientists who were attending. This Talbot obviously gave and the two men opened a studio in the York Museum. In the notice which was issued advertising the portraiture sessions, Henry was invited by name to sit but it does not seem that he accepted – which was sad for posterity even though other sitters were by no means so reluctant.[54]

Later, hopes were expressed for a collaboration between Hill and Talbot. John Murray the publisher was friendly with both men and in May 1846 he wrote to Talbot expressing the wish that 'it were possible for Mr Hill to act in conjunction with you. There are points in which your Calotypes have the decided superiority over his – there are others in which I think he excels, especially in obtaining artistic effects. A combination of the two would be a step in advance.'[55] In the same year, the *Quarterly Review* published an art review in which it expressed the hope that Talbot would bring both Adamson and Hill to London:

> To Mr Fox Talbot the happy invention is owing, but that artistic application of it, which has brought these drawings to their present picturesque perfection, required the eye of an artist, and for this the public is indebted to Mr D. O. Hill of Edinburgh, in conjunction with Mr Adamson, a young chemist of distinguished ability. It is to be hoped that Mr Talbot, in justice to his own genius, will soon invite these gentlemen to London – where they would find rather more interesting, though certainly not more grotesque subjects, than the fat Martyrs of the Free Kirk – as yet, seemingly, their favourite sitters.[56]

And what of Talbot's own skills – seemingly dismissed by the above comment?[57] From 1840 to 1846 he devoted considerable time to taking Calotypes. He travelled extensively – to Oxford (for three days in 1843 and securing twenty views a day), Windsor (with Royal permission to photograph in the private grounds), York (with the Revd Calvert Jones on one occasion: 'We took 12 views . . . today . . . most of them good – crowds of admiring spectators surrounded the camera wherever we planted it . . .'[58]) – as well as many other locations both at home and on the Continent. His friendship with Antoine Claudet extended to enjoyable photographic sessions at the latter's London studio.

Talbot's photography has for long been regarded merely as the outcome of tests conducted by a scientist interested only in chemistry and optics. His end-

K

lessly demanding family certainly took that view and stated its opinions as frankly as ever. Besides offering numerous suggestions for better subjects for the camera than those he had chosen, they criticized his efforts. His halfsister Caroline considered that he should associate himself with an artist and grew impatient when he did not do so. Kit Talbot wrote in August 1842 criticizing his cousin's choice of backgrounds – '. . . all the selections I have seen of yours seem to me to be badly chosen and not to do justice to the subjects. The article you had for background for my portrait was dark but also a reflecting surface, which is the most injurious imaginable to a background.'[59] Somewhat later Henry's mother wrote:

Lord Mount Edgcumbe was much struck with your having told him that the view of Chambord was bad because it was such a rainy day as if you could not have remained there till the weather was clear, particularly with such an interesting object before you. He thinks if you had more perseverance your success would be more complete, & that if he were you he would persevere to pertinacity. There is no doubt that if you were an artist instead of an amateur your Art would be soon at the summit of perfection.[60]

This to the man whose perseverance – to the point of obstinacy – was the great strength in everything he did.

Talbot talked little about the art of his photography – unlike some who were to follow – but what he did write deserves attention for it reveals something about the man. In one of the 1841 letters about the Calotype to the *Literary Gazette*, he answered accusations that photography was likely to prove injurious to art:

. . . there is ample room for the exercise of skill and judgment. It would hardly be believed how different an effect is produced by a longer or shorter exposure to the light, and, also, by mere variations in the fixing process, by means of which almost any tint, cold or warm, may be thrown over the picture . . . All this falls within the artist's province to combine and to regulate; and if . . . he, *nolens volens*, becomes a chemist and an optician, I feel confident that such an alliance of science with art will prove conducive to the improvement of both.[61]

In his comments in *The Pencil of Nature*, Talbot without any flourishes expressed a viewpoint which was in fact expressed practically in his photography. The bust of Patroclus demonstrated the limitless variations of lighting and subject angle and the value of soft lighting (as well as artificial fill-in where nature's sunlight was too harsh); the photograph of 'The Open Door' was presented with the words –

We have sufficient authority in the Dutch school of art, for taking as subjects of representation scenes of daily and familiar occurrence. A painter's eye will often be arrested where ordinary people see nothing remarkable. A casual gleam of sunshine, or a shadow thrown across his path, a time-withered oak, or a moss-covered stone may awake a train of thoughts and feelings, and picturesque imaginings . . .

and with 'The Haystack' he offered the view that the artist might scoff at the minute detail of the photograph as being 'beneath his genius to copy every accident of light and shade' – but yet might not the minutiae revealed by the camera 'sometimes be found to give an air of variety beyond expectation to the scene represented'. Are these not the thoughts of an artist, too – of the man who, while his feeble attempts at sketching drove him towards photography, could none the less in his younger days recognize the singular lighting effects which demanded the genius of a Claude to record? And he was not slow to criticize the conventions: 'It is . . . a pity that artists should object to the convergence of vertical parallel lines [in photographs where a camera was pointed upwards] since it is founded in nature and only violates the *conventional* rules of art.'[62] Talbot was close here to a statement that photography was a new kind of art, with its viewfinder or ground-glass screen making essentially different demands on the skills of a new breed of artist, the photographer.

There were some who saw more in his work even when it was being produced. As far back as May of 1840, when Talbot circulated some of his photogenic drawings which had been created with the coming of the spring of that year, the *Literary Gazette* wrote about the distribution of lights and shades – 'the former, in particular, are bold and striking, and may furnish lessons to the ablest of our artists'[63] while the Revd Calvert Jones, himself an artist of no mean merit, wrote on receiving some of Talbot's Calotypes the following year: 'The marble head is equal to one of M. Angelo's drawings, and the small bit of Lacock wonderfully pictorial and strong – also the large one of the backyard, sunny in the extreme, the foliage I think brighter than any one in silver that I have seen.'[64]

In the Calotypes that can with some certainty be identified as the work of Talbot, there is a variety which is greater than that found in the work of any other photographer of the 1840s – ranging from landscapes through moody records of trees to still life, and from portraits through splendidly posed –

though not stilted – groups to the microcosm revealed by the solar micro-scope. The quality was uneven* – which is understandable with the demands made on Talbot's time and the fact that some took the form of experiments – but the best did not yield to any contemporaries including Adamson and Hill. The prints included in *The Pencil of Nature* were a miniscule proportion of Talbot's total output but fortunately the centenary exhibition of some 600 or so of his pictures – selected to show both the work of the experimenter and of the photographer – will allow individuals to make up their own minds on the evidence of the actual *objets* and not on the opinion of others. With that, Talbot would have been satisfied.

It is likely that in the years ahead the reputations of others in immediate contact with Henry Talbot during the first decade of photography will be established. John Dillwyn Llewelyn and his wife Emma – Talbot's cousin – together embarked upon the demanding art and technique of photography from its very beginning. Llewelyn, the son of a scientist, brought the necessary scientific knowledge to the technique – he was elected a Fellow of the Royal Society in 1836 at the age of twenty-six – and over the years practised photogenic draw-ing, the Daguerreotype, Calotype, photo-engraving, wet-plate collodion and the oxymel process which was slower than collodion but did not need to be used wet. The subjects ranged widely over portraits and landscapes and he was one of the first photographers to devote attention to the photography of botanical specimens. Llewelyn had considerable talent, and while his corre-spondence with Henry Talbot was not prolific it is evident that they had a deep regard for each other's work. Llewelyn remained an enthusiast for the Calotype process and as late as May 1852 – on sending some specimens of his work to Talbot – he wrote:[65]

* It has been suggested that the admittedly varied quality of Talbot's work reflects the absence or presence of an 'artist'. There is no evidence to substantiate this view – indeed, the repeatedly expressed views of other members of his family that Talbot should cooperate with an artist appear to indicate that as in most things he went his own independent way. Thomas Malone later related a story[66] of Henry Collen being present during a picture-taking session when Talbot wished to point the lens upwards. 'You are not going to take it so, surely!' To Talbot's comment that it could not be taken any other way, Collen allegedly replied: 'As an artist, I would not take it at all.' Whether the story has much accuracy is open to some doubt – it seems much too pat and there is no record of Collen ever having visited Lacock Abbey – but if the occasion was the taking of the picture published in *The Pencil of Nature* as 'The Ladder' the result is adequate testimony of the virtue of Talbot's attitude in persisting.

I feel somewhat diffident in sending Talbotypes to their fountainhead . . . I have been practising sun paintings for some years and as a matter of chemical amusement have followed all the different processes on paper, silver & glass – and it is rather remarkable that the method I now follow when I wish for good views is identically the same with your old original receipts.[*sic**]

Another enthusiast from the beginning was the Revd Calvert Richard Jones, a Welshman from a wealthy family who was a close friend of Kit Talbot – the two having been at Oriel College, Oxford together and the minister having performed the marriage ceremony between Kit and Lady Charlotte Butler in 1835. Over the years Calvert Jones, who was a talented water-colourist especially in marine and figure studies, was a demanding correspondent of Henry Talbot's – requiring advice, complaining about the inadequacies of prepared paper and chemicals, passing on information about the latest progress made by other inventors (for example, in 1845, that of the Frenchman Bayard) and endeavouring to sell negatives to Talbot – which he eventually accomplished – for distribution commercially. Calvert Jones concentrated on views of Swansea and the surrounding countryside although following a trip abroad in 1845–6 he returned with numerous Calotypes of Malta, Sicily, Naples, Rome and Florence, most of which, never a modest man, he declared 'wonderfully perfect and beautiful'.[67] Most of them, in fact, *were*. Jones, while somewhat aggressive by nature and certainly demanding, had as intense a belief in the Calotype system as Llewelyn: 'The apathy of the British public about [photography] is quite inexplicable but I cannot help thinking that your agents in London cannot be very active or very proper ones . . .'[68] And later: 'I think you underrate the flattering power of the Talbotype as I do not see why its likenesses should not be as pleasing as Daguerreotype ones which persons go daily in flocks to have done.'[69] Like Llewelyn, too, that loyalty – based on hard and practical experience – continued. In 1853 he told Talbot: 'I think you may have the satisfaction of knowing that your method of photography (Talbotype proper) is superior practically to waxed paper, albumenised &c. &c. or any other that has yet been devised.'[70]

George W. Bridges was another of the pioneers who was also a clergyman. He was introduced to Talbot and the Calotype through friendship with

---

* Llewelyn may also have suffered for his photography: 'Emma has been nursing Mr Llewelyn all through the winter but he is better now . . .' wrote Talbot's aunt, Lady Mary Cole, two years later. 'I *lay* it on photography, for he is so devotedly fond of it, that he inhales too much chemical poisonous gas . . .'[71]

Caroline Mount Edgcumbe and her husband. Bridges early conceived the idea
of a tour of Malta, Italy, Greece and the Holy Land and was instructed in the
Calotype process by Talbot's assistant Henneman. (Calvert Jones also helped
with advice later.) He set out in 1846 and did not return for seven years.
During that time he had to contend with badly prepared iodized paper sent
out from England and its poor keeping qualities in Middle Eastern tempera-
tures. Moreover, as though to emphasize that successful fixing was not so easy
as photographic historians have subsequently imagined, his most consistent
problem during those years was that of the serious density loss in positive
'copies' which were, of course, still produced by printing out in daylight. It
may be assumed that Henry Talbot did all he could with advice, for towards
the end of 1852 on his return to England, Bridges wrote that he would like
to lay at Talbot's feet the results of his years of 'wandering' – he had some
1,700 pictures – and thanked him for his 'liberality'. Talbot, he said, had done
everything 'that man can do to bring it [photography] into use and fashion –
but like all great Discoverers you are defrauded of your due.'[72] Bridges's
work, as with that of Llewelyn and Jones, has still to be adequately presented.

In his photographic patent of 1843 it will be recalled that Talbot described a
system for the production of photographic prints for publication. A few
months later he began to put the plan into effect when he sent Nicolaas Henneman to Reading to take charge of what was to be the world's first mass-volume
photographic-print production facility. Henneman was a Dutchman born in
1813 who for most of his working life had been a manservant. He came to
England some time between 1835 and 1839 by which latter time he was in
Talbot's employ and known to the family as 'Nicole'. He was a slim, handsome
man who was frequently a model in Talbot's portraits and both portraits and
sitter were clearly firm favourites among the ladies of the Talbot household.
He was described by one acquaintance as 'genial and laughing' and as 'a lively,
volatile fellow . . . nothing like the typical Dutchman'.[73] He assisted Constance Talbot in the finishing of Calotypes in 1841 and when Talbot decided
to set up an establishment for the production of prints commercially Henneman
was an understandable choice.

It was between December 1843 and January 1844[74] that Henry began
organizing the new business in Russell Terrace, Reading which is now called
Baker Street. (A plaque marks the present No. 55 as the location.) The house

had formerly been a school and much of the photographic work was in due course to be carried out in a glasshouse adjoining the building and in the extensive yard. Talbot's correspondence contains no guidance on why Reading was chosen but it may be surmised that, with Henry Collen still operating in London and with the hope that the exclusive licence would pass to Claudet before too long, London was out of the question and that Reading presented a convenient location between London and Lacock on the main Great Western Railway line.

Henneman's activities created something of a stir at first. Many years afterwards a part-time helper John Henderson recalled that Henneman's movements

... were watched with some degree of suspicion, the chief reason being that he was known to be purchasing every possible variety of paper at the different stationers, and rather unusual quantities of chemicals at different shops. Added to this he lived alone in a rather large house for a bachelor, and worked all day in a sort of conservatory or small glass house at the back of his residence, which he never left unlocked, so the old Housekeeper thought him a most mysterious person, his hands being stained all shades from brown to black. He seldom appeared in public unless well gloved ...

The conclusion was 'that he was engaged in forging Foreign Bank Notes or some such nefarious pursuit'.[75]

George Lovejoy's stationery shop and library in London Street, Reading – a gathering place for many of the town's scientific and literary intelligentsia – was a major supplier to Henneman and it was from there that he enlisted two apprentices John Henderson and Alfred Harrison to assist him, together with another young man – Thomas Augustine Malone – from the shop at which he purchased his chemicals. Both Harrison and Malone subsequently became full-time employees at Reading and moved with Henneman to London when the establishment at Russell Terrace closed in 1847.

By February 1844 Henneman was producing prints but was apprehensive about the slow start of the business. His fellow servant at the Abbey, Porter, was working with him but Henneman decided by May that he or another worker would have to go – and to add to the depressing circumstances 'the weather has[sic] and is still very bad and not fit for *negatives*'.[76] The next month he wrote to Talbot:

I am ... very anxious to kno[sic] how your work has taken and in hopes that you will require a great many copies more for you must be aware I have nothing to do ... in the meantime I shall feel greatly obliged to you if you think of anything to help me on.[77]

A change was soon to come and by September Henneman was able to send Talbot a bill for £237 0s. 9½d. which included the supply of no less than 10,400 photographic 'coppies'.[78] The high level of work continued such that in October 1845 Henneman anticipated criticism from Talbot of print quality by pointing out that he was at present working on no less than 254 negatives and that 'it is impossible to get good ones of everyone'.[79] One year later, a note of print and paper production to November 1846 – although unfortunately not giving details of the precise period of production – did give a telling indication of production levels.[80]

	Iodized paper	Unmounted 'copies'		Mounted 'copies'	
		Large	Small	Large	Small
Production	2,642	7,935	5,547	8,318	4,473
Deliveries	2,628	6,728	5,107	6,896	3,510

This output of prints was directed to publication in books and the sale of individual photographs to printsellers.

Details of the first project executed at Reading very early in 1844 were subsequently given by John Henderson.[73] John Walter, an M.P. and 'chief proprietor' of *The Times*, was a frequent visitor to Lovejoy's shop, where he learned about Henneman's work and may have met Talbot. Walter's daughter Catherine died in January 1844 and her brother John prepared a memoir of her last days for circulation to her family and friends. Henderson related how he and Henneman were sent to the family's home at Bearwood near Reading to photograph a bust of the young lady and prints taken from the Calotype negative were included as a frontispiece to the privately printed *Record of the Death-Bed of C.M.W.*[81] There is no detail of this episode in Talbot's correspondence nor is any information available on the number of copies of the memoir printed – though the quantity was presumably very small. Conceivably Talbot regarded the photography of the bust and the subsequent print production as a suitable early test of the Reading establishment's capabilities – and a favour done for the proprietor of *The Times* certainly would do no harm. *Record of the Death-Bed of C.M.W.* therefore preceded *The Pencil of Nature* – but the latter was undoubtedly the first book illustrated with original photographs that was produced for sale anywhere in the world and Beaumont

Newhall has likened its importance in the history of photography 'to that of the Gutenberg Bible in printing'.[82]

In the early advertising for the new work – the title of which was not original, for it had headed a report on the Daguerreotype in the *Literary Gazette* of 2 February 1839 – Talbot took great pains to emphasize that the illustrations were not the work of the *artist's* pencil but, as the title indicated, were produced by optical and chemical means alone. Even though this was a general point which still needed to be made in 1844 so far as photography on paper was concerned, the language of protestation adopted came close to suggesting that the illustrations were *inartistic*. Thus Talbot wrote to his halfsister Horatia in February of that year:

> I have announced in Longman & Co's catalogue, or monthly list, the forthcoming appearance of a work to be entitled The Pencil of Nature. We mean to guarantee to the Public that the plates will be executed by persons who know nothing whatever of drawing; & they may have all confidence in what they find there, since no artist is to be allowed to have any hand in it.[83]

Talbot's ideas on the new work changed with time. In a note that he must have compiled at an early stage of planning in 1844, he proposed to publish six parts composed of 5, 7, 9, 9, 10 and 10 prints respectively (50 prints in all) and selling at 12s. for the first and 21s. for each of the remaining five parts.[84] With the publication by Longman in June 1844 of the first 5 prints, reference was made to the issue of the work in ten or twelve monthly parts, each containing 5 plates. In fact, *The Pencil of Nature* appeared in a far more haphazard manner than planned. Only 24 plates in total were issued – varying in size from a little under 9 inches × 7 inches to 5 inches square – and these appeared in six parts dated June 1844; January, May, June and December 1845; and April 1846. The contents were 5, 7, 3, 3, 3 and 3 plates respectively selling at 12s., 21s., and 7s. 6d. for each of the remaining four parts. The causes of this performance were no doubt Talbot's many commitments and also the problem of achieving a consistent and high-quality product at Reading.

His concern was expressed in the introductory remarks to the first part where he explained the reasons for differences in the tones of the prints and hoped his countrymen would

> ... excuse the imperfections necessarily incident to a first attempt to exhibit an Art of so great singularity, which employs processes entirely new, and having no analogy to any

thing in use before. That such imperfections will occur in a first essay, must indeed be expected. At present the Art can hardly be said to have advanced beyond its infancy – at any rate, it is yet in a very early stage – and its practice is often impeded by doubts and difficulties, which, with increasing knowledge, will diminish and disappear. Its progress will be more rapid when more minds are devoted to its improvement, and when more skilful manual assistance is employed in the manipulation of its delicate processes; the paucity of which skilled assistance at the present moment the Author finds one of the chief difficulties in his way.

Talbot always spoke and wrote with directness: in the last sentence above he was referring probably to the general advances which would result from a wider practice of photography but we may speculate on the effect of the words chosen on those working at Reading. In a more sophisticated manner, he referred to the thrill and challenge of something totally new in the Latin quotation which he chose for the title page of *The Pencil of Nature*:

JUVAT IRE JUGIS QUA NULLA PRIORUM
CASTALIAM MOLLI DEVERTITUR ORBITA CLIVO*

An historical sketch of the invention of photography down to January 1839 was written by Talbot for the first part and each print was accompanied by a caption – sometimes dealing with technicalities, sometimes with history and sometimes with aspects of artistic appreciation. As a means of demonstrating the capability of a *new* discovery there was perhaps an undue emphasis among the twenty-four images on the reproduction of engravings and also on the photogenic drawing technique of reproducing impressions of plants and lace. It was particularly regrettable that Talbot did not include any portraits from life and only one group of figures, while a photomicrograph produced by the Calotype process would have been a valuable addition. But he did at least look to the future – to applied photography – in two of his captions. A record of a cabinet of exotic china pieces (Plate 3), he suggested, was superior to a written inventory – and, should the collection be stolen, the 'mute testimony' of the picture produced in court 'would certainly be evidence of a novel kind'. A photograph of some of Talbot's books (Plate 8) suggested something even

* From Virgil, *Georgics*, III, 293, where the poet was referring to a form of poetry never attempted before. It may be translated – 'I rejoice to walk on the hills where no track of my predecessors makes its way to Castalia down the gentle slope.' (Castalia was a spring on the slopes of Mount Parnassus sacred to Apollo and the Muses.) The quotation appeared in Talbot's scientific notebook for 23 September 1839 preceded by the words 'New Art. Nature's Pencil No. 1'.[85]

more dramatic and far-seeing in the (now matter-of-fact) recording of electro-magnetic radiation beyond the visible spectrum:

Experimenters have found that if [the] spectrum is thrown upon a sheet of sensitive paper, the violet end of it produces the principal effect: and, what is truly remarkable, a similar effect is produced by certain *invisible rays*, which lie beyond the violet, and beyond the limits of the spectrum, and whose existence is only revealed to us by this action which they exert.

Now, I would propose to separate these invisible rays from the rest, by suffering them to pass into an adjoining apartment through an aperture in a wall or screen or partition. This apartment would thus become filled (we must not call it *illuminated*) with invisible rays, which might be scattered in all directions by a convex lens placed behind the aperture. If there were a number of persons in the room, no one would see the other: and yet never-theless if a *camera* were so placed as to point in the direction in which any one were standing, it would take his portrait, and reveal his actions.

For, to use a metaphor we have already employed, the eye of the camera would see plainly where the human eye would find nothing but darkness.

Alas! [he concluded in a somewhat titillating manner] that this speculation is somewhat too refined to be introduced with effect into a modern novel or romance; for what a *dénouement* we should have, if we could suppose the secrets of the darkened chamber to be revealed by the testimony of the imprinted paper.

The immediate reaction to the first number of *The Pencil of Nature* was favour-able. The *Art-Union*[86] commented that the view of Queen's College, Oxford (Plate 1) was 'the most perfect that can be conceived; the minutest detail is given with a softness that cannot be imitated by any artistic manipulation ... the whole is melted in and blended into form by the mysterious agency of natural chemistry'. The same magazine saw in the famous representation of 'The Open Door' (Plate 6 in the second part) 'the microscopic execution [that] sets at nought the work of human hands'.[87] An in-depth and more technical review of the first two parts in the *Athenaeum* stated that all who saw *The Pencil of Nature* would be 'convinced that the promise of the art is great, and its utility and excellence, in many respects, of a high order' though it confessed that 'we see illustrated [both] the beauties and the defects of photography'.[88] Thomas Moore with customary wit thanked Talbot for this 'beautiful book' and wrote:[89]

As I could not please myself in any of the trials I made to *pen* something for the Book, I am most glad that I did not send you anything at all – for, to have been in partnership with *Sol* without doing anything worthy of the connexion would never have done for a poet – or rather *would* have *done for* me entirely.*

After the appearance of Part 2, a keen amateur photographer wrote from Norfolk with the bluntness that has characterized such enthusiasts ever since:

> I hope you will not give us any but *camera views* in the next numbers of your work. The leaf in No. 2 is certainly very pretty, but not so difficult of execution and consequently not so valuable as camera views. I think also that such a picture as the bookshelves . . . hardly deserves a place by the side of such pictures as The Haystack, The Boulevards, and The Open Door & I am not alone in this opinion: from all I can learn, the feeling among the amateurs of this art is identical with my own.[90]

The family was its usual helpful, if demanding, self. Lady Elisabeth criticized Talbot's selection of subjects also but launched a personal promotion campaign amongst her influential friends and went as far as to claim – following the publication of Part 5 – that 'owing to me it [the art] is certainly becoming much more known dans le beau monde'.[91] She felt it was no good leaving the advertising to the publishers and Constance had earlier made the same point. Talbot's wife proposed to use a birthday gift of money from Talbot 'in spreading your fame, by announcing the publication of your second number. Don't please put on a cold forbidding look . . . You know the work ought to be advertised and that the *expense only* hinders you . . .'[92]

On one important point Henry Talbot was at fault. Lady Elisabeth (and others) realized shrewdly that her son's historical introduction to Part 1 was extremely valuable and had been well received. In it he had promised to continue the account in a later number but – although pressed – he never did so, and this was not the first time (or the last) when he made such a promise and failed to keep it. Doubtless pressure of work was partly to blame – as it was for the somewhat intermittent appearance of the following numbers, which may have had an effect on sales. The trend downward is evident from the sales figures opposite.[93]

It is possible that the bookbinder – Alfred Tarrant – supplied copies direct to Talbot but the figures give an accurate overall view of the commercial performance of the six-part work. Nicolaas Henneman was thus called upon to produce over 4,300 prints for which Talbot would have paid approximately

* Moore subsequently sent handwritten verses for photocopying and inclusion in *The Pencil of Nature* presumably at Talbot's request) but they were never published.

	Sales	Delivered to Talbot free	Returned to Talbot 1852	Total produced
Part 1	274	12	0	286
Part 2	153	19	5	177
Part 3	157	9	26	192
Part 4	151	10	11	172
Part 5	81	9	10	100
Part 6	73	9	7	89

£85.[94] Talbot's gross receipts from Longman were just under £290. Out of this amount, he paid separately for the mounting and wrapping of the parts which may have amounted to about £75.[95] In addition, there were the costs of overheads at Reading with which Talbot almost certainly helped Henneman and any advertising which he decided to organize privately. *The Pencil of Nature* may, therefore, have broken even as a commercial project – or even yielded a very small profit. But of its place in history there is no doubt.

While parts of *The Pencil* were still being published, Talbot issued twenty-three views of Scotland under the title *Sun Pictures in Scotland*. During his stay in Scotland in the autumn of 1844 he concentrated on photographing subjects associated with the life and writings of Sir Walter Scott and the published views included Melrose Abbey, Abbotsford, Dryburgh Abbey, Loch Katrine and the Scott Monument in Edinburgh. The work appeared in July 1845, price one guinea. One hundred and twenty volumes were bound by Alfred Tarrant representing a total order to Henneman at Reading of 2,760 prints.[96] Lady Elisabeth was once again chief promoter and a list of subscribers in her handwriting now at the Science Museum is headed by 'Her Majesty the Queen' followed by such notables as the Duke of Devonshire and Lord Dudley Stuart – the latter, a true patriot, ordering two copies! There are some discrepancies between different subscription lists but it seems probable that over one hundred copies of the total edition were sold.

Sun Pictures in Scotland had little of the variety of *The Pencil of Nature*, although the views of Loch Katrine were powerful landscapes. Lady Elisabeth deeply regretted that Talbot included no introduction for she reported that many of the subscribers believed the pictures to be engravings prepared by artists from his originals. Nor was that all – 'Many people think the 3rd [and]

4th numbers of Pencil of Nature worth all the Scotch views, and there certainly is more *clearness* in them owing I suppose to your having been in Scotland so late in the season.'[97] She saw some value in the book, however, as serving to make *The Pencil of Nature* better known.

The two other products prepared at Reading did not incorporate Talbot's own photography though both constituted firsts in their respective fields. In August 1846 an unknown quantity of a small three-plate work entitled *The Talbotype Applied to Hieroglyphics* was produced, probably at Henry Talbot's own expense. In December 1845, Anthony C. Harris had rediscovered and copied the rock *stela* of King Sethos I and his viceroy Amenemope located on a cliff some twenty-five miles north of the Abu Simbel temples. (The cliff was submerged in 1965 by the waters of Lake Nasser, newly formed by the completion of the Aswan Dam.) Harris sent a copy of the tablet to George R. Gliddon – a popularizer of Egyptology – who had a rendering prepared by a specialist Joseph Bonomi and the text was translated by Samuel Birch of the British Museum. The three Calotype photocopies comprised introductory details and the rendering of the tablet (which was dated to between 1397 and 1387 B.C.), Birch's translation, and an extract from Harris's letter to Gliddon in which he described his find. All of the communications were handwritten and the prints each measured approximately $9\frac{1}{2}$ inches × $7\frac{1}{2}$ inches. Talbot's own copy is now at the Science Museum in London. This production was almost certainly the first application of photography in Egyptology – a field where it was destined to become a tool of great importance.[98]

The fourth and last publication was a volume of illustrations to accompany three volumes of *Annals of the Artists of Spain*, written by William Stirling (later Sir William Stirling-Maxwell), the Scottish scholar and historian.[99] Just before the move to Regent Street, Henneman was commissioned to copy with his cameras sixty-six specimens of paintings, etchings, engravings, drawings and book frontispieces by Spanish artists under the direction of Stirling who recorded in the preface: 'For the following illustrations my friends are indebted to the beautiful photographic process invented by Mr Fox Talbot. They were executed here, under my superintendence, by Mr Nicolaas Henneman, the intelligent agent of the inventor...' Henneman also produced two photographic frontispiece plates for the volume of which only twenty-five copies were produced. Each of the illustrations occupied one page with a blank facing page and Stirling's desire to keep their size relatively small, incorporating a tasteful simple border, gave immense impact to the copy prints. The largest reproduction measured only $5\frac{5}{8}$ inches × 4 inches and others were in such varied sizes as $2\frac{7}{8}$ inches × $1\frac{7}{8}$ inches, $3\frac{1}{4}$ inches × $1\frac{1}{4}$ inches and 2 inches × $2\frac{1}{2}$ inches. Henneman sought Talbot's advice with some of the problems which arose in copying originals[100] and the results were impressive. The British Library's copy contains a number of prints which have faded generally and a larger number which have suffered edge discolouration. But others are perfect and one print in particular – the copy of 'Wild Boars in an Enclosure' by Francesco Collantes – is of a beautiful, reddish tint such that it appears as though it had been made at Reading but yesterday. Just as *The Pencil of Nature* was the first book published for sale to contain photographs, so three years later Stirling's work was the first book with photographic illustrations to be devoted to the fine arts.*

Henneman's primary task during these years was control of production which was a major responsibility for he was operating the Victorian equivalent of a modern 'D. & P.' (developing and printing) plant when contemporary theoretical knowledge could proffer limited assistance in solving the numerous problems that arose. Photography was and is a process acutely susceptible to variations in quality, impurities and to contamination, but much of this was only obscurely seen at that time. Moreover, the print-out method of producing positive prints could be exceedingly slow and Henneman's problems in meeting production deadlines may be imagined.

Thomas Malone, who was a capable chemist, does not seem to have been at Russell Terrace all the time – in 1844, for example, he was working with the Frenchmen Claudet and Fizeau on the production of printing plates from Daguerreotypes – but he did devote increasing time to improving the Calotype process and researching new techniques. In addition, it is to Malone that we owe an account of the basic manner in which prints were produced at Reading.[101] This generally followed the system outlined in Talbot's patent of 1843 but Malone gave insights into the manner in which the beautiful tones of the Calotypes of this period were obtained. If the prints were of a 'cold, slate coloured hue' following the sensitizing of salted paper with the ammonio-nitrate of silver, nitric acid was used as a toner. It was a remarkably hit-and-

---

* In 1849, fifty copies of a collection of photographic reproductions of seventeenth-century engraved portraits by Spanish artists were produced by Henneman and Malone and sold by Henry Graves of Pall Mall. One volume of the collection is now in the Royal Photographic Society Collection.

miss procedure. The chemist Malone wrote regretfully if not disapprovingly: 'The action of the nitric acid seemed to be an obscure one . . . And we do not know that it can be said that the process was fully under control . . .' None the less, at its best, it produced that 'rich velvety "mulberry tint"' which is a revelation still when prints unaffected by the passage of time are examined. Heat, at the fire or applied with an iron, was also used in toning the prints – and a touch of fixing liquid (hypo) left in them gave a 'purple or deep tinge'. Malone realized that tests were needed to establish how long these last prints would survive but did not appear to be unduly worried. We now know that this process would normally have had a deleterious effect on the long-term life of the finished print.

It may be assumed that the initiative in producing the illustrated books came either from Talbot or, for example, in the case of the *Annals of the Artists of Spain* from William Stirling. The promotion of the Calotype pictures for sale through printsellers' shops was more haphazard. Thus it was Calvert Jones who suggested that Winsor & Newton, the artists' suppliers, would be an excellent outlet (though in fact they sold very little and commented when returning prints that the subjects were not 'interesting to Artists and parties who visit our *House*').[102]

The first concerted drive on the printsellers took place in 1845–6 when B. Cowderoy joined the staff at Reading. Cowderoy was an accountant with a brokerage and agency business in Reading prior to his appointment: he was energetic and a good organizer. Some outlets already existed, of course, but he saw that more were needed and he advised Talbot in April of 1846, just before departing on a sales visit to Oxford and Cheltenham, that accounts should be opened 'in some 20 good towns as well as with the London houses . . .'[103] It seems that he achieved part of this objective for at the end of the year outlets existed in Eton, Windsor, Southampton, Manchester, Northampton, Cambridge, Banbury, Oxford, Gloucester, Cheltenham, Birmingham and Reading (including Lovejoy's shop), as well as a number of outlets in London in addition to one in Malta.[104] Two of the most important shops in London were Gambart in Berners Street and Ackermann in the Strand, while there were at one time two outlets in Oxford for views of the colleges. It is impossible now to reconstruct with accuracy the success and profitability of print sales – although it may be assumed that the business was not at a high level. But there were some successes at least – for example, a statement from James Gardner of London covering the year from 29 April 1846 to 7 April

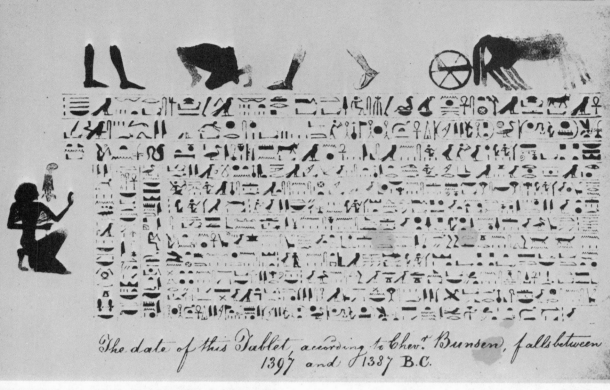

25

— The Talbotype applied to Hieroglyphics —
Tablet at Ibrim — discovered 27th Dec. 1845, by Mr. A. C. Harris — forwarded to the undersigned, and communicated by Mr. Saml. Birch to the R. Soc. of Literature, with Translation &c. — Vide Lit. Gaz, 25th July 1846 — photographed by Mr. H. Fox Talbot's kindness, from Mr. Jos. Bonomi's design ——— London Augt. 46.
George R. Gliddon

The date of this Tablet, according to Chevr. Bunsen, falls between 1397 and 1387 B.C.

25. The first of three prints comprising 'The Talbotype Applied to Hieroglyphics' produced at Reading in 1846

26. Using a solar microscope, Henry Talbot took the world's first photomicrograph with polarized light. This Calotype of a crystal, which probably dates from the early 1840s, displays features described by Talbot in Royal Society papers on the nature of crystals (page 75)

27

28

Once the Calotype had been discovered, Henry Talbot took a large number of portraits - mainly of his family and in an informal setting

29.   His half-sister Caroline Augusta, wife of the 3rd Earl of Mount Edgcumbe

30.   His half-sister Henrietta Horatia Maria

31.   Lady Elisabeth Feilding - photographed by her son as she neared the end of her life

32/33.   Nicolaas Henneman (32) was a favourite subject, but a fellow servant (33) at Lacock – who has not been reliably identified – ran him a close second. This latter picture was produced for sale, price 1s. 6d.

34/35/36.   Talbot's young family were a natural subject for his camera and for a few years in the first half of the 1840s he captured the image of his daughters as they grew older. These three portraits probably date from about 1844 when Ela Theresa (34) was nine, Rosamond Constance (35) was seven and Matilda (Tilly) (36) was five

27.   At an early stage of his researches, Talbot realized the value of the camera in copying works of art and printed pages - and careful choice of different cameras and lenses enabled the size of the original to be modified. Here is an example of 'diminishing'

28.   'Wild boars in an enclosure' (1634) by the Spanish artist Francisco Collantes was one of the works copied by Nicolaas Henneman and included by William Stirling in the fourth volume of his Annals of the Artists of Spain

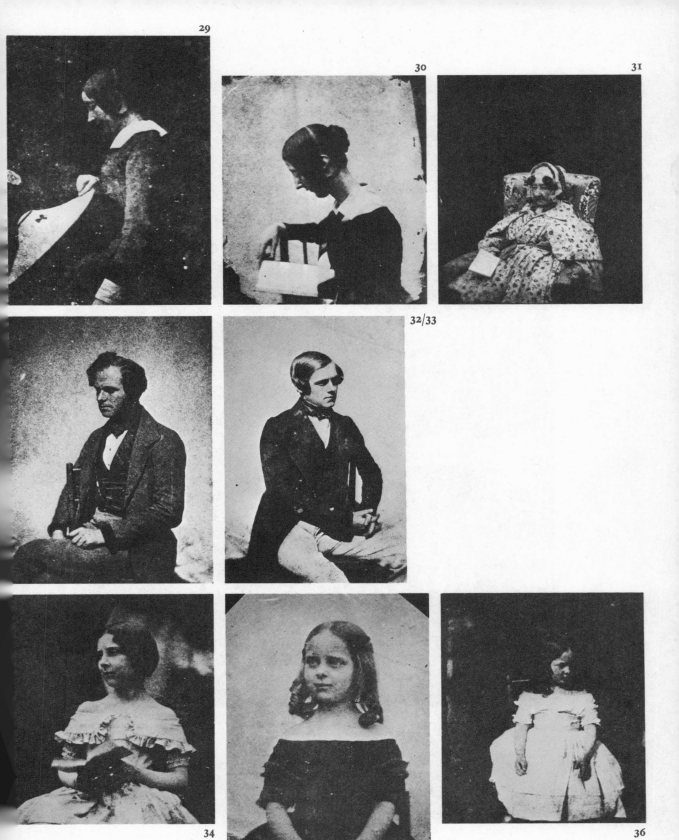

37.   *A formal studio portrait of Antoine Claudet, photographed possibly by Talbot himself. Although his visits were not frequent, Talbot enjoyed meeting Claudet at his studio in London where they joined in photographic sessions*

*In his group portraits,
Talbot frequently
managed to combine a
high degree of composi-
tional skill with an
apparent spontaneity
which belied the
relatively long exposures
still required. He
favoured outdoor compo-
sition which he may well
have believed put his
subjects at ease besides
providing greater variety
of background. Such
outdoor portraits are
rare in contemporary
Daguerreotypes which
were usually formal
studio portraits*

38.   *Caroline (left) and
Horatia, photographed in
the cloisters of Lacock
Abbey, June 1846. The
picture is technically
accomplished but has the
atmosphere of a snapshot.
By this time, Talbot's
own activities as a
photographer were
nearing an end*

39.   *Two of Talbot's
daughters and his son,
Charles Henry (just two
months old), in the arms
of a nurse - photographed
in the gardens of Lacock
Abbey in April 1842*

38

39

40. *Like many fond fathers to come in the decades ahead, Talbot carefully arranges the pose of his daughters for a portrait. This photograph was taken at Lacock Abbey in April 1844*

41. *One of a number of studies of 'The Chess Players' believed to have been taken by Talbot in Claudet's studio. Claudet himself is at right*

42. *The country seat of Sir Charles Lemon – Henry Talbot's uncle by marriage – was at Carclew in Cornwall. In this study taken at Carclew, Sir Charles is at left with Lady de Dunstanville and a Miss Dyke on the balcony*

43. *A view towards Plymouth from Mount Edgcumbe, possibly taken by Henneman and Talbot working together. The Calotype was almost certainly taken in September of 1845 when Talbot and his family visited the Earl and Countess of Mount Edgcumbe*

44

44.   *The south-west front of Lacock Abbey. Members of Talbot's family are in the foreground (with possibly Kit Talbot shown reclining at left) while gardeners are carefully placed in the background. Talbot wrote in The Pencil of Nature '. . . when a group of persons has been artistically arranged, and trained by a little practice to maintain an absolute immobility for a few seconds of time, very delightful pictures are easily obtained. I have observed that family groups are especial favourites: and the same five or six individuals may be combined in so many varying attitudes, as to give much interest and a great air of reality to a series of such pictures'*

45.   *One of the most famous pictures from The Pencil of Nature – 'The Ladder' (page 148). Nicolaas Henneman is at left*

46.   *Two servants (the seated figure is probably Henneman) in the grounds of Lacock Abbey – an example of Talbot's consummate attention to composition*

Henry Talbot devoted perhaps more time to photographing buildings than he did people. In a period of intense activity during the 1840s he visited many towns in Britain and abroad and the photographs he took – besides demonstrating his compositional skill – are now documents of considerable historical importance

47.   Northumberland House, Trafalgar Square

48.   Unfinished homes, Sussex Gardens, London

49.   York Cathedral, with Lob Lane (later destroyed) in the foreground. Talbot visited York with Calvert Jones in 1845 and their photographic activities aroused much interest among passers-by

50. *Windsor Chapel at the east end of St George's. The technical quality of this Calotype gives the lie to the assertion that the system could not resolve fine detail*

51. *High Street, Oxford. Faint images along the near pavement probably indicate the passage of pedestrians during the exposure*

52. *Magdalen College, Oxford. Perhaps because of its greater proximity, Talbot spent more time photographing scenes in Oxford than he did in his own former university of Cambridge*

53. *The Bridge of Sighs, St John's College, Cambridge*

54

55

56

54. *King's College,
Cambridge*

55. *Part of the west front
of Lacock Abbey – a less
frequent view of the
building. Lacock was the
most photographed
architectural subject in the
early history of
photography*

56. *The Boulevard,
Paris. This was probably
taken in 1843 when Talbot
visited the French capital to
instruct French business
associates in the Calotype
process*

57. *View through a
window, Rouen, May
1843. Talbot's choice of
subject and his handling
of light and shade in this
study were many years
ahead of their time*

57

58

Talbot's landscapes, although few in number, are among his best works

58. *Loch Katrine in Scotland, photographed in 1844. Several views of the loch were included in Sun Pictures in Scotland*

59/60/61. *He was fascinated by the patterns and the massing of light and shade in studies of trees. He recorded perfectly the starkness of leafless trees in winter (59/60), and, at the opposite extreme, the softness of a leafy glade (61)*

59

60

61

62. *Placing objects on sensitive paper and allowing light to act on those areas not covered formed part of Talbot's earliest photographic experiments. The shadow patterns created by lace fascinated him and he continued to experiment with pieces of lace until well into the era of the Calotype. This example can be dated probably to the mid–1840s*

63. *Talbot regarded pieces of sculpture as providing an excellent means of learning the techniques of photographic lighting (including filling in shadows) and of the positioning of the camera. His bust of Patroclus (friend of Achilles, who was killed by Hector) was one of his favourite sculpture subjects, and this Calotype was published in the first number of* The Pencil of Nature. *Another view appeared in the fourth number*

63

64. 'The Open Door' - one of the most famous
of Talbot's Calotypes, which appeared in the second
number of The Pencil of Nature (page 147).
Here Talbot's control of large masses of light and
shade was supreme: a counterbalancing object -
a piece of harness, a lantern, branches, an
out-of-focus window - prevents the masses from
overpowering the composition. His mother, Lady
Elisabeth, called this picture 'The Soliloquy
of the Broom'

65. Cart, ladder and barn - Lacock Abbey.
Another example of Talbot's compositional skill
and fine feeling for light and shade

66.   One of a number of photographs of a gamekeeper, possibly taken at Lacock. The lens used did not cover the full area of the sensitized paper in the camera and Talbot may have used this vignetting effect deliberately

67/68.   Work people featured in a number of Talbot's photographs. These studies were taken at a carpenter's shed

69

70

72

71

69/70. *Penrice Castle on the Gower coast of Wales where Henry Talbot spent many months of his early life. Below (70) is Henry's cousin Kit Talbot with Theodore and Olive, two of his children. Photographs by John Dillwyn Llewelyn*

71. *A Calotype portrait of George Pritchard, formerly British consul in Tahiti, by Antoine Claudet, August 1844*

72. *Colonel Wells, photographed by Henry Collen, who was the first man to attempt to exploit the Calotype as a medium of professional portraiture. This image was intensified at a later date*

73/74. *Two Calotypes by Robert Adamson and D. O. Hill: (73) Tomb in Greyfriars Churchyard, Edinburgh. (There is the faint image of somebody else sitting alongside the boy.); (74) A fishwife at Newhaven*

75. *Calotype portrait by Nicolaas Henneman of the Hungarian patriot Kossuth (page 173)*

76. One of the many
photographs taken by the
Reverend George Bridges on his
lengthy tour of the Mediterranean
in 1846–52. The location is
an ancient amphitheatre in
Taormina in Sicily

77. One of a number of views
of the Colosseum in Rome,
photographed by the Reverend
Calvert Jones. Some of his
negatives were purchased by
Talbot and the positives made
from them sold commercially

77

78. A Calotype of the
Exchange Building, Phila-
delphia, U.S.A., where the
Langenheim brothers – who took
this view in 1849 – had their
studio and offices. The
Langenheims purchased Talbot's
U.S. photographic patent

1847 showed that 540 out of 600 Talbotypes supplied had been sold yielding a sum of almost £50.[105]

Cowderoy's stay at Reading was the only period during the existence of the establishment when there was a sense of commercial purpose and drive. To some degree it was exemplified in the promotional leaflet for *Sun Pictures or the Talbotype* which may be dated to the latter half of 1846. After a general description of the process – where it was emphasized that the artist was not being replaced, but an aid provided for his use – the value of the Talbotype in recording buildings, studies from nature, in producing copies of metal work, glass, porcelain and furniture for manufacturers, was outlined and the intention of getting views from distant lands by well-qualified persons recorded. (This promise was partly fulfilled by the eventual sale of pictures by Calvert Jones.) The sale of prints through the publishers Gambart and Ackermann was publicized and amateurs and licensees were invited to secure their purchases of iodized paper from Reading, where they could avail themselves of 'personal instruction at a moderate charge'. On the reverse of the leaflet was further emphasis on the value of the Talbotype to the artist (as a notebook) and in exploration. There was also a perceptive forecast of the role of photography in the future:

We are in the infancy of invention with sun pictures, and no man can predict the results which may be obtained from a further advance in the paths of discovery . . . it is, in fact, an instrument of new power placed at the disposal of Ingenuity and of Art, and which, as in the case of the electrical machine and the galvanic trough, may be expected to suggest countless new applications and developments of its principle, as it becomes familiarised by use and experience.[106]

It may be that Cowderoy played some part in proposing the distribution of 7,000 Talbotypes with the 1 June 1846 number of *Art-Union* as a promotion. The value of this was evident and the journal included two well-balanced pages of editorial comment[107] which could have done nothing but good* although

* *Art-Union* compared the Talbotype favourably with the Daguerreotype, it being 'considered superior to the latter in respect of the material upon which the picture is cast, and fully equal to it in power of detail. Every means has been employed in propagating a knowledge of the Daguerreotype, and its merits have done the rest. On the other hand, the Talbotype has been hitherto only circulated in private societies, and is, consequently, less generally known. We presume, however, that the circulation of the very large number of examples with which Mr Talbot has supplied us, will have the effect of making many thousands acquainted with it who had previously only heard of it as one of the wonders of the age . . . In reducing the two inventions to a consideration of their real utilities, the preference must be given to the Talbotype. The invention of Daguerre was matured at its announcement . . . On

L

this was marred subsequently by the fading of some of the prints distributed.[108]

Cowderoy was also involved with Henry Talbot in deciding the terms of both professional and amateur licences. There is little evidence of much activity in the former in the latter half of the 1840s but the policy towards amateurs had importance for the future. A prospectus prepared by Cowderoy[109] covered the issue of a licence 'for amusement only' costing 1 guinea – although orders for 3 guineas' worth of iodized paper earned a free licence. (Lessons were also available as was equipment in addition to prepared paper.) The policy on licences to amateurs clearly varied at different times for there is at least one record[110] of a payment of 2 guineas being made and yet another – an iodized paper label issued under Henneman's name and bearing the date of 1846 in Talbot's writing – indicated that no licence was necessary.[111] Precisely which policy was adopted and for how long is a matter of conjecture but all plainly indicate that there was little to prevent any amateur engaging in the Talbotype process at this time – and the point has importance in the context of later events described in the next chapter. In these discussions with Cowderoy, incidentally, Henry Talbot revealed an interesting insight into his attitude towards the claims made in promotional literature, amending one draft on the basis that 'one should not unnecessarily *warrant* a thing to be *good*, as it may produce trouble. We make it as good as we can but it is not perfect . . .'[112]

The terms on which Henneman opened the Reading establishment are not known but incidental evidence suggests that he was a semi-independent contractor. It is likely that Talbot gave some assistance to him in starting the business but Henneman's income thereafter stemmed from the charges for prints supplied to Talbot's order. Thus large prints cost Talbot 4. 8d. each – with mounting and ruling 2½d. extra, while '¼ sheets' cost 1. 2d. each. Henneman also made 'penny sheets'.[113] In the year to end May 1846, for example, Henneman supplied Talbot with prints to a total value of £287 13s. 0½d.[114] – and this general level of payment is confirmed from Talbot's account book (with Coutts the bankers), which shows payments to Henneman of £220 in 1844, £203 in 1845 and £335 in 1846. Out of this and other earnings Henneman had to run the Reading establishment, including paying the wages of his assistants.

---

the other hand, the Talbotype, since it was first made known, has, through the unremitting labours and research of its inventor, been wonderfully improved . . .'

He clearly grew unhappy with this arrangement and, in discussion with Cowderoy in April 1846, demanded either a minimum order level per week from Talbot throughout the course of an entire year with extra payments and expenses for *taking* photographs – or alternatively £150 per annum salary, a share of profits, all rents and taxes at Russell Terrace to be paid by Talbot and the latter to pay for the existing stock of fittings, apparatus and chemicals estimated at £175.[115] Cowderoy expressed the hope that agreement could be reached because there was much doubt 'of meeting with another person so suitable in all respects'. Henry Talbot thought similarly and a three-year contract signed between them on 6 June 1846 granted Henneman his main requirements concerning salary, share of profits and other matters in their entirety.[116] A contract signed between Talbot and Alfred Harrison in mid-May granted him a minimum of £100 (basic salary and incentive payments) a year – but out of this Harrison was to pay the wages of 'two lads'.[117] Accounts at the end of 1847[118] showed Thomas Malone receiving £2 10s. od. per week, Alfred Harrison £1 18s. 5d. and his brother D. Harrison £1 10s. od. Receipts at the time exceeded payments by a healthy amount but this of course excluded Talbot's payments to Henneman, payments of rent and other items.

It seems certain that Talbot lost money on the Reading operations – perhaps quite substantially – but the new contracts showed that he still had hopes of a successful operation. He was contemplating a move from Reading to London as early as January 1846 for at that time Cowderoy calculated the budget[119] for a year's operations at an establishment in London – the total being £1,200 which intriguingly included an item of £275 for the production of a 'handbook of photography', something which Talbot never did issue in any form possibly because he thought it would weaken his patent. It was not until December 1846, however, that an agreement to rent part of 122 Regent Street at £130 a year was signed with John Newman, an instrument maker who owned the premises.[120] Presumably Talbot concluded that, since there was no Talbotype portrait operation in London with the ending of the agreement with Antoine Claudet, Henneman should be given the chance of establishing a successful portrait business. He commenced operations in the spring of 1847.

By that time Cowderoy had been dismissed by Talbot for some unknown reason, Calvert Jones had been asked to keep an eye on things in Talbot's absence abroad (and declined), and another person with business experience – one Tobias S. Telfer – had become involved only to disappear far more quickly than Cowderoy. At this distance in time and without more information, there can only be conjecture on the reasons for Cowderoy's departure – perhaps it was opposition from Henneman – but with him went the only person who had ever given a sense of commercial drive and organization to the Reading establishment.

The move from Reading to Regent Street is an appropriate juncture at which to pause and to follow broadly the fortunes of Talbot's attempts to promote the Calotype abroad – in France and the United States. A patent for the Calotype in France had been granted to Moses Poole (on behalf of Talbot) for a period of ten years on 20 August 1841 although the patent was formally transferred to Talbot's name in June of 1843.

While France was the birthplace of the Daguerreotype, a deep interest in photography on paper was shown there from the beginning. Indeed if François Arago had promoted the cause of the underrated Hippolyte Bayard with the same drive with which he fostered Daguerre's interest, the history of photographic discovery might have been significantly altered. From early in 1839 Bayard experimented with predominantly direct positive images on paper and Jean-Baptiste Biot kept Talbot fully informed of his progress – as did Calvert Jones when later he visited Bayard in Paris. The Frenchman conducted some research into negative systems as well in 1839 and after an exposure of 18 minutes in one experiment obtained an image which could scarcely be seen but which was 'developed' by exposure to mercury vapour.

On her visits to Paris Lady Elisabeth was full of enthusiasm for the opportunities in France. In February 1843 she wrote to her son 'there is at this moment an enthusiasm for [the] *Talbotype* which may subside ... I have never seen before so good a chance for your fame, don't let it slip thro' your fingers. The People here are not so slow at coming to conclusions as in our phlegmatic country.'[121] She feared that Bayard would secure precedence as the inventor of paper photography – and there was another Frenchman with the same view, Joseph Hugues Maret (allegedly the Marquis de Bassano) and a brother-in-law of the English banker Francis Baring. Early in 1843 he began communicating with Talbot on the possible exploitation of the Calotype in France through Mlle Amélina who at the time was living in Paris.*

* Earlier – in 1842 – the French instrument makers Vincent Chevalier and Lerebours had contemplated promoting the Calotype in France. They too used Amélina as an initial point of contact with Talbot.

He kept up a sustained pressure and underlined the dangers should Bayard achieve significant success – 'If Mr Talbot does not take determined action all the fruits will go to another.'[122] His ideas were expansive. With its versatility, the Calotype must be regarded as a new pencil or brush to be placed in the hands of the men of art. He envisaged a mass 'assault' in which 80 to 100 young artists would cover France to record public monuments, *'les sites les plus curieux'* and to take portraits. This would require dark rooms, the production of paper, chemicals and albums – and much capital, but would lead to *'le succès le plus complet pour son invention'*.[123] It sounded impressive and by March 1843 Bassano and Talbot had signed a provisional agreement on terms which were essentially that the patent was assigned to the Frenchman against quarterly payments to Talbot of 25 per cent of gross receipts from the sale of Calotype paper. If after the first two years Talbot had not received a specific sum (8,000 francs) the licence for operating the patent would revert to him.[124]

In May 1843 Talbot journeyed to Paris and demonstrated the Calotype process. He wrote to Constance:

> I have begun to teach the calotype to the Marquis of Bassano and his friends. Today we took four views of the Tuileries. The weather was indifferent ... The Marquis and his friends have taken for a month an isolated and lofty house that stands in the Place du Carousel fronting the Tuileries. This house will soon be pulled down by the government, as it disfigures the place. In the meantime, it has become our workshop.[125]

On 26 June, the final agreement was signed[126] and subsequently Henry gave the Frenchmen further instructions in the process.

All was enthusiasm at first. Amélina's brother was associated with Bassano and wrote excited letters about the progress being made – but Bassano never demonstrated that he had the money available that his grandiose ideas demanded. Amélina kept her English friends informed of the situation: by December no work was taking place at the Carousel 'factory' and in the months thereafter Bassano was absent so much that 'it is equivalent to total abandonment ... fiasco after fiasco'.[127] And it was. Later, an Anglo-French lawyer A. L. Bovard acted for Talbot but his services were scarcely required for under the terms of the agreement the patent reverted to Talbot in July 1845. He lost no capital – only the possibility of a considerable income if Bassano had done what he promised for (despite Bayard's work) there was no major paper rival to the Calotype in France at that time. Within a few years there was. In 1847 Louis-Désiré Blanquart-Evrard introduced a modification to the Calotype with which he was to enjoy great success. Through an intermediary, Bovard naively endeavoured to enlist Arago's assistance in the defence of Talbot's patent but the response was predictable. The distinguished French scientist stated that if Talbot went to law and his opinion was sought by the French courts he would state that there was no infringement of the patent.[128]* Moreover, he added that if Talbot endeavoured eventually to secure an extension of his patent in France he would do everything possible to defeat the plan.[129] Given this attitude – and Arago's influence in France – there was nothing for Talbot to do but withdraw.

It was not until five years after patenting the Calotype system in England that Henry Talbot contemplated its extension to the United States. In the autumn of 1846, the Revd. Bridges introduced an American R. K. Haight to Talbot who in turn commended Edward Anthony to him as 'a gentleman well qualified to extend to the New World the beautiful invention [with] which you have endowed the Old World'.[130] Anthony – at this time acting on behalf of Anthony, Clark & Company of New York – was to become a prominent figure in American photography but little progress was made in the discussions he had with Talbot. The American insisted that he must have detailed instruction on the Calotype at Reading whereas understandably Talbot was reluctant to divulge everything while the Calotype was still unpatented in the U.S. The negotiations dragged on into 1847 and on 26 June of that year Talbot took out a U.S. patent – No. 5171. Eight weeks later Anthony offered to act as a licence agent for 20 per cent of the proceeds, calculating that at least $15,000 ought to be realized – with licence fees ranging from $1,000 in New York State to $100 in such states as Delaware.[131] There was, however, never a genuine meeting of minds between Anthony and Talbot and there the matter rested between them – that is, until almost a quarter of a century later when Anthony's company suddenly wrote to Talbot[132] with a query on his experience of silver recovery!

In February 1849 Talbot received an enthusiastic letter of introduction from the Langenheim brothers of Philadelphia. William and Frederick Langenheim had been practising the Daguerreotype professionally since 1840 and were the U.S. agents for the German camera company Voigtlander. They felt that the

---

* This would be a point to be decided at law but the Académie des Beaux Arts in June 1847 reported that the difference between Talbot's and Blanquart-Evrard's processes was one of manipulation although it saw decided advantages in the French system.

Talbotype 'if properly applied, possesses extraordinary advantages over the Daguerreotype' and proposed that they act as licence agents, taking 25 per cent of the proceeds with the remainder passing to Talbot.[133] The negotiations proceeded swiftly. In April William Langenheim arrived in Lacock village and offered Talbot £1,000 for the outright purchase of the U.S. patent with payments spread over twenty-four months.[134] After deliberation Talbot agreed and wrote to Constance from London on 12 May: 'I sold [the patent] yesterday for a large sum of money to an American gentleman who expects to make his fortune by the purchase. I hope he may, as he seems a very amicable and intelligent person.'[135]

The Langenheims formed a capable team. Apart from their own portrait activities, they were probably the only professionals besides Henneman to take 'views' with the Calotype[136] – and won a number of medals for the Talbotype from the Franklin Institute and the American Institute of New York. Their hopes of licence sales were high initially and they wrote to Talbot in June 1849 that 'The Talbotypes have created a great sensation all over the United States and most papers of any standing contain favourable articles on the subject...'[137] It is hard now to see the grounds for the optimism. The Daguerreotype, which was not patented in the U.S., had been an immense success and anybody – professional or amateur – interested in the Calotype system would have been able to practise it without charge up to 1847 when Talbot took out his U.S. patent. The reaction to the Langenheims' attempt to sell licences from 1849 was therefore predictable. By September their letters to Talbot were showing a note of caution – the cholera epidemic had affected everything and all the enterprising were joining the Californian gold rush.[138] Two months later they reported that they had only sold licences in Georgia, Florida, Alabama, Louisiana and Texas and requested postponement of their outstanding payments of £400 of the purchase price otherwise they would be ruined.[139] Talbot agreed but the next year the brothers again asked for a postponement, and suggested that perhaps Talbot might purchase the U.K. rights to their albumen–on–glass system (the Hyalotype) in exchange.[140] Talbot did not wish to and in any case the Langenheims shortly afterwards went bankrupt. A foreign diplomat in the U.K., had acted as guarantor of the agreement between Talbot and the Langenheims but he died in 1851 and it appears that Talbot released the estate from any liability. He never received the outstanding payment. However the relationship survived for in 1854 Frederick Langenheim and Talbot were in contact briefly over the situation concerning the collodion process.[141] With the arrival of that system in the U.S. any hope for photography on paper in the camera died.

The Regent Street establishment was primarily a portrait studio as distinct from the emphasis on print production at Reading. Business began seriously in the autumn of 1847 at which time Caroline Mount Edgcumbe was instrumental in persuading Queen Victoria to appoint Henneman a 'photographer in ordinary to H.M.'[142] which was of obvious value in promoting the concern. The business – which also included instruction, the distribution of chemicals and equipment, and the sale of work by foreign photographers such as Marteus and Ferrier in France – seemed to progress satisfactorily* but at the end of the year Talbot took the initiative in securing an agreement with Henneman and Malone to end his direct responsibilities and commitments for the Regent Street establishment.

Virtually all the correspondence at this time was with Thomas Malone and in January 1848 Talbot wrote complaining about the delay in considering his proposals made a month before. With the London season coming on it was

. . . the most likely time for me to meet with some capitalist or other enterprising person who would take this speculation off my hands on reasonable and fair terms. It is very inconvenient for me to have the responsibility of an establishment which my not living in London renders it difficult for me to superintend . . .

Talbot went on to recommend that Henneman and Malone give attention to what should

. . . turn out to be one of the most popular and lucrative branches of the art, the copying *on an enlarged scale* of Daguerreotype portraits already existing and prized by the owners.[143]

Henry Talbot referred to the subject again with greater force in February. If his offer was accepted, he would do his best to send customers and work – he mentioned continuing *The Pencil of Nature* and a book on photomicrography – and to help by devising improved processes and instruments. But if they did

* The Science Museum in London has a bound copy of 24 Calotypes – taken by various photographers including Talbot himself, Henneman and Calvert Jones – entitled *Talbotypes: or Sun Pictures, Taken from The Actual Objects Which They Represent*. The volume bears the date 1847 and Nicolaas Henneman's name and address at Regent Street in the frontispiece. No additional information about this volume has yet been found.

not wish to accept, then he would offer the business elsewhere for he was not prepared to accept the situation any more:

> It is a constant source of dissatisfaction to me which I wish to put an end to ... At present you have few customers because to say the truth your portraits are not by any means what they ought to be with our present knowledge of photography and you suffer them to be *spoiled* by Mr Hervé [a retoucher who also coloured some of Henneman's prints] to an extent which is cruelly vexatious.[144]

However, an agreement was finally signed in June 1848 and it was on extremely generous terms. Talbot in effect made Henneman and Malone a gift of the business, paid up all salaries and debts to the date of the agreement and issued them with a Talbotype licence – all for the sum of £1,000 which was not to be repaid until the gross receipts of the business exceeded a certain level. Over and above that, if required Henry Talbot was prepared to make a loan of £500 available to the two partners. A more favourable start for Henneman and Malone could scarcely be imagined[145] but Henry Talbot's expenditures in that direction were far from being at an end.

Malone concentrated on research into chemical and materials faults as well as improved processes, and he cooperated closely with Talbot. He was a capable worker and his valuable if unspectacular role in the early history of photographic processes has been inadequately recorded. He paid particular attention to the paper base problem, visiting mills and conducting detailed study of the constituent elements. His conclusions were realistic and pessimistic: 'a pure paper has not been made these 20 years' . . . 'There must be a revolution at the mill before we obtain a perfect paper.'[146] His researches into paper, fixing and other matters were well revealed in his letters to Talbot during the period from 1848 to 1851:

> I am still perplexed with the *points of resistance* in the fibres of the paper which give a porous appearance to the image. I anticipate that we shall find this latter defect is *chemical & not dependent* on the 'make' of the papers. The presence of Hyposulphite or some other chemical salt still produces a change in the *positives we think* even after *distilled water* has been used.
>
> Several amateurs also complain. Something might be learned from an examination of pictures made & fixed by yourself *some years* since . . .[147]

And again:

[The new specimen of paper] is very sensitive. Portraits may be taken on it in half a minute on a *dull* day – with a three inch lens (double combination) six inches focus measuring from the back lens to the ground glass. There is a new lens by Voigtlander. It is very useful. It takes a picture *on paper nearly* 5×4 – without curved paper holders.*[148]

With Talbot's approval (and financial support probably) Malone travelled to the Continent where he met some of the leading scientists in photography – including Edmond Becquerel, the Abbé Moigno, Niépce de Saint-Victor, and Bayard – as well as the photographer Marteus whom he reported to be keen to become a licensee of Talbot's processes. Malone found them very 'liberal' and learned a great deal – but the Frenchmen were also impressed, Bayard for example mistakenly thinking that one of their prints from a Calotype negative must have been from a glass negative such was its quality.[149]

Malone engaged with Talbot in researching into fine porcelain as a base for sensitized emulsions but the problem of fixation was never far from his mind. He performed what were almost certainly the first quantitative tests of hypo's effect on the metallic silver of the photographic image – reporting to Talbot that in one test print he calculated that the level of silver in 56 square inches did not exceed twelve-hundredths of a *grain*.[150] Travelling about as he did far more widely amongst photographers than Talbot, he was fully aware of the adverse publicity resulting from fading ('We are constantly and unpleasantly cross-examined upon the subject.'), and by this time the fading of some of the prints distributed with the *Art-Union* in 1846 was adding to the problem. Malone believed that treatment with boiling caustic potash was one possible remedy and this was included in the patent which was taken out jointly by Talbot and him in December 1849.†

The patent – No. 12,906 – outlined a method of sensitizing porcelain with a basically Calotype procedure which employed albumen (white of egg) as a vehicle for the salts; a means of obtaining albumen-coated glass plates which

* Admitting the maximum amount of light through a lens – i.e. using it at maximum aperture – cut the exposure time but often it presented severe problems with the definition produced at the edges of the recorded image. This was overcome in some cameras by holding the sensitized paper in a curved plane as distinct from today's conventional flat plane.

† Malone continued to study the problem of print fading after he had left Regent Street and taken up the teaching of chemistry. In 1852 he proposed to Talbot that 'all pictures in which silver is used should be protected *in a very simple manner* by means of a *basic lead salt combined* with either starch gluten or perhaps still better an adhesive *resinous cement*. Pictures in books to be enclosed in a properly made cover lined with the lead compound. Pictures in frames to be protected by strips holding the lead compound on their exposed surfaces.'[151]

were processed to a primary negative image which could subsequently be modified to a positive; the preparation of varnished paper and the subsequent application of an albumen film sensitized by exposure to iodine vapour; the use of albumen to obtain images on polished steel plates; and, as we have seen, the immersion of paper images in boiling caustic potash after conventional fixing, converting the resulting greenish tinge to more conventional hues by toning with sulphuretted hydrogen. Subsequently none of these proposals was commercially exploited but Talbot by prior agreement purchased Malone's share in the patent for £100.[152]

Talbot took out another and his last photographic patent in June 1851 – No. 13,664 – but its proposals too received little or no commercial development. The main system proposed was again an albumenized glass plate yielding both positive and negative images according to viewpoint (Talbot called the process *Amphitype*[153] from the Greek base for 'both') but he departed from a Calotype formula almost entirely to use ferric iodide and ferric sulphate. A second proposal was for a unit which could be used to sensitize, expose and fix glass plates whilst attached to a camera. The idea was ingenious and if successful would have obviated the large quantity of equipment (including a dark-room tent) that had to be carried by the photographer when practising the recently announced collodion process. He subsequently modified the idea to construct what was called a 'Traveller's Camera' for exposing and processing paper and glass negatives[154] and used the unit during his stays in the Lake District.[155]

As we have seen, Talbot's practical participation in the taking of photographs was small after 1845–6 but in 1851 he conducted an experiment at the Royal Institution which received considerable attention. For many years scientists had been theorizing on how objects moving at high speed could be studied in detail – how, in effect, the high-speed action could be observed in slow motion. John Herschel and Talbot discussed this in some detail in 1833[156] and in a scientific notebook in March 1835 Talbot proposed an experiment whereby falling drops of water or pendulum movements in a darkened room could be made to appear motionless by intermittent illumination through a clockwork-driven disc.[157] In the meantime Charles Wheatstone employed electrical discharges to observe high-speed phenomena. All this was before the days of photography but Talbot brought the two concepts together on 14 June 1851. A printed paper (usually claimed to have been *The Times* but no convincing evidence of this has been traced) was fastened to a disc which was made to revolve as rapidly as possible. A battery was discharged and a positive image was obtained on an Amphitype plate.

Talbot informed Michael Faraday the next day[158] that the image of the printed letters was just as sharp as if the disc had been motionless. The plate – which despite Talbot's ill-founded impression of its high sensitivity was relatively slow as with all systems based on albumen – did not survive but to Talbot undoubtedly goes the honour of making the first photograph of an object illuminated by electric flash. In a subsequent letter to the *Athenaeum*[159] he explained 'it is in our power to obtain the pictures of all moving objects, no matter in how rapid motion they may be, provided we have the means of *sufficiently* illuminating them with a sudden electric flash'. (In his letter announcing the successful experiment to Faraday, Talbot sought advice on augmenting the brilliancy of the flash and suggested two methods that he himself thought promising.) The *Literary Gazette* was delighted. As a result of this 'great triumph of scientific perseverance', it explained:

... photographic portraits will be obtained with all the animation of full life instead of the stiffened serenity which even a sitting of a few seconds gives to the countenance. Nothing will be more easy than to take the most agile ballet dancer during her rapid movements, or to catch the image of the bird of swiftest flight during its passage ...[160]

Meanwhile the Regent Street business was progressing. Henneman received such assignments as copying pages from rare books,[161] portrait commissions were beginning to increase and Talbot (whatever his protestations to the contrary) felt sufficiently involved to pay for a series of advertisements in the *Literary Gazette*, the *Athenaeum* and *The Times*. These appeared in the spring of 1850, under the heading 'Talbotype Sun Portraits on Paper' by 'Messrs Henneman and Malone – Photographers on Paper to the Queen'. Portraits were taken in dull weather 'in much less time, and with a more natural contrast of light and shade, than formerly'. These portraits when coloured, the advertisements explained, were 'perfect and pleasing' while a copying service for Daguerreotype portraits and for portraits in oils and water colours was offered. Apparatus and pictures from Italy, Germany, France and the United States could be viewed 'gratuitously' at 122 Regent Street.[162]

The year 1851 brought the Great Exhibition – and a further assignment for Henneman to participate in photographing the exhibits for the Jurors' Reports which were to be presented at the conclusion to the representatives of foreign nations participating and other notables. Talbot waved his patent rights but was incensed by what he considered to be the Exhibition executive committee's cavalier treatment of Henneman in the prices offered for negatives and prints (though the latter were eventually produced in France). He enlisted David Brewster's support[163] in attempting to persuade the committee to increase its payments and, when he failed to achieve satisfaction, personally made a payment of £200 to Henneman to supplement the payment made by the committee.[164] As a gesture of thanks to Talbot for his action over the patent, the committee presented him with fifteen copies of the Jurors' Report with a suitably printed frontispiece. The value was put at £30 per copy or a total of £450. At one time Henneman was planning a book containing 100 views of Crystal Palace during the exhibition but it never appeared.

Another somewhat unusual event in 1851 was the portrait which Henneman took of the famous Hungarian patriot Kossuth ('the illustrious Magyar', as Talbot called him): even more remarkable was the 3 seconds' exposure claimed for these pictures which, at nearly three o'clock on a hazy November afternoon, was in Talbot's words 'putting ye power of photography to a severe test'.[165] A setback at this time, however, was Malone's decision to leave the partnership through ill health* but the business continued to expand. Henneman concentrated his print-production facilities at Monument House in Kensal Green (where he claimed he would be able to produce 18,000 prints per month) and continued to receive assignments such as making stereo pictures for Charles Wheatstone – with which, he told Talbot, Lord Lansdowne and 'a great many of the nobility' on a visit to King's College, London were delighted.[166]

The early 1850s marked Henneman's most successful period at Regent Street and in 1853 he took 833 portraits during the year – the highest number ever.[167] But an average of sixteen sessions per week was not high by reported Daguerreotype standards and thereafter in any case the business declined in the face of growing competition. Henneman was not a good organizer. John Henderson described him as 'erratic'[73] and Malone later said that he was incapable of relying entirely on himself.[168] If he had been a superb portraitist he might have overcome these weaknesses but in truth he was little more than average. He struggled on until 1856 and then gave up the Regent Street and Kensal Green businesses. Unbeknown to Henneman at that time, Talbot made

* He recovered in 1852 and, after posts at the Royal College of Chemistry and the Royal Polytechnic Institution, was for some time Director of the Laboratory at the London Institution.

a number of payments to satisfy the most pressing debtors[169] and this was yet another example of the great loyalty and generosity he showed his former man-servant, for his account books record payments to Henneman of rarely less than £100 a year even when there was no formal commitment between them.[170] Henneman subsequently joined a photographic studio in Birmingham but when he last appeared in the Talbot correspondence in the middle 1860s he was planning to leave photography and go back into service. He became a lodging-house keeper – and died in January 1898.[171]

By the time that the Regent Street business closed, Talbot had spent well over £5,000 on photography.[172] It is unlikely that he received as much as half that amount in income and in the middle 1850s he turned back to mathematics, to further research into photo-engraving and to his new and consuming interest, the Assyrian cuneiform. The Daguerreotype had caught the world's imagination as a medium for portraiture and following the unsuccessful attempts by Collen and Claudet, few professionals – with the exception of Adamson and Hill, and Henneman – favoured the Calotype. For this Talbot himself, the creator, was partly responsible. He possessed none of the attributes of the successful businessman and failed to enter into a whole-hearted pro-motion of the Calotype. In addition, he was dogged by the problems inherent in the attempted mass production of a product whose quality was highly susceptible to factors then largely unknown or inadequately realized. With the announcement of a workable and fast system based on the glass negative, the days of the paper Calotype were numbered but it had a major significance in the history of photography. The Daguerreotype was described by Oliver Wendell Holmes as 'a mirror with a memory'. This description of a beautiful system was apt, for it may be interpreted to imply that it was essentially con-cerned with the past. Indeed it was, for the Daguerreotype had no future whereas Talbot's Calotype process was the way to the future and to today's photography. Unfortunately, that way gave rise to controversy and it is to this that we now turn.

6

Photography: Of Priority, Plagiarism and Patents

In August 1854 the *Art-Journal* magazine published a fierce attack on Henry Talbot's patenting activities and on his reputation as a scientist. The path he followed, the magazine alleged, was 'degrading to the philosopher' while he appeared to believe that his patents secured for him 'a complete monopoly of the sunshine'. With a show of Victorian class consciousness, it criticized Talbot's preparedness to defend his patents at law – 'a wealthy man . . . can play with law; that which is sport to him being death to his poor victim who dares to contest his claim' – and proceeded to more general criticism.

> Reviewing Mr Fox Talbot's labours as an experimentalist, we find him industriously working upon the ground which others have opened up . . . He has no claim to be considered as the discoverer of any photographic process, but merely as the deviser of processes from the results of other men's labours.

The *Art-Journal* then returned to the issue which was the principal cause for the entire criticism, roundly declaring that 'in no respect does the collodion process [which Talbot claimed was covered by his 1841 patent] resemble the calotype'.[1]

Henry Talbot did not reply to the attack – two cases at least of alleged infringement of his 1841 patent were already at law and his lawyers doubtless advised him against any retort – but David Brewster condemned the 'disgraceful attack' which he assumed to have been written by Robert Hunt (who was a frequent contributor to the magazine) and later wrote: 'I agree with you in holding in contempt such articles as the one in the Art-Journal. It is of course the production of an interested party not seeking truth, but under the influence of self interest.'[2]

Without evaluating at this stage the detail of the *Art-Journal*'s criticisms – or of Brewster's response – the article did represent a useful summary of the views held at the time by sections of the photographically interested, both amateur and professional. The issues came to a head in the Talbot versus Laroche case which was decided in December of 1854 and an analysis of the situation leading up to that decision and its aftermath forms the essence of this chapter. Firstly, however, it is important to set the accusations which Talbot faced in the general socio-economic context of the period. A fault of photographic historians is that all too frequently they concentrate exclusively on the photographic considerations of any issue without studying wider issues which might have a considerable importance in the understanding and therefore objective evaluation of photographic matters. Thus anybody reading previous accounts of the controversy over Talbot's photographic patents might be forgiven for concluding that it was a narrowly photographic matter in which there was either agreement or disagreement with Talbot's attitudes and actions. But the fact is that the period of fierce debate over Henry Talbot's patents *was a time of great controversy over patents generally, irrespective of the detailed technical validity or otherwise of individual patents.*

That controversy was at its height from around 1850 to 1875 – as late as 1869 the London *Economist* expressed the opinion (and hope) that the patent laws would soon be abolished[3] – and other European countries besides Britain were involved. Both royal commissions and select committees of Parliament examined the British patent system on at least three separate occasions in the second half of the nineteenth century and in understanding the Talbot controversy it is significant that the first of these examinations – by a select committee of the House of Lords – was taking place in 1851–2.

The general case for patents may be stated simply: an inventor publishes details of his discovery and for so doing the Crown grants a monopoly to the patentee for a given term (which was fourteen years in the 1850s and is now sixteen years).* The grant of the monopoly was formalized in law by the Statute of Monopolies of 1624. During the early decades of the nineteenth century there was considerable pressure to reform the patent laws in favour of fairer treatment of patentees but this was in due course almost swept aside by the anti-patent movement which was part of a general and powerful socio-

* It is likely to become twenty years if a Patents Bill now before Parliament becomes law.

economic philosophy which took the practical form of anti-protectionism, free trade, and a liberalization of commercial and economic policies. That famous economists such as Jeremy Bentham, Adam Smith and John Stuart Mill were in favour of patents mattered little.

The case against patents was made in evidence to the committees of Parliament and through, for example, the columns of the *Economist*. At precisely the same time as the opposition was mounting to Talbot, that magazine published opinions such as the following:

Before . . . [the inventors] can . . . establish a right of property in their inventions, they ought to give up all the knowledge and assistance they have derived from the knowledge and inventions of others. That is impossible, and the impossibility shows that their minds and their inventions are, in fact, parts of the great mental whole of society, and that they have no right of property in their inventions, except that they can keep them to themselves if they please and own all the material objects in which they may realize their mental conception.[4]

Quoting the views of the patent abolitionist John Lewis Ricardo before the House of Lords select committee in 1851 the *Economist* wrote:

. . . nearly all useful inventions depend less on any individual than on the progress of society. A want is felt . . . ingenuity is directed to supply it; and the consequence is, that a great number of suggestions or inventions of a similar kind come to light. 'The ideas of men', said Mr Ricardo, 'are set in motion by exactly the same circumstances'. So we find continually a great number of similar patents taken out about the same time. Thus the want suggests the invention, and though the State should not reward him who be the first to hit on the thing required, the want growing from society, and not from the individual or from the Government, would most certainly produce the required means of gratifying it . . .[5]

A different approach was pursued in the *Economist* on another occasion:

The privileges granted to inventors by patent laws are prohibitions on other men, and the history of inventions accordingly teems with accounts of trifling improvements patented, that have put a stop, for a long period, to other similar and much greater improvements. It teems also with accounts of improvements carried into effect the instant some patents had expired. The privileges have stifled more inventions than they have promoted,[*] and have caused more brilliant schemes to be put aside than the want of them

* For example: Parliament extended James Watt's patent for twenty-five years in 1775. It is claimed that he grew rigid in his ideas and discouraged experimentation – and Professor T. S. Ashton has expressed the view that if Watt's 'monopoly had been allowed to expire in 1783, England might have had railways earlier'.[6]

M

could ever have induced men to conceal. Every patent is a prohibition against improvements in a particular direction, except by the patentee, for a certain number of years; and however beneficial that may be to him who receives the privilege, the community cannot be benefited by it . . . On all inventors it is especially a prohibition to exercise their faculties; and in proportion as they are more numerous than one, it is an impediment to the general advancement, with which it is the duty of the legislature not to interfere, and which the claimers of privileges pretend at least to have at heart.[7]

The opposition to patents thus took the form of both practical and moral objections and the quotations above represent a general attitude to patenting which some of the criticism of Talbot mirrored in a specifically photographic context. Indeed, while sometimes the rights of a *genuine* as distinct from a *pirating* inventor were differentiated in some of the published criticisms of Talbot's activities, it may be surmised that many of his critics, whether professional or amateur, were opposed to patents *per se*. The collodion process was not patented by its discoverer but it is a fascinating exercise to contemplate whether, if he had done so, he too would have faced a series of opponents determined to break the patent. The evidence of the history of the Daguerreotype patent, as well as Talbot's, suggests the possibility – to put it no more strongly – that this would have been the case.

For much of the nineteenth century the patentee faced major administrative problems too. There was no patent office forming the centre of a clearly defined system and in a famous article in the weekly journal *Household Words*,[8] Charles Dickens described graphically the tortuous procedures and numerous visits to the offices of various officials which were required before a patent might be taken out. The cost of patenting was high – a little under £100 for England and Wales alone and £300 including Scotland and Ireland – though knowledge of the registration procedure was so poor in political and governmental circles that a select committee in 1829 had to enquire of its witnesses what official fees were being charged![9]

An attack on the inadequacies of the then patent system formed the major part of the founding address at the British Association for the Advancement of Science meeting in 1831 at York[10] and David Brewster was a savage critic of what he considered to be the state's shabby treatment of the inventor. The patent laws, in his view, were

. . . a system of vicious and fraudulent legislation, which, while it creates a factitious privilege of little value, deprives its possessor of his natural right to the fruit of his genius, and which places the most exalted officers of the state in the position of a legalized banditti, who stab the inventor through the folds of an act of parliament, and rifle him in the presence of the Lord Chief Justice of England.[11]

More specifically, and less emotionally, Brewster and those who thought like him criticized the high initial costs of patenting;* the fact that no serious examination of the patent request took place (to establish that it was not 'frivolous'); that in effect no rights were conferred by the grant of the patent and that thereafter it could be challenged at any time – and frequently was; that such defence of a patent was extremely costly, certainly running into many hundreds of pounds; and that, if the patent were subsequently set aside after legal action, none of the high enrolling fee was repaid to the patentee. Brewster had no time for the 'remorseless pirates who are ever on the watch for insecure inventions'[12] but for the protection of both inventors and the public he did make such constructive suggestions as the establishment of a number of scientific boards whose purpose would be to become acquainted with the present and past state of the 'useful arts'. Once one of these boards determined that an invention was new, the patentee from that time on should be 'absolutely secured in all the advantages of his patent for fourteen years'.[13]

The absence of a test of novelty in an invention led to a considerable amount of the litigation during the nineteenth century and was a cause of dissatisfaction to patentees and challengers alike. It might be logically supposed that patentees who were accused by their critics of patenting the discoveries of other men – as Talbot was – would favour the ambiguous situation of the time but in a letter to the President of the Board of Trade, Henry Labouchere, in 1851 Talbot argued strongly along the lines earlier suggested by Brewster – that a Board of Patent Commissioners should be authorized to establish whether or no an invention was a novelty and that, if it was, a certificate should be issued to the patentee which would supply automatic grounds for the issue of an injunction against an alleged infringer, unless the infringer were prepared to go to law and to put up a bond of £100 which would be lost if the case failed.[14]

A new Patents Act in 1852 partially answered objections by establishing a patent covering the whole country and a Patent Office (though its functions were very limited) and lowering the initial fee of taking out a patent to £25

* The high cost of patenting was frequently defended as a means of keeping the number of 'unimportant' or 'frivolous' patents down. The cumbersome machinery, too, was defended as facilitating objections to patents. William Carpmael, Talbot's patent adviser, held such views and expressed them to the select committee of the House of Lords in 1851.[15]

with a scale of annual renewal charges for the life of the patent. But it was only a beginning and meant that the problems encountered by both patentees and those attacking 'bad' patents continued in the absence of an administrative framework in which a test of novelty would have been a principal and valuable element. Trial of complex patent issues by jury at common law was another major problem and this continued until the end of the nineteenth century. Patent cases are now heard before specialist judges in the High Court* and the patentee is likely to receive a somewhat more sympathetic hearing compared with the middle years of the last century 'when the judges seemed to bristle at the very mention of a patent'.[16]

Thus, the situation confronting the patentee was highly unsatisfactory and the cost, complexity and pitfalls which continued long after 1852 meant that only those with the most serious of intentions even contemplated taking out a patent. But even then they faced an inconsistent situation because the system of grants by government in return for the donation of an invention to the public (in much the same way as Daguerre received a pension in France) was by no means unknown in Britain. In the period up to 1815 it was estimated that £77,000 had been made available by executive grants to inventors[17] and while the usual objection to the system was the potential for abuse and corruption, other grants were made later in the century. Thus at mid-century William Snow Harris – one of Talbot's guests at Lacock Abbey during the Bristol British Association meeting of 1836 – received £5,000 and eventually a knighthood for his work on electricity and particularly in developing electricity conductors for Royal Navy ships. The Society for the Encouragement of Arts, Manufactures and Commerce (founded in 1754) was during its early history an organization devoted to the abolition of the patent system and its replacement by a system of 'rewards' for inventors, though by 1845 it had reached a stage where it opened eligibility for its prizes to patented inventions as well.[18]

For some, therefore, moderate or substantial wealth came from discovery without controversy of any kind. For others there was some material reward if controversy: amongst Talbot's associates, Charles Wheatstone was involved in patent disputes in which the extreme language used by the other side rivalled that adopted toward Talbot. But for the squire of Lacock there was controversy and little if any reward. The detail will be elaborated later but a major problem

* The Patents Bill now before Parliament proposes the formation of a Patents Court which will be part of the Chancery Division of the High Court.

faced by Talbot was that his discovery was of a kind in which any competent and interested individual could participate with as much expectation of success when sufficiently experienced as the most competent professional experimenter. Wheatstone faced the problems arising from inventions – like the telegraph – which could only be exploited by commercial organizations. Talbot's invention could be used and exploited potentially not only by commercial organizations but by individuals – so that his problems were multiplied proportionately. As we have seen, he did not patent photogenic drawing but within a matter of weeks he was having to protest in the columns of the *Literary Gazette* against the declared intention of others to patent an application of photogenic drawing to reproduce etchings and drawings prepared on glass.* Claims to have anticipated the discoveries of Daguerre and Talbot were rife and, while not concerning patents directly, a comment in the *Athenaeum* in June of 1839 highlighted what was to be the major problem for Talbot once he did take out patents – the interest of the many: 'Hardly a day passes that we do not receive letters respecting some imagined discovery, or improvement, in the art of Photogenic drawing, but the suggestions are generally far too crude to be worthy of publication.'[19]

While Henry Talbot on several occasions detailed at some length his criticism of the patent system then existing, he nowhere stated explicitly why he took out twelve patents – four of which were photographic in nature – between 1840 and 1858. The matter is of importance since his motivation in taking out patents is highly relevant to the consideration of his later attitudes and actions. Did he regard patents as a means of establishing priority, or a basis for commercial exploitation or a mixture of both? As we have seen, David Brewster recommended patenting photogenic drawing as a means of establishing both a priority of discovery of 'a more fixed character' and of securing financial benefit.[20] Priority of discovery was important to the scientist – and still is a driving force for obvious reasons – but taking out a patent was a very expensive method of formally recording a discovery when a paper delivered to the Royal Society would do equally well.

Some historians have suggested that the Calotype patent of 1841 was a form of revenge by Talbot for the relative lack of attention given to photogenic drawing in 1839 – and a means of underlining that what was good enough for

* William Havell (an artist) and J. T. Wilmore (an engraver) were two who were associated in the technique. Wilmore directed an acrimonious letter to Talbot in the columns of the *Literary Gazette* but Havell disclaimed all intention of proceeding to a patent and the matter was eventually dropped.[21]

Daguerre in 1839 in patenting his invention in England was good enough for himself in 1841. In fact photogenic drawing did receive a good deal of attention but Talbot was the first to realize and to state that it needed improvement. This he achieved and the simple fact is that with the evolution of the Calotype system he realized that he had a commercial product and decided to exploit it. For that he needed to protect the discovery and therefore took out a patent. Herschel, it will be recalled, supported that view. Commercial exploitation in fact – no matter how inadequately handled by Talbot subsequently – seemed to be the main intention behind all of his patents. Despite the sharp comments from his critics about a wealthy man demeaning himself as a philosopher by seeking financial gain, Talbot saw no reason why he should not seek material reward for his many hours of work and subsequent discoveries. His general attitude was summed up in a letter commenting on a request from an acquaintance of the Earl of Shrewsbury in 1845 for full details of working the Calotype, without any suggestion of taking out a licence: '. . . is it quite reasonable to expect that the results of a thousand experiments should be communicated to all the world? It never seems to have entered the Doctor's mind that there could be the least hesitation about showing him everything.'[22] Lady Elisabeth, it should be stressed, was determined to establish what she termed the 'fame' of her son – and to drive him to its realization as best she could – but she had no influence on his patenting activities. She was surprised that he did not take out a patent for the photogenic drawing process (through which she considered he might make a fortune) but on subsequent occasions Talbot did not even tell her that he was patenting certain of his discoveries and she learned the fact from third parties. Lady Elisabeth therefore can in no way be regarded (as some writers have done) as a driving force behind her son's patenting activities.

The manner in which the controversy over Talbot's photographic patents grew and the eventual outcome can now be related but there is a general criticism of him made at that time – and in some subsequent accounts by historians of photography – which is best analysed at this stage. The criticism, put at its starkest, is that he dishonestly appropriated other men's inventions and included them in his patents.*

There is nothing in any aspect of Talbot's life to suggest that he was a dishonest man but the charges need to be examined in adequate detail.

* In this Talbot was by no means alone: perhaps the most famous of those similarly accused was a giant of the Industrial Revolution, Sir Richard Arkwright.[23]

(a) *Hypo*. Sir John Herschel undoubtedly discovered the effect of 'hyposulphite of soda' in dissolving silver salts and its specific value as a fixative in photography. Talbot was accused of patenting the discovery in 1843. Reference to his patent, however, shows that he patented a particular application of hypo with a particular objective: 'I claim the using hot or boiling solutions of the hyposulphites in order to give increased whiteness to calotype and other photographic pictures, and at the same time make them more permanent.' The principal claim therefore was to hot hypo as a method of discharging the residual silver salts which hindered the production of positive prints. No prior disclosure of this fact has been traced and, although never tested in the courts, the claim appeared to be perfectly valid.

(b) *Positive photographs*. Much attention was paid to securing one-stage positive paper photographs from 1839 onwards and a number of workers besides Talbot and Sir John Herschel engaged in the work. Talbot included a method of obtaining positives – employing gallo-nitrate of silver – in his patent of 1841. But his claim was again specific: not positive pictures generally (which would have been invalid) but those produced by a new method which was far faster than others practised up till that time.

(c) *Photographic publication* – in books and as individual prints for sale. This was included in the 1843 patent and was for a *system* of production which included features proposed by Talbot and by others. He did not claim the individual elements as new (and therefore patentable in their own right) but the 'new and useful result' secured by combining them. This was a concept well established in patent law and again appeared valid.

(*d*) *Glass plates*. Herschel (and before him Niépce) had worked with glass plates as a vehicle for photographically sensitive emulsions which suffered none of the drawbacks of paper and the Frenchman Niépce de Saint-Victor published a practical albumen-on-glass method in 1847. Claims for images produced on principally albumen-coated glass appeared in Talbot's patents of 1849 and 1851 – but with one exception these were for detailed aspects of the process. Thus the 1849 patent indicated what parts of the process were established (or old) and which were claimed as new, e.g. a subsequent reprocessing of a negative image on glass to render it a primarily positive image. It was the *conversion* from negative into positive by chemical means which was claimed in the patent.

In the 1851 patent, albumen plates generally were not claimed for this would have been invalid. Talbot did claim the use of two chemicals (previously employed by other workers separately in different processes) *in combination* on albumen plates and also a modified method of sensitizing the plates with silver nitrate.

(e) *Sulphuretted hydrogen* (hydrogen sulphide). Talbot, together with Thomas Malone, proposed this as a toning agent in their 1849 patent for images fixed in boiling caustic potash. While the toning was not a major element in the claim, it has been objected that Robert Hunt published a use of sulphuretted hydrogen in a photographic context in 1841.[24] In the first place, Hunt's reference was not to the particular use of the chemical proposed in the patent of 1849 and, secondly, sulphuretted hydrogen was a recognized agent for toning and colouring and was included as an agent for colouring copper surfaces in Talbot's first photographic patent of 1841 which was taken out before Hunt's book was published. Hunt, therefore, cannot be said to have established any priority in the context of Talbot's use of sulphuretted hydrogen.

One or two claims in Talbot's patents do raise problems. A claim for a form of enlarged photocopying of portraits in 1843 may or may not have owed something to a previous patent by another of the early photographic workers but the description is not clear enough to give an opinion either way. (Since patents were so expensive inventors frequently included as many ideas as they could in one patent, no matter how undeveloped. Talbot was occasionally guilty of this and the 1843 claim was a case in point.) Also, one claim made in the 1851 patent for 'the simultaneous production upon glass plates of images which are both positive and negative, according to the light in which they are viewed' would probably not have stood in court as written because this was a feature well recognized in glass plates from the earliest days. The claim may have been *intended* to refer to the plates produced in the way outlined in the patent but this was not the claim made. However, it could be argued that the fault was that of the system because in his summing up at the Talbot versus Laroche trial in 1854, the Lord Chief Justice advised as a general principle against including specific claims in a patent – 'better to state the matter generally, and leave it to the court to support the patent, than to state the claim too specifically, for many a patent had been lost by its being so stated'.[25] It was almost a case of heads the court wins, tails the patentee loses!

Finally there was a problem concerning the iodized paper used in the Calotype process. Talbot did not claim iodized paper (although he described it) in the patent of 1841* – only 'the employing gallic acid or tincture of galls, in conjunction with a solution of silver, to render paper *which has received a previous preparation* [author's italics] more sensitive to the action of light'. In the Talbot versus Laroche hearings it was clear that Talbot's side made no claim that iodized paper was included in the patent but some contemporary criticism appeared to indicate that Talbot *did* claim iodized paper and there was one instance at least where his lawyers took action against a retailer offering such paper (page 194). They may have done so on the basis that the retailer was promoting the iodized paper with a heavy emphasis on the Calotype system – for which he held no licence – and that this was considered to be an infringement.

Such a list of charge and rebuttal risks becoming tedious but it is necessary in fairness to Talbot. Some of his contemporary critics made use of highly selective 'evidence' which suited their own purposes and this was an understandable tactic in the campaign to break his patents. The same tactic, in addition to advancing carefully edited quotations and even statements attributed to Talbot which he did not make, has been pursued in later accounts of the controversy by some photographic historians and this cannot be excused. Criticisms of Talbot's patenting activities certainly can be made but they do not require the laying of false evidence.

To take one further example from the case made subsequently by a number of photographic historians. As a serious challenge was mounted against Talbot's photographic patents in 1853–4 he was recommended by his legal advisers to renounce or disclaim certain of the claims – of which there were a considerable number – made in his various patents if they did not form part of the principal discovery patented. In part this was because one or two of the claims were – as earlier suggested – inadequately developed. But the main reason was that as a

---

* He did, however, claim it in his U.S. patent of 1847 (p. 166). He also claimed in that patent that gallic acid had not been used in photography 'previously to my discovery'. In England this claim would have been impossible to defend. In the American patent, however, it was almost certainly intended to refer to photographic practice *in the U.S.* This claim was valid.

matter of course in litigation any opponent would seek to discredit the validity of the entire patent by attacking *any* points in it (no matter how trivial or unconnected with the main issue) which were anything less than demonstrably well founded. With such an approach – which was standard practice then and still is now in patent disputes – it was obviously good sense for the patent holder to shed any parts of the patent, no matter how well founded, which did not form part of its major claim. Thus in March 1854 Talbot disclaimed four non-essential parts of his 1841 patent and two parts of his 1851 patent, and in March 1855 all but the claims relating to albumen glass plates in his patent of 1849. To a biased historian, however, the conclusion to be drawn was only too easy: the disclaimers were an indication of the derivative nature and the low worth of the patents. It was in fact no such thing: it was a preparation for legal battle.

Perhaps the best defence of Talbot as a man of discovery is to be found in his photographic notebooks.[26] On 18 February 1839 (that is, even before he had released details of photogenic drawing to the Royal Society) he discovered the increased sensitivity derived from the use of iodide of potassium and thus laid part of the foundation for the use of iodized paper in the Calotype system; on 3 March 1839 he commenced his first experiments in sensitizing glass plates; on 23 March 1840 he proposed the use of sulphate of iron in the photographic process; seven days later he suggested albumen* as an element in a system to 'fill the pores of paper' – a concept which was brought to a highly successful reality by the Frenchman Blanquart-Evrard in 1850; on 30 August 1840 he suggested the use of silver nitrate mixed with albumen and sensitized by exposing to iodine vapour on glass plates – seven years before Niépce de Saint-Victor introduced the first practical system of albumenized glass plates; on 13 September 1842 he proposed the waxing of sensitized paper *before* exposure in the camera (not afterwards as in current practice) – a concept which Gustave Le Gray introduced as a practical method of photography ten years later; and on 18 February 1843 he was contemplating a method of recovering silver from fixing liquid. It is not suggested that Talbot translated these suggestions into reliable practice, nor that he published the concepts thereby establishing any form of priority, nor that the notebook entries in any way reduce the deserved fame of the French researchers to whom reference has been made. But what is suggested is that the man who between 1839 and

* No claim is made that this was the very first proposal concerning the use of albumen in photography. A letter from 'H.L.' proposed its use in photogenic drawing in the May 1839 issue of *Mechanic's Magazine*.

1843 could envisage the processes proposed was in no need of other men's work to establish his own fame, nor to include in his patents save where he had improved that work and given it a new application.

Three broad categories of Calotype users could be identified. From the beginning, Henry Talbot intended that the system should be free for use in 'the scientific world' and this he put into effect.[27] On an informal level from 1841 onwards he received numerous letters from scientists (and others) praising him for the help he had given them and for the examples of the Calotype which he had sent. There were also more formal contacts and an agreement signed with Talbot by William M. Nurse of the Polytechnic Society of London in December 1841 granted free use of the Calotype for a period of three months. The usage was to include experiments and the preparation of illustrations for lectures at the Polytechnic Institution but excluded any sale or gifts of pictures to third parties.[28]

Relations with amateurs were inevitably more numerous and complex. Initially Henry Talbot did his best to respond to the numerous letters of enquiry and – as with scientists – to send samples of his work. It may be surmised, however, that this became increasingly difficult with growing volume and that Talbot decided that licences should be issued against payment. There were probably few examples of such licences in the early years for the process was difficult enough to operate for the few professionals who were attempting to earn their living by it and disappointments for amateurs must have been numerous. One individual who contemplated taking out a licence in 1842 was W. Russell Sedgfield who almost twenty years later recalled that Talbot's solicitors asked £20 for a licence – which might be withdrawn at any time – and required that any prints were neither to be sold nor given away. It is possible that over the great length of time Sedgfield's memory was at fault and that the amount asked for was £2 (which would have been in line with later practice). Certainly his attitude to the patent was revealed by his comment in 1861 that he did not take out the licence but nevertheless worked the Calotype anyhow![29] In the latter half of the 1840s, as we have seen, there was evidence that amateur licences cost £2, £1 and were eventually entirely free. In the light of this – and even if the need to secure a licence at all was irksome – it cannot be claimed that the requirement was any practical deterrent to amateurs wishing to practise the Calotype.

This was borne out by the formation of the Photographic Club in 1847 when a dozen or so amateurs 'associated together for the purpose of pursuing their experiments in the Art of Photography'.[30] Of its members Roger Fenton became the most famous – but Robert Hunt too belonged to the club which was founded by Peter Wickens Fry, a lawyer, who was to play a prominent role in opposition to Talbot in the years thereafter. It was Roger Fenton who took the lead in proposing that the informal and limited activities of the Photographic Club should be transformed into the more formal framework of an organized photographic society. Fenton later reported that it was with difficulty that he secured enough support to make the concept of such a society feasible – and it was Hunt who was primarily responsible for discussions with Henry Talbot on the question of his patent which was a matter of major importance to be resolved before the society could proceed.

Hunt's contact with Talbot on the issue began in 1851 and it was clear from the beginning that there were a number of Hunt's colleagues who were opposed to Talbot's patents on grounds of principle* as well as objecting to Talbot's detailed claims and the manner in which he interpreted them. Hunt was doubtful about the 'respectability' of the society proposed by Roger Fenton but he was a natural (and knowledgeable) choice for the role of nego- tiator with Talbot. He endeavoured to adopt a neutral position and following a meeting with Talbot early in March 1852 wrote to Fry – 'I must say that Mr Fox Talbot clearly desires to make no profit by his process where it is used for amusement only or for scientific enquiry. He appears quite disposed to put as few restrictions as possible on the progress of photography.'[31]

Hunt enumerated Henry Talbot's proposals in this letter, the chief of which was that a licence would be given to every member of the proposed society on the understanding that the society was not to trade in photographs. (Any member so trading without the appropriate licence would be expelled by the council of the society.) Talbot in fact went on to propose that members should

---

* At the Science Museum in London is a handwritten, anonymous document proposing stringent regulations for the new society on patents:

'Every member will take the engagement of forwarding by all his power the progress of photography, to make no secret of his discoveries and never to take any patent for them. Members of a scientific and liberal society must be satisfied with the honour of having been the first to make a discovery. But as in some cases it would not be just to deprive an inventor of the remuneration due to his expenses and labours he cannot be blamed for taking [out a patent] but he will give notice to the Society of his inten- tion of doing so, and this notice will be his resignation as members [sic] of the Society. The Society being established for the disinterested advancement of the Photographic Science cannot admit among its mem- bers a person who will seek other than a Scientific remuneration.'

be able to sell positive photographs at the society's rooms through the secretary and that 10 per cent of the proceeds should be paid to the society. 'Mr Fox Talbot considers,' wrote Hunt to Fry, 'a fund may thus be formed for the benefit of the Society.'*

Hunt's favourable reaction to Talbot's proposals was not shared by some of his colleagues of whom Fry was the most prominent objector. Hunt wrote to Talbot on 19 March 'to inform you that many gentlemen amateurs will not admit your right to interfere with them in any way – *as they pursue photography for their own amusement* – and they state they would not belong to a society which admitted your right by any agreement'. Hunt indicated that this view refused to recognize the applicability of the injunction Talbot had recently secured against a *professional* and continued: 'I write, I beg you to understand, not as expressing any opinion of my own, but to inform you of the opinion entertained by others . . . Allow me to assure you again that I consider your proposal most liberal . . .'[32]

Talbot replied in a restrained manner underlining that 'I have already stated to you that my desire is to give a free permission to the members of the Society to exercise the art for their amusement, they on their part acknowledging my rights as an inventor and patentee'. He added in a note headed *private* – 'I assure you that I have the best wishes for the formation of a prosperous society, but it appears to me that there is not much *reciprocity of feeling* on the part of those who would naturally take a leading part in it. However, I have done all that lay in my power.'[33] With that it is difficult to disagree – unless one's opposition was based on a refusal to recognize any rights in the matter as belonging to Talbot.

The discussions continued into April 1852 and it appears that it was Henry Talbot who persuaded Charles Wheatstone to become a vice-president of the new society if it were formed.[34] Opponents of Talbot's position, however, exerted the greatest power amongst the supporters of the proposed society and on 23 April Hunt wrote of the strength of the view that 'the Society by accepting your agreement commits itself – and strengthens your application for the renewal of your patent and this it is fairly said the Society must not be permitted to do'.[35] Later Hunt told Talbot that he personally could not support the proposal that Talbot be president of the new society – 'many members of

* The various rules proposed for the new society's constitution in 1852–3 by its supporters showed a keen awareness of the commercial aspects of photography. This gives added insight into the perfectly fair attitude adopted by Talbot as a patent holder.

which are disposed to quarrel with your patent'.[36] He was also in contact with Henry's lawyers and following a meeting of the amateur photographers confirmed that if the society were to be formed it 'must be established without any reference to Mr F. Talbot's patents'.[37] Hunt indicated more detailed objections – to the claim concerning iodized paper and the collodion process–i and added, for good measure, that there were parties preparing to practise the collodion process professionally.[38] Talbot immediately replied:

> You give me good news in saying that some parties have at length resolved to infringe my patent *openly* viz. for purposes of trade. This will give me the opportunity of obtaining the decision of a Court of Law, & of showing to the world that I claim no more than I have a right to claim *under the existing patent laws*. Should it prove on the other hand that I have been misled by my legal advisers (whose advice I have always followed) I shall submit most readily to the judgement of the Court. You cannot think how glad I shall be to have the question of my rights finally settled by a competent tribunal.[39]

And there the matter appeared to rest for the moment.*

The Royal Society of Arts, however, was keen to see a solution of the problems and Talbot proceeded to take counsel from his uncle Lord Lansdowne, Charles Wheatstone and (through Wheatstone) with Lord Rosse, President of the Royal Society. During the course of May a renunciation of the patent rights so far as amateurs were concerned was being discussed and by the end of that month Talbot had agreed – the only issue being the manner in which this should be done. Talbot favoured the form of an appeal from 'a numerous & influential body of gentlemen representing Science and Art' in the interest of the public good – otherwise 'I should undoubtedly expose myself to ridicule by relinquishing the patent right merely because a body of artists objected to it as well as to all other patents, on principle'.[40] Caroline Mount Edgcumbe was keen to involve the Prince Consort in the appeal but eventually it took the form of an exchange of letters between Lord Rosse and Sir Charles Eastlake – President of the Royal Academy – on the one hand and Talbot on the other. The form of letters was agreed in advance and publication took place in *The Times* on 13 August 1852.

* An artist – John Leighton – endeavoured to secure signatures for an appeal that Talbot be granted a barony on condition that he relinquish his patent rights. There is no evidence that Talbot knew anything of this initiative and (however well intentioned Leighton's motives) if he had he certainly would have disapproved. The appeal reportedly had little success. However, Caroline Mount Edgcumbe was of the view that her half brother should receive some honour for his discovery should it be given to the nation.[41]

The letter from Rosse and Eastlake, dated July 1852, read:

In addressing to you this letter, we believe that we speak the sentiments of many persons eminent for their love of science and art.

The art of Photography upon paper, of which you are the inventor, has arrived at such a degree of perfection that it must soon become of national importance; and we are anxious that, as the art itself originated in England, it should also receive its further perfection and development in this country. At present, however, although England continues to take the lead in some branches of the art, yet in others the French are unquestionably making more rapid progress than we are. It is very desirable that we should not be left behind by the nations of the Continent in the improvement and development of a purely British invention; and as you are the possessor of a patent right which will continue for some years, and which may perhaps be renewed, we beg to call your attention to the subject, and to inquire whether it may not be possible for you to obviate most of the difficulties which now appear to hinder the progress of the art in England.

Many of the finest applications of the invention will probably require the co-operation of men of science and skilful artists. But it is evident that the more freely they can use the resources of the art, the more it is that their efforts will be attended with eminent success.

As we feel no doubt that some judicious alteration would give great satisfaction, and be the means of rapidly improving this beautiful art, we beg to make this friendly communication to you in the full confidence that you will receive it in the same spirit – the improvement of art and science being our common object.

Talbot's reply was addressed to Lord Rosse and dated 30 July:

I have had the honour of receiving a letter from yourself and Sir Charles Eastlake respecting my photographic invention, to which I have now the pleasure of replying.

Ever since the Great Exhibition I have felt that a new era has commenced for photography, as it has for so many other useful arts and inventions. Thousands of persons have now become acquainted with the art, and, from having seen such beautiful specimens of it produced both in England and in France, have naturally felt a wish to practise it themselves. A variety of new applications of it have been imagined, and doubtless many more remain to be discovered. I am unable to pursue all these numerous branches of the invention in a manner that can even attempt to do justice to them; and moreover, I believe it to be no longer necessary, for the art has now taken a root both in England and France, and may be safely left to take its natural development. I am as desirous as any one of the lovers of science and art whose wishes you have kindly undertaken to represent, that our country should continue to take the lead in this newly discovered branch of the fine arts; and, after much consideration, I think that the best thing that I can do, and most likely to stimulate to further improvements in photography, would be to invite the emulation and competition of our artists and amateurs by relaxing the patent right which I possess in this invention. I therefore beg to reply to your kind letter by offering the patent, with the exception of the single point hereinafter mentioned, as a free present to the public, together with any other improvements in the same art, one of which has been very recently granted me, and has still 13 years unexpired.

The exception to which I refer, and which I am desirous of still keeping in the hands of my own licensees, is the application of the invention to taking photographic portraits for sale to the public. [Sir Charles Eastlake agreed that this exception was 'just and fair'.[42]]

This is a branch of the art which must necessarily be in comparatively few hands, because it requires a house to be built or altered on purpose, having an apartment lighted by a skylight; otherwise the portraits cannot be taken indoors, generally speaking, without great difficulty.

With this exception, then, I present my invention to the country, and trust that it may realise our hopes of its future utility . . .

Talbot must have derived some perhaps paradoxical pleasure from the situation because it was essentially the Calotype system that was practised by amateurs and the pressures on him that had built up were a measure of its growing popularity at long last. But the policy which he had hitherto pursued towards amateurs was a liberal one and it is hard to see how this attitude was curbing the progress of photography in Britain. Talbot's claim that the collodion process was covered by his Calotype patent was another matter entirely – but this was of primary concern to professionals and there can be no doubt that the professionals used the formation of the Photographic Society as a tool with which they hoped to force Talbot to free even professional use from his patents. In this immediate objective they were disappointed. Although both sides agreed to the form of words in the letters exchanged in August 1852, the sentiments expressed (as Talbot indicated in his letter to Charles Wheatstone of 29 May) owed more to the general campaign being waged at that time against all patents in the country at large[43] than to sins of omission or commission on Talbot's part.

The presidency of the new Society was declined by Talbot and accepted by Sir Charles Eastlake in his stead. At the inaugural meeting in January 1853 Sir Charles stated:

I think it right on this occasion to remind you that we owe the invention of that form and application of the method which have already been carried to such prefection in this country, to the gentleman I have already named – to Mr Fox Talbot; and to him we are also indebted for the liberality with which he has thrown open his invention to the enterprise of men of science, of amateurs and of artists.[44]

Some of his audience would not have agreed with him and an animosity towards Talbot on the part of the Society continued for a number of years. In February of 1861, for example, the death of Peter Fry was recorded at a meeting of the Society's Council. The chairman of the meeting recounted the part that Fry had played in the formation of the Society and how 'professing liberality to the young Society [Talbot's] conditions were in every way so stringent, that it was resolved (mainly on the representations of Mr Fry) to reject the offer...' To Fry's work, the chairman continued, was owed 'the ultimate removal of the objectionable restrictions, and the freedom of photography from the shackles of the patent law'. Thomas Malone was present at this council meeting and bitterly criticized the chairman for permitting such an attack on Talbot. Malone – like those expressing support for Fry – was an interested party but it was significant that the editor of the *Photographic News* supported Malone's protest. Without taking sides on past controversies, an editorial considered that Malone's protest was 'a most legitimate one'. It was one thing to praise the dead but 'to offer a direct and most uncalled for affront to a living gentleman, and one to whose researches the art and science [of photography] is perhaps more indebted than to any other man alive is a circumstance that we must confess we cannot reconcile with our ideas of propriety and decency'.[45] Attitudes changed with the passage of time, but not before the Photographic Society had joined certain professional photographers in their fight against Talbot's patents.

As was seen in Chapter 5, portrait photography – the principal professional activity – was dominated by the Daguerreotype in the 1840s. It took time for practice and experimentation to refine the Calotype and the attempts by Henry Collen and Antoine Claudet to practise portraiture with the system may be considered in retrospect too premature to have been successful. An artist, Thomas Wyatt, also took out a licence for the Calotype in Manchester but was as unsuccessful as the others – not even recouping his initial expenses.[46] Towards the end of the decade Henneman had a measure of success at Regent Street but this may be considered a reflection of improvements in the Calotype system secured by then and of the special relationship which he enjoyed with Henry Talbot.

Because professionals worked principally with the Daguerreotype few major attempts to evade Talbot's 1841 patent were made in the decade and it was Richard Beard, the Daguerreotype patent holder, who faced the onslaught. (It needs to be emphasized that there was no doubt as to his rights over that

N

system in England but that did not preclude attempts to break his patent – another reflection of the general anti-patent attitude existing at that time.) It may be supposed that amateurs practised the Calotype both with and without a licence. Occasionally a semi-professional might complain about the restrictions of the patent – as did William Collie of Jersey when he retrospectively related how 'the patentee, Mr Talbot, interfered with the sale of them [Calotype scenes] in England; I had therefore to content myself with little fame and less fortune'.[47] There was of course no reason why Collie should make money from the Calotype without reference to the patentee but his attitude yet again underlined the strongly felt opposition to patent restrictions of any kind.

Talbot and his lawyers appear to have moved against only one alleged infringer of his patents in the 1840s – a firm of opticians at 98 Cheapside in London, Thomas and Richard Willats. Willats published a *Photographic Manual* commencing in 1844 and in that the validity of a number of Talbot's patent claims was challenged.[48] The basis of the action, however, centred on the Willats sale of iodized paper and although it is now difficult to assess the precise grounds for Talbot's move against them (p. 185) his lawyers were in no doubt. In November of 1845 Willats responded to a letter from the lawyers by expressing regret that an unintentional infringement of a patent had taken place; promising to discontinue; expressing gratefulness for the courteous manner in which they had been treated; and seeking information on what terms Talbot would grant a licence.[49]

Talbot commented:

I am glad that Mr Willats has had the good sense to submit, as I have no wish to go to law with anybody. I will consider and send word in a day or two on what terms I could give him a licence.

I wish you would ascertain whether the successors of Mr Palmer in Newgate Street, I believe No. 102, sell my iodised paper, and if so, let some one purchase a packet of it for evidence, and that being done, I should wish a similar letter to be written to them. I am not able to point out any other parties by name, who I think are likely to be infringing the patent, but when I return to Town next week I will cause proper enquiries to be made, and take steps accordingly . . .[50]

The contents of this letter are revealing for (besides indicating Talbot's lack of forward planning in deciding the terms to be offered in different licences) they emphasize the problems faced by a patentee in endeavouring to protect a patent – in particular, the continual need to search out infringers and to secure the evidence of actual sale or practice which it was claimed constituted the infringement. It was a never-ending task – and in June 1846 there were still strong suspicions that the Willats shop was continuing to infringe Talbot's patent.[51]

Negotiations on licences were frequently indeterminate in nature and the lack of decisiveness on Talbot's part in business exchanges was matched frequently by an apparent lack of genuine intent on the part of those negotiating with him. In 1849–50 there was a drawn-out negotiation between Thomas Malone acting on Talbot's behalf and a number of persons sometimes acting separately and sometimes in concert. These were Edward Harper – seeking a licence in Lancashire and Yorkshire, Richard and Lebbens Colls who were 'artists' in Middlesex and Robert Jefferson Bingham of London.* At various stages of the discussions, Talbot appeared to require a bond of £1,000 from the Colls (which probably demonstrated his lack of faith in their intentions) and down payments of £400 and £500 on signature of the agreement. For their part, Harper claimed that the glass process he planned to patent was much better than that in Talbot's and Malone's 1849 patent and that 'knowing the difficulties attendant on substantiating and protecting a patent' it would be far more sensible for Talbot to ask a lower price for licences (a view which had some validity) while Bingham stated that Talbot's claim to gallic acid in the 1841 patent was invalid because of prior discovery. It was all singularly unproductive[52] but, at just about the time these discussions were failing, an event took place which was to transform the situation.

Frederick Scott Archer was a sculptor who took up the Calotype as an aid to his work. He became a member of the Photographic Club and began photographic experimentation, turning in 1849 to the use of the recently discovered collodion (a form of gun cotton in ether) on glass. Archer began publishing his results in the *Chemist* in 1850 and full details of the collodion process appeared in the same magazine in March 1851, with a manual of the process being published separately in 1852. Archer carefully cleaned a plate of glass and coated it with collodion containing potassium iodide. When the ether had nearly evaporated, the plate was immersed in a bath of silver nitrate thus forming light-sensitive silver iodide. The moist plate was loaded in the camera,

---

* The Colls were to figure in an injunction obtained by Talbot in 1852 (p. 198). Robert Bingham had some training as a chemist and was author of another photographic manual – that produced by George Knight and Sons in Cheapside, instrument makers whose premises were close to Willats. The 1850 manual *Photographic Manipulation* referred to the use of collodion in photography and Bingham later made some claims on Scott Archer's discovery of the collodion process.[53]

exposed, developed – normally using pyrogallic acid – and fixed. The plate lost its sensitivity to light rapidly when dry and was therefore exposed moist: hence the description of the 'wet collodion process'. The method of preparation was cumbersome, requiring the operator to carry a darkroom tent with him wherever he went, but the speed of the plate and the use of glass, which yielded a clear negative base, were major breakthroughs whose potential was realized almost immediately. (At first the quality of wet-plate collodion could by no means match that of the albumen-on-glass processes but the relative lack of sensitivity of the latter was a disadvantage which collodion triumphantly overcame.) As a person Scott Archer was universally liked by all who met him but despite the immediate recognition of the value of the collodion process he died in 1857 a poor man with none of the relative wealth which the users of the process were securing.

And Talbot? At the end of 1851 he was of the view that the albumen process to which he gave the name of *Amphitype* was 'a species of the same genus' as collodion in 'a scientific classification of photographic methods'[54] but sometime later concluded that there were features of the collodion process which brought it within the terms of his 1841 Calotype patent. It was this attitude which brought the previous dislike and sometimes scorn for his patent activities to a head and led to major confrontations at law. Talbot's claim to the collodion process – which was a system by which the professional portraitist could produce negatives and positives at much lower cost than by using the patented Daguerreotype – began to be made actively in 1852–3 and the reaction of some professionals may be imagined. Here was a process which promised great commercial success and which moreover had not been patented by Scott Archer. Inevitably, therefore, it appeared at first that it would be completely 'free' – but then Talbot claimed that a licence from him must be taken out before it could be worked.

Some photographers agreed to this without demur and a record of the dues paid to Talbot between 1851 and 1854 survives.[55] The statement does not differentiate between licences to work the established Calotype or collodion processes but it may be assumed that many of the dues paid in 1854 – accounting for around three quarters of the total income from the four years of £857 9s. 6d. – were for the latter. Nine different licence holders existed in that year, including the Royal Panopticon of Science and Art at Leicester Square in London, the Brighton photographic concerns Grey and Hall, and Hennah and Kent, the painter-turned-photographer O. G. Rejlander and Philip Delamotte of

New Bond Street. Payments were usually staggered, the highest total for 1854 being the Panopticon at £131 5s. od.* and the lowest Rejlander at £13. The rounded nature of most of the payments suggested fixed fees and not payments on a print or assignment basis. Delamotte advertised his business energetically and in the *Journal of the Society of Arts* in May 1853 announced that he had 'just concluded arrangements with H. F. Talbot patentee to take portraits by the newly discovered Collodion Process'.[56] It was a statement which drove some of his fellow professionals to new heights of anger.

The action of Talbot's lawyers against alleged infringers of his Calotype patent extended during this period to those employing the collodion process and one or two stories (usually told long after the events occurred) have come through the history of photography to portray the apparent ruthlessness of the approach. In 1902 details of a letter from a photographer called Cogan were published in the *British Journal of Photography* in which it was stated that Talbot's lawyers demanded £300 per annum for a licence to work the collodion process. Then in 1930 the same journal published a more detailed account drawn from the diaries of a Welshman Thomas Sims who in 1853 set up two studios in London. Sims asserted – in a reconstruction of an interview with one of Talbot's lawyers – that the latter claimed 'that Mr Talbot's patents embrace and include every branch of photography, even the Daguerreotype' and that a licence for Sims's two studios would be £200 and £150 respectively per annum.[57] In both cases full allowance should be made for the reactions of men faced with what they considered to be a threat to their livelihood – and also for possible excesses on the part of lawyers acting for Talbot. But the point must also be made that two of the three sums mentioned in the stories were far higher than any known to have been actually paid by Talbot's biggest licensees and that the reference made in Sims's story to Talbot's claim to the Daguerreotype must throw some doubt on the validity of the rest of his story. None the less, that there were interviews which the photographers found most unsatisfactory, to say the least, is not in doubt.†

A rare contemporary reference to these activities was contained in the August issue of the *Art-Journal*.[1] It related how the lady Daguerreotypist

* Previous discussions had indicated a proposed licence payment rate by the Panopticon and other licensees of 100 guineas for the first year of the licence and £150 for each succeeding year.[58]

† The Sims case apparently went no further at law though Sims claimed to have received an injunction and the *British Journal of Photography* article noted certain subsequent stories that the case went to the Queen's Bench. No evidence for either claim has been found. There was but one brief reference to Sims – dated to February 1855 – in one of the bills from Price & Bolton to Talbot for services rendered.[59]

turned collodion photographer Miss Wigley rejected threats from Talbot's lawyers and how the 'maiden hero was too much for the hero of Lacock Abbey and the bachelor succumbed'. The story, possibly, was no more accurate than its description of Talbot's marital status.* And in recounting these various stories, historians have not been aware (or cared to publicize) that there were at least two occasions on which the allegedly ruthless Talbot granted free professional licences to exiles from Hungary.[60]

One action was taken further, however, during this period and it concerned Richard and Lebbens Colls the two brothers who had figured in the abortive negotiations with Talbot mentioned earlier. The brothers operated a 'Gallery of Art' in New Bond Street from which they sold paper prints and it seems likely that these were Calotype products and not produced by the collodion process. Since the Colls had not taken out a licence Talbot considered their operation an infringement of his patent and he succeeded in obtaining an injunction in the Court of Chancery on 22 January 1852. J. H. Bolton reported to Talbot two days later that the case had been reported in *The Times*, the *Morning Chronicle*, the *Morning Herald* and the *Daily News* thereby implying that it would constitute a strong warning to others.[61] This was the injunction which preceded Talbot's important discussions with Robert Hunt on the formation by amateurs of a photographic society – and which the amateurs refused to interpret as affecting them. As the months went on and collodion demonstrated that it was a major step forward in photographic technology, professional photographers increasingly turned to the process and were determined to defy Henry Talbot. This issue came to a head in 1854 with Talbot as equally determined to defend what he considered to be his just patent rights and the interests of those who had purchased licences from him.

James Henderson was a professional portrait-photographer operating the collodion process in a studio in Regent Street. He did not take out a licence from Talbot who in 1854 obtained evidence that the photographer used the collodion process to produce paper prints for sale and moved to obtain an injunction in the Court of Chancery. Affidavits were secured on both sides – those for Talbot being made by David Brewster and John Herschel and those

---

* Several brief references to Miss Wigley appeared in a statement of account from Talbot's lawyers for the period 1851–2, including a comment that he wished to treat her 'with indulgence' and intended to postpone action 'for the present'.[62] Thomas Malone wrote to Talbot about this sole woman professional photographer in February 1850: 'Mr Beard regrets giving a licence to Miss Wigley. The badness of her pictures & the absurdity of her advertisements tends to bring the Daguerreotype into disrepute. Such is the opinion of Mr Claudet, Kilburn [another professional Daguerreotypist] and Beard himself.'[63]

for Henderson including a joint statement by Robert Hunt and Charles Heisch, who was a lecturer in chemistry at the Middlesex Hospital.[64] Talbot won his injunction from Vice-Chancellor Sir W. Page Wood and Henderson was restrained under a penalty of £5,000. Talbot's lawyers immediately took advertisements publicizing the fact and advised that 'Artists and others desiring to practise this branch of the photographic Art [i.e. the collodion process] are requested to apply to us. All infringers of the patent rights will be proceeded against.'[65] Talbot wrote to Constance immediately after securing the injunction that they had had a 'grand field day' in the Court of Chancery and that the affidavits of Brewster and Herschel had 'demolished the affidavits of my opponents, as heavy artillery does the weak defences of the Chinese'. Such however was 'the anomalous state of British law, that the defendant Henderson may appeal if he pleases to the Court of Common Pleas and have another trial with a jury to decide upon it'.[66] Despite Talbot's enthusiasm, Vice-Chancellor Wood had agreed that although the injunction should be granted (and the Colls injunction of two years before exerted some influence on him in reaching that decision) there was nonetheless 'a serious point to be tried at law between the parties'.[67] Henderson chose to fight on but before the case came to court that of Talbot versus Laroche took place in the Court of Common Pleas. It is the latter which has gone down in photographic history but a regrettable feature of this case is that no official, manuscript legal records have been traced. All that exists of the record of the trial are a necessarily short account in the columns of *The Times*, with lengthier accounts in the *Journal of the Photographic Society* and the *Art-Journal*. These magazines were anti-Talbot and the reporting showed some bias (as well as inaccuracy in the *Journal of the Photographic Society*) but the *Art-Journal* did contain a valuable and apparently verbatim report of the Lord Chief Justice's summing up.[68] Fortunately the legal records of the Talbot–Henderson case are far more extensive and since the photographers' defence was basically the same in each, Talbot's case and the nature of the objections raised to his patent by his opponents may be described in detail with some authority.

Martin Laroche was the professional name of William Henry Silvester. He was a jeweller-turned-Daguerreotypist who by November 1853 was advertising in *The Times* that he took portraits by the new collodion process. Talbot's initial steps against Laroche were taken in December 1853 but, with evident signs of a major challenge to his position developing, he took time to disclaim all but the most important parts of two of his photographic patents

(p. 186). It was not until May–June of 1854 that detailed exchanges between the legal representatives began – with both sides blaming the other variously for undue haste or delays in bringing the proceedings on.[69] It was at this time that Talbot gave notice in the *London Gazette* that he intended applying to the Privy Council for an extension of his Calotype patent which was due to expire in February 1855.

Laroche wrote to the Photographic Society on 27 June outlining both the action which Talbot had brought against him and the fact that he had entered a *caveat* (protest) against the extension of the patent term – trusting 'that I may meet with the well-wishes and support of all who are interested in the art of photography'. A meeting of the Photographic Society was held on 6 July to discuss the issues and predictably severe criticism of Talbot was forthcoming. Peter Fry (as a lawyer and a member of the firm – Fry & Loxley – which was acting for Laroche) pointed out that all the issues which members of the Society were protesting would be considered by the courts but that 'he thought that the expense of defending this action ought not to fall on Mr Laroche alone, as his means were moderate, and he was not defending his own interests only, but those of the art'.[70] The meeting was preceded and followed by strongly worded letters in the *Journal* alleging that Talbot's invention had not been original and therefore should never have been patented.

But not all the voices in photography were of the same view. The *Liverpool Photographic Journal* adopted a noticeably objective attitude towards the dispute throughout and reminded members of the Photographic Society in an editorial that 'The history of the steam engine and other discoveries . . . will shew that the person who reduced previous discoveries into practical application has always been considered and treated legally as the inventor' – while noting in passing that present attitude in society generally which appeared to call for 'every literary and scientific individual . . . to be sacrificed to the so-called *public* benefit'.[71]

In addition, Talbot had at least one supporter on the Council of the Photographic Society itself: Nevil Story-Maskelyne – a grandson of the famous Astronomer Royal – graduated in mathematics at Oxford University but had a lifelong interest in chemistry. As a young man of twenty-two in 1845 he had confessed his dedication to photography to Talbot and a continuing friendship had developed. Story-Maskelyne kept Talbot informed of developments and endeavoured to express a view in the Council of the Photographic Society which could not have been a popular one. 'My own belief is that this is an ungenerous and immoral combination to deprive you of what the men who make it are most deeply indebted to you for their having at all',* he wrote to Talbot just before the trial commenced[72] – adding later 'I suspect it is but a very few, and those, individuals who are connected with the management of the Society, who take active part in the attack'. He identified Peter Fry as 'especially your enemy' and stated that he would watch carefully any attempt made by members of the Society to use its funds in the anti-Talbot cause.[73] Talbot himself had no doubts about the strength of the feeling against him: just before the trial commenced he wrote to Story-Maskelyne that he understood from Henneman that at its next meeting the Photographic Society intended to make 'final arrangements for my destruction at the trial. It is evident they will do their uttermost (the same body that asked me to be their President!).'[74]

The usual tactic in meeting an action for infringement of a patent was firstly to challenge the validity of the patent itself (on innumerable grounds ranging from technical faults in drafting to major issues of prior discovery by others) and secondly to claim that, even if the patent were valid, the matters at issue did not constitute an infringement. Talbot's case was relatively straightforward. In the 1841 patent his two principal claims were 'employing gallic acid or tincture of galls, in conjunction with a solution of silver, to render paper which has received a previous preparation more sensitive to the action of light' and 'the making visible photographic images upon paper, and the strengthening such images when already faintly or imperfectly visible by washing them with liquids which act upon those parts of the paper which have been previously acted upon by light'. In including these within a patent, the implication at law was that he was the discoverer of the techniques referred to or that, if he were not, details of them had not been published by another party before the patent had been taken out on 8 February 1841.

As to the Calotype and collodion processes, Talbot claimed in essence that the latter was covered by his patent because in both – (a) the substance to be rendered highly sensitive was a 'neutral' iodide of silver; (b) the liquid rendering it highly sensitive was silver nitrate; (c) an invisible image was formed on the 'activated' silver iodide and (d) the latent image was developed by gallic acid or pyrogallic acid. He argued that the glass base used in the collodion process

---

* Others, though less knowledgeable, were as loyal. In offering to help her half brother with his trial expenses, Caroline Mount Edgcumbe commented that 'your adversaries in the law suit are the most dishonourable, shuffling people I ever heard of but you can scarcely expect lawyers to be scientific . . .'[75]

had no function other than that of being a vehicle for a coating of iodized collodion which was directly comparable to iodized paper. (A sheet of ordinary writing paper coated with iodized collodion could be used in the Calotype process in lieu of a sheet of iodized paper.) And, whatever preparation was used, both were developed by two liquids – gallic acid or pyrogallic acid – which had similar photographic properties, the only significant difference being that pyrogallic acid worked faster.

The attack on Talbot's case both in Henderson's affidavits and by witnesses for Laroche was on a wide front – forty-two objections to the patent being lodged in the latter.[76] The quality of the objections varied immensely. Those by Hunt, Heisch and William H. Thornthwaite* against Talbot were detailed and knowledgeable documents which required careful consideration on the part of those acting for Talbot – though all three, and particularly Hunt with his knowledge of early photographic techniques, could scarcely have believed genuinely in the claim that there was any meaningful comparison between the technique of latent-image development discovered by Talbot and the means by which Daguerre or Niépce 'developed' images in their process. Other objections – and notably those advanced by Henderson himself – were poorly conceived, as for example:

I have been informed and believe it to be true that the results which in the said specification are stated to be obtainable by the use and application of the means and processes therein described cannot be produced and in that respect I believe that the contents of said specification are not true but save as aforesaid I do not know and cannot set forth of my belief or otherwise in what particulars they are not true.[77]

Henderson affirmed in other words, that Talbot's method did not work but he could not say how or why.

However, without any doubt the major challenge to the validity of Talbot's claim to be the discoverer of the Calotype technique came in the testimony of the Revd J. B. Reade, a man whose true contribution to the history of photography has taken longer to define with some reliability than probably any other single person in photographic history.[78] Joseph Bancroft Reade was of the same generation as Talbot. He was ordained in 1826 but the major interests

* Hunt, Heisch and Thornthwaite made affidavits on Henderson's behalf and appeared as witnesses for Laroche. Thornthwaite was a photographic-manual author and a partner in Horne & Thornthwaite of Newgate Street in London – a firm which supplied iodized collodion and which therefore had an understandable commercial interest in joining the fight against Talbot. In 1851 Talbot was seriously contemplating taking legal proceedings against this concern.[77]

of his life were chemistry, astronomy and microscopy. (He was a founder of the Microscopical Society and in 1870, the year in which he died, was the Society's president.[80]) In 1838 he was elected an F.R.S. and early the next year commenced experiments in photography. Though subsequently remembered for little scientific originality, Reade did make an intelligent deduction from Wedgwood's experiments at the beginning of the century – in which leather was found to be more sensitive than paper in photographic experiments – by applying a tanning solution to paper by means of an infusion of galls.[81]

As we have seen (p. 128) Talbot began photographic experiments with gallic acid shortly after announcing photogenic drawing and a reconstruction of the role of Sir John Herschel and Reade – as well as that of Talbot himself – can be made now with some confidence. Herschel alerted Talbot to the possible value of 'gallate of silver' in a letter dated 28 February 1839 and evidence given by Andrew Ross the London instrument maker at the Laroche trial – though both he and Talbot advanced different and erroneous estimates of the date in court – may be interpreted to mean that sometime between 26 March (when Reade achieved improved results using nut galls) and 29 March[82] Reade told Ross of his work and that Ross passed the information to Talbot. This course of events seems to be confirmed by Talbot's letter to J. W. Lubbock bearing the pencilled date March 1839 in which he referred to the use of gallic acid having been mentioned to him by Herschel 'and another experimenter'. Talbot moved quickly for he ordered some crystallized gallic acid from one of his suppliers on 30 March and referred to Reade's discovery of the light-sensitivity of silver nitrate in association with gallic acid in his notebook on 5 April 1839.* Subsequent statements by Sir John Herschel – in his February 1840 paper to the Royal Society and his affidavit in Talbot's favour in the Henderson case in 1854 – appeared to indicate that he did not pursue any significant researches in the photographic use of gallic acid.

For his part, Reade communicated an outline of his photographic work to E. W. Brayley† in a letter dated 9 April 1839[83] (which was evidence in the

---

* Talbot's notebook Q at the Science Museum presents a tantalizing puzzle in that references by name to gallic acid on 20 September and 21 September 1840 – when he discovered the 'exciting liquid' which led to the Calotype system – were subsequently and neatly cut out from the page. There are no clues as to why this was done or by whom. The action is difficult to understand because Talbot had referred to gallic acid in full in notebooks before the two September dates – and did so afterwards though then he usually employed the typical abbreviations 'G' or 'GNS' (the latter for gallo-nitrate of silver) which were an obvious form of shorthand.

† An editor of the *Philosophical Magazine* (p. 74) who used the information in lectures given on 10 April and 2 May 1839.

Laroche trial) and claimed to have shown examples of his work at a soirée held by the Marquis of Northampton, President of the Royal Society, later that same month. However, he did not contribute any papers on the subject and no examples of his work have been traced subsequently. It may be concluded, therefore, that Reade did not pursue his researches (which were primarily directed at securing solar-microscope views) very far and they certainly did not arouse any public interest at the time.

There Reade's photographic work rested till David Brewster – who as the leading editor of the *Philosophical Magazine* was possibly informed about Reade's work by Brayley – later wrote an article on photography in the *North British Review* in which he referred to Reade's 'first public use of the infusion of nut-galls, which is an essential element of Mr Talbot's patented process' and for good measure dated Reade's use of hypo on the basis of a mistaken date for the Brayley letter to before published references on such use in photography by Herschel himself.[84] (The latter claim was in complete error but was an important element in the story of Reade as an independent inventor of photography for many years thereafter.) The potential implications of Brewster's comment about Reade's work with infusion of galls began to be realized as the 1840s neared their end and, once Talbot's patenting activity became a matter of serious controversy, Reade's evidence of the use of gallic acid years before Talbot registered his 1841 patent became a vital weapon in the attack on the patent. But in letters to Robert Hunt in 1854, at the Talbot-Laroche trial and for many years thereafter, Reade added another factor – that his experiments were conducted in 1836-7, i.e. that he discovered a form of photography before it was announced by either Daguerre or Talbot. Subsequent research has demonstrated reliably that Reade's experiments *followed* Henry Talbot's January 1839 announcement of photogenic drawing but that after the passage of almost fifteen years the events of January 1839 and February 1841 coalesced in Reade's memory and he projected his experiments two years forward from early 1839 instead of early 1841.* Similarly mention of the use of hypo which Reade communicated to Brayley in April 1839 was after publication of its photographic use by Sir John Herschel in his paper to the Royal Society in the previous month.

But all this was reconstructed painstakingly many years later. In the psycho-

---

* A letter in the Royal Society Collection – dated 28 February 1839 – in which Reade communicated details of his experiments to officers of the Society provides firm evidence that Reade's discovery was made after Talbot's announcement.[85]

logically intense and electric days of 1854 and at the Court of Common Pleas, the fact that an outward going, affable and modest amateur scientist – a comparison was bound to be drawn with Henry Talbot – had apparently experimented in photography with galls two years before Talbot announced photogenic drawing in 1839 let alone the Calotype in 1841 was a bombshell. That the *system* devised by Talbot owed to Reade only what it owed to Herschel – a mention of the possible use of gallic acid; that in devising his system Talbot could have derived no additional knowledge from Reade since the latter did not publish any experimental details concerning his experiments with a form of iodized paper until he mentioned them at the trial; and above all that Reade admitted that he had no knowledge whatsoever of the existence of the latent image (in which he was in company with Herschel) tended to go unnoticed.* That Reade in March 1839 used nut galls in photographic experimentation before Talbot seems certain: but that Talbot and not Reade had the scientific insight and deductive talent to evolve a practical photographic system embracing a concept still used in photography (the use of a developing agent after exposure) is equally certain. In the atmosphere of December 1854, however, and with Reade's unintentionally false evidence concerning the date of his work, it must be stated bluntly that Henry Talbot was fortunate to be left with the validity of his patent intact – even if on the slim technicality of non-publication by Reade of an alleged prior discovery.

The trial before Lord Chief Justice Jervis and a jury at the Guildhall in London took place from 18 to 20 December 1854. While Reade's testimony was directed against Talbot's claim to the patent, Robert Hunt† and a number of

---

* Talbot stated the situation well in a letter to Nevil Story-Maskelyne: 'Mr Reade's process was only an approximation toward a true system of photography – a step in the right direction, no more.' Henry initially found that Reade's process (without the use of iodized paper) 'failed entirely' – and that later, when he secured a result, the advantage in favour of the Calotype was near to '1000 to 1'.[86]

† Hunt has an established place as an early chronicler of the history of photography and as an energetic experimenter who also contributed to the study of light. His appearance for Laroche therefore was important. Notwithstanding, Story-Maskelyne – who was a capable experimenter and scientist in his own right – was highly critical of Hunt. '. . . he has written so much nonsense that it is no wonder that he has forgotten the glowing terms in which he describes your discovery in one of his earliest productions in which he speaks of the marvellous discovery by you of the possibility of a latent image being formed in the camera! . . . Why does Mr Hunt say nothing in that work of Mr Reade's process if it was known? This Mr Hunt ought to be shewn up. The means of doing so are easily reached. Ask every scientific man you put in as a witness what Mr Hunt's thousand announcements of discoveries come to. I am sure no one person will give him a word of support. For my own part, though I believe him to be really an amiable man, I have long been out of patience with him for the months of toil I wasted in trying to work his processes and never succeeded in bringing one of them to completion.'[87]

other chemists (of whom three were from London hospitals) concentrated on the dissimilarities between paper and collodion and between gallic acid and pyrogallic acid. Although the action of the collodion was still incompletely understood, Hunt argued that there were important differences in the methods of preparation, the degree of sensitization and the nature of the chemical reaction. Another witness for Laroche described the differences between gallic acid and pyrogallic acid as like those between 'sugar and vinegar', a comparison which lightened the gravity of the proceedings for a moment besides making a graphic point. The defendant's case was without doubt competently put even if – with the exception of Reade, Hunt, and perhaps Andrew Ross – few of the witnesses for Laroche left any prominent name in history.

Talbot's side, by contrast, contained some very famous names. One of his counsel was William R. Grove, F.R.S., a highly talented physicist and chemist, who was subsequently knighted and himself became a judge. (It was later stated that Talbot wished Grove to lead for him but that he was persuaded otherwise by his solicitors.[88]*) Witnesses for Talbot – who also gave evidence on his own behalf – included Dr Miller, Professor of Chemistry at King's College, London; Dr William Hofmann, Professor of Chemistry at the Metropolitan School of Science; Antoine Claudet; and W. T. Brande. William Thomas Brande had succeeded Humphry Davy as Professor of Chemistry at the Royal Institution in 1813 and was the author of the monumental text book *A Manual of Chemistry* (the fifth edition published in 1851 ran to 1,470 pages) which was a standard reference work for much of the century. His preparedness to give testimony on Talbot's behalf was an immense *coup* which made it all the more significant that the two lengthy accounts of the trial subsequently published virtually ignored his presence and evidence.* Even the young men appearing for Talbot – notably Nevil Story-Maskelyne and William Crookes – were later to achieve considerable scientific eminence. Their role was principally to report on practical experiments and to demonstrate the similarity between collodion and iodized paper, and between gallic acid and pyrogallic acid.

The debate on these technical matters was long and need not be recapitulated

---

* Talbot's leading counsel was Sir Frederick Thesiger. It was a difficult case for a non-scientist and Grove would certainly have been more effective. The *Art-Journal*, however, was guilty of partisan reporting when it claimed in its report on the trial that, 'In many of the scientific statements made by Sir Frederick Thesiger there was much want of accuracy.'[89]

* Brande later refused any fee for appearing as a witness – requesting instead a 'veritable Talbotype as a memento'.[90]

here other than to indicate that there was a considerable scientific basis for Talbot's contention that the Calotype and collodion were of the same genus. Both had features in common, both relied on physical development of the latent image, and although gallic acid and pyrogallic acid *were* in fact different chemicals their action was identical. But the case was a matter of legal interpretation as much as scientific fact and here the role of the Lord Chief Justice was of paramount importance. In his summing up before a no doubt confused jury he confessed on three separate occasions that he did not understand the subject and that on one occasion during the trial period it 'kept me awake all . . . night'.[91]

None the less he made a brave effort to simplify things for the jury, and his examination of the detail of the four claims made in Talbot's patent was both fair and sound. It was obviously proper, for example, that Talbot's claim to 'obtaining portraits from the life by photographic means upon paper' should be defined more narrowly as referring only to the methods appearing in the patent. In evaluating Reade's evidence, the Lord Chief Justice tended to play down the totally new aspects of the Calotype system patented by Talbot in 1841 – and particularly the existence of the latent image – and placed emphasis instead on Reade's failure to publicize discoveries which the latter described during the trial to be broadly in line with Talbot's. When the jury brought in its verdict under this head, they followed the judge's guidance. In answer to his question: 'Do you find that Mr Talbot was the first and true inventor?' the Foreman replied, 'Yes, the publisher.' The Chief Justice continued: 'That is within the meaning of the Patent Laws: that is, the first person who disclosed it to the public' – 'Yes.'[92] In fact, Talbot's achievement with the Calotype was far greater than being merely a matter of priority of publication.

As to the second issue – whether the collodion process infringed the Calotype patent – Chief Justice Jervis must have taken both sides by surprise for at the most critical point of his summing up he indicated that the claims and counter-claims made about gallic acid and pyrogallic acid were not the crucial issue, for the Calotype was developed by gallo-nitrate of silver and the collodion by pyrogallic acid – and *nowhere had any witness claimed that the gallo-nitrate of silver and pyrogallic acid were chemical equivalents.* Jervis went further: if iodized paper needed an application of gallic acid before exposure and collodion did not then they were not the same or equivalent. That iodized paper and collodion on paper both produced images when acted upon by gallo-nitrate of silver – which had been an important demonstration in Talbot's case – only proved that collodion was not spoiled by the application, which the Lord Chief Justice claimed did not prove that they were the same. Jervis nonetheless had doubts about his interpretation and he concluded his summing up by supposing that the action would proceed elsewhere: 'I have endeavoured to explain it as well as I can, and it is a question open I dare say to many difficult and serious objections which I have no doubt will be taken advantage of hereafter by the parties; and I hope they will do so.'[93]

None the less his interpretation of the chemical factors for the guidance of the jury (which took no account of the fact that gallic acid and silver nitrate could be applied separately in the Calotype process) was crucial – and the jury's finding that the defendant Laroche was not guilty was almost inevitable. That decision, the *Journal of the Photographic Society* recorded with some satisfaction 'was greeted by an attempt to applaud by several persons in court . . .'[94]

Talbot was bitterly disappointed by the result. 'This will I am afraid lead to fresh litigation,' he wrote to his wife on the same day. 'The jury understood little of the subject, but trusted to the judge, and the judge fell into awful mistakes, not being able to comprehend the process, *which* he had never seen tried . . . It is impossible we can rest content with the summing up [of] the judge.'[95] His bitterness continued for some time and a little later he wrote to Lord Lansdowne:

Nothing could be more illusory than such a trial. Neither Judge or Jury understood *anything* of photography . . . it was as if I or any other landsmen were called upon to hear evidence and pronounce judgement, on the conduct of a naval captain in a gale of wind. In that case I should doubtless err greatly in my conclusions yet not so greatly as the Lord Chief Justice the other day. At any rate I should not confound the mainmast with the mizenmast. I should know stem from stern. Would it be believed that *etiquette* prevented my counsel from interrupting the judge in summing up, and pointing out to him that he was going quite astray.[96]

It was little consolation to know that William Grove – who combined both expertise in science and law with marked objectivity so far as patents were concerned – also felt that the Lord Chief Justice had erred greatly in his summing up.[97]

There were still legal decisions to be made, however. The trial at the Guildhall had been a *nisi prius* hearing in which the jury only pronounced upon matters of fact, judgement being given when the jury's findings were passed to another court. Talbot could object and request a new trial. There was in addition the application to the Privy Council for an extension of the patent which was due to be heard before the Council's Judicial Committee on 10 January 1855. Despite his initial inclination to fight on, Talbot decided by the end of the first week in January neither to contest the decision of the trial nor to continue with the application to the Privy Council. Cost was an important factor for he calculated that renewal of the patent – which was of doubtful commercial value if collodion was not covered by it – would amount to some £500.[96] By coincidence £500 was the upper limit of the estimated costs faced by Laroche and – by April 1855 – only £105 had been contributed to the defence fund launched on his behalf.[98] Thus did his colleagues show their regard for his stand against Talbot.*

The Henderson case – which had been interrupted by the Laroche trial – had still to be concluded and with the Talbot defeat in the trial it was a matter of agreeing the level of costs and compensation for Henderson. The two sides could not agree and it went to the Court of Chancery. There was again a parade of affidavits (principally to establish how much loss Henderson might have suffered by the original injunction) and in March of 1856 Talbot was required to pay £150 in damages with the taxed costs in favour of Henderson being £210 3s. 6d.[99] By this time Henderson was living in Launceston and from there in April he wrote a letter to Talbot describing how much he had suffered from the case, declaring that he had not wished to infringe the patent and hoping that 'a gentleman of your standing would not wish a poor man like myself to be the sufferer'.[100] There is no record of Talbot's reply but we may surmise it was brief and to the point!

Talbot continued to take an active interest in the question of pictures on glass for some time since he still had two patents on the subject but collodion swept all before it in professional circles and in December 1855 he wrote to his lawyers announcing his intention to give up all his existing photographic patent rights. Among his last actions over these patents was the repayment of some licensees' fees – perhaps arising from the collodion decision, possibly from his abandonment of the other patents. His legal costs (including the Henderson

* There were some intriguing undertones in professional photography at this time. Whilst news of whether the jury's findings in the Laroche trial would be accepted or not was still awaited, a *Liverpool Photographic Journal* editorial noted: 'We know that many of the most skilful of the professional photographers are beginning to hope that he [the Vice-Chancellor] may decide in favour of Mr Talbot's claim, as they see the danger of throwing open the art to general inexperience in its present state; and fear that it may be annihilated in public favour by the vulgarising it would be sure to undergo in the hands of the unskilful practitioners who are ready to rush in . . .'[101]

O

payments) in the period from January 1855 to the middle of 1856 alone were
£742 5s. 0d.[102]

In the intense disappointment of this period Talbot could take some consolation from the attitude of those around him. The family was a great support
and Caroline fulfilled her promise to help with his legal expenses. However,
perhaps most of all he may have appreciated the very genuine expression of
sympathy from Nevil Story-Maskelyne:

I hope you will now let your mind grow quiet on the subject. I fear it must have cost
you much, not in pocket only but in time trouble & wearing anxiety, and not a little in
that mistrust and bitterness against one's fellow men, which this kind of annoying & really
selfish assaults upon one is so apt to engender.

From the beginning – since I became a man – I have always looked on the Photographic
idea as one of the true poet-ideas of this marvellous age – and on you as its herald and
enunciator. My sympathy is of little value to you – but you will always have it.[103]

As the years passed opinions were still offered on the outcome of the trial –
a Scottish academic in 1858 declaring that Talbot would have won his case in
Scotland because Scotland's judges and men of law 'know and practise'
photography[104] – and even further on Talbot, if he had known of it, might
have gained some satisfaction from the comment in his obituary in *The Times*
that the case was 'somewhat unsatisfactorily decided'.[105] Talbot and Scott
Archer never met but in 1857 Thomas Malone and Talbot discussed various
patent matters and the subject of Archer arose. Malone felt that:

Archer should have had some *reward* or *share of profit* from his labours in finding &
practically using the *best vehicle* for your gallo-nitrate and iodised silver. He might *I think*
have patented collodion as an improved vehicle and required your licensees to come to
him for this article. Or you might have found it convenient to arrange with Archer . . .[106]

Talbot replied:

With respect to Mr Archer, if he had patented his collodion process, early enough, the
result would probably have been that he would have acquired a large fortune by it. But on
the other hand he would have lost the credit which he now has, or ought to have, of having
presented the invention gratuitously to the Public. So there is something to be said on
both sides of the question.[107]

So Talbot was not blind to the glory that might accrue from presenting a discovery free to the public. But his own attitudes remained unchanged, for the

year after this exchange of letters he took out his twelfth and final patent – that for photoglyphic engraving (Chapter 9).

The attempt has been made in this chapter to analyse the controversy that arose around Talbot's photographic patents and which gave rise to criticism both at the time and since. Allegations of dishonesty cannot be substantiated. He genuinely believed the collodion process to be basically similar to the Calotype – and the other claims made in the four patents were with rare exceptions very specific and did not cover the vast areas of photography which his critics (few of whom probably knew the detailed contents of the patents since they were not easily available until the Patents Act of 1852) claimed. Indeed some of his claims were so narrow and specific that it is doubtful whether on their own they would have formed a commercially exploitable product and therefore ones which – paradoxically – there was much purpose in patenting. On those occasions where a claim became erroneously more general he had the Lord Chief Justice of England's advice as a form of exculpation!

In retrospect it can be argued that this was a regrettable chapter in Talbot's life which besmirched his great achievements – that this perhaps pedantic and stubborn approach to his patents (particularly in the 1850s) showed a lack of balance and judgement.* We have seen that there was a strong feeling at the time that was opposed to patents in general as an affront to the developing 'liberty' in which the new Victorian society was revelling and this fuelled the specific objections which some interested in the new art and science of photography felt about Talbot's actions – whether through genuine belief or simply because they were not prepared to pay patent fees where it was easy to argue against the patent validity for some reason. With a new invention which essentially affected *individuals* – amateur or professional – the patentee faced what seemed to some then, and certainly appears so now, a fight on so

---

* This inflexibility – which was out of character when judged by Talbot's general attitudes and outlook on life – was revealed elsewhere in a photographic context. At the York meeting of the BAAS in 1844, for example, he became involved in an exchange with Robert Hunt and others on the proliferation of 'new' photographic techniques which he regarded as being basically variations of the Calotype system and which yet had been given exotic new names – Hunt's *Energiatype* and Dr Thomas Wood's *Catalysotype* being typical examples. (Talbot's main objection in fact was to the proliferation of *names*.) It was a shortsighted and unwise approach: he should have let the 'inventors' have their day and leave time to take care of the rest for few of the systems introduced were successful and virtually all disappeared from photographic history with scarcely a trace left.

widespread a scale as to make defence impossible and costly, and ultimate defeat inevitable. Talbot chose to fight on – and the manoeuvres required to locate infringers and to move against them might seem distasteful and certainly wearisome. The only people to benefit were the lawyers. But not to agree with the deeply held beliefs of some sections of the society in which he lived was not a crime even if in retrospect it may seem not worth the anguish and controversy that resulted and Talbot was far from being alone amongst scientists and inventors in believing in the patent system and facing the troublesome results. The point needs to be stressed that the patent system did survive in Britain and it was and is for individuals to decide whether to patent or to give their discoveries free to the public with the approbation which that might bring. Moreover, we are what we are and the stubbornness of which Talbot can be accused arose from the character trait displayed as persistence in experimentation which led to the shape of modern photography.

There is one final and important aspect of Talbot's photographic patents to be considered. In their *History of Photography* Helmut and Alison Gernsheim claimed that Talbot's patents had a severe effect on the progress of photography in Britain – 'a most serious check' and a 'crippling effect' were typical phrases used.[108] Subsequently this judgement has been incorporated into other accounts of the history of photography and of science. But how valid is it?

The progress of the Calotype, as was seen in Chapter 5, was extremely slow in the 1840s – partly because of the need to gain practical experience in the process and improve its reliability, partly because of Talbot's inadequate commercial exploitation. The drive, organization and inspiration to promote the new process were missing. Talbot never devised a consistent scheme of fees for professionals (which should have been low enough to attract greater numbers) and the absence of an authoritative manual on the technique which would have improved the satisfaction achieved was a weakness. At the professional level therefore, the Daguerreotype was not seriously rivalled for portraiture until the arrival of the collodion wet process. Thus, if Talbot had a patent (and later took out three additional patents) which he failed to develop commercially with full vigour it may be regarded as axiomatic that photography would be prevented to some degree from fulfilling its potential – although it could be argued equally that a practical system of paper photography might not have arrived as early as 1839–41 if Talbot had not invented it. However, it is not so much the lack of progress of the Calotype itself in the 1840s which has formed the substance of the accusations against Talbot but his claim to collodion and the alleged curbs resulting from his later patents which included albumen on glass and other techniques. These must be examined as they affected different sectors in photography.

Before the 'renunciation' of 1852, amateur licence fees were either very low or non-existent. Whether it concerned Calotype photography only or the later developments which included glass plates (assuming at the worst that Talbot would have regarded the latter as being included generally within his patents) can it be argued seriously that such payments required of the members of the rising middle classes and others were substantial enough to check the development of amateur photography in Britain? It seems most unlikely though the need to secure *any* form of licence was irksome to some.

The practice of photography for scientific experimentation was never curbed in any way by Talbot, which leaves the major issue of professional photography. With Scott Archer's announcement of collodion in 1850–51, a lower priced and less elaborate process than the Daguerreotype was placed in the hands of the professional portraitist and there can be no doubt that the fees required by Talbot must have restricted to some degree the numbers of portraitists taking up the new medium. If a rapid expansion of professional portraiture is to be interpreted as 'progress' – an interpretation with which not all would agree – then this was a restriction on progress.

Statistics are notoriously malleable in support of arguments but it is pertinent to refer to figures quoted by the Gernsheims concerning the number of portrait studios in London.[109] Between 1851 and 1855 (which could only include a very few months of freedom from the effects of Talbot's patent) there was a more than fivefold increase – from 'about a dozen' to 66. Between 1855 and 1861 there was only an approximately threefold increase – from 66 to 'over 200' – whereas with an absence of any patent restrictions during the entire period a far greater comparative rate of growth might have been expected. These figures are not advanced as evidence to exonerate Talbot but only to show that the situation was by no means as clear cut as the Gernsheims have argued.

But there is an even more important factor which has been left out of consideration and this stems again from the failure of photographic historians generally to put the history of photography in its wider context. As the 1840s advanced, the progress of the British economy quickened – albeit not consistently – and by the time of the Great Exhibition of 1851 was set fair for major expansion. As often happens, it took time for the country to realize that within its grasp were the organizational and technological skills upon which a surge forward both at home and as an imperial power could be based – but within a few years the economic horizon appeared unbounded. Economic statistics for the period are relatively limited but the quickening of the economy at home is suggested by the indicators for 'real wages' in the United Kingdom which rose from an index of 94 in 1855, to 105 in 1860 and 117 in 1866.[110] If the life of the working man was still extremely hard, the growing professional, skilled and clerical classes – who were the natural target in the exploitation of innovations – certainly shared in the increase in wealth. Here was the professional portraitists' major market and here was the source of the growing army of amateur photographers. Thus the growth in photography generally in the 1850s and beyond must reflect at least in part the growth of prosperity and it is at least possible that a major expansion would have taken place whether Talbot's patents had remained in being or not. The extent of that increase is impossible to calculate and more research is needed on this important aspect of the history of photography before the situation may be outlined with a greater degree of sureness. The point is, however, that whatever restrictions may have resulted from Talbot's patents, and the unwillingness of some professional photographers to pay licence fees, to attribute the expansion in photography from the 1850s onwards solely or even to a considerable degree to the ending of those patents is unproven supposition.

There is one last part of the case against Talbot to be considered. It was argued at the time (and since) that Henry Talbot's patenting activities restricted the progress of photography in the sense that those workers who discovered improvements did not publish because they feared that Talbot might patent the improvements. There was a suggestion of this thinking in the Rosse–Eastlake letter of 1852 when reference was made to the 'difficulties which now appear to hinder the progress of the art in England'. The point has already been made that the pressure exerted on Talbot at that time – when a select committee of the House of Lords was examining patent matters – probably owed as much to general reservations about the patent system *per se* as to specific objections to the situation in photography. But in any case, there was surely one irrefutable proof of the validity or otherwise of the anti-Talbot argument: following 1854–5 and the abandoning of the photographic patents there should have been a surge of new discoveries published by inspired researchers and inventors who, the argument ran, had only been waiting for the tyranny of Talbot's rule to end. One or two years might be allowed for the pace of invention to quicken but by 1856 or 1857 an explosion of meaningful and important innovation should have been apparent. In fact the popular photographic products of the period from about 1855 onwards – collodion positives, tintypes and the *cartes de visite* – were all discovered in the period before 1855 and very few major photographic innovations took place in Britain between the ending of Talbot's patents and the suggestion by Dr Richard Leach Maddox of gelatin dry plates in September 1871 – sixteen years later. How can this be interpreted to support the thesis that Talbot's patenting activities restricted the progress of photography?

It is possible that Henry Talbot's patents did exert an untoward influence on the development of photography in Britain although it would require extensive and careful research to distinguish cause from effect in the complex socio-economic–technical conditions of mid–century Victorian England. His soundness of judgement in some directions may be challenged, and the views of those opposed to patents on deeply felt philosophical grounds had a considerably persuasive attraction. But the sweeping generalizations made by some historians – and notably the Gernsheims – have been based on the obviously self-interested, one sided anti-Talbot arguments of the 1850s and such statements as 'Understandably, *everyone* [this author's italics] interested in photography was indignant at Talbot's patenting activities,'[111] are the language of the propagandist rather than the objective historian. And it simply was not true.

Roger Fenton, a famous name in Victorian photography, corresponded little with Talbot but it was noticeable that he clearly had – and continued to have – a considerable admiration for Talbot and his achievements.[112] There was also one other figure in photography – Antoine Claudet – who stood over all others in terms of achievement, scientific accomplishment, and knowledge of the various forms of photography. He gave evidence for Talbot on several occasions during the patent litigation and in 1855 he declined the offer of a fee for his assistance in words which form a fitting conclusion to this chapter:

[He] has been only actuated by a wish of helping Mr Talbot against those who have had the injustice of trying to encroach upon his rights & who instead of remunerating him for his beautiful discoveries in Photography have endeavoured to deprive him even of the honor of being the inventor of the art by which they wanted to get their living. Mr Talbot like many other great men has been shamefully and ungratefully treated by his countrymen and his age & I have been happy to be able to raise my voice, as feeble as it is, in endeavouring to support his noble and just cause. As a photographer & a disciple of Science I only fulfilled a duty towards the Philosopher, father of Photography in England, and this requires no fee.[113]

Having taken the account of Talbot's purely photographic work to its conclusion, we must return now to the year 1840 to follow his many other activities.

7
Applied Science and Etymology

In the decade following the discovery of the Calotype process and all that ensued in photography, Henry Talbot was busy in other applied scientific fields. Here too he took out patents – six in all – but happily they did not result in the controversy aroused by the photographic patents.

One area of his work was in what would now be called industrial coating technology and was concerned in particular with *electrolysis* – the chemical decomposition of substances (usually in a dissolved or molten state) by an electric current when passed through them. The decomposition of water and of metallic salts by the passage of an electric current was observed very shortly after the appearance of Volta's pile in 1800 and as early as 1805 gilded silver medals had been produced by immersing the medals – as the negative electrode (or *cathode*) of a voltaic pile or battery – in a suitable salt of gold.* However, it was not until about 1837 that a number of workers, including the German physicist and engineer Moritz von Jacobi and Thomas Spencer of Liverpool, realized that copper deposited on objects in a cell or battery was an exact replica of the surface of the plate, could be stripped off, and that non-conducting surfaces could be prepared to receive metallic deposition by dusting or rubbing with graphite. It was a short step to the preparation of moulds upon which

---

* The basic process of electrolysis may be most easily understood by imagining a simple electric cell. In one compartment a zinc electrode is immersed in, say, sulphuric acid and a current is generated. The current passes via a wire to an object – perhaps a medal – which is immersed in a metallic salt, copper sulphate. In such a case copper is released by decomposition and is deposited on the surface of the medal. This may be left as a form of coating or plating or be removed when it forms a 'negative' mould of the original surface. If the process is repeated using the mould, a facsimile of the original medal will be produced in copper.

electro-deposition took place although Spencer concentrated initially on the production of plates which were selectively built up by deposition and then used as printing plates. This process of producing copies of articles by the electrolytic deposition of a metal layer on a previously prepared surface or mould came to be called *electrotyping* – and the actual deposition of the metal *electroplating*. As the techniques evolved, increasing attention was paid to the electrolytic method of depositing one metal on a different metal. The serious problem of the early years was the period of time taken for the deposition process – a matter of days – but a contemporary work on electro-metallurgy[1] described the years after 1839–40 as seeing an 'electrotyping mania'. Between 1839 and 1841 at least ten patents were taken out and one worker – a Dr Leeson – was reported to have embraced in his patent almost every metal which could be deposited and almost all known solutions of their salts.

Talbot was fully aware of this intense activity and while the two patents he took out in 1841 and 1842 were not concerned primarily with electrotyping as such, they were intended as ancillary processes to be employed (hopefully) in the new industry. As such they owed much to his knowledge of photographic chemistry.

The first patent had the short title *Coating and Coloring Metallic Surfaces* (No. 9,167) and was taken out on 9 December 1841. It was in four parts. (*a*) Talbot proposed the addition of a solution of gallic acid to a metallic solution – for example of silver, gold or platinum – to facilitate the precipitation of the appropriate metals upon other metallic surfaces and 'coating them therewith'. (*b*) For the silvering of metallic surfaces, freshly precipitated silver chloride was to be dissolved in sodium hyposulphite (or any other liquid hyposulphite). The plate to be coated was immersed in the solution and electrolysis could be used to obtain thicker coats of silver. Talbot claimed as part of the patent the use of a battery for obtaining thicker deposits of silver, gold or platinum but only when used with the liquids described.* (*c*) When ornamenting surfaces of brass or copper with a gilded pattern, it was suggested that the object be washed with a solution of platinum chloride which would have no action on the gilt surfaces, but would give a dead black appearance to the rest of the surface, thus enhancing the brilliancy of the gilt. (*d*) Talbot finally proposed the colouring of polished copper surfaces by exposing them to the vapour of hydrogen sulphide, any of the liquid sulphides or to the

---

* James Napier specifically rejected this silvering method in his account of current industrial processes on the basis that light decomposed the solution depositing silver as a 'sulphuret'.[2]

vapours of iodine, bromine or chlorine. Various colours could be obtained and 'by partially protecting the surface of the metal according to any determinate or ornamental pattern, very pleasing effects are produced, exhibiting great contrast of colors in a little space'. White was one of the colours that could be obtained and Talbot suggested that electrotyped copper mirrors for telescopes could be treated in this manner (p. 249).*

   Gilding and Silvering Metals was the short title of the second patent (No. 9,528) taken out on 25 November 1842. There were six parts. (*a*) It was proposed that improved gilding would result from a pre-silvering of the object – the silver coating to be very thin and hardly visible. (*b*) Prior to gilding or silvering, an article should be cleaned electrolytically – by attaching it to one of the electrodes of a battery and then plunging both the poles into a vessel containing a mixture of water with any appropriate acid or salt – although not gold, silver or any other metal in solution.

   The battery must be so arranged that decomposition of the water in the vessel may ensue, and that the article operated on may give off hydrogen gas ... It is then to be quickly detached from the battery and immediately thrown into another vessel containing a proper solution of gold or silver, whereby it soon receives a coating of one of those metals. It is then taken out and washed in a third vessel, containing pure water. [The coating could be built up by repeating the entire process.]

(*c*) In gilding metallic surfaces, a mixture of gold and a solution of one of the baser metals (for example zinc iodide) should be employed in a progressive coating process in which the proportion of gold was increased. (Talbot specifically excluded mercury from the claim since gilding using an amalgam of gold and mercury was an established process.) (*d*) When gilding articles of brass or other metals using a solution of gold chloride, the addition of boracic acid, it was suggested, produced a more pleasing colour than the chloride alone. (*e*) Sometimes the colour of gilded objects was too dark. Talbot proposed that they be dipped into a very weak solution of mercury nitrate in water 'which soon causes the surface to brighten and acquire more lustre'. The process could be repeated and any excess of mercury removed electrolytically by placing the article in a battery circuit. (*f*) Gilding or silvering could be facilitated by

* In April 1841, Charles Wheatstone proposed that some of his electrotyping 'improvements' be included in Talbot's forthcoming patent but the contents of the latter indicate that the idea was not pursued. Regulating equipment for use in electrotyping was included in a Wheatstone patent (No. 9,022) taken out in July 1841 so it is possible that it was to this that he referred in his April letter to Talbot.[3]

ensuring that articles were dipped intermittently in different solutions of silver or gold or of some other metal – a slight coating of which being obtained by electrolytic action. This was a means of overcoming the slowing down (or cessation) of the coating process which occurred when the metal on the surface of the article being coated became too similar to that in the solution.

Talbot's two patents stemmed partially from his awareness of current industrial processes – and presumably the gaps in them; his experiments in photography; and his general chemical experiments over several decades – it was, after all, a gilding experiment which resulted in the explosion at Harrow School in 1812. Apart from the possibility of the industrial exploitation of any of the proposals, it may have been that he was aware of the extreme health hazards inherent in existing processes and was therefore proposing some which were less dangerous alternatives. One of the methods of gilding employed industrially even after the adoption of electroplating was to brush an amalgam of gold and mercury over the object at high temperature. Volatile mercury was given off and a contemporary writer described the results as 'most pernicious' and 'destructive to human life'.[4] Mercury insinuated itself into the bodies of workmen, he continued, notwithstanding the greatest care. 'Paralysis is common among them, and the average of their lives is very short: it has been estimated as not exceeding 35 years.'

The methods of gilding and silvering by electrolysis were also not without dangers. The electroplating solutions were prepared by dissolving silver cyanide or a gold oxide in potassium cyanide. The same writer stated that he could not 'stand as an advocate' of the 'ominous gas' given off during the process and stressed the need for effective ventilation. From first-hand experience he described the effects of inadequate ventilation – bleeding from the nose, giddiness, blindness and languor.[5] Some, at least, of Talbot's proposals were less hazardous to health.

They were not, however, taken up commercially. In the spring of 1843 an editor of the *Polytechnic Journal* asked for details of the first patent which he considered 'may be applied to most extensive and important uses'[6] and as late as 1848 a Birmingham company was proposing a meeting to arrange a licence from Henry Talbot for the use of his 'electroplate patent'.[7] There were apparently no further developments although Henry continued to conduct coating experiments for some time. Some of these significantly included the use of potassium bichromate[8] – which was doubtless to provide valuable experience for the later researches in photo-engraving.

Electricity presented the same challenge to Henry Talbot as to many other experimenters of the period and in the course of a dozen years from 1840 he took out four patents on various aspects of motive power. His first – dated 1 October 1840 (No. 8,650) – described three different types of motor each of which was intended to convert electrical energy into mechanical energy.

Two of the motors were attempts to make closed-cycle heat engines in which the heat to the working fluid was provided electrically. Unfortunately on the evidence of the specification Talbot seemed to have forgotten that a heat engine was only able to do work by virtue of absorbing heat at a high temperature from a heat source and rejecting it at a lower temperature into a 'sink'. His motors had a heat source but there was no provision for a heat sink.

In the first motor, hot gas was provided in two stages. Firstly an electrolyte (acidulated water) was decomposed by the passage of an electric current into oxygen and hydrogen. The two gases were then recombined by heating a platinum wire and exploding the gas mixture at an appropriate moment. The piston would then move under the influence of the short explosion product – in this case steam – to the extremity of its stroke. This was sound but when the piston made its return stroke it would recompress the water vapour and the work necessary to do this would equal that obtained during the expansion stroke – hence the water vapour would end up at the same temperature as before. In other words, no net work would have been done during the complete cycle of expansion followed by compression. To make a practical engine of the kind outlined by Talbot, it would have been necessary either to exhaust the water vapour at the end of the expansion stroke to the atmosphere or to cool the water vapour during the compression stroke. Both solutions would pose practical problems rendering any motor working on these lines more complex than he had envisaged.

The other heat motor was somewhat similar to the first except that heat was imparted to the working gas via a platinum filament heated by an electric current. The gas then expanded driving the piston upwards but once again no provision was made for any heat removal at the end of the expansion stroke. Unless Talbot deliberately left out detail to hinder any competitors it must be concluded from the patent that his knowledge of heat engines was limited – and, in any case, this type of engine when constructed would suffer from a characteristic disadvantage: the low conversion-efficiency of heat into available mechanical energy for doing work.

No such disadvantage attached to the third motor described in the patent – an electromagnetic device in which an electric current was used to produce a magnetic field at the poles of an electromagnet. The electromagnet attracted a keeper or armature to itself, and by coupling this armature to a wheel and crank mechanism, useful work could be done as the electromagnet was switched on and off. A further refinement of the idea was to have a number of electromagnets connected to the same bar which operated in sequence so that force could be produced over a longer stroke. Talbot's proposals for this motor were more soundly based than those for the heat engines even though there were few, if any, individual points of originality to distinguish his ideas from those circulating generally at the time.

Almost five years passed before the next patent (No. 10,539) was taken out on 3 March 1845. No less than eight different ideas were included and it may be assumed that Henry Talbot had determined to limit the costs of patenting by embracing a number of quite diverse subjects in the one patent.

The first three proposals related to heat engines and developed themes from 1840. In the first, he employed a frozen solid – carbonic acid, i.e. frozen carbon dioxide – as the medium. This was to be heated electrically and the expansion of the resulting gas used to do work. The idea was somewhat similar in principle to using an electric kettle to boil water and then to use the steam to drive the steam engine – not a very effective or efficient way to convert electrical energy into motion. The second idea showed that Talbot's ideas on heat engines had advanced since 1840 for he now realized that a heat engine needed a sink as well as a heat source. He proposed the liquid and gas phases of carbonic acid to achieve this – which would have meant the whole engine being subjected to high internal pressures in order to keep the carbon dioxide liquid. His third proposal envisaged using an expandible liquid as a working medium for a heat engine, an idea which could no doubt have been made to work in some way but as expressed in the patent demonstrated little regard for practical considerations.

The following three parts of the patent were devoted to electromagnetism. Two of the proposals were somewhat vague and scarcely developed but the third was an extension of his idea to produce an attractive force by means of an electromagnet and then convert that force into rotary motion. The problem with his 1840 electromagnetic engine was that it exerted a large force over a small distance. In the new patent, he proposed to overcome the disadvantage by placing a large number of electromagnets mechanically in series. The result that he intended was to couple say 100 magnets together, each of stroke one tenth of an inch and so to obtain an overall stroke of ten inches. (That is, the total motion of the end magnet would be ten inches when magnetized, this magnet being attached by a rod to the crank of a fly wheel.)

Unfortunately such an arrangement was not of itself stable unless some mechanical constraint was introduced – such as keeping the change in the relative air gaps between each and every magnet the same at all times. As described and without any apparent mechanical linkage – for instance some form of 'lazy tongs' device to which all the magnets were attached – the application of current to the electromagnets would result in unbalanced magnetic forces and consequent instability. (Evidently Talbot had not put his idea fully into practice for he would have discovered the difficulties immediately and mentioned in the patent the need for a restraint of some kind.) The principal interest of this proposal, however, was Henry Talbot's specification of *surface magnets* – putting conductors into slots instead of winding them around discrete iron cores which was the conventional method. Burying the conductors in slots is modern machine practice and the impression is sometimes given that the practice dates from the 1880s. That this was not the case is demonstrated by the fact that in 1845 Henry Talbot did not claim the idea as his own – and, indeed, it had featured in an earlier Wheatstone patent.

As if to underline his versatility, the last two parts of the patent described a horizontal axis windmill – in which it was not necessary to screen the blades from the wind for part of their rotation – and a number of improved methods of sealing the tube of an atmospheric railway. In the latter, Talbot was shrewdly making proposals concerning an issue of great topical interest, since 1845 marked the peak of excitement in atmospheric railways as a possible rival to the steam railways.* In the system a long tube was laid between the rails with a leather seal along the top. Into this tube a piston was inserted with a projection which came out at the top of the tube through the leather seal and was attached to the train. A partial vacuum of about 35 centimetres of mercury was

---

* Four operational railways were built in the period from 1844–60 totalling thirty miles of single track. They were the first to provide a fast, frequent, cheap and clean urban commuter rail service and caused the first experimental underground lines to be built both in Britain and the United States. The system worked well but was expensive to build, needed much developmental work before it could become truly efficient, had operating inconveniences (a single track working made junctions and stations a continual source of problems) and had virtually all of the vested interests of steam – including Robert Stephenson himself – ranged against it. The ultimate failure was perhaps inevitable. (For an account of their history see *Atmospheric Railways – A Victorian Venture in Silent Speed* by Charles Hadfield: David & Charles, 1967.)

created on one side of the piston by a suction engine at intervals alongside the track and the normal air pressure on the other side was then sufficient to propel the train. The seal was a potential weakness of the system and it was to this that Talbot directed his proposals which included a modified positioning of elastic cushions in the operation of the tube and a method of moving aside the elastic cushions before the train's connecting bar reached them thus removing the friction.

Talbot was in contact early in 1846[9] with Hallette's Atmospheric Railway and Canal Propulsion Company – a British subsidiary of France's biggest steam-engine manufacturer and one of the companies promoting atmospheric railways. Hallette had patented its own valve system so the company's obvious concern for the integrity of the tube meant that Talbot's approach was a wise one. However no practical results ensued. Indeed, none of the proposals made in the 1845 patent were developed commercially, and the vague if not impractical nature of some of the concepts included underlined his diversity and lively imagination rather than his seriousness at the time as a practical experimenter and innovator in motive power techniques.

In the following year (patent No. 11,475 taken out on 7 December 1846) Henry Talbot added another rider to his work on heat engines. Instead of heating liquids or inflammable gases, he now proposed the introduction of discrete charges of explosives (specifically gun cotton) into the cylinder. The charges were contained in cavities in a rod which was introduced into the cylinder at the appropriate instant and then detonated electrically – the detonations operating a piston arrangement as before. Again there was no indication that the proposed unit was constructed and since the principle of the internal-combustion engine was known by this time the new proposals demonstrated a sense of loyalty to heat engines rather than any great novelty.

But the fourth and last motive power patent – No. 1,046 dated 13 December 1852 – was important for it was almost certainly the first to be devoted exclusively to a linear electric motor. A large number of electromagnets were arranged in a line with their pole faces uppermost. A large diameter iron cylinder – which could be hollow – was arranged so as to run on the surface formed by the electromagnets. On either side of the running surface were two commutators one for running in each direction. Their function was to excite the electromagnets just ahead of the iron cylinder, thus providing a source of attraction which enabled the cylinder to roll towards the energizing magnet. Once over the energized magnet, the commutator switched off the current and energized the adjacent magnet so moving the cylinder on by a further stage. When the cylinder reached the end of the row of electromagnets the process was reversed – instead of the magnets being energized in the order 1, 2, 3, 4, 5 . . . they were energized in the sequence 5, 4, 3, 2, 1 . . . The whole distance traversed by the moving cylinder communicated motion to the rest of the machinery, its axis being attached to a crank and fly wheel.

What Talbot proposed in fact was the production of a travelling magnetic field and the use of an iron cylinder was reminiscent of the cylinder in one of Charles Wheatstone's electric 'eccentric' engines* built some years earlier – Talbot's machine being in effect an unrolled form of the same principle. Wheatstone had contemplated such a modification in his patent of 1841 and recent research has shown that he built a linear motor some time in the 1840s.[10] Only he and Talbot of the early inventors of electric motors devoted attention to the problem of obtaining linear motion (as distinct from rotary) over a considerable distance. The concept was eminently sound and the idea of a travelling magnetic field is fundamental to the modern alternating current generator and motor – for instance, the rotor of an induction motor is dragged round by a moving magnetic field in a rather similar way that the tides are made to move around the earth under the influence of the gravitational field of the moon.

No practical applications of Talbot's (or Wheatstone's) linear motor proposals took place in the 1840s but considerable attention has been devoted to the concept in recent years. Linear motors are used in situations – in crane drives for example – where it is necessary to move a load along a long beam, but the greatest current research effort is without doubt being directed to the use of the motors in high-speed transport.

It seems that only one electric motor was built to Talbot's specification – that contained in the 1840 patent – and fortunately Robert Hunt gave a brief description of it in a comprehensive paper on *Electro-Magnetism as a Motive Power*[11] that he delivered to the Institution of Civil Engineers in 1857:

---

* The basic idea behind eccentric motors was to convert the short stroke of an electromagnet into the equivalent of a long stroke. Wheatstone proposed to do this by means of an eccentric motion such that instead of an inner cylinder (the rotor) being concentric with an outer cylinder (the stator) with magnets on it that were energized in sequence to attract the rotor, the latter was arranged to act as if it were rolling around the bore of the stator. (Imagine a 10p piece sliding around inside a very small diameter jam-jar lid.) Since the centre of the cylinder forming the rotor was moving on a small diameter circle, the force of motion had to be picked up by means of a crank or 'eccentric'. Such motors were intriguing but were not in the main-stream development of electric motors.

P

Mr Talbot's engine was 3 feet 6 inches long, and 2 feet 6 inches wide; when excited by a Grove's battery, consisting of four cells with double plates of zinc 9 inches by 6½ inches, platinum plates 9 inches by 5½ inches, excited by diluted sulphuric acid in the proportions of 1 to 4, and concentrated nitric acid, it drove a lathe, with which was turned a gun-metal pulley 5 inches in diameter . . .

The motor was made for Talbot by William T. Henley – who was an experimenter in electromagnetism in his own right as well as a first-class 'instrument maker' and whose name is chiefly remembered now for his part in the later manufacture of telegraph cables. Henley completed the motor in August of 1842 and commented that it worked well and possessed considerable power – indeed, with some modification to the contact breaking apparatus, he later thought that it developed more power than the eccentric electric motor he had built for Charles Wheatstone.[12]*

Early in 1843 Francis Watkins – another instrument maker from whom Talbot purchased much of his electrical equipment – was negotiating on his behalf for the renting of a room at the Adelaide Gallery† in which to demonstrate the engine but nothing apparently came of the idea.[13] It was also Watkins who suggested to Talbot that a discourse on electromagnetic engines which William Grove was giving at the Royal Institution on 10 February 1843 would present a good opportunity to introduce the motor to the scientific world. Talbot proposed the idea to Grove – expressing the belief that the engine was 'more powerful in proportion to its size than any hitherto made' but expressing some doubts whether the engine would be ready for the lecture since it was undergoing some modifications.[14] Grove welcomed the proposal and the prospect of a discussion with Talbot on the subject but it is not clear whether the motor was included in the lecture.[15]

Although there were no practical results, Talbot's ideas clearly came to the notice of engineers and industrialists both in England and on the Continent. In February 1846 a cotton-mill owner expressed interest in carbonic gas as a source of power[16] but it may be assumed that the matter went no further since Talbot was asked about other mills already incorporating his ideas and it was

* While there was no disagreement about the power developed by the motor Talbot did criticize the construction as not being to his specification. Henley and he could not agree on the matter and it went eventually to lawyers before payment of £56 was made by Henry in 1843.

† The full title of the gallery was the *Gallery of Practical Science* and it was located in Adelaide Street close to the Strand in London. It was established by a group of wealthy benefactors for the education of the public in science and engineering.

bluntly stated that no order would be placed 'without having a sufficient guarantee that it will work well' – a guarantee he probably could not have given. The proposals about the use of gun cotton attracted interest in Switzerland and joint developmental work was proposed in 1847.[17] There were however already considerable demands on Talbot's financial resources and he could not contemplate the idea.

Only one problem arose over alleged patent infringement. At the end of 1842, the talented Scotsman Robert Davidson staged an exhibition devoted to electromagnetism as a motive power at the Egyptian Hall in Piccadilly. This included an electric locomotive engine carrying passengers on a circular railway but Talbot considered that a smaller motor driving a small circular saw infringed his 1840 patent. He asked his lawyers to contact Davidson but stressed:

. . . that it is not at all my wish to prevent the exhibition . . . on the contrary I will with pleasure give Mr Davidson my licence and permission to continue to exhibit [the machine], as I believe him to be a very ingenious man, provided that he will give me an undertaking not to make any other Engine or mould in the principle of my patent in England and Wales without my written licence and permission so to do.[18]

It was a wish that Davidson promptly agreed to and – in his own words – 'cheerfully' so.[19]

The first contact between Charles Wheatstone and Talbot was an unpropitious one and took place in the pages of the *Philosophical Magazine and Journal of Science*. In a paper 'On the velocity of electricity'[20] Talbot had referred to some 'ingenious' experiments which had recently been made by Wheatstone to determine the velocity of an electric spark passing through air and then proceeded to outline his own ideas for determining the speed of electricity through a conducting body by means of a revolving mirror. Wheatstone replied sharply in the next issue[21] that from the beginning his experiments were intended to extend to the passage of electricity through solid conductors, that he had already communicated his intention of conducting a major experiment (along the lines suggested by Talbot), that he had delayed communicating an incomplete record of his experiments to the Royal Society, and regretted:

. . . that this delay should have occasioned my experiments to be so far misunderstood, that one of the earliest which suggested itself to me, and which I have always considered to be of primary importance in the series, should be proposed elsewhere, several months afterwards, as an experiment yet to be tried, and be presented also as having entirely escaped my attention.

Wheatstone's response was somewhat unjust since there was no reason to believe that Henry Talbot knew of the future experiments that he had planned nor was he making the implied criticism of Wheatstone's experimental obtuseness which the latter supposed. Talbot none the less came back and – on the evidence of Wheatstone's statement – yielded him priority in the large-scale experiment to determine the velocity of electricity using a revolving mirror.[22] Evidently, the disagreement was amicably resolved for Wheatstone was one of the leading scientists who accepted an invitation to stay at Lacock Abbey before the Bristol meeting of the British Association for the Advancement of Science in 1836 (p. 80).

By then Wheatstone had been appointed Professor of Experimental Philosophy at King's College, London and had already established a considerable reputation for himself as an experimenter in sound and electricity though his major work in telegraphy still lay in the future. Like others he devoted attention to electric motors and it was in their development that he and Talbot cooperated in the early 1840s. The relationship was an interesting one because it not only involved exchanges of ideas but Talbot's financial support of some of Wheatstone's experiments.

As early as December 1840, Wheatstone was writing to Talbot:[23]

I have consulted an intelligent workman who says he will undertake to make an electrolytic engine with a single cylinder according to the drawing I showed you, for ten guineas, and he seems to be quite confident that it will succeed and be a good working model. All the funds that I can command at present are employed in the improvement of my telegraphic apparatus, and I have none to spare for other purposes; but if you are still inclined to defray the expenses of the experiment I will put it in hand immediately. When it is completed we shall see whether anything is to be expected from the application of the principle.

The 'electrolytic engine' (now in the Science Museum – Plate 15) was duly completed, Talbot paid the money and by February 1841 a memorandum of agreement[24] between the two experimenters appears to have been drawn up. Talbot was clearly worried about some safety aspects of Wheatstone's engine for the latter wrote on 1 March 1841:[25]

I had foreseen the liability to explosion from the cause you mention and had requested the workman to furnish the model with a safety valve, but as I found the expense would be thereby augmented I resolved for the present to do without it. I intend to keep at a respectful distance during the experiment and to use one of my telegraphic connectors so that I may break the circuit from a distance before I have occasion to approach the instrument. It may however be as well to take the additional precaution you suggest. I have devised an extremely simple safety valve for the engine itself, but I do not think it can be added to the present model.*

The two men corresponded on a number of topics – including electrotyping, as we have seen – but it was the eccentric engine which was the major interest of the relationship. Although no fully signed and dated copy of the agreement between them has been traced, a letter from Talbot's lawyer and a draft agreement suggest that they entered into a form of partnership in 1841.[26] This was the year that Wheatstone took out the patent which included specifications for eccentric engines and the draft agreement provided for Talbot to bear the full cost of the patent in which he was to be granted a one half share, to finance experiments for further improvements up to a total of £500 (the experiments to be at Wheatstone's discretion) and for joint exploitation of any proceeds resulting from the application of the patent.

Unfortunately it is impossible to distinguish the respective contributions of ideas that the two made to the partnership. Talbot told Professor Grove in January 1843 that 'Wheatstone's eccentric engine is a joint invention of Professor W and myself; if it were worthwhile we could point out the share which each of us had in it' – and continuing: 'Practically speaking I think my arrangement [his own motor specified in his 1840 patent] most likely to produce a real working engine.'[14] Wheatstone was enthusiastic about the eccentric engine's potential and whatever Talbot's doubts may have been he was true to the agreement for his account book for 1841–2 showed payments to Charles Wheatstone of at least £410. But, like all the proposed electric motors of the period, nothing commercial developed from either engine and after 1843 the contact between the two men grew more infrequent, though they remained

* It was during this period that Henry Talbot was providing photographs for Charles Wheatstone's stereoscopic experiments (page 131). In this same letter Wheatstone referred to the impact caused by a new photograph of Talbot's at a soirée given by the President of the Royal Society and added:

'The artists generally greatly preferred it to the more elaborately finished Daguerreotype portraits which were also exhibited there. One academician said it was equal in effect to anything of Sir Joshua's [Reynolds].'

friendly and of course continued their independent researches. Almost a quarter
of a century later (in 1866) Wheatstone wrote to Talbot[27] explaining that he
was conducting some experiments in electromagnetism and that the large
circular flat electromagnet 'made for my patent of 1841' would be useful if he
could borrow it back from Henry. Even later – in 1874 – Wheatstone regretted
that he met Talbot so rarely and remembered with pleasure his stay at Lacock
'in those remote times'.[28]

It has been noted on several occasions that none of the electric motors built
in the middle decades of the nineteenth century were used more practically
than as 'philosophic toys' to use a phrase of the period. The potential of the
motors was obvious – their versatility, compact size, general cleanliness (compared with steam) and the ability to switch them off and on easily as distinct
from the lengthy process of raising steam. The early experimenters were encouraged by the improvements in batteries in the 1830s and also by the large numbers of accidents experienced with steam boilers. As a result, there was no short-
age of attempts to employ the motors for useful work. An American Thomas
Davenport obtained the first patent for an electromagnetic 'engine' in 1837 and
he used it experimentally to drill holes in steel. With a grant from the Czar of
Russia, Professor Jacobi experimented with an electrically driven boat on the
River Neva and in 1842 Robert Davidson (whose electrically driven saw has
already been mentioned), with some assistance from the Royal Scottish
Society of Arts, constructed an electrically driven carriage for operation on the
Edinburgh and Glasgow Railway.[29]

However by the end of the 1840s brilliant work by Joule (principally) and
others demonstrated convincingly that to convert chemical energy into electrical energy in a battery and to use that in a motor was infinitely less efficient
than to burn coal to drive a steam engine or even to grow oats and use it to
feed horses. Robert Hunt expressed it in his 1857 paper – 'Animal power
depends on food. Steam power depends on coal. Electrical power depends on
zinc' – and the comparison was greatly against zinc for it had been calculated
that one grain of coal would raise a weight of 143 lb one foot high whereas
one grain of zinc could only raise 80 lb one foot high. Moreover at a price
ratio of 35:1 to the disadvantage of zinc it was obvious that the time was not
yet ripe for electromotive power.*

* Batteries, of course, became quickly drained and Hunt's description of Talbot's electric motor per-
forming useful work by operating a drill concluded with the words – '. . . but in three-quarters of an
hour the battery was quite exhausted'.[30]

That time came in the last decades of the century with the invention of the incandescent lamp and of efficient generators. The attractions of electric light demanded the construction of power stations using coal and the transmission of electric energy over relatively long distances – and it was but a short step to the realization that the new network could transmit *power* to factories and homes as well as a form of light. It was then that the electrical motor came into its own.

Henry Talbot's researches into motive power did not contribute any major discoveries in the history of the electric motor – nor did Charles Wheatstone's and many other workers – but they were part of that history and contributed to the store of knowledge which could be exploited once cheap electric power became available. Surviving bills for 'voltaic batteries', electromagnets and galvanometers form the minutiae of Talbot's interest and electromagnets and other items are on display at the Museum in Lacock. A number of his batteries were used by one Joseph Jennings in the early 1850s in an attempt to resuscitate dead persons which was sufficiently noteworthy an event to form the subject of a paper to a scientific society.[31] Earlier William Horner Fox-Strangways had underlined the fascination of researches in electricity for his nephew with a characteristically felicitous, if not completely accurate, statement: 'Henry I believe has given up Flora for Electra.'[32]

Although much of Talbot's work in the 1840s was of an applied scientific nature he continued to pursue academic research strongly in one direction – and that was his old favourite of etymology. As we have seen, he published three slim volumes of miscellanea in the late 1830s which dealt with varied aspects of etymology – though with the emphasis on classical languages – and a series of notebooks from the ensuing decade testify to the energy of his researches despite the demands of photography. These researches eventually reached a stage where he decided to gather more than 1,000 etymologies of English words together and publish them.

English Etymologies appeared at the turn of 1846–7 and was published at Talbot's expense by John Murray. The print order was for 500 volumes and the book was considerably more substantial in physical terms than Henry's earlier efforts, running to just under 500 pages. Murray had agreed to handle it in the spring of 1846 when he advised that it displayed 'much originality & ingenuity – though you must be prepared for criticism & dissentient voices'.

The appeal would be limited inevitably but a selling price of 12s. would do 'quite well'.[33]

The volume was generally well received. The *Literary Gazette*[34] in a lengthy review deemed it 'the most interesting work on the derivation of the English language which has appeared for many years; and perhaps the most entertaining that has ever been published on the subject'. The review took issue with Talbot on a number of points in a frank but fair evaluation – and concluded: 'We would willingly break a few more lances with Mr Talbot in the . . . attractive and exciting arena of etymological tourney.' Talbot's private correspondents also sang the book's praises. Macaulay discussed numerous points of agreement and disagreement before pronouncing it 'eminently ingenious and interesting'[35] whilst Kit Talbot entered with energy into an analysis of his cousin's etymologies (frequently disagreeing) and concluded that it had much amused him having 'the great merit that one may begin at the end or in the middle, which is an arrangement of reading I am much given to'.[36] George Butler, ever the headmaster, eulogized the work of his former pupil and commented: 'I am really astounded at the variety of your intellectual pursuits, as well as the acuteness which you display in bringing them to a conclusion.'[37]

However, late in 1847, the *Quarterly Review* published an extensive and abusive criticism of *English Etymologies* by an anonymous reviewer.[38] Talbot was accused of innumerable failings – inadequate knowledge of the languages from which he quoted, incompetence in the arrangement of the book, bringing forward apparently conflicting etymologies from other scholars – and the major failing in that of all his etymologies not one was either new or correct. Etymology was (and in a number of areas still is) a subject *par excellence* for detailed disagreement. Talbot was prepared for that – but not for the abusive nature of the *Quarterly Review* criticism, even if numerous detailed points of disagreement were valid. He wrote to a university acquaintance that he had been 'knocked down by a ruffian' and that he was not formerly aware that he had 'a personal enemy in the literary world or that a great Review would allow itself to be made a vehicle of private hostility'.[39] Despite numerous enquiries, he never did find out the identity of his violent critic.

The editor of the *Literary Gazette* – who was unashamedly sympathetic to Talbot's cause – persuaded him to compose a lengthy reply which was published on New Year's Day 1848.[40] It was impossible to deal with every point and doubtless Henry had no wish to do so where the anonymous reviewer had made valid criticisms. But he delivered some telling blows of his own –

occasionally sarcastic* but more frequently casting doubt on the reviewer's knowledge and soundness:

... surely a Reviewer can only lose credit by asserting (what no one will believe) that the industry and acuteness of the German scholars have been employed for so many years on the comparison of languages without producing any results which can be considered of much importance.

One aspect of the exchange, however, revealed a surprising naivety on Talbot's part when in effect he defended the book on the grounds of its lack of importance. In his *Literary Gazette* reply he referred to a 'small volume' which was 'not very likely to interest the public, and certainly not intended or expected to receive much notice from the reviews of the day' and which was 'pursuing the noiseless tenor of its way towards that sure and quiet asylum, the library shelf'. In a letter he referred to it as a 'comparatively unimportant volume', a 'desultory and rambling' work which, if he had been aware of the 'villainy' of some literary men, he would not have published before a 'really important [volume] on European philology'.[39] It is difficult to sympathize with Talbot in this approach. There was no justification whatsoever for the nature of the *Quarterly Review* criticism but it was (and still is) typical of some academic exchanges. But, more important, if he considered it worthwhile to publish his researches they should have been significant and substantial enough for him to have desired that they be noticed in the reviews and (hopefully) to have been regarded as a useful addition to contemporary etymological research. Talbot seemed, however, to want the best of all worlds – the modest honour of another work published and placed on the shelves of libraries yet for it not to be subjected to serious scrutiny on the grounds that it was a relatively unimportant miscellany. In fact *English Etymologies*, if frequently incorrect, was by no means as insignificant at the time of its appearance as he appeared to believe.

A detailed analysis of the volume and his later notebooks from the standpoint of today's knowledge confirms the soundness of the general evaluation of Talbot's etymological work contained in Chapter 3. His acute and critical intellect, allied with an extensive knowledge of classical and other languages, frequently led him to propose etymologies which were stimulating and cor-

---

* 'It seems that I know next to nothing of the Greek language – hardly anything beyond the alphabet. This is indeed a most unfortunate deficiency. The University of Cambridge should have looked to it, when they adjudged to me the Porson prize.'

rect. He saw many of the difficulties which existed in accepted etymologies and proposed solutions – some of which were sound and others of which could be as erroneous as those they were intended to replace. Superficially his writing on the subject was most impressive, showing a considerable grasp not only of his main languages such as Latin, Greek, French and German but of Hindustani, Breton, Celtic and even Icelandic. Sometimes his ingenious, fire-cracker mind hit upon the right solution – but what was missing was a framework of knowledge, a scientific philological approach which would enable a more systematic, more comprehensive analysis of the subject to take place. Against Talbot's intuitive skills must be set numerous examples of false *a priori* reasoning, false analogies, a sometimes extensive citation of languages which had had very limited influence on the vocabulary of English (he had a great readiness to refer to *any* language which offered a word that looked or sounded similar to the one he was discussing), a lack of consideration for semantic relationships, and perhaps – most important of all – a cavalier approach to the sound rules which he knew were being evolved in Europe. For example, in *English Etymologies*, he indicated that 'crouch' was derived from 'couch', conveniently forgetting the missing 'r'; he proposed that 'greet' was derived from the Anglo-Saxon 'grith' without explaining how 'th' became 't'; that 'patter' came from 'bespatter' without explaining the 's'; and derived 'racket' from the Italian 'lacchetta' without commenting on how 'r' came from 'l'.[41]

Talbot was aware of the etymological work being done in Europe and particularly by the German philologers – he attacked his *Quarterly Review* critic on this ground. He knew that exciting discoveries were being made – his notebooks showed that he had read some at least of Rask's work (p. 90) – and had a notion of systematic sound correspondences and of hypothetical roots from which cognate words in different languages were independently derived.* These and other concepts provided that scientific framework for comprehensive study whose absence was noted above.

But however acute and shrewd Talbot's suggestions were – and to be fair the elaboration of the new learning was still taking place in the second half of the nineteenth century – he made no sustained or systematic attempt to master

---

* The concept of a hypothetical source or parent language that no longer existed – which began with Rask, was developed by Bopp and others in the 1830s and 40s and was not fully propounded until the work of Schleicher in the 1860s – was still not widely understood at this time. Henry Talbot was aware of the concept and a letter from Kit Talbot[42] revealed that Henry was defending the concept against his cousin's scepticism. But in practice Henry Talbot and most of his contemporaries still seem to have thought in terms of identifying the source language among *existing* languages.

the subject and therefore he belonged essentially to the pre-scientific age of etymology. In this, as has already been suggested, he may have been the victim of his own wide range of interests which left inadequate time for the assimilation of the new European thinking on etymology which would have demanded virtually full-time professional application. As such, despite the power of his knowledge and intuition and the entertaining and frequently ingenious way in which he presented his ideas, he left no lasting mark as an etymologist. But Henry Talbot at least had the last laugh over his reviewer adversary for *English Etymologies* sold quite well and by the time the accounts were closed in 1857 well over 80 per cent of the original print order had been purchased by private subscribers and libraries. It was the most successful by far of his written works.

8

Mid-Century: Family, Astronomy and Botany

Henry Talbot's researches and patent affairs, together with the attempt to promote the Calotype, required a heavy outlay of money. The major, regular source of his income continued to be Lacock rents, modestly increased by occasional sales of timber. A detailed account book for 1843[1] showed a total actual income from rents during the year of a little over £3,000 with arrears of about £200 outstanding. Tithe payments and other casual income brought the total rental for 1843 up to £3,298 11s. 10d. Outgoings on the estate and household expenses at the Abbey were at a substantial level. The 1843 account book showed maintenance, repairs, insurance, and tax payments of a little over £1,000 and payments of almost £600 to Lady Elisabeth. (These payments ceased on her death in 1846.) Although there is a risk of some duplication, an estimate of total outgoings may be made based on a statement of household expenses for 1856[2] written in Constance Talbot's hand and including such items as servants' wages,* food, wine, holidays, coal, 'amusements' and education bills. These expenses totalled £2,083 1s. 3½d. so it may be assumed that, together with the upkeep of the estate, the outgoings balanced the rental at between £3,000 and £3,500 per annum.

Talbot's research, photographic and patent expenditure, it must be concluded, was derived from income on stockholdings, sales of stocks and other

---

* Census returns give details of the size of the household. That for 1851 showed nine servants in the house (including two men servants), while a later return included one two-wheel carriage, two four-wheel carriages and three horses. There was also a permanent gardener and possibly two or three part-time gardeners.[3]

large if incidental income such as the sale of livings in his possession. No comprehensive account of his stockholdings has been traced but they were evidently large and there was much activity in them. Thus in 1839 he purchased £1,000 worth of annuities[4] – but in one of his later accounts was shown as having sold stock worth around £2,000 in the years to 1851. One of the banks which he used failed in 1840 and he lost a little money but he was much too careful in money matters to have relied exclusively on one concern.[5] (He also had an informal arrangement with West Awdry, his influential steward, who advanced loans from time to time against the security of income from the rentals.) In some ways this carefulness was allowed to go too far. It clearly took Constance some time to convince Henry that regular payments should be made from the estate into a bank account in her own name (though this was possibly very enlightened for the times) and he must have been one of the most inveterate late payers of society membership dues and newspaper bills – two or three years being quite normal – which was probably due more to absent-mindedness than to meanness.

In sum, while the evidence is not complete, there is every reason to conclude that although Henry Talbot was not very wealthy, he and his family could live a comfortable and active life in which they were denied little if anything. The estate was well maintained and indeed as late as 1852 West Awdry was negotiating a further purchase of land at the edge of the estate.[6]

One major item of income in 1848 derived from the expansion of the railway system. The Great Western Railway line from London to Chippenham and beyond was opened as early as 1841. By 1844 there were plans to extend a branch line under the control of the Wilts, Somerset and Weymouth Railway down through to Salisbury and Weymouth via Corsham, Melksham, Devizes and Westbury. The plans had to go before Parliament and it was to be many years before the project was completed. However the initial stages of the new track went ahead quickly and this followed a line which included Lacock. The company entered into compensation negotiations with Talbot and its principal negotiator was the redoubtable I. K. Brunel. Talbot was as ever a difficult, not to say exasperating, negotiator for, while there was every reason for him to expect the company to pay a fair compensation, he kept going back over points which the other side had thought to be agreed and raising fresh objections. Talbot laid down strict requirements about the minimum distance the line was to pass from Lacock Abbey, the appearance of earthworks, the behaviour of the navvies and had some of these objections raised by friends and relatives in the parliamentary debates on the Act proposing the new railway.

The exchanges were fierce: Lady Elisabeth warned her son[7] about 'Railway *Sharks*' but Henry needed no urging to adopt a militant approach. 'The Railway people & Brunel have taken the field, and fired a volley of notices at me. I suppose I shall have as much trouble as last year with them.'[8] In 1846 he accused the company of trespass and deviation from the agreed line but in 1848 the matter was finally concluded[9] with a compensation payment to Talbot of £5,005 14s. 3d. which must have been a welcome sum as his photographic and patent expenses grew.

In general Talbot was a keen supporter of the railway expansion. While all her life Constance was afraid of travelling by rail and fearful for her husband's safety in his many journeys,* Talbot would have none of it. In 1831 he wrote excitedly about his first journey on the new Liverpool to Manchester railway, and was full of praise for its comfort and feeling of safety.[10] His sense of pleasure and excitement continued throughout his life and the railway provided a limitless source of humorous anecdotes – as, for example, in 1845 when he related the experience of Calvert Jones at the conclusion of the rail journey to York where the two of them were to take photographs:

> . . . the luggage on the roof of the railway carriage caught fire and immediately a gentleman exclaimed Oh! the gunpowder! for he had four pounds of powder in his portmanteau; fortunately they were near York and the train stopped before the fire had communicated to his fatal portmanteau . . . [otherwise] the York terminus was nearly being *his terminus*![11]

However, the anecdote with the greatest significance for social and railway historians stemmed from Kit Talbot, a close associate of Brunel. He wrote to his cousin Henry in 1853:

> Did you but know how your life depends on the steadiness of the signalmen at the parts where other railways meet and cross! I said one day to Brunel while we were coming up [to London] 'I am always glad when we have passed the Reading points, they are so complicated . . .' I wanted his assurance there was no danger but his reply was 'And so am I".[12]

Talbot's researches were given priority whenever possible but there were

---

* There was some ground for Constance's pessimism. As late as 1872, railway accidents were of 'such frequent occurrence that unless a number of people are killed or seriously injured, no notice is taken of them'.[13]

events and responsibilities which demanded attention. Thus in 1840, he was appointed High Sheriff of Wiltshire – a largely ceremonial post, and expensive for the holder, whose tenure lasted one year. Talbot detested the ceremonial, the expenses and the whole paraphernalia of arranging special clothes for foot-men, fitting out coaches and officiating at meetings in most of which he had no interest whatsoever. It was a post which it was not proper to refuse, which he accepted with the greatest reluctance, parted from with genuine pleasure – and yet performed well. The only permanent and not unpleasant memory he retained from his year's duty was a well-known Calotype print of a footman and coach awaiting the High Sheriff at the door of Lacock Abbey (Plate 95).

In his steward, West Awdry, Talbot possessed a distinguished and talented deputy who relieved him of most of the detailed responsibilities in the village and county. Only occasionally did Talbot himself *have* to take decisions on the eternal problem of the poor. Sometimes he was reproved for this attitude. A very active worker in parish affairs, T. H. S. Sotheron of Bowden Park (who subsequently became M.P. for the northern division of the County of Wilt-shire), on one occasion wrote to Talbot:

> The business on which the vestry was assembled today affected you as a principal Land-owner in the Parish, more than anyone of us who attended it and as gentlemen of Infor-mation like yourself are much wanted, for the purpose of instructing and guiding the many, I was very sorry to receive your note [of absence].
>
> Notwithstanding your indifference to Parish matters, I think you will be glad to hear the result of our . . . resolutions.[14]

The criticism was somewhat unjust. Talbot was certainly not an active or demonstrative leader in parish affairs – his interests lay elsewhere and that was not his style anyhow – but he did everything that was asked of him and he was far from being unmindful of the problems his tenants faced. In 1851 he supported the plan to extend the school and a year or so afterwards made land available at a low cost for a new cemetery. From time to time religious prob-lems arose – at the end of 1850 the vicar turned to him during a period of 'popish controversy' in the village and in 1854 Constance urged him to act in an issue involving the curacy because 'it is very troublesome but essential to our own comfort that you should interfere'.[15] Talbot, however, was generally loath to do so, partly by natural inclination but also because he considered it improper, save in exceptional circumstances, for a squire – even though he did own the living – to interfere in such matters.

The intensity of Talbot's work is indicated by his wish – expressed in a letter to his mother early in 1846 – that he might be able to imitate 'the Enchanter in Southey's poem, who changed himself into seven Enchanters of equal power with himself & thus was enabled easily to overcome the difficulties which had previously been too much for him'.[16] He continued to seek solitude for his studies and the ladies worried about his not visiting them frequently enough, not eating, not keeping sufficiently warm, not taking enough exercise, and working far too hard – just as they had done from his schooldays onwards. He continued to be criticized for writing too little (in 1845 Lady Elisabeth referred sarcastically to her gratitude for a letter knowing as she did 'the violence it does you to *write*')[17] – but the number of letters written by Henry Talbot which still exist underline the monstrously insatiable appetite of the other Talbots, Fox-Strangways and associated relatives for letters rather than any dereliction of duty on his own part. There was more justification for criticism from Lady Elisabeth about how frequently her son was away from the Abbey but – as we have already seen – Talbot very early in life had decided that he needed to be alone to work satisfactorily and he held to this resolution for the rest of his life. Indeed, it is likely that he was away from home and from all his close relatives for at least six months in each year and possibly nine months in some.

Such an arrangement made for tender contact when he was with his young family and his mother and halfsisters – and for splendid letters. The classicist addressed Horatia in 1841:

[Greek] is a much finer language and flows like the Muses' native tongue, while the Latin poets did little but translate & imitate the Greek. Could their own native Italy furnish them with no subjects of interest? No class of writers are so destitute of originality as the Latin poets, it is most rare to meet a sentiment not translated from the Greek.[18]

Talbot the mathematically orientated, walking guide-book wrote to his wife Constance later:

When you are at Bath you will find it easy to see Glastonbury for there is a new railway open from Bristol to Glastonbury all the way. It turns off from the Exeter line, 12 miles beyond Banwell station. Distance from Bristol to Glastonbury 40 miles: time 2 hours & a quarter. Adieu.[19]

And Talbot, the amused and amusing observer of life and manners, wrote to Horatia prior to a visit to Lacock Abbey that a new carriage that would be sent to meet her and Lady Elisabeth at the railway station 'has a semi-omnibus appearance, & you will probably be hailed by persons enquiring how much you charge for a ride?'.[20]

But Lady Elisabeth's days were numbered and after a short illness – which she realized would be her last – she died peacefully in Henry's arms in the early hours of 12 March 1846. Although a man then of middle-age and experienced in life, Talbot felt her death deeply. It was symptomatic, however, of his love for his own children that he wrote to Constance shortly before his mother's death: 'I am afraid dear Rosamond's birthday will be clouded but you must give her *many* kind words from me, & tell her I had thought of her and prepared a little present for her which I will give her some other day.'[21] But deeply as Henry and Caroline felt Lady Elisabeth's death they both had families and both were busy – Henry with his work and Caroline with her duties at Court – whereas Horatia, who was now thirty-six years old, had spent most of her life with her mother and was alone. Her half brother realized this with greater perception than anybody else and his letters and expressions of fondness for Horatia – which had always been warm – grew even warmer. She was ever a romantic and an emotional woman and Henry's words were shaped for her moods and at the same time intended to cheer:

Yesterday evening I was romantically inclined, with a feeling for the grander scenes of nature, so I went to see the sunset from the summit of Primrose Hill! where by the way I never was before. Or perhaps it was that I thought a long walk would do me good. However that was, the wind was uncommonly keen & gave me such a hoarseness that I can hardly articulate today.[22]

And again, posing the possibility of a holiday far afield in the West Indies or Ceylon, he wrote to her:

O! that I were a cinnamon planter! taking my coffee in a bungalow overshaded by tamarind trees, with a learned Pundit expounding to me the meaning of a Pali manuscript and a distant view of Adam's Peak and the Sugar Candy Mountains of the interior . . .[23]

Horatia recovered her spirits and joined Caroline for a lengthy stay in Europe. But even then Talbot could not rest easy over the welfare of his sisters for whilst in Sicily they were overtaken by the flood of revolution which swept through Europe in 1848. He wrote a series of letters urging their immediate return to England but he underestimated the resourcefulness of the

Q

women and the effect that the presence of British warships at that time had on such situations. While an official British diplomatic delegation was awaited in Sicily, Caroline, representing Lord Mount Edgcumbe and attended by Horatia, held court for the rebels. (Talbot declared that he would not be surprised to find Mount Edgcumbe elected King of Sicily 'especially as Caroline would make an admirable and most ornamental Queen'.[24]) From Sicily they moved to Rome, where they were immediately caught up in riots directed against the Pope, Pius IX, civil war between the Italians, and the invasion by the French. It was not until 1849 that, much to Talbot's relief, his sisters arrived back safely in England.*

For a brief period, better times were in store for Horatia. In 1849 came her engagement to Thomas Gaisford – a member of an old Wiltshire family – and Henry took responsibility for the wedding settlement. The marriage took place in January 1850 at Lacock and Horatia and her new husband set up home in London. Doubtless much relieved Henry could give wholehearted attention to his work. 1851 promised to be a good year. There was the Great Exhibition to visit; he planned to observe a total eclipse of the sun in Europe (p. 250); and he conducted the first experiment in flash photography (p. 171). Talbot's numerous letters describing his visits to the Great Exhibition gave a fine impression of the excitement of the occasion. Presumably his natural repugnance for such occasions was overwhelmed by his interest in the many wonders and examples of Victorian technology on display.

On 30 April 1851 he wrote to Constance:

I peeped in thro' a window at the east end of the Crystal Palace, and found myself in the

* The letters in the Lacock Collection throw interesting light on the momentous events in Europe in 1848 as seen through the eyes of an English family. Following a letter describing some unrest in England, Talbot wrote to Horatia on 27 March 1848:

'The world has turned topsy turvy and inside out – all the wise heads and the long heads, the statesmen of fifty years experience are puzzled and confused. Their calculations, predictions & expectations are not better – not so good – as those of the ordinary bystander . . . Whatever may be in reserve for England, it is a most glorious thing that she has stood unmoved at the first shock of such an earthquake, which had laid thrones in ruin on every side. The fall of Metternich [the Austrian Chancellor] is almost the most portentous event of modern times.'[25]

Although he referred slightingly on one occasion to 'pseudo-patriots',[26] Talbot was a firm supporter of the liberal cause in Europe. A copy note still survives of a letter – almost certainly written in 1848 about events in Sardinia and possibly sent to his uncle Lord Lansdowne who was at that time Lord President of the Council – in which he took the Government to task for contemplating intervention should the King of Sardinia invade Italy to fight the Austrians:

'. . . the sympathies of almost the whole of the English nation are quite the other way. The House of Commons would never endure it. War against Italian liberty! Incredible!'[27]

territories of the United States, who ought rather to have been located in the Far West of the building. Outside . . . a chaotic confusion of packing cases, straw and trampled mud. Crowds of people asking unnecessary questions of impatient policemen. Foreigners jabbering broken English, good-natured Englishmen trying to interpret for them but failing to understand.[28]

A day later he described how because of a traffic jam of carriages, he walked from a hotel in Jermyn Street in half an hour to get a position in the gallery looking down towards the throne:

I had some difficulty in maintaining my post . . . against the assaults of Goths & Vandals & still more difficulty to resist the appeals of fair ladies who however by a delightful caprice soon 'were sure they could see better further on'.[29]

Afterwards he recounted to Constance the Royal opening at length:

The scene was remarkably interesting and exciting; I got a little over-fatigued with walking, pushing & being pushed and gazing at a thousand sights, so that I passed almost a sleepless night, as I dare say was the case with many others . . .
[The crowd] . . . remained in quiet expectation. Except that a few individuals of short stature who could see nothing, behind other people, gave fees to sundry policemen & workmen to fetch empty packing cases, on which they reared themselves, in unstable and tottering equilibrium. This was called 'taking a private Box' . . . Prince Albert then advanced with a paper in his hand and made a speech, of which we could not hear a word but which we comprehended to be an account of what the Royal Commissioners had done . . . The Queen made a reply, which I have no doubt was a very gracious one. The Archbishop of Canterbury then rose at a considerable distance from the Queen on one side with an open book in his hand and addressed Her Majesty. The solemn tones of his voice reached us, but we could not tell what he said . . .
[The Royal procession moved off around the exhibition] . . . Of course we in the Gallery all scampered down into the aisle, to get a near view of the procession – in which we succeeded perfectly. All round the building the cheering was immense that followed their progress . . .[30]

A pleasant indication that the normally ice-cool, collected Talbot could get excited like many of his fellows.

His flash experiment took place just over four weeks later and then he set out for the Continent. It was whilst abroad that he learned that Horatia had given birth to a son on 28 July but had died eleven days later.

For Talbot there was solace in his own family. A fourth and final child –

Charles Henry – had been born to Constance and Henry on 2 February 1842 and the family was a close and happy one. Mlle Amélina came back from France in 1846 and was to remain as a companion to Constance and the girls for the rest of her life. The relationship between Constance and Henry continued to be a loving one in which she worried about the stresses to which she knew he was being subjected – particularly during the period when his patents were challenged – and did her best to help. There was no disguising the genuine nature of Talbot's response when on receiving birthday congratulations from Constance on one occasion he replied: 'A thousand thanks for that delightful birthday present, *your letter* which did me all the good in the world and made everything appear this morning *couleur de rose*.'[31]

Although normally seeking Henry's approval for major changes or decisions, Constance was very much in charge of household affairs – not being slow (with the greatest show of deference) to change any decisions made by her husband in her absence with which she did not agree, occasionally using sarcasm to get Henry to come to a decision, and being swift to stamp out any undesirable attitudes amongst the staff.*

The children were a delight to both husband and wife and the letters exchanged through the years described their progress – a progress which was recorded by Henry Talbot's own camera, much like tens of thousands of fond fathers since. On his journeys from home in the early 1840s, Talbot and the girls exchanged kisses – in March 1843 Constance wrote: 'Matilda has just discovered that I am writing to you & sends you a kiss *here*. Rosamond sends one *here*. You know their plan is to *kiss the paper* in the hope that the person to whom the kiss is sent will take it off in the same way.'[32] Birthdays were normally joyous events with their father and much excitement over gifts. Father left riddles to be solved in his absences (when mother also conducted simple scientific experiments for them) and the youngster Charles Henry was not left out of things. ('Charles sends his love to you and bids me describe how he is at this moment engaged – he is sticking Peacock's feathers all about my room . . .'[33])

As the girls grew up, they displayed vivacious personalities. All three demonstrated that they had inherited their father's skill in letter writing and Rosamond

* In September of 1859 Constance announced to Henry the immediate departure of a servant called George Hallam on the grounds that he was a 'confirmed Radical and Chartist' so 'the sooner he goes the better'.[34]

developed talents as a water colourist far above those of the normal amateur. All three showed an interest in politics too and expressed their views in a forceful manner.

Talbot's son Charles was in a different mould from his sisters – and his problems as the son of a brilliant father must not be underrated. He went to his first preparatory school in 1850 and to Harrow in 1855. He was a competent scholar, though never such a hard worker as his father. Reports from his various schoolmasters adopted a guarded attitude but he was clearly a lonely boy with a sensitive nature and an occasionally explosive temper. He wrote well and frequently from Harrow to his father, who had a fond regard for Charles's interest and was certainly no Victorian tyrant driving his son on to emulate his own achievements.

The pattern of the 1840s and 1850s for the family was one of lengthy holidays at home for Constance, Amélina and the girls, with Henry Talbot joining them for very brief periods interspersed with long periods of work in London and at Lacock Abbey as well as occasional trips to Europe. Initially houses were taken in the West Country – at Weymouth and at Clifton – but by 1850 the West had been supplanted by the Lake District, where Sir David Brewster and his daughter visited them. Five years later began the pattern of a decade – several months spent in the Lake District followed by an entire winter in Edinburgh. Talbot as a young man had found Edinburgh a delightful city, and as his contacts with Scotland's capital city grew so did his regard for Scottish scientists and universities. The renting of a house and all the other expenses were costly – Constance estimated £600 for four months in 1859[35] – but Talbot had no qualms about the cost for his wife and the girls obviously enjoyed themselves immensely, and he had the occasional *pied-à-terre* for visits to David Brewster and other Scottish scientists.

The Talbots – and particularly the girls – became very much a part of the Edinburgh scene, sometimes poking gentle fun at their Scottish hosts in the letters which they wrote to keep their father informed of their parties and gay life:

We had a very fine and good supper, to which the company did ample justice; indeed supper is never thrown away upon Scotch people, who consider eating by no means the least agreeable part of a ball. Dancing was kept up till three o'clock, and everybody looked remarkably gay and en train [sic]. The reels were most furious, as there was an unusual number of Highlanders in costume, and they always dance so much better, seeming to take pride in showing off, when they appear in Highland dress.[36]

In 1858 there were the first mentions of a young man John Gilchrist-Clark in the letters – and in the spring of 1859 Matilda's engagement to him was announced. Gilchrist-Clark was at the time a lawyer of somewhat modest means but it was a love match upon which Constance and Henry were delighted to pronounce their blessing. The wedding took place on 16 June 1859 and Henry settled £5,000 on his daughter. She was the only one of his children who married.

Astronomy and botany were two lifelong passions of Henry Talbot and at this mid-century point, it is appropriate to look both back and forward over the years at the nature of their attraction for Talbot and his achievements in them.

Astronomy impinged upon him at least as early as that day in May 1808 when he ran about the library of All Souls at Oxford and examined an orrery there. Within a few months his interest was sufficient for him to begin and continue a notebook of astronomical drawings. From then on astronomy frequently featured in the letters that passed between members of the family and Talbot. Comets – spectacular phenomena if visible to the naked eye – were popular subjects and for a time Lady Elisabeth Feilding could hold her own with her son on the subject. Thus in 1811 they debated the appearance of the tail of a comet which appeared in that year. Lady Elisabeth disagreed with Henry's representation of the shape, and offered one of her own – adding . . . 'the tail has perhaps increased since then, as it becomes more visible after the comet has passed its perihelion, from not being lost in the superior brightness of the Sun'.[37] Six years later Talbot's mother had to defer to her son for a definition of *angular velocity*[38] – and by then he was issuing advance notices of forthcoming astronomical events to all the family, something he was to do until the day he died:

Tell Caroline and Horatia that they may see Mercury on the 19th and for some days before and after – in the west after sunset, about nine o'clock. But if they may not sit up so late [they were nine years and seven years respectively] don't give my message.[39]

Occasionally he became depressed by the problem of observation in England's cloudy skies but his spirits always revived quickly and he was off again, furthering both his own knowledge and that of his family. In 1831 he exchanged views with his sister Horatia[40] on how cometary tails, aurorae and nebulae might have similar physical origins. Constance and their children (when they were old enough) all fell under the spell. In March 1858 he advised Constance that 'the greatest eclipse that will take place in England during the 19th Century' was to occur on 15 March and be seen along a narrow path across the country. With that typical scepticism about matters ordained by experts he added:

Calculation shows that Lacock is about two miles outside [of the path] but the tables of the Moon cannot be depended upon to this degree of nicety and the calculations may prove erroneous to the extent of several miles.[41]

His daughter Rosamond was busy about Europe painting, and observed to her father that San Remo was a fine place for astronomy: '. . . the atmosphere [is] so magnificently clear that the moon is sharply visible when only a mere thread'.[42] His youngest daughter Matilda was at that time having astronomy taught to her family in Scotland, and – as though to demonstrate the enduring interest – Caroline Mount Edgcumbe wrote about an eclipse of the moon just a few weeks before Henry Talbot died: 'What a very curious colour the moon becomes! No wonder the Ancients fancied such a phenomenon portended disaster & bloodshed.'[43]

At the professional and scientific level, Talbot was in contact with many of the leading astronomers of the day. We have already seen that he worked for some time alongside François Arago at the Paris Observatory in 1825 when he conducted intensive observations of Jupiter and Saturn – and also studied the nebula in Orion. In the 1830s he was corresponding with G. B. Airy (a near contemporary at Trinity College) who at the time was Plumian Professor of Astronomy at the University of Cambridge and Director of the newly erected Cambridge Observatory. These exchanges continued over the ensuing decades after Airy had become Astronomer Royal. Inevitably astronomy was a topic in the correspondence between Talbot and Sir John Herschel – for example in 1843 Henry was disputing Sir John's views on the nature of the zodiacal light.[44] In later life Talbot was also to become a friend of Charles Piazzi Smyth, Astronomer Royal of Scotland and Professor of Practical Astronomy at the University of Edinburgh. Foreign astronomers were amongst the scientists whom Talbot met on his tours abroad – these included the talented physicist, Léon Foucault, and Jean-Joseph Leverrier,* the brilliant mathematician – astronomer.

Henry Talbot's notebooks and, more important, his published papers, provide the basis for an evaluation of his astronomical work. Astronomical entries in the notebooks and in separate notes extended from 1822 to at least 1858. Comets were the most frequent subject. He spent considerable time (particularly in the early years) calculating and reporting their orbits and speculating on their composition – particularly that of the diffuse tail. Talbot was aware of current thinking on the subject and he mirrored this rather than contributing anything significantly original.† He made observations of Halley's Comet during its appearance in 1835 and could not resist the impish comment that whereas three predictions had made the comet pass *below* Ursa Major, it had passed *above*.

Henry Talbot had an early fascination[45] with experiments to demonstrate the rotation of the earth with pendulum devices. His ideas were ingenious but he never appeared to test them in practice. Such a demonstration did not take place until 1851 when it was performed in Paris by Léon Foucault – since when his name has been given to a 'Foucault pendulum'. In 1851 he suspended a 62-lb iron ball from the dome of the Panthéon in Paris by a wire 220 feet long which was kept in motion by a mechanism. Foucault showed that as the pendulum swung to and fro in a plane, the earth rotated beneath it so that relative motion existed between them – in fact at Paris the pendulum rotated clockwise at more than 11 degrees per hour taking 32 hours for a complete rotation. (The rate of rotation depends on latitude – the rate slows as the Equator is approached and at the Equator a pendulum does not rotate at all.) The theoretical basis of the experiment did not convince Talbot. In a privately printed paper[46] – the substance of which was given to the British Association for the Advancement of Science meeting by Sir David Brewster in 1851 – he suggested conducting

* Talbot was almost certainly introduced to Leverrier for the first time by Sir David Brewster at a scientific meeting in Oxford in 1847. The Englishman John Couch Adams – Leverrier's equal in mathematical brilliance – was also there and presumably the subject of the very recent discovery of the planet Neptune was the most topical and exciting subject on the agenda.

Adams and Leverrier had independently predicted the existence of an unknown planet which would account for perturbations in the orbit of Uranus. There was a subsequent controversy over priority – in which the two men themselves were scarcely involved directly – and Arago once again adopted the role of defender of the honour and genius of French science.

† Occasionally there was a surprise insertion in the notes, as in 1825[47] when he appeared to indicate some support for the Cartesian philosophy of a universe composed of whirling vortices (*Théorie des Tourbillons*) – a philosophy long since supplanted by Newton's theories of gravitation even in France where they had taken longer to become established.

further experiments in which a rigid horizontal bar would be laid so as to balance precisely across the top ('a true mathematical point') of an upright bar. (For the purposes of the experiment he proposed that all consideration of the earth's annual motion and the resistance of the atmosphere should be omitted.) He regarded this as a much simpler experiment than Foucault's and proceeded to argue that he was convinced that it would fail – even though it was based on the same *a priori* reasoning as Foucault had adopted and which had led to a successful outcome of the Paris pendulum experiment. The British Association meeting discussed Talbot's views but was inclined to disagree – most members felt that if the problem of friction could be overcome the experiment would indeed succeed.*

Henry Talbot's first formal astronomical paper was delivered to the British Association in 1842.[48] It was devoted to the production of reflecting telescopes – and more particularly to the copying of specula (reflectors) by the electrotyping process. '[If] . . . an electrotype cast were taken from a perfectly polished surface, the cast was also perfectly polished . . .' Yet electrotypes were normally made in copper which reflected little light. Talbot related that Charles Wheatstone had some months before proposed making specula of platina, palladium, silver or nickel – and that he (Wheatstone) had produced a mirror of platina which appeared 'to have quite brilliant polish enough, and to be white enough to answer the purpose . . .' Talbot, however, had persevered with copper – endeavouring to find a way of whitening it. This he did by exposing a speculum of bright, polished copper to the vapour of hydrosulphuret of ammonia which did not injure its polish, but after passing through a series of varied colours (scarlet, blue etc.) rendered it very white'.† This speculum had not changed in quality over the course of a year and thus this appeared to be a method by which important results could be obtained. 'There was no danger of such a speculum being oxidated by the air, since it was already in combination with sulphur, a more powerful chemical affinity than oxygen.' Talbot went on to review the electrotyping methods adopted by Professor Steinheil at Munich, in particular his innovatory technique of precipitating gold backed by copper.

[Professor Steinheil] first precipitated gold from cyanide of gold, and he mixed with it cyanide of copper, and kept gradually increasing the quantity of the latter, so that an alloy

---

* Foucault's experiment is demonstrated in the entrance hall of the Science Museum in London.

† This method of producing metallic specula was included in Talbot's patent of 1841 (No. 9,167) – *Coating and Coloring Metallic Surfaces.*

was precipitated, which was continually increasing the copper with respect to the gold, till he had a speculum whose surface was gold, and which then became an alloy, the quality decreasing, till, at the bottom, it became pure copper . . . He thus obtained a speculum with a face of gold & a back of copper.

He concluded with some opinions on the operation of very large telescopes.

The value of this paper was the manner – and this was by no means unusual with him – in which Talbot had reported his own work and that of others in an area of great topical interest. Electrotyping was regarded in this case as a means of producing relatively low-priced reflecting telescopes.*

On 28 July 1851 parts of Europe experienced a total eclipse of the sun. Talbot's second paper, contributed by previous arrangement to a special Royal Astronomical Society volume on the subject,[49] constitutes a fine example of his scientific writing at its best: literate but full of sharply observed detail and interesting theoretical speculations.

After describing the setting at Marienburg, where he was making his observations, he described his equipment and then his apprehensions concerning the weather which were fortunately not fulfilled. Observations then began and in Talbot's words:

The sun's disk [sic] was unusually free from spots. I observed only two small groups. One of these, consisting of two spots and some *faculae*, was situated near the western edge of the disk; the second was a larger and blacker spot, of elongated form, close to the eastern edge . . . I mention the spots more particularly, because I am convinced that they have some close connexion with the rosy flames which are seen in total eclipses to issue from certain points of the circumference of the disk.

Precisely at the expected moment, 3h 32m, I observed the first impression of the lunar disk. In about two minutes afterwards, the first group of solar spots was occulted. The eclipse then advanced steadily for some time, giving occasion for no particular observation beyond the gradual diminution of the brightness of the daylight . . . A few seconds, however, before the total immersion, a thick fold of cloud obscured the crescent, and the observation of the immersion was lost. I instantly withdrew my eye from the telescope to contemplate the scene around me. Before me rose the towers of the feudal castle, seen in a gloomy and livid light, such as, perhaps, never before had shone upon its walls. The sky overhead was hung with lurid clouds, but in the distant south-eastern horizon there was a clear band of sky, which I had seen not a minute before, of its usual blue colour. This was now changed into a deep orange-yellow. It is difficult by description to convey any idea

* In the event, the methods described were not proceeded with for later both Steinheil and Léon Foucault discovered a method of surface-silvering glass. Once glass mirrors were available it became preferable to make mirrors and then silver them than to try to make electroplated replicas.

of this awfully darkened landscape. Some have compared it to the effect of a thunder storm at sunset. I shall not attempt any comparison. A hurried glance at the scene presented at that moment was all that time permitted. I now made haste to observe, as accurately as I could, the degree of obscuration which prevailed. The printed papers lay ready at hand. The type of ordinary size was very plainly legible, and therefore at once thrown aside. I then took up the types of decreasing size, and carefully noticed the smallest of these which was legible.*

A total obscuration of the sun had been predicted of about three minutes at Marienburg. Not more than one had elapsed, while making these hasty observations, when I was startled by a bright light which shone forth suddenly in the clouds. My first rapid impression was that the sun was emerging, and that the predicted time had proved erroneous; but instantly applying my eye to the telescope, I saw that it was the corona around the moon, which was seen through an opening in the clouds. My whole attention was instantly absorbed by this spectacle. The whole of the moon's disk was displayed, as black as ink, against a luminous background. At the point nearly where the first contact had taken place, two red flames or firey eminences appeared upon the edge of the moon. One of these ascended to a great elevation, and then curved itself at right angles in a most extraordinary manner towards the other, which was altogether detached from the disk, and floating in the air like an island of light. I saw no other than these two; perhaps, because I was so entirely absorbed in their contemplation. A veil of cloud now again began to pass over the lunar disk, which, while it perplexed the observer, at least enabled him to observe and chronicle the fact that the bright red eminences are visible through very considerable thicknesses of cloud. The cloudy veil then again became thinner, and a very strong concentration of light was seen in one point of the corona, conveying the impression that the sun was about to emerge at that point. Just before the emersion of the sun, a multitude of small red flames started suddenly into view upon the edge of the disk, like a jagged or serrated line of fire. This new and interesting spectacle had, however, hardly lasted two seconds, when the disk of the sun reappeared in a very brilliant line of light, broken into many portions, and put an end to this series of curious and wonderful phenomena ...

By a careful observation of the time when the printed papers became illegible in the evening twilight, I arrived at the conclusion that the darkness which prevailed at Marienburg during the total eclipse of the 28th July, was about equal to that which occurred one hour after sunset the same evening.

Talbot then gave his conjectures on the causes of some of the observed phenomena: the 'solar spots' and 'firey eminences'. In his speculations he was in reasonable agreement with advanced contemporary opinion. While the paper thus contained no point of striking originality, it was the work of a first-class observer who had a considerable depth of theoretical knowledge.

* The legibility of printed papers with different type sizes was one method for measuring the degree of darkness during an eclipse.

Before the eclipse Talbot had been in contact with the Astronomer Royal, G. B. Airy, on general matters concerning the event and, more interestingly, on possible photographic coverage. Airy was keen that Talbot should organize 'a brigade of Talbotypists or Daguerreotypists' along the track of the eclipse with exposures being made at different times – and concluded:

I wish much that you could be induced to give so much attention to the process as to make it practicable for some observers. I do not suppose that you can make it practicable for *all* observers, but probably you might for persons who have dabbled a little in photogenic operations.[50]

Henry Talbot may have had a hand in the brief comments on photography which appeared in some *Suggestions to Astronomers* for the eclipse published internally by the British Association for the Advancement of Science. But he took no pictures at Marienburg. In his exchanges[51] with Airy, Talbot was somewhat pessimistic – underlining the fact that to stand any chance of success the observer would have to devote himself exclusively to photography and ignore all other observations (which clearly he deprecated); that the lack of sensitivity to red light of the available plates and papers constituted a severe handicap in recording the moment of full eclipse; and that the possibility of driving the camera by clockwork synchronously with the movement of the sun would be highly inconvenient save in an observatory. One positive suggestion he made was for a battery of cameras, operated by a single exposure mechanism, to overcome the possible failure of a single exposure in one camera.

Talbot subsequently advised Lord Rosse on photography of the moon and also Warren De La Rue (the successful stationer) who in his spare time was turning himself into an astro-photographer respected by professional astronomers. Once improved materials became available and experience of the techniques grew, the advantages of photography over other means of recording the appearance of astronomical bodies were self-evident. John Herschel and others had by this time recommended photographic surveillance of the sun and with funds provided by the Royal Society De La Rue designed a special photographic telescope – a *photoheliograph*. During the eclipse of the sun in 1860, De La Rue succeeded in obtaining a series of more than thirty images before and after totality and, even more importantly, he secured two albeit overexposed pictures of prominences. These were the beginnings of an application of photography which expanded rapidly and without which many contemporary astronomical studies would be impossible.[52]

Twenty years were to pass before the appearance of Talbot's third and final astronomical paper – which was given to the British Association meeting at Edinburgh in August 1871. It was 'On a method of estimating the distances of some of the fixed stars'[53] and intriguingly the method was based on spectral analysis – a study begun by Talbot almost fifty years before.

He proposed the simplest case of two stars, equal in mass and brightness and revolving in circles about the common centre of gravity, with the plane of their motion passing through the earth's. This last being the case, from earth the stars would appear to move in straight lines and at intervals come into apparent conjunction. Employing spectral analysis, Talbot further proposed that a certain, 'standard' ray be chosen and be observed carefully at various times in each of the stars of the binary system over several years. He then explained:

At the time of their conjunction, or near it, neither star would be approaching the earth, consequently the observed deviation of the ray X (if any) from its normal position would be due to the *proper motion* of the system of the two stars relatively to the earth, which is a constant quantity to be allowed for in all other observations. Now suppose another set of observations to be made at the time of the greatest elongation [i.e. the apparently furthest point appearing as a straight line as seen from earth] of the two stars. At that time each of the stars is apparently stationary, but in fact one of them is approaching and the other receding from the earth with a maximum velocity. The observed deviation of the ray X will therefore be different in the spectra of the two stars, and (allowance having been made for the proper motion of the system) it will appear at once which of the two stars is approaching the earth, and the question of its direct or retrograde orbit will be resolved. At the same time the distance of the two stars from the earth will result from the calculation.

The paper was topical – William Huggins had already begun his great work on the spectral analysis of stars – well argued and ingenious. But the proposal needed to be developed further and there were practical problems. For example, for the system to work spectroscopically the pair of stars would have had to be of nearly the same brightness – a difference of more than 2.5 times would have made the method impossible to work. For this and other reasons the number of binary systems that could have been measured by Talbot's method would have been negligibly small and his suggestion was not followed up – at least in this form.

None the less this proposal merited a reference in Agnes M. Clerke's classic account of astronomy in the nineteenth century[54] – and Talbot would have been interested to know that within a decade of his death spectral analysis had been used to locate binary star systems (designated *spectroscopic binaries*) whose pairs of stars were relatively so close that they could not be resolved by practical visual means.

Agnes Clerke's attitude represents a fair evaluation of Talbot's contribution to astronomy – he did not contribute ideas of lasting or great importance but his observations and theories were regarded with justifiable respect by professional astronomers. The pity was that he presented papers on the subject so rarely, for his writing – particularly in the case of the account of the 1851 eclipse – has a pleasantness and vivacity, as well as scientific interest, which lives to this day.

Henry Talbot's contribution to botany was more substantial and needs to be set in its context. The nineteenth century was a period of intense activity amongst European botanists. Building on the solid foundations laid by Linnaeus (the Swede Carl von Linné) who organized and standardized the system of plant classification during the previous century, professional and amateur botanists alike set about naming new species, compiling extensive herbaria,* cultivating botanic gardens and publishing illustrated reference works concerning every branch of the plant kingdom. This was the era of the great voyages of scientific exploration, and a steady flow of specimens and seeds of exotic plants from distant lands provided much excitement for the enthusiastic naturalists of the age.

In the late eighteenth century the Linnean Society was formed in London, based upon the complete collection of plant specimens and manuscripts of the great naturalist. These had been purchased by the Society's first president Dr (later Sir) James Edward Smith for the sum of 1,000 guineas from Linnaeus' widow. The Society provided then – as it still does – a common meeting ground for eminent British and foreign naturalists and in 1838 it became deeply involved in the controversy which eventually succeeded in making over to the nation the Royal Botanic Gardens at Kew. The first director of the Gardens, Sir William Jackson Hooker (1785–1865), who was perhaps the most widely respected and ardent botanist of the age, rapidly expanded the area of the Gardens from eleven to six hundred acres and built extensive hothouses to accommodate the ever-increasing quantities of exotic new plants which the public were eager to view. He also compiled with the help of his son, Dr

* The herbarium was a collection of dried, pressed plants which was the standard reference tool of taxonomists – specialists in *classification*

Joseph Dalton Hooker (who later succeeded him as director), the largest single collection of herbarium specimens in the world which has now expanded to number at least six million.

The published theories on evolution of Charles Darwin and Alfred Russel Wallace had their influence on botany. Linnaeus had possessed a clear perception of reality but had believed in the immutability of living things. A century after the publication of his *Species Plantarum*, Darwin and Wallace provided a new dynamic of interpretation and the classification of plants proceeded with a fresh awareness.

At the more amateur level, 'botanizing'* was one of the few activities that was regarded as respectable for young ladies and young gentlemen alike – and such was its popularity amongst respectable families in the nineteenth century (of whom the Talbots, Fox-Strangways and their friends were highly enthusiastic examples that to this day it has the image of a leisurely drawing-room pursuit. Hence many modern universities feel constrained to advertise their courses in botany as courses in *plant science* to underline its academic and scientific status.

As a schoolboy Talbot went straight to the experts. Undaunted, he adopted the policy of corresponding with the highest botanical authorities of the country in order that they might advise him of relevant publications on the subject and confirm or correct the identifications he made on the specimens he had collected. His particular interest was the British mosses – and in this he may have been influenced by the fact that William Hooker, who became a frequent correspondent, began his botanical career with the discovery of a rare new moss *Buxbaumia aphylla*. The mosses are a difficult group of plants for laymen to identify and by commencing his botanical studies with them Talbot showed his typical approach to learning.

The first eminent botanist whom Talbot consulted (Chapter 2) was Lewis Weston Dillwyn, a fellow of the Linnean and Royal Societies and an amateur botanist of great talent. In 1805 Dillwyn had published the *Botanist's Guide through England and Wales* with Dawson Turner, the Yarmouth banker and leading cryptogamist,† who was William Hooker's patron and father-in-law.

Dillwyn regarded Henry Talbot's interest in botany with utter seriousness.

---

* Strictly speaking, the reference should be to *collecting and classification* only and 'botany' is used in this somewhat loose manner throughout the chapter. At the specialist level, the discipline was already subdividing in Talbot's time into, for example, plant physiology, anatomy and histology, and genetics.

† The cryptogams are the lower plants, including algae, mosses and liverworts.

In October 1814 he wrote to the Harrow schoolboy who had been criticizing his published work:

> I accept of your proposed correspondence with pleasure, & shall be very happy to render every assistance in my power to your botanical pursuits. Next winter I hope that you and Christopher [Kit Talbot] will pay me a visit, and if you are forming a Hortus Siccus I can then give you specimens of several of the rarest British species. I will now look over your supplement to Glamorganshire, and make such remarks as may occur.
>
> *Carduus eriophorus* I long ago observed in this county and though it is hardly sufficiently rare it ought to have been mentioned in Glamorganshire as it has been thought worthy of notice in other parts of the Guide.
>
> *Oxalis corniculata* I believe has never been found *wild* in Britain except in Devonshire, & I cannot help suspecting either that you have made a mistake, in that the plants which you found had escaped from Lady Mary's [i.e. Henry's aunt] Garden. In the neighbourhood of such a general collection as hers care must be taken to discriminate between such *escapes*, & those plants which are the real *natives* of the place. I strongly suspect that *Funaria lutea*, *Linum catharticum* . . . & the double variety of *Saponaria officinalis* must come under the former denomination & are therefore not entitled to a place in the Guide. *Anthemis nobilis*, *Mentha rotundifolia*, *Equisetum fluviabile*, *Orobanche elatior*, *Scutellaria minor* & *Festuca vivipara* shall all be mentioned in the next Edition if another should ever be published. The white varieties of *Erica cinerea* and *tetralix* are occasionally found *hic & ubique*.
>
> I shall be glad to receive your list of the rarer Harrow plants whenever it may be convenient for you to send it. Doctor Smith's is the best arrangement of the British Mosses tho' it is far from perfect, & the Flora Brittanica is a work which you most undoubtedly ought to have. The musci [mosses] are rather a difficult tribe and if you are determined to master them you had better come & shut yourself up for a fortnight in my library where you will find a tolerably good collection which will materially assist.[55]

It was significant that in this formal age Dillwyn concluded: 'Yours very sincerely.'

Walter C. Trevelyan – Talbot's contemporary and botanical co-worker at Harrow – maintained contact in subsequent years.* Like Talbot, he was to become a man of considerable and varied talents but in spite of his extensive contributions to botany (his major work *Vegetation of the Faroe Islands* was published in 1837) he was never elected to the Fellowship of the Linnean Society. When Trevelyan went up to Oxford in 1816 they continued to compare notes on their investigations and it was obviously important for Talbot to be able to discuss his botanical exploits and discoveries with a contemporary who was his equal in knowledge of the science. It is evident from one of

* Over half a century later, on 12 September 1871, Trevelyan wrote to Talbot to say that he had presented a copy of their schoolboy 'catalogue' of flora to Harrow School.

Trevelyan's letters that the study of botany at Oxford left much to be desired:

... I hope you were pleased with your visit to the Continent, I suppose you had not much time to spare for botanising. I hope you saw the Botanical Garden at Paris. That here [at Oxford] is pretty good in the collection of hardy plants, but very bad houses; all the *trees* are to the south so prevent the Sun from shining on the rest of the Garden. They very seldom have a lecture as nobody scarcely will attend.[56]

Talbot, however, relished referring his questions and discoveries to those whom he knew would always give wise and well-considered comments on his efforts – and after the early contact with Dillwyn this meant increasingly the Revd. James Dalton and William Hooker. Dalton, the vicar of Croft in York-shire who was a friend of Hooker's and expert in the study of sedges and mosses, became concerned at what he saw as Talbot's over-enthusiasm for the mosses and urged him to broaden his interests. In nearly every letter he wrote to Talbot during their brief period of frequent correspondence (1816–17) this exhortation was found in some form and at first he met with little response: Henry wished to master the mosses completely before turning to the higher plants.

It was William Hooker who introduced Dalton to Talbot and this may be interpreted as an indication that Hooker – already a highly regarded botanist – had recognized that Talbot was a potentially able fellow-worker despite his tender years. Hooker's willingness to guide and help was typical of the charac-teristic modesty and generosity of the man who was to become the greatest British botanist of the century, rivalled only perhaps by his son. These qualities shone in all his letters and they won him the deserved respect of scientific and lay society alike.

None of Talbot's early letters to Hooker have been traced but a letter of August 1816 from Hooker to him demonstrates the relationship:

You will I am sure be much surprized at my not having written to you: but I have as yet been home but a short time and no sooner did I return to Halesworth than I had an unexpected visit from a foreign botanical friend. He has just left me and his stay has so thrown me out of my usual botanical employment that I must work a few days incessantly at my Flora Londiniensis before I can attend to any other employment. I had already laid by some mosses for you and by the latter end of this week I shall not fail to complete the packet and dispatch it to Lady E. Feilding in Town. I can however delay no longer sending you a few lines if it be only to notice your papers of *Phasca* which I had examined previously to leaving town. And first I must tell you that you have completely set me right with

R

regard to *P. rectum* and *P. auricollum.* Your specimens are quite satisfactory and I have made drawings from them which I shall publish ... Your *P. alternifolium*, however, is quite another thing and I fear only barren shoots of *Bryum carneum*: and your *P. piliferum* is no other than male plants of *Bryum bicolor*, or some species nearly allied to it. Indeed *P. piliferum* itself I am afraid is but a variety of *P. cuspidatum*.

Mohr's H. Crypt. Germ. I am sorry to say is not to be procured at any booksellers. My copy was given to me by a friend in Switzerland and I believe is the only perfect copy of it in the kingdom. Were I not in such constant, I might almost say, daily, use of it I would send it to you for a few weeks. I have, however, laid by for you copies of his Generic characters, his remarks upon them and of the species of his Genus Phascum, which may be of some service to you.

I have just purchased a duplicate copy of Hedwig's Stipes which being offered to me for £9 I could not refuse. I have therefore my former copy at the disposal of anyone who wishes to purchase it for what I gave for it, which is £12. There are two volumes done up in one volume in boards.

I am glad you like Mr Turner's Muscologia Hibernica. I wish he had time to publish a new edition, in which the number of species might be greatly increased. I am not sure however that *Bryum stellare* is a native of that country. I should like very much to see your specimens and I beg you will have the goodness to communicate anything to me that you may think interesting.

I wrote to my valued friend Mr Dalton respecting you and he tells me that you have promised him the pleasure of your company in the Autumn. You will be much gratified, I trust, in his acquaintance. Unfortunately he lives in a country not very favourable for mosses, but it is no great distance from Teesdale where there must be a vast field, hitherto unexplored. Mr Dalton was himself once an excellent muscologist and with his acuteness, had he continued with ardour the study would have been, ere this, the first in this or perhaps any other country. I shall write to you further with the packet.[57]

Hardly any direct, detailed record of Talbot's early botanical exploits has survived but it may be assumed that he spent much of his spare time collecting specimens, consulting works of reference and annotating his collection, for without such hard work, he scarcely could have earned the respect and confidence of so many eminent botanists at such an early age. Most important of all, he developed during this period the keen powers of observation and accurate description which are so essential for botanical work. Thus during a trip to Italy in 1823, he made field notes that in their detail had some lessons for the modern botanist. For example:

Gentiana asclepiadea. Named from its resemblance when out of flower to the *Asclepias vincentryicum.* Flowers sessile. Corolla has five points with intermediate smaller ones. Anthers coherent. In G. ciliata and *amarella*, not so. Interior of corolla speckled. Stamina smooth, 5 in number coherent in their lower part with the tube of the corolla. Capsule stalked, compressed, seeds placed horizontally, surrounded with a broad membranous border, which is curiously reticulated. They are very numerous. Calyx has only four teeth of which two opposite ones are larger than the other 2. The calyx is tubular, the teeth short and subulate. Anthers white. Leaves undulate at the margin, very pointed, broader than common in this genus.[58]

The language of botanical description may seem dry to the non-botanical reader – but Talbot was by no means insensitive to the more aesthetic aspects of plants and their habitats. In the staccato style he sometimes adopted, he wrote to his mother in 1817:

You want to know what there is in my garden: Imprimis – some immense Roman nettles which sting everybody. Some gigantic coriander and stately mallows – verdant millet – pretty antirrhinum – shewy scorzonera – curious briza, quizzical Claytonia – humble aretotis.[59]

Over forty years later, the excitement and pleasure in plants and their setting continued unabated. From the Pyrenees in the summer of 1860 he wrote to Constance:

Today I took a drive & walk to see le pas de Roland, 5 miles from here. The heat was great but the walk over rugged paths by the side of a beautiful mountain river was very pleasant. On the rocks by the river I found some plants, which also grow in England, but these specimens were larger and more abundantly in flower than I have seen in England. There was great abundance of *Anagallis tenella* (grows at Grasmere on the hill beyond the cottage) – of ivy-leaved *Campanula* which I remember Mary Talbot showed me on the hill above Llanelay [Glamorgan], and of *Pinguicula lusitanica* (which I have only seen in the New Forest in Hampshire).[60]

Even when on other business – for example during the trip to Germany in 1851 to observe the eclipse of the sun – his eye was ever open for flowers: 'The woods of North Germany are very gay with flowers of *Epilobium augustifolium*, commonly called French willow-herb.'[61]

Henry Talbot's early training in botany was to serve him well for the rest of his life. There is no doubt that had he so desired, he could have entered the ranks of the eminent professionals, but this was rendered impossible by the multiplicity of his interests. So botany ran throughout his years as a subject of continuing delight and interest – but with apparent surges (during the mid-

1820s, the 1830s and the 1860s) when he felt relatively free to concentrate on botanical studies* or when stimulated by important events.

His interest in his garden was lifelong too. At Lacock Abbey he planted the seeds and bulbs of plants he collected on his travels abroad in 1823 and 1826, and also the material sent to him by the many fellow botanist members of his family and professional and amateur collectors of his acquaintance. Talbot compiled a list of the trees he planted at Lacock and many of them are still standing. On the left of the main drive to the Abbey there is a tulip tree – grown from seed by Talbot – which now stands some seventy feet high. This overlooks the walled garden which was once the site of his botanical garden but which now consists of allotments for the village of Lacock. In a small note-book which survives he meticulously recorded daily events in the garden during 1828 and 1829. On 15 April of the latter year he noted:

Two large Box trees planted at the angles of the terrace. *Orobus vernus* in flower. A *ranunculus* in the shrubbery now in bud, which I do not know, perhaps *R. auricornus*? Wild *Ornithog. umbellatum* in the meadow but it shews no appearance of flowering. Wild violets blue & white have been in flower some time. *Tussilago*, *Petasites* and *Nepeta violacea* in flower.[62]

His absence on trips abroad or in England did not lessen his thought about the garden and greenhouses at Lacock. In May 1847 he requested Constance:

You will find some seeds on my library table, besides those I gave you. I wish you to sow them *in pots* which may stand in the old greenhouse till the new one is ready. One kind is from Mr Bridges from Mt Etna . . . Round the brickwall of the greenhouse I wish for a trellis or lattice with sweet peas. This will require a bed of earth 6 inches wide and will narrow the gravel walk to that extent.

I wish Charles to sow a bed of lupins for me somewhere in my botanic garden and water them when they come up. If he is not inclined to be a gardener let Matilda do it. There are 8 kinds of lupins in my packet – the one which is written illegibly is *Rose* lupin.[63]

Some time later he sent an invitation to Horatia:

I am putting plants into my new conservatory – would you like to visit Henderson's in Pine Apple Place and choose half a dozen of your own favourites to be added to the collec-

---

* Talbot was sometimes inaccurately accused by the ever-demanding members of his family of having given up botany. During his first year at Cambridge, for example, his cousin Jane Talbot in Wales accused him of having 'such an immoderate *love* of Euclid as to pretty nearly fill up all the gaps you used to have for Botany'.[64]

tion? In that case you should select the identical specimens you wish for, which should be vigorous young plants . . . They must not require stove heat.[65]

There was scarcely one member of his family with whom he did not correspond on botanical matters, but his most serious contacts were with his uncle William Fox-Strangways. In Fox-Strangways' letters there was a greater intimacy – natural for one so closely related – which was absent from the more formal exchanges on botany with William Hooker.* The style of their correspondence was unrestrained and their excitement over the discovery of a new plant or travelling in an unknown region still communicates itself. Fox-Strangways, like Talbot, was able to devote only a part of his life to botany and his level of accomplishment in the science was comparable. He was a Fellow of the Linnean Society, contributed to the *Gardener's Magazine*, and was eventually accorded the honour of having two genera of plants named after him – *Stranvaesia*, a Chinese genus of the rose family, and *Foxia*† of the lily family. There is no evidence, however, that he named any new plants himself.

During Fox-Strangways's sojourns abroad as a diplomat he often became homesick for his garden at Abbotsbury in Dorset – in spite of being surrounded by so much unfamiliar Continental vegetation. Writing from Vienna in 1836[66] he lamented: 'My dear Henry, I wish your letter told me more of your garden' – but soon launched into an enthusiastic description of the Viennese botanic gardens for he was too vital a man to be downcast for long. He made dramatic plans – few of which were ever realized. In January 1826 he had[67] 'a great mind to offer to go with Lord Ponsonby to explore Patagonia. I hope some botanist goes out in the ships to survey T. del Fuego' – the latter sentence forming a wistful afterthought for he realized he had too many commitments for such a venture. Perhaps he was trying to persuade his nephew to go: it was not the first occasion on which he had attempted to get Henry Talbot to journey to exotic places but usually without success. That same letter did, however, plant in Henry's mind the idea of a botanical trip to Corfu and the Ionian islands.

While planning this journey, Talbot wrote to Sir James Smith, enquiring about botanical works of reference which might be of assistance in his studies. By this time he knew the President of the Linnean Society and his family well

---

* Fox-Strangways was also able to ridicule Henry Talbot's weaknesses more forcefully than anyone else. From the Pyrenees in June 1857 he wrote: 'You will not believe your eyes when you see the date of this letter. I am here without waiting for you, as if I had waited, I should never have arrived.'[68]

† Now incorporated in the genus *Hyacinthus*.

and Smith was eager to be of assistance. (In 1829 Talbot was elected to the Fellowship of the Society and was thus acknowledged to be amongst the most distinguished botanists of the time.)

Regrettably there is little information relating to Talbot's work in Corfu and the Ionian islands. Perhaps some of the letters he sent never reached their destination – but what is certain is that he did not find sufficient time in the ensuing years to work vigorously on his Ionian collections. However in 1833 he wrote to Hooker about some 'new plants I have discovered in the Ionian islands . . . which I have named *Silene cephallenica, Silene integripetala, Delphinium graecum . . . Sideritis purpurea*'.[69]

This is the first indication of Talbot having the confidence to name new species without consulting an eminent botanist first. In fact most of these names were either not accepted or did not withstand the test of time. According to the international convention, the Latin binomial* of a plant is suffixed with the surname of the botanist who was responsible for its designation as a species: *Sideritis purpurea* Talbot – a small purple-flowered herb – is the only remaining plant species which bears his name in this way. In 1834 he again wrote to Hooker[70] – who at that time was Professor of Botany in Glasgow – and suggested that he should publish his Graecian plants in Hooker's botanical journal. It seems, however, that this never came about.

Four years later Henry Talbot made an historic contribution to botany for which he has never been given full credit. For many years, it had been the dream of the sixth Duke of Bedford – himself an ardent botanist – that the Royal Gardens at Kew be established as a national botanic garden, and he had promised William Hooker the directorship should such a post become available. In 1837 – before his wish had been fulfilled or even publicized – the Duke died and soon afterwards the Lord Steward, Lord Surrey, began to visit the Gardens with the object of assessing their suitability for conversion to vineries. At this time the greenhouses were filled with the plants that Sir Joseph Banks had collected during his historic voyage to the Pacific islands and Australasia with Captain Cook, and many of these plants were lost as Lord Surrey began to implement his plans.

News of this spread rapidly and the national newspapers joined the battle. On 8 March 1838, Talbot wrote to Hooker that: '. . . it would be a pity if Kew Garden were to be sacrificed to a pitiful and false economy.'[71] Since the

* The first name is that of the *genus*, the second that of the *species*. This was the system inaugurated by Linnaeus.

issue would have to be resolved in Parliament, Talbot approached the Chancellor of the Exchequer (T. Spring Rice) to find out whether pressure from a learned society would have any influence on the parliamentary decision. On receiving a favourable reply, he 'therefore petitioned to the Council of the Linnean Society to present a petition to the House of Commons, recommending that Kew Garden be converted into a national garden; the suggestion was unanimously adopted by the council'.[72] In May he again wrote to Hooker informing him that 'the Chancellor of the Exchequer spoke confidently to me last night that something satisfactory be done about Kew Garden, and I am pleased to see that he takes a great interest in it'.[72] The Linnean Society's petition and other opposition to the Lord Steward's plans had the desired effect and William Hooker was appointed the first director of the new National Botanic Garden. Thus was Hooker's early encouragement of Talbot's schoolboy botanical exploits rewarded by an important contribution on Talbot's part to furthering botanical science.

Sir William's respect for Talbot as an influential botanist was further underlined in August 1845 when he requested him to supply a testimonial for his son,[73] Joseph Dalton Hooker, who at the time was applying for the Chair in Botany at Edinburgh University. Talbot had, in fact, become firmly established amongst the eminent botanists of the time. Among his correspondents were John Lindley, Professor of Botany at London University; Stewart Murray, curator of the botanic garden at Glasgow; George Bentham, who was later to produce, with Joseph Hooker, the monumental *Genera Plantarum*, which is still a standard reference work; and John Hutton Balfour, who was the successful candidate for the Edinburgh Chair. He also corresponded with the prominent Italian botanists Tenore and Bertoloni,* of whom he commented to Hooker:

He [Bertoloni] is the best botanist they have in Italy. Tenore is led away by the vanity of making new names. Bertoloni admits no species into his Italian flora of which he has received no specimens, but not content with this he goes to the absurd length of admitting no habitat of any species unless he has a specimen from the locality.[74]

The 'vanity of making new names' was an easy trap for nineteenth-century botanists and species were often named on the basis of a single dried specimen.

---

* Antonio Bertoloni was one of the numerous contacts at home and abroad to whom Talbot later sent photogenic drawings and Calotypes. One photogenic drawing of Lacock Abbey sent to Bertoloni and in the possession of the Metropolitan Museum of Art, New York is reproduced in Beaumont Newhall's *Latent Image* (Plate 9).

Talbot himself was over-cautious when it came to names and describing new species and he usually relied on others if he was in doubt over an identification. (Only very occasionally did he dispute Hooker's opinions – writing, for example, in December 1835: 'I cannot help thinking you are in error with respect to your *Orlaya grandiflora*.'[75]) There was one occasion, much later in his life, when Talbot made an attempt to describe a new plant. He had obtained seed from a collector who had travelled in the Cape region of South Africa and raised the plant in the garden at Lacock. In December 1866 he sent a living specimen to Professor Balfour in Edinburgh for the Botanic Garden:

> It is the one you investigated last year and which I afterwards took to Kew, where it was examined by Professor Oliver, Mr Bentham and others. The plant is undescribed. I propose for it the *provisional* name of *Vellozia elegans* by which it may be designated for the present in your collection. We propose to have it figured next time it blooms, in the Botanical Magazine.
>
> It is a native of South Africa. As no other species of *Vellozia* is found in Africa, and this one diverges in important characteristics from the Brazilian species described and figured by Martius,* it is at present open to question whether it is not a new genus. At any rate it is very pretty when in full flower, and quite different in aspect from anything in the Gardens.[76]

Vellozia is a genus of the Velloziaceae, a small family with members occurring in South America, South Africa, Madagascar, and Arabia. At the time when Talbot grew his plant, the genus *Vellozia* had only been found in the Americas and so he was understandably suspicious of ascribing the same generic name to a plant originating in South Africa. In a further letter to Balfour,[77] he compared the plant to the genus *Xerophyta*, also Velloziaceae, which was known to occur in both Africa and America but pointed out once more that there were important differences in the floral structure which made its inclusion in this genus unlikely. He balked, however, at going so far as to give it a new generic name and so in 1867, Professor Balfour named it in his honour *Talbotia elegans* Balfour.

Joseph Hooker was not satisfied with Balfour's opinion, and wrote an article in the *Botanical Magazine*[78] returning the plant to the genus *Vellozia*:

> ... it appears to have been overlooked that an African (Madagascar) genus of *Vellozia* had already been described by Commerson, under the name of *Xerophyta* ... Commerson's

---

* A German botanist who collected primarily in South America. Talbot visited him on at least one occasion (June 1842) in Munich.

plant agrees with *V. elegans* in the principal character by which I find *V. elegans* to differ from its Brazilian species viz., the length of the filaments. As, however, *Xerophyta* is reduced by Endlicher to *Vellozia*, it appears clear that *Talbotia* should go with it, and that Professor Oliver's original name of *V. elegans* should be retained for this plant.

Joseph Hooker's judgement appeared to be final and the plant remained *Vellozia elegans* Oliver, its original discoverer forgotten. However, there has been a recent revision of the Velloziaceae, which has reversed this judgement and proved Talbot's original suspicions to be correct: the plant was indeed a separate genus and the name *Talbotia* has been restored thereby commemorating a highly talented botanist who was too modest about his own ability. This was surprising for outwardly Talbot never lacked self-confidence – but it may have been that, since the time he could devote to the study of botany was limited, he felt that it was the business of those who had made botany their profession to make decisions regarding plant classification. But he was never slow to supply them with material for study and most of his letters from professional botanists contained notes of thanks for specimens he had sent them or for publications to which he had drawn their attention. His principal botanical role was that of a man in the background who indirectly made a considerable contribution to botanical science in the nineteenth century.

It was entirely appropriate that it should be Talbot who proposed the use of photographic techniques in botany. As early as March 1839, he had written to Hooker: 'What do you think of undertaking a work in conjunction with me, on the plants of Britain, or any other plants, with photographic plates, 100 copies to be struck off, or whatever one may call it, taken off, the objects.'[79] Sadly no volume was ever produced but in June of the same year William Hooker gave his opinion on the photographic process:

I am extremely obliged to you for your kindness in sending me the specimens of photogenic drawing. They are very curious and ingenious. But what I was most pleased with was the imitation of an *etching*. Can that be made available for botanical drawing? Plants should be represented on paper, either by *outline* or with the shadows of the flower (which of course express shape) *distinctly* marked. Your beautiful *Campanula hederacea* was very pretty as to general effect – but it did not express the swelling of the flower, nor the calyx, nor the veins of the leaves distinctly. When this can be accomplished as no doubt it will, it will surely become available for the publication of good figures of plants.[80]

Hooker obviously recognized that the science of photography – which was still at the stage of photogenic drawing – had not yet progressed sufficiently for the publication of botanical reference works. More importantly, he saw the drawback in the photographic representation of plants for the purpose of identification and reference – a drawback which is still pertinent today: the impossibility of representing in a single photograph all the features of a plant which distinguish it as a separate species. Although more time-consuming, an accurate line drawing in which the artist can bring all these features into view is nearly always more satisfactory than a photograph. None the less, Hooker later pointed out the supreme advantages of photography in botany which, also, are equally valid today:

... I must confess that I should much prefer photographic *landscapes* to the kind of representations you allude to. By landscapes I mean not only home and distant scenery, mountains, buildings etc, but portraits of Trees, such as cannot be done from specimens. When he [his son Joseph Hooker] is at Borneo, for example, how interesting it would be to have faithful representations of the Palms, the Climbers ... which abound in that country. We can indeed have the details in our Herbaria, but nothing else.*[81]

It is regrettable that ultimately Hooker did not publish a work in conjunction with Henry Talbot. It would have been a lasting symbol of their close cooperation over nearly fifty years and possibly could have formed a partial record at least of Talbot's contribution to botanical science in the nineteenth century – a contribution which it has taken more than a century to re-establish.

* Following the invention of the Calotype in 1840 Talbot took some fine studies of trees (Plates 59, 60 and 61).

9
Photographs in Printers' Ink

In the early years after the discovery of photography, the prime concern was the improvement and perfection of the photographic process itself. It was however only a matter of time before attention became increasingly drawn to combining the skills of the photographer, engraver and printer in the production of images from the printing press – images which could be numbered in runs of hundreds, then thousands and ultimately millions. Of course, illustrations of drawings and paintings had been produced by the engravers' skills for centuries – each requiring to be engraved or etched upon the printing surface in a technique whereby the engraver was endeavouring to recreate the original. For simple line illustrations the task was not difficult – particularly for a skilled practitioner – and could be accomplished in a short time. But for complex originals and, even more so, for artistic works of genius the task could be daunting and might take many months to accomplish. Moreover, the printed reproduction would only be as good as the engraver's skill which for optimum results was required to be as high as the original artist: sometimes, indeed, they were one and the same person.

The coming of photography presented those who began experimenting in the reproduction of the images via the medium of printer's ink with a supreme opportunity and a supreme challenge. The opportunity was the existence in one picture of the world of detailed reality, captured in a relatively short instant of time. For reproduction in works of art or science, and eventually newspapers, the value of the photographic image was evident and of potentially immense significance. Today, we are still debating the effects and implications of its electronic equivalent – the TV picture. But the challenge was immense, too. In presenting reality, the photographic record must be transformed into a printed record with the utmost fidelity – and that meant not through the engraver's tools such as the scribe, the graver, or the dry point, but through the action of light and chemistry which had created the original. That original was composed of tones which could vary from full black through varying shades of grey to white – this type of image came to be described as *continuous tone* – and it was representing the full range of tones in a photograph which was the experimenters' greatest difficulty. In reproducing tones in artists' illustrations, engravers had evolved skilful techniques of varying the depth, width and arrangement of engraved or etched lines to suggest the effect required. In addition, before the birth of photography, they had evolved chemical etching techniques which would prove useful in reproducing the photographic image. But it was to be the end of the nineteenth century before the potential may be said to have been realized.

Contemporary printing technology offered Talbot and other photographic experimenters three different types of printing surfaces – all of which still exist today. In what we now call *letterpress* or *relief* printing, the areas of a plate which carry ink are higher than the non-printing (highlight) areas. In *planographic* printing the entire surface is flat and printing is accomplished by treating it so that some parts repel ink and others accept it. (Lithography is a major form of planographic printing and was discovered at the end of the eighteenth century by Alois Senefelder in Bavaria working on a surface of absorbent limestone.) In the *intaglio* (or incised) technique – which is broadly the opposite of relief or typographic printing – the ink-retaining areas are cut or etched beneath the surface of the plate which is wiped clean and therefore represents the highlight areas of any illustration. Most of the work done in Talbot's lifetime in photomechanical reproduction concentrated on the lithographic and intaglio techniques.

Nicéphore Niépce himself – as part of his photographic research – inaugurated the photomechanical age probably as early as 1826. He discovered that bitumen of Judea (which was already used by etchers as a 'resist') hardened when exposed to light and became insoluble in oil of lavender (or animal oil) in which it was normally readily soluble. Niépce used this knowledge to produce an etched plate – on various surfaces including copper, pewter (tin) and stone – in which the initial stages differed radically from traditional techniques. In these techniques – for example, in transferring a line drawing to a plate for etching – a copper plate was coated with a resist or acid-resistant 'ground' which could be composed of wax, gum and asphalt or bitumen. The etcher or artist then drew the design to be reproduced on the plate with a sharp instrument which removed the ground and laid the surface bare beneath. Nitric acid was applied which attacked the copper where lines had been drawn, and etched into it. When completed, the plate was cleaned, ink was applied (thereby filling the etched furrows), the surface was wiped clean of ink and paper brought into contact with the plate. The paper absorbed the ink and thus reproduced the original drawing.

Niépce, however, took an existing illustration – an etching or lithograph – varnished or oiled it to make the base as translucent as possible, laid the illustration on a prepared plate and exposed it to light.* The areas of the coated surface under the lines of the original received no light and were therefore unaltered, remaining soluble: the areas under bare paper were exposed to light and the bitumen became insoluble. When the plate was washed with oil of lavender the bitumen that had been under the lines of the original illustration dissolved – and etching could proceed by the traditional methods. There were numerous practical difficulties with Niépce's *heliogravure* (as it came to be called) and it was incapable of reproducing intermediate tones – but to him undoubtedly went the honour of the discovery and application of the principle of the light-sensitive resist which formed the basis of later photomechanical systems.

Shortly after Henry Talbot announced photogenic drawing at the beginning of 1839, wood blocks were sensitized to receive images of plants and lace which were then engraved by hand – the first results being published in the *Magazine of Science* of 27 April 1839. Even earlier, Dr Andrew Fyfe of Edinburgh had combined photogenic drawing with lithographic techniques to produce the images of ferns.[1] But in their reliance on hand techniques both events looked back rather than forward – and the first really significant attempts to combine photography and engraving skills to produce a close representation of the original images centred on the Daguerreotype. It was a natural development. In the first place the fact that the Daguerreotype was unique was usually considered to be a weakness which could be removed if a way could be found to transform the plate into a printing surface capable of reproducing copies. In the second, the Daguerreotype already consisted of a silver-coated copper

---

* According to a review of photo-engraving techniques by Thomas Malone in 1857, light did not have a visible effect on the bitumen in Niépce's system – unlike later light-sensitive grounds used in photomechanical reproduction – and the effect of the exposure to light was usually only revealed by the action of the solvent.[2]

plate which although somewhat soft offered a limited potential as a printing surface if it could be engraved or etched to accept ink. Daguerre himself would have none of this:

> Today, now that the process has reached greater perfection and gives a fineness of detail, as proved by the magnifying glass, I am more than ever convinced of the impossibility of engraving a plate which will produce prints that even approach the maximum image perfection of this technique.[3]

Reproducing the detail of the Daguerreotype original was indeed a severe task but this was not the first occasion on which Daguerre pronounced himself satisfied with the status quo and refused to countenance development work of considerable potential importance.

The earliest experiments in etching Daguerreotypes to form intaglio plates were conducted by two doctors of medicine – Dr Alfred Donné in Paris and Dr Josef Berres in Vienna. Although the techniques varied in detail, both depended on the action of nitric acid in etching the silver (or shadow) areas of the Daguerreotype. The results were imperfect – particularly in the reproduction of middle tones – but Donné was able to draw a reported forty impressions from his plates[4] and Berres (whose plates were solid silver) up to 500.[5] The latter published a booklet on his work in August of 1840 – *Phototyp nach der Erfindung des Professors Berres* – which contained five illustrations and which thus qualified to be regarded as the first publication ever to make use of photomechanically produced pictures. (Moreover, at least one of Dr Berres's reproductions was more obviously photographic in nature than many of the attempts that others were to make in the years after.*) W. R. Grove experimented with the etching of Daguerreotypes by electrolysis and later Alphonse Poitevin as well as Paul Pretsch directed their ingenious minds to the subject. But without doubt the best results were achieved in the early 1840s by the French physicist Hippolyte Fizeau, who was associated with Antoine Claudet in the technique which was subsequently patented in England. (Thomas Malone later reported that in about 1844 he had been instructed in the process by Fizeau and worked on it for some months – a further reminder of his varied photographic experiences.)

Fizeau etched the Daguerreotype plate with a mixture of nitric acid, potassium nitrite and sodium chloride – which left the highlight areas covered by

---

* Berres sent a copy of this engraving to Talbot. It is now in the Lacock Collection (LA6148).

mercury amalgam unaffected. Silver chloride was built up in the areas lightly etched by the solution and this was removed by washing with a solution of ammonia – the etching thus being gradual and repeated in steps. According to Malone,[2] the etchant solution eventually began to affect the highlight areas and this was countered by placing the plate in a strong, boiling solution of caustic potash. The highlights were subsequently further protected by electroplating with gold and the plate was dusted with fine, powdered resin – a technique borrowed from the already established *aquatint* method of the engravers. Stronger etching of the shadow areas between the particles of resin was continued with nitric acid to create small, deeper recesses capable of holding ink. As further protection for the soft silver surface, the Daguerreotype was electroplated with copper which could be repeated when the copper began to show wear. This made print runs of hundreds and even thousands perfectly feasible.

Daguerreotypes etched by Fizeau's method resulted in the highest-quality reproductions ever obtained from the unique originals and some examples of his work showed satisfactory tonal range.* But other attempts were far less satisfactory, demanding extensive assistance from hand-engraving techniques. In general, the processes were involved; the softness of the silver-coated plate (despite protection) was a weakness and was also a limitation on the potential print run; nobody save Fizeau could come close to reproducing the continuous tones of original Daguerreotypes; and the risk that a unique original of great value might be irretrievably damaged during the etching process was always a possibility. Etching Daguerreotypes was a quite logical step in the history of photomechanical reproduction – but across the Channel in England Henry Talbot was already beginning researches which would point the practical and successful way forward for the future.

Talbot was well aware of the work being carried out on the Continent in etching the Daguerreotype. Later he praised the 'considerable success' of some of Fizeau's 'beautifully distinct' specimens but noted the 'great uncertainties' which the experimenters faced.[6] During the 1840s he must have regarded the improvement of the Calotype system as taking priority but the problems of mass-producing purely photographic prints at Reading and the threat of fading made photo-engraving an attractive area for research. At least as early

* The range of quality – including examples of Fizeau's work – was demonstrated in *Excursions daguerriénnes: vues et monuments les plus remarquables du globe* published in parts by the French instrument maker N. P. Lerebours in Paris between 1840 and 1844.

as 1847[7]* he was considering the theoretical possibilities of 'transferring photography to steel engraving' (the choice from the beginning of steel – a metal which would bear long print runs – was a shrewd move) by means of electro-chemistry and his ideas even included a proposal for printing from Daguerreotypes in colour. Whether Talbot conducted actual experiments along these lines is not known for after 1843 he ceased to keep scientific note-books. But writing in the spring of 1853 about the new photo-engraving techniques that he was then announcing (which owed nothing to electro-chemistry) he referred to his researches having begun 'some months ago' which could well have indicated some time in 1850 or 1851.[6]

Whenever the numerous experiments began, it could not have been long before Talbot sensibly felt the need for the advice of a skilled engraver and this was supplied by George Barclay of Gerrard Street in London who for some years thereafter offered his frank and sometimes humorous comments and advice to the experimenter. The first contacts between them occurred in 1852 (before Talbot's patent was taken out) when Barclay supplied a wealth of information about the treatment of plates, the nature of different inks and the working of printing presses. 'You will find great facility in cleaning off the superfluous ink by making the plate warm . . .' and '. . . You must not expect that the man who knows how to make a printing press has any more idea of "how to print" than an elephant' – were typical comments from Barclay's pen.[8] He also offered to spend a week giving Talbot a general insight into etching and printing 'without at all enquiring the bent of your ideas'[9] – so it was evident that at that stage Henry Talbot was not revealing the nature of his researches.

Those researches concentrated on the intaglio system – where the ink-carrying areas are below the surface of the plate – and before describing his patent proposals it is appropriate to briefly detail the problems of reproducing a full range of photographic tones by this particular system. Highlight areas of the original photograph presented few problems because they were represented

* Talbot's notebooks contained various references to reproduction techniques at earlier dates. Thus on 21 January 1838 (Notebook O) he noted: 'Let a shadow of a plant be thrown on a copper plate covered with wax or something more fusible so that the heat of the sun may uncover the plate by melting the wax. Then let it be etched with aqua fortis.'

He also had a full awareness at an early stage of the problem of retaining ink in shadow areas: 'Take a mezzotint copper plate [a plate with a burred surface], silver it, form a D'type picture on it, then precip. tin or some other metal by galvanic action on the [high] *lights*, so as to fill up the cavities of the surface. Then print off impressions with ink' (Notebook Q: 16 July 1840). No evidence of practical experiments along these lines has been traced.

by the level surface of the plate which was wiped clean of ink before printing. At the opposite extreme, areas of full black in the original were represented by deep etching of the plate. If these areas were limited in lateral extent (a mere line) then ink was retained quite well – but if the areas were broad then the wiping of the surface areas was always liable to remove ink from them in addition and to cause variations in tone on the printed page. Finally, there was the most difficult problem of all – how to achieve precise, differential etching so that the levels of grey between white and black in the original photograph could be faithfully reproduced in copies produced by the printing press? With an eye on the future the problem could be stated more comprehensively – how could the full range of tones be reproduced faithfully and consistently, in copies printed in large quantities and at high speed?

Talbot's patent *Improvements in the Art of Engraving* (No. 565) of 29 October 1852* was aimed squarely at 'producing or obtaining etchings or engravings by photographic and chemical means alone upon plates of steel'. The steel plate was dipped initially in a mixture of vinegar and sulphuric acid, then wiped clean and dried. A solution of gelatin was prepared, to which was added about half its volume of a saturated solution of potassium bichromate. The steel plate being slightly warmed, the prepared solution was poured over it and spread with a glass rod. Superfluous potassium bichromate sensitized gelatin was poured off and the plate heated gently to dry it, the process being carried out away from strong daylight. When dry, the solution was a bright yellow colour and the surface smooth. Assuming that the subject for etching was a plant leaf or item of lace, this was placed upon the surface of the sensitized steel plate and exposed to daylight in a photographic copying frame for a time varying from 30 seconds to 5 minutes or more. Light darkened the surface of the plate not covered by the object to a brown but the area under the object remained yellow.

When the plate was dipped into cold water for one or two minutes, all of the potassium bichromate and much of the gelatin was removed from the area unaffected by light (i.e. the area under the object being copied) which was thereby whitened. The plate was then dipped into alcohol briefly and placed in a vertical position to dry. This completed the photographic part of the process. Talbot proposed a solution of platinum bichloride as the etchant – a relatively expensive chemical but one which did not attack the remaining

---

* The patent was dated 29 October 1852, was sealed on 24 January 1853 and the detailed specifications filed on 29 April 1853.

S

areas of hardened gelatin on the plate with the speed of the more common nitric acid.*

A small amount of this etchant solution was poured on the plate and spread with a brush. (A greater depth of etchant would prevent the operator from seeing the process proceeding.) There were no objectionable by-products of the reaction, Talbot said, and within a minute or two the photographic image on the plate was seen to blacken – experience indicating when the process had gone far enough. The etchant solution was then poured off, all traces of it removed by washing with salt water, and the plate rubbed with a wet sponge or cloth which eventually removed the remaining gelatin.

Talbot then continued:

When the etched parts are both broad and uniform, as in the case, for instance, when the object is an opaque leaf of a plant, although the etching holds the ink pretty well, yet when printed off, the effect is not always satisfactory. I proceed therefore to explain a useful modification of the process. In order to which I must observe that when the object placed on the steel plate to be engraved is a piece of black crape or gauze, an engraving of it is obtained in the way above mentioned, which truly depicts the object, representing every thread in its proper place by a corresponding engraved line; but when two or three thick-nesses of this gauze are employed instead of one, and are placed obliquely to each other at various angles, then the resulting engraving offers a mass of lines intersecting each other in different directions which cover the whole plate, and which, when printed off upon paper, produce a result which, to an eye at a little distance, appears like a uniform shading. Now let us suppose that we have in this way covered a prepared steel plate with two or three folds of black crape or gauze and placed it in the sunshine. When taken out of the sunshine and the crape removed, let the broad leaf of a plant, or some other object of irregular out-line, be placed upon the centre of the plate, and then let the plate be replaced in the sunshine for three or four minutes. When it is removed for the second time, and the object detached, it will be seen that the light of the sun acting upon the parts of the plate exterior to the object has wholly obliterated the previous effect produced by the gauze, and has converted that part of the plate to a uniform brown colour, while the central part of the plate offers, the image of the leaf, upon which the crowded intersecting lines produced by the gauze are still seen. The plate is now to be etched as previously described, and the result is, that an etching of a leaf is produced covered with engraved lines, which lines are entirely wanting on the rest of the plate. When this is printed off, the impressions offer the appearance of a leaf nearly uniformly shaded. But in order to obtain greater perfection in this respect, it is

* Letter to the *Athenaeum* of 30 April 1853. In this letter – and an earlier one to the *Athenaeum* of 9 April – Talbot gave an excellent background to the researches leading to the new patent. There was one dis-appointment in the 30 April letter: he stated that adding remarks on the theory of the process would make the length of the letter too great and that they would be better deferred till later. But he never did expand on the theory of the process.

only necessary either to manufacture on purpose some pieces of more delicately woven fabrics, or to cover a sheet of glass by any convenient method with fine opaque lines to intercept the light, or with a powder adhering to the glass, consisting of distinct opaque particles, and very uniformly diffused over the surface. These things, which I believe have not been heretofore used in the fine arts, I would denominate photographic screens or veils.

He indicated that an aquatint ground* was another method of achieving the effect – but that a different ground had to be laid for each plate whereas the same piece of veil served for any number. 'The method of engraving which I have here described as applied to steel plates is also applicable to plates of zinc. Lithographic stones are also readily engraved by the same process.' Positive copies of photographs 'either upon glass or upon paper of good uniform texture and moderately transparent' could be engraved but he indicated that the prepared steel plates were not a practicable proposition for use directly in a camera.

Quite apart from such improvements as the use of a more selective (albeit expensive) etchant as platinum bichloride, the major advances in the patent were Talbot's discovery that an emulsion of potassium bichromate sensitized gelatin hardened and became insoluble (or less soluble) in water when exposed to light, and the discovery of what effects could be achieved using a screen or veil to create ink-retaining cavities which gave an impression of unbroken tone in broader areas.

Potassium bichromate was one of the compounds figuring in Talbot's chemical experiments at least as early as 1831[10] but there was no indication that he conducted any tests for light-sensitivity at that time. Dr Gustav Suckow of the University of Jena in the following year noted the light-sensitivity of chromates when mixed with an organic substance – and Mungo Ponton, before the Royal Scottish Society of Arts in May 1839,[11] announced his findings that paper soaked in potassium bichromate and exposed to light with an object on it went deep orange while the paper under the object remained the original colour of bright yellow. When immersed in water, the area not exposed to light was rapidly dissolved out and the picture was 'fixed' as a white drawing on an orange ground. Ponton – who noted the cheapness of potassium bichromate compared with silver nitrate – was unable to explain the correct nature of the chemical reaction involved and subsequent investigators –

---

* Dating from around 1765, this method consisted of applying particles of resin to the plate's surface in some suitable manner. The etchant then acted on the parts of the plate not covered by the particles.

such as the French scientist Edmond Becquerel and Robert Hunt – did not advance the study in this direction significantly. It was Talbot who tied the various clues together, was the first to understand the characteristics of gelatin (and similar organic compounds) in association with potassium bichromate and who moreover applied those characteristics to a practical end which has altered comparatively little to this day. The point is stressed because some photographic historians have belittled Talbot's achievement.* However, J. M. Eder was in no doubt.[12] He roundly declared Henry Talbot to be the discoverer of the light-sensitivity of a mixture of potassium bichromate and gelatin – and the publisher of the fact that the chromated gelatin became insoluble in light, that is it lost its capacity of swelling in cold water. It was this discovery, in Eder's view, which formed part of Talbot's claim to 'outstanding merit' in the evolution of photographic engraving.

The concept of a contact 'veil' or 'screen' – again a Talbot innovation which was carried through to the present day – was a brilliant stroke which may have resulted initially from an acute observation of the results obtained in photogenic drawings and Calotypes of lace, which was a favourite Talbot subject. The wording of the patent indicated that he realized the relatively coarse and geometrically regular veil patterns in the finished product were noticeable, hence the need for finer woven fabrics or fine ruled lines on glass.† In fact Talbot used numerous variations, from yellow (as distinct from the usually black) gauze in a transparent, flexible film, and black lines ruled or scored on different surfaces to an aquatint ground printed on paper made translucent by waxing. He did not elaborate sufficiently in his own writings on the manner in which the exposure of light through the screen affected the hardening of the

* Talbot explained the basis of the patent claim well in correspondence with Col. (Sir) Henry James of the Ordnance Survey in Southampton in 1860. James – in reply to a Talbot letter indicating that the process of photozincography (a transfer photolithographic technique used by the Survey for printing maps and manuscripts) touched on his rights under the 1852 patent – advanced the names of Ponton, Hunt, and Becquerel and asked what Talbot claimed under his patent. Henry Talbot replied that no claim was made for the use of potassium bichromate *alone* for such a claim would be invalid. The claim was for the employment of a *mixture* of potassium bichromate and gum or gelatin in photography. The 'introduction of the gum renders a new class of useful processes possible, which is a good test of a real practical invention'. Many of the most important patents on record, he continued, were for a *combination* of two inventions both of which were known before but had never been combined. Such a claim was valid even when the result of the process was the same as before though perhaps better and cheaper. As to the issue of photozincography, Talbot was prepared to defer to William Carpmael's opinion which was that there was no infringement – and there the matter ended.[13]

† In experiments before the patent was taken out, Barclay supplied Talbot with finely ruled steel plates which were used twice to produce printed proofs of a 'screen', with one set of lines at right angles to the other.

sensitized-gelatin surface (and therefore its solubility) and this needs some explanation.

If we assume that a positive photograph was to be etched, the two exposures – one through the positive and one through the gauze – would have resulted in hardened gelatin with the highest resistance to etching in those areas completely clear (i.e. highlight areas) in the original. Areas of full black in the positive would have prevented light reaching the gelatin underneath – which would therefore not have been hardened – but the exposure through the gauze would have caused some hardening in the gelatin under the gaps of the gauze with a continuing complete absence of hardening under the strands of the gauze. Hence, the gelatin under the strands would have been almost completely removed by the subsequent immersion in water and the steel or copper underneath exposed immediately to the full power of the etchant solution. As for the areas of intermediate tones in the original, Talbot may well have theorized that the combined exposures through the positive photograph and gauze would have resulted in a layer of protective gelatin in direct ratio to the tone and therefore capable of ultimately yielding an ink volume in the etched areas similarly in ratio. In practice this theory was borne out imperfectly – varying characteristics of etchant and the sensitized gelatin with temperature and storage conditions would have had an important effect, for example – and Talbot in due course turned to other methods. None the less the potential remained.

In the absence of notebooks, Talbot's researches cannot be reconstructed in detail but the experiments with the screen alone must have been exhaustive before he could gauge relative exposures correctly, to say nothing of achieving the optimum strengths of potassium bichromate and gelatin solutions and platinum bichloride. And this was only in the period to 1852 preparatory to the drawing up of the first photo-engraving patent. In his letter of 9 April 1853 to the *Athenaeum*, he wrote of the multiplication of difficulties in his researches which had results that 'were most anomalous and contrary to all expectation' – including etched plates that were half positives, half negatives. He also underlined the challenge presented by the continuous tone of the photograph – 'because the gradations of shadow and the depth of the etching upon the plate are found not to follow the same law as they do upon the original photograph. There is a much greater difference on the plate than exists on the original: the shadows are too deep, and the lights are too strong.' In fact, the problem was not so much a matter of different laws as of complex technological problems in achieving a facsimile of the original. None the less, the process did reveal according to Talbot a 'reasonable degree of certainty' which he modestly felt would 'doubtless be soon and greatly improved by other experimenters'.

Once the patent was secure, Talbot sent many examples of his photo-etchings – almost all of leaves, plants, line drawings and similar objects it may be assumed* – to friends, relatives and fellow researchers including Brewster, Biot, Hunt, Lord Rosse, Wheatstone, Fenton, Claudet and Herschel.[14] Herschel replied:

> This great step will render possible the *publication* of miniature books – even of miniature facsimiles of original Mss &c. &c. and I congratulate you on having arrived at so great a result in itself independent of the innumerable applications which it is capable of.[15]

Hunt noted: 'They are exceedingly delicate and beautiful and even in its present state the process appears applicable for many very important purposes,'[16] while Roger Fenton was as enthusiastic as anybody. He looked forward eagerly to 'the perfect result' of the researches being carried out by Talbot and others which would solve the problem of fading photographs. 'I hope that the honour of finally solving this question will by your researches be won for this country. It would be a rare good fortune for the same hand to have commenced & completed the structure of photographic art.'[17] Some of the proofs of this early work were even put to good use in raising funds for a local charity.

The general reaction then was favourable and hopeful but Talbot realized that much needed to be done – and the forthright George Barclay underlined it. Whilst realizing the potential ('after what you have . . . done everything is possible')[18] he offered a stream of criticism and advice which on occasion must have depressed Talbot but which equally must have played an important part in the practical evolution of his photo-engraving process. Around the time of the announcement of the first patent,[19] Barclay criticized the 'tameness' and absence of 'spirited touches' (he meant shallow etching) in Talbot's plates. This was a subject to which Barclay returned repeatedly in the early period and he provided guidance that emphasized Talbot's inexperience as a practical engraver:

---

* In May 1853 Kit Talbot wrote: 'If the art can be extended so as to embrace landscape and figures, the discovery will be invaluable.'[20]

You are in error in fancying the lines should be close for a dark tint. They must be fine and tender for light tints and wide and stronger . . . for dark . . . Could you discover any means by which the surface extension could be stop'd and the depth proceed it would be hailed with delight by the present race of engravers and with much complacency by those who will thereafter adopt your process . . .[18]

Talbot's inexperience clearly worried Barclay and in one lengthy letter emphasizing the need for differential etching of varying tone areas, he stated firmly that it would not be by Talbot's own labours that the 'perfectibility' of the process would be decided.[21] On a later occasion when Talbot requested guidance on printing Barclay answered that it was needed not in printing but in engraving.[22] But he praised where he felt it due and it would be fascinating to know which of Talbot's plates Barclay described as 'elegant in the extreme'.[23]

The 1850s witnessed the beginning of extensive research in photo-engraving techniques both in England and on the Continent, some of it doubtless inspired by Talbot's work but much of a totally different kind. France was the main centre of the research. In 1855, Alphonse Louis Poitevin in studying the reaction of chromates with organic substances in light introduced what later came to be called the collotype system and pigment printing – and extended the idea to produce high quality photolithographs (with a grained stone to produce the tones) which were printed by Lemercier, a noted Paris lithographer. However, although of superior quality, these were not the first photolithographs published in Paris. This honour fell in 1853–4 to Lemercier, Lerebours (an optician and instrument maker), Barreswil and Davanne (both chemists and amateur photographers) who used the asphalt process with which Nicéphore Niépce had experimented many years before. The distinction of producing the first book of photographs by photolithography in Britain nominally falls to John Pouncy who in 1857 published *Dorsetshire Photographically Illustrated* – the originals being based on his own pigment printing process – but the photographic positives were so heavily retouched by the engraver as not to be recognized in the volume as photographs.* Pouncy none the less was a prize-winner in a competition (in which Poitevin won the gold medal) organized by the Duc de Luynes in Paris to encourage the production of permanent photographic prints.

Charles Nègre and Firmin Gillot cooperated in the difficult task of producing half-tone pictures by the typographic system of printing at this time but Henry

* Not surprisingly a number of the reproductions showed houses associated with Henry Talbot and his family, including Melbury, Moreton and Stinsford (the last being a Strangways seat).

Talbot was most interested in the results being obtained by Nicéphore Niépce's cousin Niépce de Saint-Victor. Using light-sensitive asphalt on steel, he succeeded in etching only outlines at first but in 1853 began to achieve good half-tone results with only limited help from the retoucher by making use of the aquatint technique. Niépce de Saint-Victor was joined in this work by the engraver Lemaître and later by Charles Nègre, and Eder described the results eventually achieved by the process as being unquestionably the most beautiful examples of half-tone etching on metal for intaglio processes at the time, 'showing a surprising perfection in the delicate middle tones'.[24]

Talbot was aware of Niépce de Saint-Victor's progress for they exchanged examples of their work through John Murray the publisher.[25] (Murray also sent Talbot some of the Lerebours–Lemercier photolithographs.)* Henry was careful to send Jean-Baptiste Biot examples of his own engravings and an account of his researches for presentation to the Academy of Sciences in Paris as soon as the patent specifications were filed – and Biot did this on 2 May 1853. The Frenchman reported that the members were impressed and that Arago had announced that M. Niépce had been working on a process partly analogous to Talbot's for some months – but this was mentioned only to show that Niépce was not guilty of any plagiarism and it would have 'no effect on your rights as first inventor . . .'[26]

However, a challenge to what Henry Talbot considered to be his rights as an inventor did arise unfortunately in a different context – and the issue continued until into the 1860s. Paul Pretsch was the son of a Viennese goldsmith who spent his whole life in printing during which his work took him over much of Europe. After learning electrotyping as a means of printing, he entered the Government Printing Office in Vienna where he was subsequently given responsibility for studying the applications of photography to printing. The work of this department in producing Talbotypes and other forms of photography earned a medal at the Great Exhibition of 1851 where Pretsch was in charge of the Viennese Government Printing Office representation. He was a highly talented and knowledgeable worker and two or three years later he threw up the job in Vienna to go to London to exploit his experience in photography and printing technology with the system which he named

---

* The work of Lemercier, Lerebours, Barreswil and Davanne formed the earliest portfolio of photo-lithographs with reasonable reproduction of tones. The large reproductions featuring photographs of architectural subjects appeared in 1853–4 under the title *Lithophotographie; ou, Impressions obtenues sur pierre à l'aide de la photographie*.

Photogalvanography. He took out a British patent for the process in November 1854.

The first part of the process was substantially like Talbot's in the use of potassium bichromate and gelatin save with the addition of a silver salt (silver nitrate) and potassium iodide. Pretsch however made use of the swollen gelatin produced under toned areas of a positive original – the gelatin rising into a relief pattern which was in ratio to the various tones and which was granular in nature (providing an ink-retaining potential) possibly as a result of the silver salts present – to make moulds and produce either intaglio or relief (typographic) plates by conventional electrotyping techniques.

The production of an electrotype was a lengthy process taking days and sometimes weeks, and while the assistance required of the engraver's retouching skills varied, it was often substantial. None the less a photo-electrotype certainly took a much shorter time to produce than hand-etched plates – and the existence of a master from which numerous electrotype copies could be made solved any problems of wear on a plate, from each of which 300 to 400 impressions could be taken. A company – the Patent Photogalvanographic Company – was formed in London. It included Roger Fenton among its executives and in 1856 commenced the publication of a series work *Photographic Art Treasures* produced from intaglio copper plates. The large-size illustrations included photographs by well-known photographers of the day (including Fenton himself) as well as reproductions of paintings. Other examples of Fenton's work were issued separately.

It seems that Henry Talbot was not aware of Pretsch's system until the spring of 1856 when he read an account of a meeting which Pretsch had addressed at the Society of Arts.[27] At that meeting Pretsch had stated that his process used some materials of Talbot's process 'although in another way and for another result'. Clearly the electrotyping parts of Pretsch's patent owed nothing to Talbot but the latter considered that the initial stages of the process were based on his patent. He sought an opinion from William Carpmael and the response was categorical:

I entertain a strong opinion that no person has a right without your licence to use gelatin mixed with bichromate of potash applied to a surface in the dark and then to take a picture by the camera or otherwise by the aid of light and then wash off by water the parts not acted on by light.[28]

By the time he received this opinion Talbot was already in contact with

Pretsch and a friendly exchange of letters ensued. Talbot referred to Pretsch's 'well known talents and ingenuity',[29] assured him there was no wish 'to depreciate your ingenious experimentation but merely to establish my own rights in the matter as an inventor', expressed himself 'desirous of proceeding in the most amicable manner',[30] and suggested that Pretsch's company ought to discuss the taking out of a licence under his own patent of 1852. For his part, Pretsch – while admitting differences of opinion 'on the points to which you have politely called my intention' – expressed appreciation of Talbot's conciliatory spirit and hoped that whatever the outcome 'it will not alter the kind feelings which you have pleased to express on my behalf any more than it will diminish the sentiments of respect which I in common with lovers of science entertain for your most valuable labours'.[31] With that they agreed to let their solicitors settle the issue – with predictable results.

The record is not complete but by February 1857 proceedings had been instituted on Talbot's behalf against the Patent Photogalvanographic Company for infringement of his patent.* In April of that year Fenton contacted Talbot direct and indicated that the Company was prepared to take out a licence but that it could not be more than a nominal amount since the prospects of the organization were not good enough.[32] Most of the exchanges, however, were between Talbot's lawyer J. H. Bolton and Fry and Loxley – acting for the company. Among the ideas canvassed were Talbot's proposal that a 5 per cent royalty be paid to him on the company's gross sales but with a waiving of the royalty until 3,000 copies had been sold from plates; a company proposal that a payment be made in respect of the use of potassium bichromate and gelatin of £50 per annum rising to £100 per annum when a net profit of £2,000 was achieved; another company proposal that Talbot join it; and a Talbot offer to purchase Pretsch's patent for a sum not to exceed £500.[33] All of these came to nothing for the company was in severe difficulties which had nothing to do with Talbot. Its management was at loggerheads and as early as May of 1857 its losses were reported to be around £4,000.[34] By November it had been wound up.[35] The patent was kept in being against future possible use but the litigation lapsed. There the matter rested for the time being but George Barclay – while he had hoped that the two sides could reach a workable solution – took Henry Talbot to task for not placing his process in the hands of skilled engravers long

---

* At the same time *The Liverpool and Manchester Photographic Journal* (15 March 1857) reported that 'Herr Pretsch threatens M. Poitevin with legal proceedings for a trespass on his patent . . .'!

before competitors had appeared. It was his view that by so doing the technique would have been perfected by early in 1854.[36]

But Talbot did not believe that the techniques included in his first patent would be perfected by engravers but by himself – and on 21 April 1858 he took out a second patent.* The first part of the patent describing procedures up to the start of etching was in essence like that in 1852 but thereafter the technique diverged widely. In the first place Talbot stated there was no need to wash the plate after exposure of the object or photographic positive – on the contrary, much more beautiful engravings could be obtained because the more delicate lines and detail of the picture had not been disturbed at all. A more important departure was the careful spreading on the exposed plate of a 'little finely powdered gum copal' or, failing that, common resin. The application of an aquatint ground was different in that Talbot secured a greater degree of control by laying it on the gelatin and not the surface of the metal plate itself.† The plate was then held horizontally over a spirit lamp to melt the copal – which Talbot stressed would not harm the image – and subsequently allowed to cool.

He did not specify the manner of applying the resin ground and his son Charles later described a modification introduced by his father after the 1858 specification was filed. Common resin and camphor were dissolved in chloroform and the solution poured over the gelatin surface of the plate after exposure. The chloroform immediately evaporated, leaving a film of resin and camphor on the surface. When the plate was warmed the camphor in turn evaporated leaving an even distribution of minute particles of resin. According to Charles Talbot, this was a 'much better and very ingenious method' compared with the original one which was 'uncertain and troublesome'.[37]

The etching solution and method of etching proposed in the patent were brilliantly conceived: they form the basis of the technique applied to this day and were included with the use of potassium bichromate sensitized gelatin as the basis upon which Eder praised Talbot's 'outstanding merit'. He chose ferric chloride as an effective and safe etchant which was used in varying strengths. Three solutions of the etchant were prepared – No. 1 was a saturated solution

* The patent – No. 875 – was sealed on 15 June 1858 and the detailed specifications filed on 14 October 1858. In his provisional specification Talbot included an electrotyping proposal but this was not included in the final specification.

There is some evidence that at one time he was contemplating taking out patents in France and Belgium for the new developments but he did not proceed with the idea.

† In the intaglio process of Niépce de Saint-Victor and Lemaître, resin was applied to the partially etched plate. Copal is a resin obtained from certain tropical trees.

of ferric chloride; No. 2 consisted of five or six parts of the saturated solution and one part of water; and No. 3 of equal parts of water and the saturated solution. Talbot indicated that a number of tests were necessary to establish the proper strength of solutions before attempting any engravings of importance. In such tests, solution No. 2 was brushed on the plate with a camel-hair brush. If the etching proceeded too rapidly the solution should be altered by adding some of the saturated solution (No. 1) and, if too slow, water should be added. Assuming the right strength of No. 2 was found, all of the details on the plate would appear in about 2 or 3 minutes, the operator stirring the liquid all the time with the brush 'and thus slightly rubbing the surface of the gelatin, which has a good effect'. When the etching was deemed complete, the liquid was wiped off with cotton wool, the plate subjected to a stream of cold water and rubbed to remove the gelatin.

Talbot then outlined a somewhat different technique which had major significance for the future since it concerned not only differing strengths of etchant but local action on areas of the plate requiring particular attention:

When the plate is ready for etching, pour upon it a small quantity of the liquid (No. 1) [the saturated solution]; this should be allowed to rest upon the plate one or two minutes; it has no very apparent effect, but it acts usefully in hardening the gelatin. It is then poured off from the plate, and a sufficient quantity of solution No. 2 is poured on. This affects the etching in the manner before described. And if this appears to be quite satisfactory, nothing further is required to be done. But it often happens that certain faint portions of the engraving, such as distant mountains or buildings in a landscape, refuse to appear, and as the engraving would be imperfect without them, I recommend the operator in that case to take some of the weak liquid No. 3 in a little saucer, and without pouring off the liquid No. 2 which is etching the picture, to touch with a camel-hair brush dipped in liquid No. 3 those points of the picture where he wishes for an increased effect. This simple process often causes the wished for details to appear, and that sometimes with great rapidity, so that caution is required in the operator in using this weak solution No. 3, especially lest the etching liquid should penetrate to parts which ought to remain white [i.e. the highlights]. But in skilful hands its employment cannot fail to be advantageous, for it brings out soft and faint shadings, which improve the engraving, and which would otherwise probably be lost. Experience is requisite in this as in most other delicate operations connected with photography; but I have endeavoured clearly to explain the leading principles of this new process of engraving according to the mode which I have hitherto found the most successful.

It may seem strange at first that the weakest solution of ferric chloride acted most vigorously but the greater amount of water would cause the solution to be absorbed more quickly by the gelatin and thus commence etching first. With a more saturated solution the swelling of the gelatin would take place at a slower rate.[38]

While again no detailed and comprehensive record of Talbot's researches exists, the plates and proofs taken from them which survive are testimony to his labours. He coined the word *photoglyphic* to describe the new process of engraving – the second part of the word coming from the Greek verb 'to engrave' and the whole having an analogy which Talbot wished to make with hieroglyphics.*[39] The scientist in him delighted at the progress made and even in the appearance of the engraved plate in its own right. He wrote at this time:

> The engraved steel plate is itself a beautiful photograph bearing microscopic examination. The impression with ink on paper loses some of the minuter detail – this is the nature of things & cannot be helped . . . The scientific facts upon which the process is founded are among the most beautiful in photography which is an art fertile in singular novelties.[40]

Throughout much of the 1850s (and this continued into the 1860s) Talbot sought his photographic subjects for engraving not from his own camera but from others – for example the Paris photographers Soulier and Clouzard and later from Ferrier and Soulier. He had a close and friendly relationship with the latter in particular who supplied him with innumerable positives on glass, though waxed paper negatives were in Talbot's view acceptable save when the waxing made the tones appear too faint by transmitted light.[41] From the time of the first patent he had been content that examples of his work should be distributed widely – but not formally published. This attitude changed, however, once he had evolved and patented the new process, and the first photo-glyphic engraving to be formally published appeared in the newly launched *Photographic News* of 12 November 1858.

The editor of the *Photographic News* was the twenty-six-year-old William Crookes, who had appeared for Talbot in the Laroche trial, and who was subsequently to edit *Chemical News* and the *British Journal of Photography* before going on to achieve even greater fame as a physicist and chemist, the discoverer of the metallic element thallium and to receive a knighthood in 1897 for his services to scientific knowledge. In the spring of 1858 Crookes's contacts

---

* The term *Photoglyphic engraving* has frequently been used in the context of Talbot's first photo-engraving patent: this is incorrect.

informed him that Talbot had made an important new discovery* (the provisional specifications of the patent were placed at the Patent Office in April)
and he immediately wrote to him asking for details. There began a very
friendly exchange of letters which lasted for some years – and Talbot revealed
that the new discovery was in photographic engraving. When Crookes was
appointed editor of *Photographic News* in August 1858 he requested permission
to publish examples and information on the new process and Talbot was only
too happy to oblige once he had secured the French photographers' permission for printing from their originals. His only condition was that the
printing be carried out by T. Brooker of the Copper and Steel Plate Printing
Office in Margaret Street, London who by this time appeared to have largely
replaced George Barclay as an adviser on engraving technology. When the
first etched plates were delivered, Crookes pronounced himself 'quite astonished
at their perfection and sharpness of detail. I have seen specimens of all the
processes . . . but never saw anything to equal these. The difficulty has been
in the half tones but the beautiful pictures which I now have before me leave
scarcely anything to be desired in that way'.[42]

An article on photoglyphic engraving appeared in *Photographic News* under
Talbot's name on 22 October 1858 and the actual specimens of the process
followed three weeks later.[43] Seven architectural subjects from Madrid,
Granada, Seville, Valladolid, Prague and Paris were chosen† – all from Soulier
and Clouzard originals. Publishing seven different subjects was an obvious
tactic to increase sales but Crookes explained it by identifying difficulties 'with
our circulation' of getting all the issues out in time with just one plate and
claimed that any problems in the wearing out of a single plate were removed.
In addition, the selection gave a better indication of the extent and variety of
subjects that could be reproduced. The impressions were made on an attractive
cream paper and the quality was good: the middle tones were reproduced and
details held even if there was a lack of strength in the shadows. There were no
blemishes and no retouching was visible in the examples examined. The
plates were, however, small – that of the Institute of France, Paris, for example
measuring $2\frac{7}{8}$ inches wide $\times$ $2\frac{3}{8}$ inches deep. (George Barclay, in one of his last
letters to Talbot, praised the quality but asked why the plates were so small.[44])

* Interestingly, the rumours flying at the time included one that Talbot had succeeded in obtaining
naturally coloured photographs.[45]

† Emma Llewelyn, Talbot's Welsh cousin, must have echoed the view of many others when she expressed delight at some specimens that Henry had sent but asked '. . . how about Lacock rather than
Paris'.[46] (See Plates 83–86.)

Brooker indicated at the time that 6,000 prints had been run but gave no indication of the maximum printing from any one plate.[47]

The reaction was generally good and Crookes reported that 'nearly all the daily and weekly London papers noticed the subject together with upwards of 100 provincial papers and the remarks on the novelty and importance of the process were very favourable . . .'[48] There were inevitably some criticisms but Talbot took a very enlightened attitude to them, writing to Crookes on one occasion: 'Please inform me who is your "Contemporary" who speaks ill of the invention. I should wish to send him a few good specimens. If after that he remains obdurate, I leave him to his own opinion.'[49]

The publishers of *Photographic News* were sufficiently pleased with the result to ask Talbot to produce another and single subject for September 1859 (the Tuileries in Paris) to encourage buyers as the magazine entered its second year. This time the steel-coated copper plate ('[steel] does not injure the impressions . . . it causes a slight improvement in the tone'[50]) gave a picture $6\frac{1}{2}$ inches $\times$ 6 inches in size. It was carried in the 16 September issue and whilst Crookes referred to the 'superiority of this print' and the great power of producing an unlimited number of photographs that the process conferred, it must be stated frankly that the examples examined were not good. The etching was exceedingly uneven and there were numerous processing blemishes. Talbot had worried about the quality of the plates he had etched months before printing took place (he spoke apologetically of being out of practice and 'not being a good manipulator, but getting speedily tired, which a good photographer ought never to be'[50]) and was very doubtful when he saw the proofs Brooker was producing. But he allowed himself to be persuaded by Crookes and his publishers and the publication went ahead. On this occasion it was not a good advertisement for the process.

There was however plenty of encouragement from other quarters. Talbot had sent some 'photoglyphs' to Prince Albert, whose private secretary replied that the Consort had 'watched with the deepest interest the progress of your improvements in an art which is destined to be of so much service to the world'.[51] Charles Wheatstone had one eye at least on business possibilities. He had been disappointed with the heavy retouching of some prints produced for him of stereoscopic slides by Paul Pretsch but believed Talbot's process could produce pictures for the stereoscope which ought to meet with a considerable sale: 'My large stereoscope, far superior as it is to the others, has never become popular on account of the expense of the pictures.'[52]

The family was delighted with the results of the new discovery but none more so than Emma and John Dillwyn Llewelyn, who were without doubt the most accomplished husband-and-wife team in the early history of photography and who took up the new process with great enthusiasm, desiring to know all the technicalities. Emma wrote to Henry: 'I have been sole printer (with nitrate of silver) for Mr Llewelyn . . . I am delighted to think we shall have such an interesting amusement as your new art to add to our occupations . . .'[53] Llewelyn himself – whom Talbot invited to visit Lacock Abbey for a few days' instruction in manipulation – also, like Charles Wheatstone, compared the new technique favourably with Paul Pretsch's system:

> The simplicity of the manipulation strikes me very forcibly. Unless I had seen it, I could hardly have believed that a metal engraving could have been produced so quickly and so easily. What a contrast the new process offers in those respects to the complicated and laborious photogalvanography, the manipulations of which were as long as its polysyllabic name. Besides which your engravings are all genuine photographs while the photogalvanographs were all more or less assisted by the engraver's tool. There can indeed be no doubt of the importance of the great step which you have gained in the advance of this most interesting art. I look forward to see all illustrated works printed in this manner for who will accept the work of men's hands when they can have the work of the sun's rays.[54]*

Llewelyn was a distinguished scientist and innovator in his own right but lest his evaluation be thought biased, the opinion of one Francis S. Beatty, an engraver and printer in Dublin, may be quoted. He considered photoglyphic engraving so far above all others that the Queen should confer 'some distinguished mark of her favour'[55] on Talbot.

Unfortunately Talbot continued to demonstrate his lack of business flair. Despite George Barclay's prompting he admitted as late as August 1858 that he had not yet decided what to do with the invention though 'perhaps some of the leading Publishers & Printsellers might be invited to form a company (limited of course) to carry it out, in conjunction with other persons'.[56] Two months later he was still talking vaguely along the same lines and on this account was reluctant to discuss the matter of licences though he had no objections to amateurs experimenting with the process. In February 1859 Talbot wrote to Crookes asking whether his publishers could find a post for Henneman who had been staying on in London hoping that a company would be formed

---

* To be fair to Pretsch, much of his work was of excellent quality but surviving examples examined do not look like photographs. See, for example, the reproduction of a photograph by O. G. Rejlander in the *Photographic Journal* of 15 September 1859 (p. 28) which looks like a first-class artist's etching.

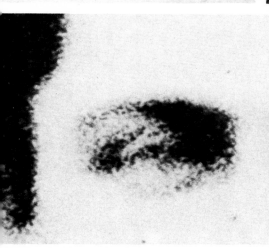

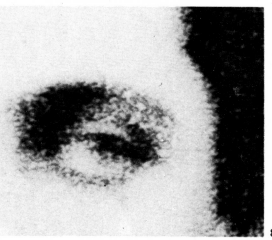

79/80/81. *Enlargements from three subjects demonstrating some of the techniques by which images were built up in Henry Talbot's method of photo-mechanical reproduction: (79) makes use of a 'screen' of opaque squares and clear lines, (80) of a screen with diagonal clear lines added and (81) of an aquatint ground formed from powdered resin*

82. *A piece of the gauze which Talbot used to create a screen in his early photo-engraving experiments. The resulting prints would have differed from the effects shown above, since the (highly irregular) squares would have been clear and the lines opaque*

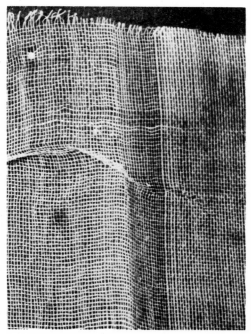

83

84

85

86

83/84/85/86. *Four of the photographic prints distributed with copies of* Photographic News *on 12 November 1858. The original photographs were by the French photographers Soulier and Clouzard and Talbot made the photoglyphic engravings from which the prints were made.* (83) *Bridge over the River Moldau, Prague,* (84) *Institute de France, Paris,* (85) *the Congress of Deputies, Madrid, and* (86) *a court in the Alhambra, Granada*

87

87/88. *Two later examples of Talbot's photoglyphic engravings - (87) the church of St Maurice at Vienne and (88) the portal of St Trophimus at Arles, both in France. The pictures dated from 1866 when the prints were being publicized as 'photo-sculpsits'*

88

89

Latticed Window
(with the Camera Obscura)
August 1835
When first made, the squares
of glass about 200 in number
could be counted, with help
of a lens.

90

92

91

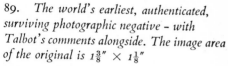

94

89.   *The world's earliest, authenticated, surviving photographic negative – with Talbot's comments alongside. The image area of the original is $1\frac{3}{8}'' \times 1\frac{1}{8}''$*

90.   *Although its date cannot be fixed definitely, this pale lilac positive image of Constance Talbot may well be the world's first photographic portrait on paper. Talbot's notes show that he took two portraits of his wife by the newly discovered Calotype process on 6 October and 8 October 1840. Both portraits were made 'without sun' and the exposure was five minutes in each case. A subsequent portrait taken on 10 October (which is now in the Royal Photographic Society Collection) was made in thirty seconds in bright sunlight*

91.   *The world's first group portrait on photographic paper. Talbot's notes recorded on 13 October 1840 'C E and R 1' 30″ – meaning, Constance, his wife, and daughters, Ela (right) and Rosamond, photographed with an exposure of one minute thirty seconds*

92.   *The essence of Talbot's photographic achievement – a developed Calotype negative. The yellow tone of the ground and highlights was typical of iodized paper. The original measures approximately $1\frac{1}{4}'' \times 2''$*

93.   *Possibly the earliest surviving Calotype (on the bottom of this positive in Talbot's hand is '3' cloudy . . . Sept. 1840'). Talbot wrote in his notebook on 24 September 1840, 'In 3 minutes a singular picture was obtained, the sky a deep fiery red [in the negative] especially by transmitted light, against which the roof almost white contrasted as if covered with snow'*

94.   *Mlle Amélina – 13 October 1840. An exposure lasting three minutes*

95.   *'Footman at Carriage Door' – 14 October 1840. A three-minute exposure*

98-102. *Following the announcement of photogenic drawing in 1839, Talbot continued with some established practices - such as reproducing the outlines of flowers on photogenic drawing paper (98) - but in the winter/spring of 1840 he began a major programme of experimentation to improve the system. The results, while falling short of the later Calotypes in quality and, more importantly, in relative shortness of exposure, were sufficient to impress discerning critics such as John Herschel. Exterior and interior views as well as still life compositions were subjects for Talbot's cameras. Shown here are (99) a view of Lacock Abbey (13 April 1840); (100) one of the galleries at Lacock Abbey (23 November 1839 or 2 March 1840); (101) a table still life (24 April 1840) and (102) an exterior composition, a style unique to his own photography at this early period in the history of a new art form*

97

96/97. *Both at the Reading and Regent Street establishments, Henneman had coloured versions of Calotype portraits and scenes produced. Henry Talbot did not approve of the results. Shown here is a copy of a Calotype original of Henneman (left) and a fellow servant in the role of woodcutters - and a coloured version which sold for 3s. 6d.*

98

99

0

101

102

103

104

105

I

107

103. *Henry Talbot, aged three. Artist unknown*

104. *William Davenport Talbot, Henry's father*

105. *The arms of the Talbot family. (From a document, dated 1778, granting royal authority for William Davenport to adopt the surname of Talbot and to bear the family's arms)*

106. *Henry Talbot's two Royal Society medals: (left) the Royal Medal of 1838 for his mathematical researches and (right) the Rumford Medal awarded in 1842 for his photographic researches*

107. *Talbotia elegans – a plant named in Talbot's honour by Professor Balfour of the Royal Botanic Garden, Edinburgh. (Illustration by W. H. Fitch from* Botanical Magazine *1869 – no. 5803)*

by Talbot to exploit photoglyphic engraving. Henry explained that the hope had not been fulfilled because of his own ill health over the winter and that most likely some months would elapse before he was able to take any action in that direction.[57] He never did – but the intrusion of the world of business inevitably raised the subject of patents again.

After the publication of Talbot's photoglyphic engraving in *Photographic News* in November 1858, Paul Pretsch, whose patent had lapsed earlier that year because he could not afford the annual payments, requested Crookes to extend the same publicity to his technique. There then began three more years of desultory and unproductive exchanges between Talbot and Pretsch (either directly or through third parties) which revealed something of both their characters. Talbot had believed from the first that part of Pretsch's system was based on his first patent. That belief had been confirmed by what Talbot considered to be reliable expert advice and he was adamant that his work should be suitably acknowledged. Whatever may have been said about the high fees asked for Talbot's photographic licences, it seems clear that in photo-engraving he was more concerned with the question of *acknowledgement* than securing fees, although the latter obviously arose in the discussions. For his part, Pretsch was not prepared to agree to the public declaration that his system derived or was partly derived) from Talbot's patent even though he seemed near on occasion to agreeing to pay for a licence from Talbot. The two views were incompatible despite the intercession of others.

Thus when Crookes told Talbot of Pretsch's approach about publishing pictures in *Photographic News*, Henry explained the situation but said that Pretsch could have a free licence to publish provided he would write direct or via Crookes to request it.[58] A similar situation arose with the *Photographic Journal* early in 1859 but here it was the journal's editor who sought permission to publish which Talbot 'liberally accorded'.[59] At the end of that year Pretsch proposed that a works be established to operate both their systems with Henry granting a licence on 'liberal' terms. But as to the demand that there be an attribution on the plates to Talbot's licence Pretsch insisted, 'I think, taking a licence from you, should be enough satisfaction and you ought not to demand from me that I shall give myself a box behind the ear.'[60] This was not good enough for Talbot. He wanted a public admission of his patent priority – and thought in any case that his system was much superior to Pretsch's. As a result he was not prepared to operate any other process conjointly.

In 1860 and 1861 Pretsch worked on a system for the production of plates

T

for typographic (as distinct from intaglio) printing[61] and was also associated for some time with Warren De La Rue, the businessman–scientist and astronomical photographer. The commercial exploitation of photo-engraving was raised again in 1861 when J. Hogarth – who had his eyes set firmly on the potential market represented by such magazines as *Illustrated London News* – proposed that Pretsch, Talbot and he be associated in a new company.[62] Various financial arrangements were proposed and rejected but the critical issue remained. Pretsch wrote (quite rightly) of the great future which lay ahead in photo-engraving, of the many disappointments and setbacks he had encountered over the years which he had not considered he had deserved, and indicated that his resources were virtually exhausted: could not some form of cooperation be arranged?[63] Talbot was adamant: he did not wish to join Pretsch because it would interfere with any company he himself later established but – more to the point in his eyes – Pretsch was posing as the 'sole inventor' of his process which simply was not true.[64] Pretsch finally left England in 1863 and continued his researches in Vienna where he died in 1873. It would have been no consolation to him but it should be stated that he suffered far more at the hands of some of his business partners than he did from Talbot who after all had an arguable case even if his inflexible, uncompromising attitude over 'priority' precluded the possibility of a mutually beneficial outcome. Where the Lacock man could most definitely be faulted – as in photography – was in the failure to think out a clear-cut scheme for business exploitation of his invention (with or without his own participation) and seek to promote it.

Talbot's experiments continued in the early 1860s* and Brooker was joined as an engraving and printing adviser by W. Banks of Edinburgh. It was Banks increasingly who sought plates and paper of the quality Talbot wanted, who removed from plates the evidence of Talbot's false starts when an etching proved unsuccessful and who participated to some degree in the actual experiments. Thus in 1861 he wrote about the difficulties in producing a ruled-line glass screen requested by Henry and a little later it was evident that Talbot was experimenting with a transfer printing system based on asphalt.[65†]

* One aspect of Talbot's engraving work which still remains to be fully researched is his production of plates without any kind of resin ground. His notes on proofs made from such plates in the Lacock Collection confirm that the plates were made without a resin ground but tantalizingly give no details of how they were produced.

† At various times during his experiments with steel Talbot's ingenious (if occasionally fanciful) mind saw other possibilities – for example, creating photographic effects on steel dotted with platina and treated with acid solutions which resulted in the steel background becoming very dark and the platina very bright.[66]

In January 1862 he bought his own 13-inch copper-plate printing press and proceeded to enjoy himself immensely – sending one of his first successes to his daughter Tilly in Scotland. It is not clear to what extent the prints produced from Talbot's etchings during this period issued from his own press but some extremely praiseworthy specimens were circulated. In 1862 he was invited to submit prints to the International Exhibition in London: these showed further improvement in the control of tones in particular and he was awarded a medal, one of the official reporters at the Exhibition (H. W. Vogel) commenting: 'Talbot has opened a new field of photography and the graphic arts by his heliogravure . . . and he has justly earned the prize which the jury has awarded him.'[67] (Pretsch also received an award for photo-electrotype and typographic plates.) In 1863 he prepared a plate of Mount Guajara in Tenerife for a report[68] published by his friend Charles Piazzi Smyth, Astronomer Royal of Scotland.

Piazzi Smyth's expedition to Tenerife in 1856 was intended to demonstrate the superiority of astronomical observations from high altitudes – up to 10,700 feet in this case – and as a keen photographer* he took a series of photographs of different peaks about four miles away to prove the clearness of the air compared with records taken from sea level. When published in 1863 the report included five pictures: four photographic prints produced at the Stationery Office 'Talbotively' (to use Piazzi Smyth's phrase)[69] and one from a Talbot etching on steel. The original negative from which Talbot worked was not a good one by Piazzi Smyth's own admission but Henry eventually produced a plate which measured $6\frac{3}{4}$ inches $\times$ $4\frac{1}{4}$ inches and bore 500 impressions. It was not one of his best but Piazzi Smyth was delighted. He wrote that 'to the inventor alike of photography and photoglyphy' it probably did not matter which method was used, but from the point of view of permanence 'to readers in a future century it may make a great difference' – and added the opinion that for scientific purposes 'definition and minute linear accuracy appear almost better in the photoglyph'.[68]

It was about this time that a writer preparing an article on engraving wrote to Talbot for information and a typical photoglyphic plate, commenting: 'To write an article on chemical engraving without giving you a prominent place

---

* At this time he was experimenting with enlarging up to 8.5 diameters from his collodion negatives. In the context of the Guajara engraving, he asked Talbot whether the grains of silver seen in the enlargement could be used directly in some way instead of an aquatint ground.

In 1865 Piazzi Smyth mounted an expedition to the Great Pyramid in Egypt and under most trying conditions obtained numerous photographs – some from the inside of the Pyramid using magnesium ribbon.[70]

in it would be like writing a treatise on the law of gravitation and omitting the name of Newton.'[71] But his family's ever-demanding attitude never ceased and in thanking her half brother for an example of photoglyphic engraving sent in November 1863, Caroline Mount Edgcumbe continued:

> It is very soft and pretty – but is it not the same sort of thing you did 3 or 4 years ago, & that you got the medal for at the Exhibition last year? Will you explain this – because I am anxious you should *now* try your hand at something on a larger scale, to make you a *name* for photographic engraving among the Public in general . . .[72]

Perhaps even she would have been reasonably pleased when in 1865 Talbot's engravings won a prize at the Berlin International Photographic Exhibition.

Talbot continued to be supplied with original photographs by both foreign and home photographers – the latter including his former assistant Henneman and the Edinburgh portraitist John Moffat – and it was a sign of changing times when Moffat criticized the *British Journal of Photography* in 1865 for not printing a photoglyphic engraving of his portrait of Talbot (p. 319): 'It would have been so much more in keeping with our art than the wretched wood cut they put forward.'[73] In 1866 Brooker pronounced some of Talbot's plates the most successful he had ever done and thought some later efforts capable of providing 3,000–4,000 impressions.[74] Talbot also kept in contact with the leading workers in the field: for instance, Joseph Swan[75] (who had earlier introduced a pigment-transfer process and was later to introduce important improvements in photographic printing paper, plates and screening techniques, as well as earning a knighthood for his invention of the incandescent lamp) and F. Joubert, the talented French engraver and inventor.[76] However, there were no further developments and Talbot's time must have been increasingly devoted to his Assyrian and mathematical researches for there was little sign of active research into engraving from the mid-1860s onwards. But even then his typical versatility could not be quenched entirely for in 1875 he was proposing a new method for securing 'superior photographic veils'[77] and in the year of his death was producing a photoglyphic engraving for a book (p. 322).

But the vital breakthrough to essentially modern techniques was to be made by others. Two years after Talbot's death Karl Klič in Vienna transferred a pigment image to a grained copper plate, washed the print in warm water and then etched the plate with ferric chloride solutions of different strengths.[78] This was close to modern intaglio (*photogravure*) printing – and in 1890 Klič is credited with adopting a positive cross-line screen (with transparent lines and opaque dots) to make his process suitable for high-capacity rotary presses. Thus he created *rotogravure*.* In typographic printing – with its immense potential of printing both type and half-tone illustrations at the same time – the American Frederic Ives, after continuing research by a number of workers,† introduced in 1886 the cross-line screen on glass which, with appropriate camera procedures and calculation of screen–plate distances, yielded images composed of dots of varying size and distribution much as we see them in many of our newspapers to this day.

Might Talbot's photoglyphic engraving have become a commercial success if he had been prepared to have professional engravers develop it and to place it in the hands of capable businessmen? It is a possibility, even though it would be wrong to underestimate the continuing problems in achieving comprehensively satisfactory results with a wide range of subjects, the conservatism of those using non-photographic etched-line techniques or the challenge in illustrating books represented by such excellent if limited application processes as Collotype and Woodburytype.[79] Talbot, however, was what he was: an obstinate 'loner' and in that lay the reason for his research successes as much as the possible failure to exploit the photoglyphic engraving process. But, as in photography, his was the way to the future – combining light-sensitive bichromates with gelatin, the screen, the use of ferric chloride and differential etching – and for that he has a secure place in the history of photomechanical reproduction which is second only to that of his place in the history of photography itself. The importance of his contribution for the future was assessed in perceptive terms when an acquaintance commented in 1867[80] on examining one of Talbot's etchings that now 'he should not despair of being able to *fly*'.

* Adolf Brandweiner in Vienna independently discovered the technique in 1892 and took credit for first publishing details.

† Others may have anticipated Ives's discoveries but it is his name which is still associated with the process, and that of Max Levy who is credited with the perfecting and commercial manufacture of cross-line screens.

10
Numbers and Assyrians

From the later 1850s onwards Henry Talbot again began publishing on mathematics. After his papers on integration – which were so highly regarded by the Royal Society – his notebooks show that he turned to the theory or properties of numbers. Once again this was a subject bristling with unproved conjecture and one which had occupied some of the greatest mathematical minds of the eighteenth century. Correspondence in 1847[1] indicated that he was giving the subject serious consideration then – but he did not publish until 1857,[2] almost twenty years after his previous paper to the Royal Society in London.

His subject was one of Fermat's* theorems, which he introduced to the Royal Society of Edinburgh thus:

It is well known that no satisfactory demonstration has ever been given of Fermat's celebrated theorem, which asserts that the equation $a^n = b^n + c^n$ is impossible, if a, b, c, are whole numbers, and n is any whole number greater than 2 . . . Fermat himself was in possession of the demonstration, or at least believed himself to be so, and he describes his demonstration as being a wonderful one – *mirabilem sane*. He does not say that the theorem itself is wonderful, but his demonstration of it; from which I think it likely that he meant to say that it was very remarkable for its shortness and simplicity.

Since, however, subsequent mathematicians have failed to discover any demonstration, much less an extremely simple one, of this celebrated theorem, it has been surmised that Fermat deceived himself in this matter, and that his demonstration, if it had been preserved to us, would have proved unsatisfactory . . .

* Pierre de Fermat (1601–65) is chiefly remembered for his role in the foundation of analytic geometry, theories of probability and modern arithmetic. His work was usually contained in correspondence where he was prone to state theorems without advancing *proofs*.

Nevertheless . . . I have found that there is one case in which Fermat's theorem admits of a singularly simple demonstration; and as I do not find it noticed in any mathematical work to which I have been able to refer, I think it worthy of being brought under the notice of mathematicians. It may possibly prove to be a step in the right direction towards the recovery of Fermat's lost demonstration. It is, moreover, in itself a very extended and remarkable theorem, although less so than that of Fermat.

The case was that in which one of *a, b, c* was a prime number. This proved, in eighteen lines, he went on to provide his own extension to Fermat's theorem, namely that $a^n = b^n - c^n$ is also impossible (*a* being prime) except when $b - c = 1$.

In this paper, therefore, as well as in the paper entitled 'On the theory of numbers'[3] given to the Royal Society of Edinburgh in 1862, he was still challenging or improving on the findings of accepted authorities. The 1862 paper began: 'The object . . . will be, to give a connected view of some theorems of importance, which are often found in books rather obscurely demonstrated, and in some cases are inaccurately given, or are liable to exceptions which are not mentioned.' Not a favourable view of contemporary text-books.

The subject was a new proof of another of Fermat's theorems: 'If *p* is a prime number, which does not divide *a*, it necessarily divides $a^{p-1} - 1$' and the derivation from it of Wilson's theorem, 'If *p* be any prime number, the product of all the numbers less than *p*, or 1. 2. 3. . . . (p − 1), augmented by unity is divisible by *p*.' Talbot continued with a new view of Euler's 'associate numbers', or rather an alternative system. The paper ended with a criticism of the demonstrations of Peter Barlow in his *An Elementary Investigation of the Theory of Numbers* of 1811, in which Talbot pointed out some errors 'lest they should acquire credit, by having appeared in a work of authority'. (Barlow's Tables are still reprinted.)

The essay 'On Fagnani's Theorem',[4] given to the Royal Society of Edinburgh in 1863 was not a return to integration, but was an original piece of analytical geometry applied to confocal conics. Fagnani's theorem itself stated that the difference between the lengths of two arcs of an ellipse could be expressed as the length of a related straight line. A special pair of such arcs defines *Fagnani's point* on the quadrant of the ellipse. This point had been shown to be the intersection of the ellipse with the rectangular hyperbola having the same foci as the ellipse. The geometric properties of the system, as Talbot wrote, had been investigated by Graves, MacCullagh and Brinkley, contemporaries who were all connected with the Royal Irish Academy. Talbot characteristically added his own observations to prove new theorems about confocal conics – and an afterthought on the subject[5] was read at Edinburgh in 1865.

Between these two papers he published 'Researches on Malfatti's problem'.[6] This contained an original proof entirely by Euclidean geometry – and that was its importance – of a known construction: 'In a given triangle to inscribe three circles touching each other, and each of them touching two sides of the triangle.' It was a condition of the acceptability of such a construction that each step – point, line or arc – had to be validated by mathematical proof: the Italian geometer Malfatti himself, having propounded the problem in 1803, gave the correct construction and a proof which was based on trigonometric formulae and the solution of equations. Up to 1865, however, wrote Talbot (again disregarding the eminence of earlier writers who attempted solutions):

> Although it is a question of elementary geometry which can be solved by a simple and elegant geometrical construction, yet no *geometrical* proof has ever been given, as far as I am aware, of the truth of this construction. It has been established hitherto only by a very elaborate use of algebraic analysis, in the course of which, however indisputable the result may be, all *geometrical* perception of its truth is lost. And yet there can be little doubt ... that a *geometrical* reason must exist for any simple series of facts belonging to elementary geometry ... I now offer the Royal Society a purely geometrical solution of the problem ...

Thus complete geometric proof had eluded some of the the greatest geometers: Steiner of Berlin, Zornow of Königsberg, and even Plücker, one of the greatest names in contemporary geometry.

Henry Talbot proceeded in his typically painstaking way, over eleven *lemmas* or propositions, to establish his basic simple facts and then to complete his proof, which, as he claimed, was simple and wholly Euclidean.*

Two years later – in April 1867 – Henry Talbot again addressed the Royal Society of Edinburgh, this time 'On cubic equations'[7] showing a method of

---

* Talbot's construction was as follows: 'Bisect the angles of the triangle ABC, by the lines AO, BO, CO. In two of the smaller triangles thus made AOB, BOC, inscribe the circles γ and α. From D, the point of contact of α with the side BC, draw a line DY, touching the circle γ. Then DY will touch one of the required circles also; which circle also touches AB, BC, two sides of the triangle, and is therefore wholly determined.'

Dr Hart, in the *Quarterly Journal* (as quoted in Casey's *Sequel to Euclid*, 1886) had anticipated Talbot by a few years, but the proof – although purely geometrical – assumed many facts to be known which Talbot worked out in his eleven lemmas.

dealing with a certain class of cubics. In introducing it, he insisted that to find one root by inspecting and substituting (the simplest way of finding a root) was not a *scientific* process of solution. The equations dealt with, however, were of special form and the essay did not advance the theory of equations significantly.

His last mathematical paper in Edinburgh – read in April 1875 – was an 'Essay towards a general solution of all degrees having integer roots'.[8] This again did not advance theory – but it detailed an original method of simplifying calculations where large numbers were involved. During its preparation Talbot indicated to Philip Kelland that he had met certain difficulties, but Kelland replied that whatever the problem, in Talbot's hand the subject would 'be approached with uniform clearness of perception'.[9] Such was his reputation with the scientists and mathematicians of Scotland gathered in the Royal Society of Edinburgh which in 1858 had elected him an honorary fellow – an honour limited to twenty British subjects and which Talbot shared with Charles Darwin, James Prescott Joule, T. H. Huxley, J. A. Froude, Thomas Carlyle, Alfred Tennyson and the mathematicians John Couch Adams, J. J. Sylvester and Arthur Cayley.

What was Talbot's contribution to mathematics over his lifetime? A striking attribute was his capacity for clear thought and lucid expression. This, as he almost said explicitly, was not present in some contemporary exponents. The number of topics which interested him was limited, but within it his gift of seeing into a complicated problem, clarifying it in his own mind and setting the solution down very simply, placed him on equal terms with the better known minds of his circle, such as Herschel, Peacock and Lubbock – and indeed with many of the continental writers of the time.

Few of Talbot's contemporaries at Cambridge gained fame exclusively as mathematicians. Some certainly (for example Peacock) became teachers, but it was their pupils who were really to bring English mathematics back into the European mathematical community. This was not entirely accidental when it is remembered that the background of the undergraduate studies of Talbot and his friends was still limited to a preference for synthetic (or geometric) over analytic (or algebraic) method. Liberation was not to be achieved overnight by a rejection of Newton and a text-book of analysis.

The limitations upon mathematicians of Talbot's era were bound to increase as the subject progressed and as analytic methods were increasingly applied during a period when all branches of mathematics were re-thought from their fundamentals. The years 1820 to 1840 saw the foundation of modern geometry and analysis, the work of Poncelet and Plücker in the former, and of Abel, Galois and Jacobi in the latter – often anticipated by the monumental and omniscient Gauss. A theorem in integral calculus, however general, still based on the arcs of curves for its interpretation – which condition Peacock had required and Talbot had accepted – was by 1837 outdated. By then, although the Royal Society rightly recognized Talbot's inventive genius by awarding him the Royal Medal, his essay was no longer in the main stream of development.*

It is probable that Talbot himself saw this – that mathematics was going in a direction where he could not wholeheartedly follow. The later notebooks showed an attempt at further development and his correspondence with Herschel demonstrated that mathematical problems were still being discussed. But Talbot's days of *important* mathematical achievement ended in the 1830s – even if two decades later he was again immersed in mathematical ideas, still stimulated by the challenge of unsolved problems and by impatience with apparently lengthy or inappropriate or inaccurate methods.

His genius in mathematics was an exceptional craftsmanship in devising original methods of attacking existing questions rather than the invention of new concepts. It is probable that had he started as a young man from a modern mathematical grounding, he could have absorbed and amplified many of the ideas which have arisen since his day – but he would have wanted to work them out for himself from first principles and to apply his own original methods. Moreover he would have been highly selective of those which appealed to him, for his horizons were far wider than the world of pure mathematics.

In the 1850s Henry Talbot began work, which was to continue for the rest of his life, on a subject that was one of the romances of the nineteenth century – the re-discovery of the great Assyrian Empire after millennia of obscurity.[10] To this he was to contribute much of value.

Assyria was located in northern Mesopotamia – present-day Iraq – with the major sites of Nineveh and Nimrud situated on the higher reaches of the River

---

* None the less, in a major work on differential and integral calculus, published in 1870, Talbot's contribution was reviewed with those of such names as James Bernoulli, Steiner, Pascal, Fagnani and Chasles.[11]

Tigris. For part of the second millennium B.C. it was a dependency of Babylonia, whose capital city was on the Euphrates to the south. But Assyria subsequently became independent and went on to become a major power throughout Mesopotamia spreading into present-day Syria and Armenia. Its days of great-ness were to reach their height in the period of the so-called Neo-Assyrian Empire when, between 750 B.C. and 612 B.C., Assyrian fighting prowess gave it control of an area covering most of the Near East, stretching from Egypt in the west through to the Persian Gulf. During that period King Sennacherib destroyed Babylon – but Babylon was to rise again under the Chaldeans to destroy Assyrian power and Babylon's power in its turn was later to yield to the Persians under Darius and Xerxes.

In 1840 little was known of Assyria – its laws, customs, kings and its superbly barbaric art some of which can now be seen in the British Museum. Within little more than a decade, however, the archaeological excavations of the Frenchman Paul-Emile Botha and – even more so – of Austen Henry Layard were to lead to a revolution in knowledge. In 1839 Layard set off for what was intended to be an overland journey to Ceylon and with hopes of securing a post in the diplomatic corps. But – several years later – encouraged by Sir Stratford Canning, British Ambassador at Istanbul, and by Henry Rawlinson, then British Consul at Baghdad, he devoted his intuitive mind with its acute artistic awareness to excavations first at Nimrud and then at Kuyunjik (to the north of Nimrud) which proved to be the site of Nineveh. By 1847 the first tablets and inscriptions from Nimrud excavated by Layard were received at the British Museum – and they were the first of thousands upon which the study of Assyriology was to be based. Fortunately work on an equivalent of the Rosetta Stone had already been continuing for some time: the decipher-ment and translation of Assyrian cuneiform writing was to establish Major (later Sir) Henry Creswicke Rawlinson alongside Layard as a co-founder of Assyriology.

About twenty miles from Kirmanshah in Persia – on the old highway between Persia and Babylonia – is the Great Rock of Bihistun, which is part of a low mountain range and reaches a height of a little over 3,800 feet. On the rock, perhaps 400 feet from the ground and occupying a prepared surface about 60 feet wide by 23 feet in depth, is a sculptured bas-relief and trilingual inscrip-tion. It was executed at the command of the Persian King Darius I (522–486 B.C.) and shows him before rebels who are submitting to his power. This inscription was of critical importance to the early Victorian researchers: it comprised 414 lines of Persian cuneiform, 263 of Elamite cuneiform which contained a translation of part of the Persian text, and 112 lines of Babylonian cuneiform which similarly formed a translation of part of the Persian cuneiform text.

Discovering the key to the thousands of tablets being unearthed at Nineveh and Nimrud (and thus to the story of a lost empire) was somewhat more complex than in the case of the Egyptian hieroglyphics and the Rosetta Stone, for Greek appeared on the latter whereas the Bihistun inscription was in three languages all of which were entirely unknown. An additional difficulty was the problem of copying the inscription at Bihistun for it was in a position relatively inaccessible for close study. The latter however was overcome by the athleticism and application of Henry Rawlinson and those who assisted him.

Rawlinson was a brilliant linguist, athlete, soldier and diplomat. To the Greek and Latin learned during his schooldays were added later Persian, Arabic and Hindustani – his knowledge of Persian and Persian poems in particular making him a welcome visitor to the Shah's court when on diplomatic business. In 1835 he was posted to Kirmanshah to act as military adviser to the Shah's brother who was governor of the province. On his way there he copied the Persian cuneiform text at Mount Elvend but it was the inscription at Bihistun to which he devoted most of his attention. By 1839 he had painstakingly copied 200 lines of the Persian text and over a number of visits in the period from that date to 1847 – interrupted with service on the Persian side in the Afghanistan War and as British representative in Baghdad – he completed copies of all three texts making up the inscription. A translation of part of the Persian cuneiform was completed by Rawlinson and sent to the Royal Asiatic Society in London early in 1838. Within another year he had completed deciphering and translating nearly all the 200 lines he had copied up to that time.

Some work had already been done on the decipherment of the Persian cuneiform. In the eighteenth century the German scholar Karsten Niebuhr had recognized at Bihistun three distinct systems of characters (though not the fact that they were giving the same subject matter), suggested values for certain signs and correctly identified that the script was read from left to right and not perpendicularly. G. F. Grotefend, working on other Persian inscriptions, had identified the signs for rulers' names such as Darius and Xerxes and Rawlinson's continental contemporaries Eugène Burnouf and Christian Lassen had added further to the knowledge of Persian cuneiform. But it was Rawlinson who over the course of a decade virtually completed the decipherment with 'a wonderful faculty for divining the correct values of the signs, for restoring broken words, and for grasping intuitively the general meaning of a passage'[12] and who proceeded with a considerable programme of interpretation and translation. In his genius for decipherment Rawlinson was matched by Dr Edward Hincks – rector of a remote country parish at Ardtrea in Ireland – who quite independently had arrived at similar results to those of Rawlinson and who on occasions was able to suggest solutions which Rawlinson had not seen. Hincks however was less interested in translation as such and it was capability for both decipherment and translation which placed Rawlinson in a class on his own.

Old Persian cuneiform – the word comes from the Latin *cuneus* (a wedge) after the shape of the components of the script pressed into clay – was almost entirely *syllabic and phonetic* in composition, that is individual signs had no individual meaning only an individual phonetic value. The first key came from the correct identification of the individual signs making up the names of known kings – and thereafter, through skill and luck, phonetic values were assigned to other individual signs until eventually decipherment was virtually complete. One important element in this decipherment was the amount of text that had become available, which not only aided the decipherment process as such but enabled correct decipherment to be verified. But perhaps the most important element of all was the application of the relatively new tool of comparative philology – in which known languages from a similar group (for example Sanskrit and Avestan in the case of Persian cuneiform) enabled the scholars to assign phonetic values (and thus eventually meaning) to cuneiform syllables in the necessarily cumulative process of decipherment. They were assisted in the task by the relatively limited number of syllabic values in Persian cuneiform.

By 1847 Rawlinson, Hincks and others had turned their attention to the Babylonian cuneiform inscriptions on the Rock of Bihistun,* without which decipherment the many recently discovered relics from Assyria would not yield their knowledge. But the task was to prove much more difficult – and in a very real sense the decipherment of the Assyrian and Babylonian cuneiform is still continuing. To a considerable degree the problem stemmed from history.

---

* The third cuneiform inscription on the Rock – Elamite – originated from an area of south-west Persia. The language was a development from Babylonian cuneiform so once the Babylonian decipherment was complete that of Elamite could be accomplished.

The civilizations of Babylonia and Assyria were built on the earlier civilization of the Sumerians* – a non-semitic people who invented the cuneiform system of writing on tablets. Babylonian and Assyrian were different dialects of a language which came to be called Akkadian† and both adopted cuneiform (as did the Hittites and Persians). But the Babylonians and Assyrians were semitic peoples and there were inevitably complications when they adopted cuneiform script to express their own speech. Their script was infinitely more variable than the later Persian cuneiform: it was syllabic and an individual sign in the script could have in some cases a dozen possible syllabic values, the correct value being determined by the context (i.e. the word) in which it occurred. But at the same time there was often a different sign for each syllable. Thus whereas in Persian cuneiform there were perhaps thirty or so signs to be deciphered, at any given period in Babylonian–Assyrian there were possibly between 300 and 500 signs.

There were additional problems where decipherment merged into transliteration and translation. The cuneiform script did not mark the end of a word, so it was a matter of interpretation where successive syllables formed a whole word. And, once an individual word had been isolated from other signs in the text, there was the problem of identifying its meaning by comparison with similar sounding words in its 'family' group of languages which were already known – Hebrew, Aramaic and Arabic.

In the late 1840s and early 1850s Rawlinson and Hincks independently worked on the decipherment of the Babylonian cuneiform,‡ with Edwin Norris, as an assistant secretary and librarian of the Royal Asiatic Society, frequently acting as an informal link between the two.§ Working on the Bihistun inscription, Rawlinson informed the Society in 1850 that he had identified about eighty proper names, and that, working through the Persian text, had compiled a list of about 500 Babylonian words of which he knew the meaning certainly and the phonetic values approximately.[13] Hincks's papers on the Babylonian and Assyrian syllabary in the period of 1846–50 demonstrated

* Sumer was situated around the delta of the Tigris and Euphrates in southern Iraq.
† Akkad was to the north in the area of Babylonia.
‡ However, the inscriptions found by the excavators of Assyrian sites comprised *Assyrian* historical texts and *Assyrian* copies of Babylonian literary texts. It was on these that the early scholars – including Henry Talbot – worked.
§ Norris used to see Rawlinson's various papers through the press (often with suggestions for improvements). He became an authority on cuneiform, and was working on his Assyrian dictionary when he died in 1872.

that he had a more accurate knowledge of the use and values of the characters and their nature than Rawlinson. It was Hincks who first published a list of characters (a good number of whose values proved to be correct), identified the signs of the vowels – and who deduced too that the Babylonians and Assyrians had borrowed their writing from a non-semitic people. He also first distinguished the essentially syllabic nature of the signs. Rawlinson freely admitted in 1850 that Hincks knew more about the Bihistun inscription languages than anyone else – but once again proceeded to demonstrate that he was the supreme decipherer *and* translator.

It was one thing for Rawlinson, Hincks, Norris and a few others including Henry Talbot to be sure that the decipherment of Assyrian-Babylonian cuneiform had been well begun, but quite another matter to convince the less knowledgeable who were asked to believe that one sign could have perhaps a dozen different syllabic meanings. As late as 1862 Talbot reported in a letter to Hincks that:

... the Professor of Hebrew at the Sorbonne at Paris, Monsr Bargès, has declared himself fully convinced by ... arguments of the entire futility of the pretended cuneiform discoveries. He estimates that one-fifth of the French Academy admits the decipherment to a certain extent, while 4-5ths remain incredulous.[14]

But he drew consolation from the fact that one of the sceptics also rejected Champollion's discoveries in hieroglyphics even though 'nothing can be more certain than the general soundness of Champollion's system'.[15] He was none the less sharply aware of the problem – and later the same year wrote to Hincks:

The polyphone values [i.e. representing several sounds] are among the chief difficulties of the language and I am persuaded they *must* have occasionally caused embarrassment to the Assyrians themselves. Probably the bulk of the population was uneducated, and unable to read and write: but those persons who could read a little only, must have been sadly puzzled by the polyphones and the other peculiarities of the language. I am not surprised that modern literati are reluctant to admit the fact of their existence, so opposed to all the former facts of philology.[16]

In the 1850s, therefore, Rawlinson was understandably cautious in making any general claims for the success of the work – particularly perhaps as the history of the Assyrian and Babylonian Empires touched frequently on events recounted in the Bible which was an eternal source of fascination for the general public as well as scholars. Asked to make some general pronouncement, he refused stating that there was a great deal more to find out and that until he had studied all the tablets from Nineveh and Babylonia he would say no more.

The next move was made by Henry Talbot. He had followed Rawlinson's and Hincks's brilliant work with critical admiration and great interest, while his knowledge of Hebrew was an advantage in evaluating their results. Talbot ranked Edward Hincks as the *first* discoverer – i.e. decipherer – of the Assyrian language though he agreed that Rawlinson's work was completely independent. He maintained contact with Samuel Birch at the British Museum* and it was almost certainly Birch who arranged for Talbot to have some access to tablets before they were released in copy form to the public. In September 1854 Henry Talbot privately published *Notes on the Assyrian Inscriptions* (material prepared for the next meeting of the British Association for the Advancement of Science) and the paper gave a good brief description of the state of the researches in Assyriology generally and some typically lively Talbot ideas on both the language and geography of the inscriptions. A few months later Birch informed Hincks that Talbot had made '*great* progress in the Assyrian'.[17]

Henry hoped that the publication of Hincks's independent work would convince the doubters that Assyrian cuneiform was being deciphered and translated correctly but the British Museum at this time was not able or prepared to publish the work which Hincks had lodged with it in London. So Talbot proposed another tactic. He had been given access to a recently discovered clay cylinder dating from the reign of the Assyrian king Tiglath-Pileser I† and on 17 March 1857 he sent to the Royal Asiatic Society his translation in a sealed packet together with a letter in which he wrote:

Many persons have hitherto refused to believe in the truth of the system by which Dr Hincks and Sir H. Rawlinson have interpreted the Assyrian writings, because it contains many things entirely contrary to their preconceived opinions. For example, each Cuneiform group represents a syllable, but not always the same syllable; sometimes one, and sometimes another. To which it is replied, that such a licence would open the door to all manner of uncertainty; that the ancient Assyrians themselves, the natives of the country, could

---

* Birch was an Egyptologist who none the less fully supported the work being conducted on Assyriology. He wrote over 200 books and papers and ultimately became Keeper of the Department of Oriental Antiquities at the British Museum.

† Tiglath-Pileser (now dated to 1115–1077 B.C.) was King of Assyria during its expansion into Armenia and Syria, and during a major conflict with Babylonia, when he occupied north Babylonia and plundered the city of Babylon itself.

never have read such a kind of writing, and that, therefore, the system cannot be true, and the interpretations based upon it must be fallacious.

Experience, however, shows that the uncertainty arising from the source is not so great as might easily be imagined. Many of the Cuneiform groups have only one value, and others have always the same value in the same word or phrase, so that the remaining difficulties and uncertainties of reading are reduced within moderate limits.

Practically speaking, and considering the newness of the study, there is a fair amount of agreement between different interpreters in their versions of the Assyrian historical writings of average difficulty.

It is with the hope of showing that such agreement exists, that I have ventured to offer this translation to the Society.

It is well known that Sir H. Rawlinson has announced his intention of publishing translations of these lithographs, and also transcriptions of the same into the ordinary European letters. Now, assuredly it will not add much to the authority of his translations if other scholars, after their publication, shall say that they are disposed to concur in them. Those who doubted before, will continue to doubt afterwards, attributing the agreement less to independent conviction than to the great and deserved influence of Sir H. Rawlinson's authority.

But it is evidently quite a different thing, when a translation has been prepared by another hand *before* the appearance of Sir H. Rawlinson's translation, and without any communication with him. All candid inquirers must acknowledge that if any special agreement should appear between such independent versions, it must indicate that they have Truth for their basis. Moreover, the inscription of Tiglath Pileser I treats of very various matters, changing abruptly from one to the other; it abounds in proper names and statements of specific facts. It is, therefore, well suited for a comparison of this kind. I think it probable that there will be found a general resemblance between Sir H. Rawlinson's translation when published, and that which I have now the honour to offer. In proportion as this shall prove to be the case more or less completely, the argument which I wish to found upon it will be stronger or weaker; but, at all events, I hope it will be sufficient to prove that a true basis of interpretation has been established by Hincks and Rawlinson, upon which other investigators may confidently reply.[18]

The idea appealed greatly to the Council of the Royal Asiatic Society, which agreed that the comparison should be made – and invited not only Rawlinson but Edward Hincks and Jules Oppert* to submit translations.

Talbot was pleased with the addition of Hincks in the demonstration and wrote:

There will doubtless be errors in all the translations – but this is of small importance

* Oppert (1825–1905) taught languages and devoted his spare time to oriental languages (he spoke and read Arabic, Persian, Turkish, Greek and Armenian as well as five or six European languages). In 1869 he was appointed Professor of Assyriology at the Collège de France.

U

compared with the fact (which I confidently anticipate) that certain passages of importance will be rendered in the same way by all the translators, although relating to affairs previously unknown, and the absence of all bias upon the minds of the translators will render this agreement a proof positive of the truth of the system, in the opinion of all candid archaeologists.[19]

He was less pleased with the relatively short time given for the translation to Hincks and Oppert; that what he considered to be essential notes and explanations were deleted from the published report when it appeared; and that Oppert chose to work from a different copy of the cylinder inscription – but the result was none the less impressive. The distinguished members of the small panel invited by the Royal Asiatic Society to examine the translations reported separately and cautiously but their general conclusions were clear:

> . . . the Examiners certify that the coincidences between the translations, both as to the general sense and verbal rendering, were very remarkable . . .
> . . . the resemblance . . . is so great as to render it unreasonable to suppose the interpretation could be arbitrary, or based on uncertain grounds . . .
> Upon the whole, the result of this experiment – than which a fairer test could scarcely be devised – may be considered as establishing, almost definitively, the correctness of the valuation of the *characters* of these inscriptions . . . At the same time the differences prove that much remains to be effected before the sense of every term can be confidently rendered.

Two of the panel commented upon the close agreement between the translations of proper names and concluded that 'this agreement is no doubt, in part at least, owing to their adoption of the values proposed previously by Sir H. Rawlinson and Dr Hincks'.[20]*

Talbot was later praised for this idea which 'contributed more than anything else, to allay the doubts which had been circulated with regard to the truth of the translations of the Assyrian inscriptions'[21] and Wallis Budge wrote that it had 'a very good effect on the opinion of the learned world, and produced in the minds of the general public a keen sympathy, which had been hitherto

---

* This last was a valid point and requires some comment. Rawlinson and Hincks had deciphered a body of the Assyrian characters; Talbot and Oppert would have followed the meaning of characters established generally by Hincks and Rawlinson. (It is thus an error to describe Talbot as a *decipherer* of the Assyrian cuneiform.) The argument presented by Talbot in proposing the test was that if four people acting independently could produce approximately the same result – which was both plausible and meaningful – then the principle of the original decipherment and transcription of the texts could be regarded as sound, even though problems remained in the translation of individual words.

lacking'.[22] Immediately after the test, Henry Talbot wrote to Edward Hincks optimistically:

I have no doubt that our experiment will convert a large number of candid and learned persons who have hitherto been sceptical, and that if they will closely examine the translations and transcriptions they will find still more reason to be satisfied of the correctness of the system discovered by yourself and Rawlinson.[23]

Hincks remained somewhat jaundiced at the diversity existing in the translations from the Assyrian (as compared with the general agreement as he saw it between Egyptologists) – a frame of mind which was partly shaped by the manner in which he believed the British Museum favoured Sir Henry Rawlinson and ignored himself. Talbot remained hopeful, despite being aware of the problems in transcription and translation of Assyrian cuneiform that continue to this very day. He kept up the practice of never studying a new translation released by Rawlinson until he himself had translated it independently and he went on submitting sealed translations so that another scholar might compare his work with Talbot's translation, which with 'writings of such extreme divergency and complexity . . . cannot fail to be of utility'.[24]

From the early 1850s until his death Henry Talbot continued to correct and improve his earlier translations – notes in his hand abound in his own copies of his printed papers. Although his publications – more than seventy separate papers – are not used today because knowledge of Assyrian has moved on, he played a considerable part in the exciting and yet demanding new world of Assyrian cuneiform translation which unfolded in the nineteenth century. Moreover, while some students were content to work and not to publish or only to publish to a very limited circle of specialists, Talbot showed an acute awareness of the value of publishing as widely as possible, and with copious notes, to ensure that the new science of Assyriology would go from strength to strength by securing public interest and support – and he supported the policy from his own pocket by encouraging others. Nowhere was this seen to better effect than in his attitude to George Smith.

Smith (1840–76) started work as an apprentice to a bank-note engraver – where it was forecast he would have a brilliant future – but a keen historical interest in the Bible, coupled with studies of the discoveries and researches of Layard, Rawlinson and others, led to his spending every available free moment in the sculpture galleries at the British Museum. The frequency of his visits and his rapidly growing knowledge came to the notice of Samuel Birch and Smith was eventually employed officially as a 'repairer' of tablets from Nineveh. In this task his ability to read cuneiform developed rapidly and Wallis Budge commented that 'like Rawlinson, he *felt* what an inscription must mean; and his instinct was rarely at fault'.[25] Smith was corresponding with Talbot from about 1868 and in January of 1870 he wrote requesting Talbot's support for his application to join Birch's department at the Museum as an assistant.[26] This Talbot was delighted to do – as were Layard and Norris – and with Birch keen on the appointment Smith's success was a formality. Smith began work on the preparation of selections of the cuneiform inscriptions being published under the general direction of Sir Henry Rawlinson but also pursued his own researches.

In 1870–71 he prepared for publication a volume on Ashurbanipal* but despite financial support of £150 from J. W. Bosanquet – a banker and student of Assyriology – the cost of the project mounted and Smith appealed to Henry Talbot for assistance. Talbot sent two payments totalling £75 and also assisted Smith in checking the proofs (making numerous useful suggestions). The published preface included the comment 'the completion of this work was provided for by Mr H. Fox Talbot, the Assyrian scholar'. Smith was a compulsive worker whose health was not strong and the problems of working on inscriptions in the British Museum without the aid of electric light were severe. When he was seriously ill in 1871 Henry Talbot wrote to him encouraging him to get better and to continue his work, for the Lacock man had no doubt of the future that lay ahead for Smith.[27]†

It was indeed a brilliant future. Before 1871 was out, Smith had succeeded in partially deciphering the classical Cypriote script while working on a Cypriote–Phoenician bilingual text – but an even greater triumph came in the following year, when he recognized that one of the cuneiform tablets at the Museum contained an Assyrian account of the Deluge. Smith read a paper on the discovery before the Society of Biblical Archaeology on 3 December 1872

---

* Ashurbanipal (668–627 B.C.) was the last of the great kings of Assyria. He was a soldier and the administrator of a far-flung empire but, most importantly for the scholars of the nineteenth century, he was a man of learning who collected a vast library, the remnants of which were to play an important role in assisting the decipherment of the language of the Assyrians.

† Smith was not the only scholar to receive encouragement. In November 1861 Talbot wrote to a Jules Oppert deeply depressed by the attack of non-believers in the cuneiform decipherment that Champollion had suffered the same sort of attacks with his work on Egyptian hieroglyphics: 'Therefore you should not be discouraged if your valuable labours are not properly appreciated now. You are labouring for the future and posterity will do justice to them.'[28]

and in the party on the platform, with such notables as Sir Henry Rawlinson and the Prime Minister William Gladstone, was Henry Talbot. In the next few years Smith made three archaeological expeditions to Assyria (financed by *The Daily Telegraph*); published *The Chaldean Account of Genesis* in 1875; and died in 1876 as the result of cholera contracted during his third expedition to Mesopotamia.

Talbot kept his wife Constance and other members of the family informed of such major developments and the excitement he felt was evident in his letters. In one he described important discoveries:

... likely to excite universal attention especially in the religious world. It appears that the Babylonians possessed writings handed down from great antiquity, relating to the early history of the world and that the Jews and other nations accepted more or less of these histories as true, adding nevertheless traditions of their own which they thought equally trustworthy.

Mr Smith has recently published the *Deluge Tablet* in the original Cuneiform characters and I have been studying it. I agree with Mr Smith in all the essential points, the building of the ship, the deluge, the letting the birds out of the ark to see if the land was dry, Noah's sacrifice of thanksgiving on coming out of the ark &c. &c.[29]

Talbot had an abundant correspondence in these years with other Assyrian scholars – amongst whom he appeared to be on the closest and most friendly terms with Edwin Norris – but the subject frequently arose in correspondence with scientists and scholars in other disciplines who clearly had a high regard for his knowledge. He continued to bring the work of foreign scholars to the attention of his British colleagues;[30] he urged Samuel Birch that it was time photographers were employed on excavations in Mesopotamia to take copies of inscriptions instead of employing 'copyists' who of necessity worked laboriously and slowly;[31] and must have had some satisfaction when in 1872 a volume of *Photographs of the Collection in the British Museum* taken by Stephen Thompson was issued.

In December of 1870 the Society of Biblical Archaeology was set up, with Samuel Birch the moving force, supported by Henry Rawlinson and Henry Talbot. The need for a new society had been discussed for some time since the prime interest of the Royal Asiatic Society was the study of India, Persia and China and that of the Society of Antiquaries was in British antiquities and ecclesiology. A new specialist organization devoted to Egyptology and Assyriology would bring philologists and theologians together and ensure the prompt publication of their papers. After a refusal from Rawlinson, Birch asked Talbot to accept the position of the first president of the Society – a measure of his regard – but Talbot also refused.[32]* However he contributed to the Society's two publications *Transactions* and *Records of the Past*. He also played a financial role in keeping the Society and its publications solvent which cannot now be detailed but which was evidently very important and greatly appreciated.

After his death in 1877 a letter of sympathy to Henry Talbot's family described him as 'one of the greatest Assyrian scholars'.[33] In such letters and obituaries a slight degree of exaggeration may sometimes be suspected. Talbot himself would doubtless have appreciated most the obituary written[34] at the time of Henry Rawlinson's death in 1895 in which there was no risk of exaggeration in the evaluation of his own contribution to Assyriology. After referring to the earlier work of Grotefend, Burnouf, and Lassen, in Europe, the anonymous writer indicated 'three other honoured names' as being connected with Rawlinson – Edwin Norris, Edward Hincks and Henry Talbot. With that appreciation Talbot would have been well content.

* Talbot was, however, a vice-president of both the Royal Society of Literature (which published a number of his papers) and the Royal Asiatic Society.

11
The Final Years

The comfortable domestic arrangements of the Talbot family which were
established in the 1850s and which constituted a congenial background for
Henry's researches continued throughout the following two decades. Constance, Ela and Rosamond very much enjoyed the lengthy winter stays in
Edinburgh, where they could be close to Tilly and her rapidly growing family,
and in 1864–5 Constance eventually prevailed upon Talbot to purchase a
house in Edinburgh – 13 Great Stuart Street.

The annual visits to Edinburgh and the Gilchrist-Clark homes at Speddoch
and Dabton (near Dumfries) continued until 1866 and then in the following
year Constance and the girls left for Europe. She did not return until the
summer of 1869 – her time abroad including a severe illness – and Rosamond,
together with Mlle Amélina who had become her inseparable companion,
continued on in southern Europe until 1870 when they were caught up in the
events of the Franco-Prussian War. Talbot himself spent periods at Lacock
Abbey on his own, as well as in London where he stayed usually at the
Athenaeum, but the lengthy periods during which the Abbey contained no
Talbots led Kit Talbot on one occasion to ask his cousin whether he was ever
going to live at Lacock again.[1]* In fact as the years passed, Henry spent increasing time at Lacock which came to mean more to him – rather as it had to his
mother as she grew older. The visits by Constance and the children to Europe
broke the habit of staying in Scotland and in the late 1860s and 1870s Bath
and Bournemouth became favourite wintering locations.

---

* Kit added: 'I often wonder what the attraction of Scotland in winter can be'!

Henry Talbot's lifetime habit of seeking solitude with occasional, brief returns to the bosom of the family continued – indeed it appeared to intensify. His trips to Europe were solitary ones save for the rare occasions when some of his many relatives were travelling there and meetings could be arranged. During the decade of the 1860s he journeyed to France, Italy and Switzerland six times – and it appears that a trip in 1869 to Italy (ever his favourite) was the last occasion on which he crossed the Channel.

To strangers, Talbot's attitude was cool, not to say brusque, and even over-bearing: to fools he was cutting. But for those with whom a continuing relationship developed, he became the helpful, loyal and even loving man known to his family. He was never the heavy-handed Victorian father with any of the children and he was rewarded with a great depth of love, from the girls in particular. As he and Constance grew into the quieter years of late middle age and beyond they were both kept younger in outlook by the lively and spirited characters of Ela and Rosamond – who never married – and Tilly, who was busy raising a family which would eventually number four girls and two sons. Talbot doted on his grandchildren[2] of whom he saw so little despite Tilly's continued requests, not to say demands, that he visit Scotland more frequently. To them he was a very distant, very famous but a very loving figure.*

Ela, Rosamond and Tilly – as the 1860s wore on they all entered their thirties – were talented women. They were all above average artists (in this they followed Constance rather than Henry who, if it had been otherwise, might not have given the world the negative-positive system of photography) but Rosamond was undoubtedly pre-eminent as artist, letterwriter and in her ability to deal with her father. From San Remo in 1867 the artist in her wrote to her father:

The sunrises are sometimes splendid – on the shortest day the clouds of crimson and gold were particularly gorgeous, and exactly at half past seven, the sun itself like a ball of fire rose straight out of the sea, without a speck or vapour to dim its brilliancy.[3]

And from Naples over two years later she commented on murals in the museum there: 'There is a wonderful spirit and movement in the attitudes of both men and horses, and the tints are as delicately shaded as anything which

---

* His fame did not prevent the various Talbot ladies requiring him on his travels about England to deliver to relatives the kittens produced by the Abbey's considerable cat population.

could be produced in the present day.'[4] Great was her pleasure when later she could announce to her father that she had sold paintings to the value of £10 15s. od. at a London exhibition and that she was as a result 'rapidly growing rich'.[5] Rosamond had a measure of steel in her make-up and she did not hesitate to make good-natured fun of her father's failings. Talbot was a master of writing wise words about events after they had happened and Rosamond told him firmly on one occasion: 'I am not at all satisfied with your prophecies for they always come after! You always say "that is just what I expected" when the news has come!! But you should tell us *beforehand* what will be the denouement of all this . . .'[6] It was not only Henry Talbot who felt his daughter's forthrightness. In 1870 there was a minor scandal in Lacock involving the vicar of the day. When it was rumoured that he was going to leave and apply for the chaplaincy of a lunatic asylum, Rosamond commented: 'It would just suit him!' – and, when the vicar's resignation was confirmed, added: 'We ought to light a bonfire & ring the bells . . .'[7] Rosamond was not only lively in word but also in deed. On holiday in Bath in 1872, she took great delight in experimenting with a fire extinguisher in the garden – firing a jet of water fifty feet in the air and watering the neighbours' gardens on both sides. 'Luckily [perhaps Rosamond felt tempted to write 'unluckily'] no one was walking there!'[8]

Charles Henry Talbot was in a greatly different mould from his sisters. It has already been noted that he had a shy, introspective personality and had encountered some problems at school. As the time grew near to follow his father's footsteps to Cambridge, he developed a condition which made it difficult (according to his own claim) to concentrate mentally or to read for any length of time. Doctors were consulted and recommended plenty of physical activity with little mental exertion. Constance worried about her son and talked of hypochondria; Rosamond simply criticized his idleness; and Talbot was perplexed and thoroughly saddened. His son went up to Trinity at the end of 1860 and in the spring of the following year – anticipating a poor performance in the college examination – Henry wrote to William Whewell, his old friend and the Master at Trinity, asking him to take the most indulgent view of the case possible:

He is often unwell, but even when well he finds himself almost incapacitated from reading. It is a thing to be pitied and not blamed for it does not arise from idleness. Never having experienced anything of the sort myself, I cannot well understand his state of mind.

He says 'I experience a complete want of mental energy – the effort of *serious* thinking is what I cannot stand; and the attempt to do so confuses my head'.[9]

It was a loyal and not unsympathetic reaction on Talbot's part – and the outcome was not as poor as Charles himself had feared, for in the mathematical tripos in 1864 he achieved the status of a junior optime.*

It is now impossible to diagnose Charles's illness – physical, mental or purely imaginary – but he was no fool. He had inherited some of his father's mathematical skills and, following instruction for some years in an architect's office after coming down, he developed a talent for what might be termed the philosophy of architecture. He also became extremely knowledgeable in matters of mediaeval and church architecture.

In the middle 1860s he spent much time at the British Museum, attended lectures at the Royal Institution and British Association meetings and conceived some imaginative ideas. After one period of study in the British Museum, he wrote to his father about the vulnerability of the Assyrian sculptures: 'I think they ought to be all photographed and then photoglyphically engraved in order that if they do get injured there may be an exact record of what they were.' He applauded the way in which the Assyrians had depicted the events of everyday life on their monuments and added: 'Why don't we do the same? Why don't we represent omnibuses & railway trains & walking advertisements . . . ?'[10]

Charles practised the collodion photography of the period and immediately realized the potential of photography for enlarging and reducing architectural plans. In addition, he researched family history and gave short shrift to the family practice of adopting the Talbot name whenever necessary – 'I consider the Margam family as Ivorys and ourselves as Davenports.'[11]

We may assume that Henry Talbot was not displeased by the young man's activities and ideas – and that he welcomed without any reservation Charles's preparedness to act increasingly as his representative in the life and affairs of Lacock village, from presiding over ploughing matches to monitoring the progress of the school.

In these later years the economic situation of the village did not receive the frequent mention in family letters that occurred in the earlier periods and – while there were the customary acts of a good squire's family such as giving

* Honours candidates were divided into wranglers, senior optimes and junior optimes. Other candidates sat an examination but did not seek honours.

seed potatoes to the poor when crops had failed and supporting individuals who were in severe difficulty – it is a fair assumption that the condition of the villagers at this time was reasonable. The family obtained apprenticeships for young men in other parts of the country, a servant was nursed through five years of terminal illness and major new developments in village life – such as the extension to the school in 1868-9 – were supported financially. West Awdry and then Charles Talbot took virtually the whole burden of being Lord of the Manor from Henry's shoulders but occasionally he would make his presence felt – as when he disagreed with structural work at the church of St Cyriac in Lacock in the early 1860s. Whilst it was totally against his nature to obstruct anything desired by the villagers or their representatives, he denounced the wholesale modifications as being too costly for the village to afford and the fact that the initially proposed *repairs* had become in his view undesirable *alterations* – a view with which posterity might well agree since the work none the less proceeded.[12]

That general refusal to interfere was a trait of Talbot's character and his philosophy in life. He was in the non-political sense a moderately compassionate and intellectual *liberal* with an ability to see other persons' points of view in the minor and major affairs of life. Thus at one extreme he expressed genuine regret in 1869 that the Senior Wrangler at Cambridge that year – who was a Jew – would on account of his religion be unable to secure the fellowship which he deserved.[13] At the other extreme, he wrote to Constance in the previous year from his hotel in St Moritz – 'I had got so far in my letter when noisy people entered, so I took a turn out of doors in the humid atmosphere, till they were gone . . .'[14] Talbot would not dream of protesting.

With the sole and important exception of his attitude over patents – where paradoxically he displayed an inflexibility which was generally alien to his character – Talbot allowed the waters of life to flow about him, yielding where necessary to ease the strain of impact but managing generally to stay on the course he had chosen. He was, in a sense, an observer of life's pattern, and though far from being without feeling, maintained the air of a detached and unbiased onlooker. Thus he was in no way affected by the continual criticism he received throughout life about not visiting his relatives more frequently, any more than he appeared to be emotionally or spiritually affected by matters of religion. He went to church and analysed the sermons for intellectual or historical content but nowhere did Talbot give a clue as to the deeper effect on him – if any. No sign of spiritual commitment was ever revealed publicly.

While it is impossible to know what thoughts passed in the secret recesses of the mind, he appeared to turn his back on death and refused to attend funerals. Indeed, it was an intriguing feature of his letters that he rarely looked back to lament the passing of time in his own life – rather he concentrated on the present and future and it was perhaps in the beauty of flowers that he saw both most clearly.

Whatever Rosamond's strictures about her father's past-future forecasts of events, Henry continued to be acutely interested in political and international events. He refused to vote in one county election on the admirable grounds that he did not care for either candidate[15] but his strongest comments were reserved for the Irish question:

All the time of our House of Commons is occupied with Irish affairs, to the neglect of our own. At last ministers are beginning to display a little commonsense and have asked for power to suppress treasonable newspapers. If they had done this ten years ago, they would now have a tranquil Ireland . . . For months past, the Irish papers have daily advocated ARMED Rebellion![16]

Events abroad, however, attracted the most attention. Talbot wrote at length about the events in the United States. On the outbreak of the Civil War he commented:

Republicanism has lost all its prestige, now that it is seen by so striking an instance that a nation cannot go on long without a king and aristocracy. Where all men are equal none will obey and therefore when a crisis comes all is discord and each man judges for himself.[17]

Four years later he wrote:

What an event is the assassination of President Lincoln! And who can tell what consequences may follow! Poor man! I rather liked him, he was so honest and well intentioned and acted as well as he could, in a very difficult position . . . How hard upon him to be cut off in the moment of his triumph![18]

Talbot's work in photo-engraving, Assyriology and mathematics in the 1860s and 1870s was by no means the entire story, though other published papers were few. These were concentrated into a short period and were published in the *Proceedings* of the Royal Society of Edinburgh for the 1870–1 session.[19] In a short 'Note on some anomalous spectra', Talbot related aspects of his work on spectroscopy of thirty years before to recent experiments in Europe in which 'instead of proceeding regularly from the red to the violet like the ordinary solar spectrum, [the spectrum] stops at a certain point, returns backward, then stops again and resumes a direct course to the end'. A 'Note on the early history of spectrum analysis' was an account of the work of Wollaston, Fraunhofer, Brewster, Herschel and himself written for a new generation – and, while its subject was quite deliberately the experiences of the *earlier* years, a sense of disappointment may be felt by the reader that Talbot did not continue the story through to Kirchhoff's and Bunsen's work since on no previous occasion had he given an appreciation of their experiments.

'On some optical experiments' included a report on an improvement in the Nicol prism in which the prism was constructed half of calcareous spar and half of glass (instead of two pieces of calcareous spar) which improved its polarizing characteristics. A second report again dealt with earlier experiments in which Talbot had noted how the 'mere presence of a chemical substance in a flame frequently suffices to cause the appearance of its characteristic rays, and that it is not at all necessary that the substance should be consumed and dissipated'. He took his observations an important step further, however, in proposing a method for the analysis of substances of which only very small quantities were available. His own work, carried out at the Physical Laboratory of Edinburgh University, was concerned with the then rare metallic element thallium which William Crookes had discovered in 1861 and some of which he later sent to Talbot for the purpose of spectral-analysis experiments.[20]

Talbot's system was to seal the specimen, and a drop of water, in a strong glass tube with platina wires inserted at each end and to ignite it by means of an electric current. The tube (insulated as necessary) was immersed in water to prevent it from overheating and exploding. He described the effect:

The bright light given off under these circumstances by strontia, sodium, thallium, and many other substances, is very beautiful, and so permanent that at the close of the experiment the original grain or half grain of the substance does not appear diminished, and even the drop of water is found remaining unchanged. Provided always that the chemical substance is one not liable to decomposition under these circumstances of heat and moisture ... This method might be usefully applied to the illumination of microscopic objects by homogeneous light. If the tube were placed immediately under the stage of the microscope, the full intensity of the yellow light would fall upon the object.

His extensive researches in other subjects in these later years left little time for optics but as late as his seventy-fifth year Talbot was requesting Constance to purchase supplies of coloured gelatin in Bath for optical experiments. His fascination with such phenomena as phosphorescence and crystallization as well as the techniques of spectroscopy remained unabated. His continuing versatility did not go unnoticed by fellow scientists – in May 1871 Charles Piazzi Smyth wrote:

When I saw recently, almost simultaneously, a paper on spectrum analysis by you before the Royal Society of Edinburgh and also a paper on an Assyrian eclipse before the Society of Biblical Archaeology in London I was lost in wonder as to where you might be in bodily presence . . . [I hail] with delight your return to vivify these parts with intellectual light.[21]

Talbot never lost the scientific approach. When his wife returned from the Continent on her last trip there after a prolonged period of ill health he urged that she take the greatest care: 'You should not remain on deck if there is any wind, or if the weather is anything but a calm warm day. For the boat goes 17 miles an hour through the air, which *added* to the velocity of the wind if contrary, makes it often bitterly cold . . .'[22]

Henry Talbot indulged in virtually no practical photography after 1851: in the subsequent years his enthusiasm for the beauties of a scene was expressed in purely verbal and never photographic terms. But years later, in 1865, hopes that he might be working on a system of colour photography were expressed by the editor of the *British Journal of Photography*, John Traill Taylor:

I have been informed that you are making some experiments in photography in natural colours. I should feel extremely obliged by your sending me some account of your experiments, and if your success has been such as to warrant your indulging the hope that this desideratum is not quite impossible.[23]

In a letter written some months before, Charles Talbot had made an ambiguous reference to a 'new process in photography'[24] evolved by his father and it is possible that Henry had thoughts on the subject, although no evidence survives to indicate that he ever began practical work on colour photography. None the less, Traill Taylor's faith in Talbot's capacity to do so continued, and over ten years later he wrote that no man was better constituted for undertaking investigations in 'heliochromy'.[25]

But the photography which he had done so much to create as a practical system intruded frequently into the life of the family. In the 1860s the girls caught the *carte de visite* craze and Talbot's visits to London were accompanied with requests that he obtain the latest sets of pictures featuring members of the Royal Family and other notables. An enterprising cleric even sent a *carte de visite* of himself when applying to Talbot for consideration for the post of curate at Lacock!

Talbot himself was a reluctant sitter* – which was consistent with his character – but in the 1860s three photographs were taken of him which still survive. In March of 1864 he and Sir David Brewster were photographed together by the light of burning magnesium by the Edinburgh photographer John Moffat at a meeting of the Photographic Society of Scotland of which Brewster was president; a few weeks later Talbot sat for Moffat in the more formal setting of his studio, some of the results being printed as *cartes de visite*; and later – probably around 1866 or 1867 – Constance, Ela, Rosamond, Charles and Henry posed for family portraits by J. H. Blomfield of Hastings in the cloisters of Lacock Abbey. With his unkempt clothes and hair, Henry Talbot appeared in each of the photographs to be suffering the experience with little pleasure – and at best it may be assumed that he thought a show of Gladstone-like severity was appropriate.[26][†]

Over the last two decades of Talbot's life – as his photographic work in particular could be set in perspective and as memory of the patent controversies receded – the tributes and awards for his achievements increased. As distinct from the Royal Society's contemporaneous award of the Rumford Medal in 1842, these later tributes came mainly from abroad and from Scotland. In 1855 a Grande Médaille d'Honneur was awarded in Emperor Louis Napoleon III's name by the international jury of L'Exposition Universelle in Paris. Three years later the Photographic Society of Scotland awarded Talbot its gold medal for his discoveries in photography (a letter announcing the award referred to him as 'the great discoverer of photography')[27] and later still – probably in 1862 – the Council of the Edinburgh Photographic Society awarded him a medal and admitted him to honorary membership.[28] It was

* In 1856 Constance wrote from Edinburgh that she and the girls had visited an exhibition of work by Edinburgh's 'best portrait painter' Sir John Watson Gordon. 'I recollect now that he is the man to whom Sir D. Brewster wished you to sit for your picture.'[29] Talbot obliged Brewster in many things but this was not one of them.

† Three other portraits of Talbot from this later period exist – all by unknown photographers. A modern print of one is in the possession of Harold White who attributes the copy (made perhaps in the 1930s) to Herbert Lambert of Bath. Talbot appears to be around fifty-five years old in this study. The Science Museum has two collodion glass negatives of portraits of Talbot, which may have been exposed a year or two after the study copied by Lambert. (Plates 2–6.)

the French who again honoured Talbot in 1867 when the Société Française de Photographie awarded him a medal as *'un des inventeurs de la photographie'* though the Society's officer M. Laulerie in communicating the good news to Talbot[30] inadvertently referred to the award as a testimony of recognition *'à l'inventeur de la photographie'*!*

The marks of esteem were not always of such a formal kind. André Adolfe Disderi – who made the *carte de visite* popular – requested a portrait for displaying in his new salon.[31] The distinguished Scottish scientist Dr Lyon Playfair, in inviting Henry to be a judge in the appropriate class of the 1862 International Exhibition in London, wrote: 'A jury of photography on a great ... international occasion without your name in it would be to everyone like the play Hamlet with the part of Hamlet omitted.'[32] (Talbot declined on the grounds of having paid insufficient attention to photography since 1851.) Numerous photographic magazines – at home and abroad – requested his portrait but the most distant evidence of fame in the late 1860s was the address of a successful photographic company in Simla in India – 'Talbot House'.[33]

Throughout his life Henry loathed personal participation in ceremonial – there is no evidence that he received even one of his earlier awards in person – but in 1863 he was finally prevailed upon to accept the Doctorate of Laws of Edinburgh University and be present at the investiture. The Principal and Vice-Chancellor of the University at the time was David Brewster and Talbot's companion for the honour was the Prime Minister Lord Palmerston. In presenting Talbot as worthy of the degree, Professor Muirhead – Dean of the Faculty of Law – was in part as chauvinistic and as inaccurate in his references to Niépce and Daguerre as was François Arago toward Talbot and other foreigners in an earlier year but the expressed reason for the award was balanced and accurate – and as true now as then. Muirhead referred to Henry Talbot's 'pre-eminence in literature and science, and the benefits his discoveries have conferred upon science' and to the fact that, whatever the contribution of other early pioneers in photography:

... it was Mr Talbot who first made known that method of photogenic operation which however imperfect originally, has yet formed the basis of all that is valuable in the subsequent development of the art. The photography of the present day – far still no doubt from perfection yet productive of exquisitely beautiful results, and capable of application to innumerable industrial and aesthetical purposes – owes its existence to him.[34]

* All of these awards are displayed in the Museum at Lacock.

Caroline as ever wrote directly and succinctly about her half brother's investiture with the blue hood of an Edinburgh LL.D. – 'I honour Sir D. Brewster & the other Savans for their judgment and discrimination in selecting you as a colleague to Ld. Palmerston, no less than for the energy & skill they must have employed in making you accept.'[35]

William Grove was less successful when he endeavoured to persuade Talbot to accept the presidency of the British Association for the Advancement of Science in 1868–9. (The annual meeting was scheduled to be held in Exeter in the latter year.) In sending advance notice of the unanimous decision to invite him to become the next president, Grove admitted that Talbot's inclination would be to refuse but stressed his pre-eminent qualifications for the appointment, the opportunity it would afford to express important views on science and education, and on a personal as well as scientific basis begged Talbot: 'Don't say No and disappoint us all.'[36] But although aware of the honour accorded him, Henry did disappoint Grove and his colleagues – and on this occasion he had a valid excuse in Constance's serious illness while abroad in Europe and his need to be with her.

In 1873 the Photographic Society in London finally recognized Talbot's work formally when it altered its rules to make him an honorary member – along with Robert Hunt, which may have brought a wry smile to Talbot's lips. Whatever the relations in earlier years, the *Photographic Journal* – the organ of the Photographic Society – was unstinting in its welcome for the new honorary member: 'There is no other man living, either in this country or any other, that photographers would desire to honour more than Dr Fox Talbot, and certainly none more deserving of our homage . . .'[37] A few months later Talbot was invited to attend a display of his work which was being planned and the Secretary wrote, 'It needs no assurance on my part to say how warmly you would be welcomed by the present generation of photographers with whom your name is a household word.'[38] A leading part in these moves was taken by John Spiller, a vice-president of the Society, and it was Spiller who on his own initiative in 1874, at a time of some crisis in the affairs of the Photographic Society, sounded out Talbot on the possibility of his becoming president. But even if it had been made official the request would have received an inevitable, negative response.

In his last few years Talbot's lifelong habit of frequent visits to London became an impossibility as rheumatism and, even more important, a serious heart condition restricted his mobility. Eventually he was confined for lengthy

2A

periods to a wheel chair. Even before this period, time had taken its undeniable toll of the family and friends around him. Cousin Mary Talbot in Wales died in 1861, William Horner Fox-Strangways (the fourth Earl of Ilchester) in 1865; 1868 saw the deaths of David Brewster and Charles Lemon; a few years later Thomas Malone died; and in 1874 J. H. Bolton – Talbot's lawyer of many years' standing – and another Welsh cousin Jane Nicholl died. Then in September 1876, at the age of seventy-eight, Mlle Amélina died peacefully.* Caroline wrote of 'our dear, affectionate friend . . . of 56 years! . . . I grieve much for you all, as well as myself.'[39]

The memories of time past – childhood days in Wales, numerous plants carefully tended in the gardens – lengthened, and were recalled mainly by the ageing ladies of the family. But Tilly's lively children, although only rarely visiting Lacock Abbey, introduced the spirit and energy of youth into the family circle. They loved their grandfather and he loved them – with a devoted concern for their well-being and progress. It was typical for example that Henry – with memories of his own schooldays – should applaud the desire of his daughter not to send her son Jack to Eton too young: 'Small boys might be lost in a school of *nine hundred*.'[40]

The family spent the early months of 1877 at Bournemouth to which Caroline supposed Henry had carried off some of his Assyrians.[41] As the year wore on, his endeavours in that direction were underlined for in the seventh volume of *Records of the Past* no less than six papers were published under his name. Henry etched at least one steel plate for publication and – probably around this time – his cousin Emma Llewelyn wrote about photography with an eye both to the past and the future:

> Mr Llewelyn looked out some of his best negatives to show Ela but she could not appreciate them I am sure, so well, as if she had been your printer in bygone days. I exhorted her to get *you* to look over your old stores . . . if your negatives are still in existence some prints from them would be valuable – *invaluable* I mean.[42]

Talbot was involved with photography in another direction for he had agreed to write an appendix on the early history of photography to appear in a revised English edition of *A History and Handbook of Photography* by the Frenchman G. Tissandier. The original was written very much from the

---

* In her will, Amélina left a bequest to Talbot as a mark of appreciation for the many years of happiness spent with the family. It was used to pay the costs of installing central heating in the Abbey.

French viewpoint and the publishers wished to restore the balance of the new edition both by including Talbot's appendix and a new chapter on the English inventors by the editor John Thomson.* In his chapter Thomson wrote: 'Talbot was, indeed, the Caxton of sun printing. Daguerre caught the sun's messages, Talbot printed them.'[43]

The appendix was to be in three parts, the last of which would cover photo-engraving. Understandably Talbot based his account on his published papers of 1839 and 1840 and there was no great originality in his writing. On 12 September 1877 he wrote to the publishers: 'I have not been well, which has delayed my sending you the rest of my paper. I now send the *second* part . . . The third part is in preparation and will complete the Appendix.'[44] In fact he never completed it† for two days later he was taken seriously ill, and after appearing to rally, died in his study in the early hours of Monday, 17 September 1877.

In the weeks and months that followed, a flood of obituaries were published in the journals of the learned societies, *Nature* ('a wonderful man'), the *British Journal of Photography* and newspapers from *The Times* and *The Daily Telegraph* to the *Wiltshire Telegraph*. Most concentrated on his scientific and photographic achievements, on their value to society – and occasionally referred to controversial matters such as why he did not receive at least a knighthood for his photographic discoveries. But his local newspaper the *Wiltshire Telegraph* perhaps came closest to the man and to the villagers' attitude to him and his death:

There was laid in the grave in the pretty cemetery of this parish, yesterday, one of whom it may be said that he was the originator of one of the most wonderful discoveries of the present age . . .

Mr Talbot was essentially a scientific man; his whole life was passed in the study of one or other of the natural sciences; and to his love for these studies may probably be attributed the retired life which he led. Perhaps there is no gentleman occupying the position in society which Mr Talbot held who was personally less known to the general public; but at home, in his own neighbourhood, no gentleman could be more respected, or more esteemed. We will take upon ourselves to say that no Lacock person ever made an appeal at the Abbey and came away empty. In Mr Talbot not only the poor, but all his numerous tenantry, knew and felt they had a friend. He was in every sense a good landlord – one who

* Thomson himself achieved fame in photography by his pictures of foreign lands and his celebrated *Street Life in London* which was published at this time.

† Charles Talbot wrote the third part of the appendix which included two photo-engravings (one of a map and the other of a view in Java). The book was published in 1878.

never interfered with his tenants in the smallest degree. Claiming a right to his own opinions, he scrupulously avoided interfering with the opinions of others. Many a time has he been known to go to the poll in company with those who might be said to be dependent upon him and whilst he has entered the booth of one party, they have gone into the booth of the opposite side . . .

[On his death] the inhabitants of the little town had hardly come downstairs before the melancholy news spread from house to house, and never was regret more unfeignedly expressed. Every shop was partially closed, and every window had its blinds drawn; and in this state they remained until yesterday (the day of the funeral) when business was entirely suspended, all the shops were closed, and a Sabbath stillness pervaded the streets.[45]

Talbot's achievements remained uncommemorated for almost twenty-five years but as the new century dawned, the idea of restructuring the chancel of Lacock church as a memorial to his memory was revived. The centenary in 1900 of his birth provided a modest surge of publicity – a leader in *The Times* was perplexed by the lack of recognition of his achievements[46] – but it was significant that almost three quarters of the final cost of the Lacock church memorial of over £1,300 was contributed by the family, a few friends, and the proceeds of visits to Lacock Abbey. The mass of photographers showed as much regard for Talbot's memory as they did the poverty of Scott Archer's family when he died after creating the concept of wet-plate collodion photography.[47] Perhaps it was, as *The Times* suggested in 1900, that in order to be recognized by the public and government Talbot should have been a showman 'versed in the methods of advertisement' like Daguerre but, equally, may it not be a reflection of the differences between national attitudes?

On the occasion of the centenary of Talbot's death, his life and work are thankfully now commemorated in a most fitting manner at the Talbot Museum in the village of Lacock. Hopefully this volume – the first comprehensive biography to be published – will also contribute to establishing at long last Henry Talbot's rightful position in the history of nineteenth-century science and learning.

Some members of his family during his lifetime – and others since – argued that if Talbot had been less versatile and had concentrated on fewer disciplines his achievements in them might have been even greater. This may have been so – and perhaps, for example, a practical system of colour photography might have been advanced by some years. But there is something sublime in the attitudes, the learning and the enjoyment of the Renaissance-type man who can illuminate such diverse subjects as spectroscopy, botany, the origin of words, the history of the Assyrians and the limits of pure mathematics as well as giving the world a new applied science.

Talbot wrote few words on the meaning and the philosophy of science – but he never lost his sense of wonderment at the worlds which his researches revealed to him and which engendered a sense of true scientific humility. As the creator of photography as we know it to this day, he marvelled at Nature's gifts – and yet, in a sense, looked forward to both the benefactions and the dangers of technology:[48]

You make the powers of nature work for you, and no wonder that your work is well and quickly done . . . There is something in this rapidity and perfection of execution, which is very wonderful. But after all, what *is* Nature, but one great field of wonders past our comprehension?

Notes

The source of all documents, unless noted otherwise, is the Lacock Collection, Talbot Museum, Wilts. 'T.' stands for 'Talbot'.

CHAPTER 1
AN ABBEY AND ANCESTORS

An outline account of the history of Lacock Abbey and its owners, together with a bibliography, is given in the National Trust booklet *Lacock Abbey* written by Janet Burnett-Brown.

The details given in this chapter of the Talbot and Fox families have been drawn, to a considerable extent, from the unpublished researches of Miss Thelma Vernon of Lacock and the Dowager Viscountess Wimborne respectively.

1. Reference in LA58–39 – 2 April 1858.
2. *The House of Commons 1715–1754*, I, by Romney Sedgwick: The History of Parliament Trust/HMSO, 1970.
3. For an account of the personal and political aspects of the relationship, see *Lord Hervey* by Robert Halsband: OUP, 1973.
4. 18 October 1798 (from a Digby relation).
5. 17 November 1816 (from G. O. Paul).
6. 28 March 1796 (Lady Susan to Lady Elisabeth).
7. 20 July 1796 (Lady Elisabeth to Lady Harriet Fox-Strangways). All letters

quoted in this section are from the Lacock Collection.
8. 27 June 1799 (Lady Elisabeth to Lady Harriet).

CHAPTER 2
MINORITY, CAMBRIDGE
AND THE 1820S

1. 'Statement as to the Title of William Henry Fox Talbot Esquire to the Manor, Rectory & Abbey of Lacock, and divers Estates in Wilts; and Narrative shewing the comparative situation of that property on 31st July 1800 and February 1821': quotations are from this document unless otherwise indicated. (Generally reliable, if somewhat over-zealous in defence of Lady Elisabeth and in criticism of others.)
2. LA21–6 – 11 February 1821.
3. LA08–2.
4. LA08–5 – 27 May 1808.
5. LA08–9 – 11 September 1808.
6. LA08–10 – 17 September 1808.
7. LA09–3.
8. LA11–3.

9. 9 March 1811.

10. LA11–6 – 23 June 1811 (Hooker to Charles Feilding).

11. LA11–7.

12. LA14–5 – 1 October 1814 (T. to Charles Feilding).

13. LA12–15 – 24 May 1812.

14. The original letter has not been traced: it exists only as a copy.

15. LA12–10 – 27 April 1812 (T. to Lady Elisabeth).

16. LA15–7 – 13 August 1815 (T. to Lady Elisabeth).

17. 29 September 1814.

18. 29 July 1813 (T. to Lady Elisabeth).

19. 17 October 1811.

20. Lacock Collection.

21. LA17–15.

22. LA17–18 – 11 March 1817.

23. LA17–8 – 11 February 1817.

24. LA17–25 – 19 May 1817.

A number of volumes – besides those given below as specific references – provide useful background on Cambridge University during the eighteenth and nineteenth centuries. These include *Unreformed Cambridge* by D. A. Winstanley (CUP, 1935); *Reminiscences of the University, Town and County of Cambridge from the Year 1780* by Henry Gunning (Bell, 1854); and *The Student Sub-Culture and the Examination System in Early 19th Century Oxbridge*, by Sheldon Rothblatt in *The University in Society* (Volume 1) edited by Lawrence Stone, Princeton University Press.

For details of the Newton–Leibniz controversy see *History of the Study of Mathematics at Cambridge* by W. W. Rouse Ball, (CUP, 1889); *Men and Discoveries in Mathematics* by Bryan Morgan (John Murray, 1972); and *Their Majesties' Astronomers* by Colin A. Ronan (Bodley Head, 1967).

25. LA20–24 – 29 December 1820 (T. to Lady Elisabeth).

26. LA20–23 – 7 December 1820 (T. to Charles Feilding).

27. *Early Victorian Cambridge* by D. A. Winstanley: CUP, 1955, p. 18.

28. *Alma Mater*, by a Trinity Man [subsequently identified as J. M. F. Wright]: Black, Young & Young, London 1827, pp. 124–5.

29 LA18–11 – 23 April 1818 (T. to Lady Elisabeth).

30. LA20–9 – 21 June 1820 (T. to Lady Elisabeth).

31. LA20–16 – 18 August 1820 (T. to Lady Elisabeth).

32. LA19–15 – 20 November 1819 (Lady Elisabeth to T.).

33. Lacock Collection.

34. LA18–23 – 29 August 1818 (Charles Feilding to T.).

35. 3 June 1820 (Caroline to T.).

36. LA19–18 – 26 December 1819 (T. to Lady Elisabeth).

37. LA20–12 – 30 June 1820 (T. to Charles Feilding) and Lady Elisabeth to T. dated, probably mistakenly, 19 June 1820.

38. LA21–18.

39. LA21–15.

40. LAM–103. The assessment is undated and unsigned.

41. LA20–11 – 26 June 1820 (Awdry to Charles Feilding).

42. LA22–4 – 8 January 1822.

43. 25 November 1822 (W. H. Awdry to T.).

44. LA24–12 – 30 January 1824.

45. LA27–23 – 14 November 1827.

46. 8 July 1830 (Horatia to T.).

47. LA28–62.

48. LA30–35 – 12 July 1830.

49. LA30–40.

50. LA29–149 – 19 December 1829 (Horatia to T.).

51. LA30–11 – 20 February 1830; LA25–8 – 21 May 1825 (both Lady Elisabeth to T.).

52. See Chapter 8, pp. 261–2.

53. LA26–16 – 30 March 1826 (T. to Lady Elisabeth).

54. LA26–20 – 16 April 1826.

55. 10 February 1833 (Caroline to T.).

56. 6 June 1826.

57. LA29–77 – 16 August 1829 (T. to Lady Elisabeth).

58. 25 November 1823 (T. to Charles Feilding).

59. *Hermes*, No. 2 (1839), pp. 164–5.

60. The original copy of the letter has not been traced but extracts were published in French in a biographical memoir of T. by Richard Cull which appeared in *Trans. Soc. Biblical Archaeology*, VI, Part 2, 1879.

61. See *Traité des courbes spéciales rémarquables,* Teixeira, Madrid, 1897.

62. Royal Society Collection: 17–263 – 22 May 1827 (T. to Herschel).

63. Royal Society Collection: 17–261 – July 1826 (T. to Herschel).

64. Lacock Collection: the extracts are from Notebooks C, D, D, D, F and D respectively. Some of the views expressed – for example, that on the nature of the thunderstorm – are largely erroneous in the light of present knowledge.

65. *Edinburgh Journal of Science*, V, 1826, pp. 77–81.

66. A comprehensive review of this is contained in *Nineteenth Century Spectroscopy* by William McGucken: Johns Hopkins Press, 1969.

67. *Edinburgh Journal of Science*, ibid., p. 81.

68. LA30–10 – 25 February 1830.

69. LA30–37 – 15 July 1830.

70. LA30–44 – 14 September 1830.

CHAPTER 3
THE CREATIVE DECADE

Captain Swing by E. J. Hobsbawm and George Rudé (Lawrence & Wishart, 1969) is a full and detailed account of the events of 1830–2. A useful account of the Swing Riots is also contained in *English Country Life 1780–1830* by E. W. Bovill (OUP, 1962).

1. LA30–52 – 27 or 28 November 1830 (Charles Feilding to T.).

2. LA30–48 – 27 November 1830 (Lady Elisabeth to T.).

3. LA30–49 – 29 November 1830 (Lady Elisabeth to T.).

4. LA30–56 – 2 December 1830 (Horatia to T.).

5. LA30–62 – 20 December 1830.

6. LA(H)33–3 – 13 February 1833 (T. to Charles Feilding).

7. LA(H)33–5 – 19 February 1833 (T. to Charles Feilding).

8. LA31–28 – 16 April 1831 (to T. from his bailiff).

9. See, for example: *The Age of Reform 1815–70*, by Sir Llewellyn Woodward: OUP, 1962; *The Age of Improvement*, by Asa Briggs: Longman, 1975; *The Passing of the Whigs 1832–1886*, by Donald Southgate: Macmillan; *An Encyclopaedia of Parliament*, by N. Wilding and Philip Laundy: Cassell, 1968.

10. LA31–10 – 2 March 1831.

11. 18 December 1823.

12. 16 May 1831.

13. LA(H)32–5 – 14 July 1832.

14. LA(H)32–14 – 26 November 1832 (T. to Charles Feilding).

15. LA(H)32–11.

16. LA32–66 – 17 November 1832.

17. LA32–72 – 27 November 1832.

18. LA(H)32–19 – 23 December 1832 (T. to Lady Elisabeth).
19. LA(H)33–2 – 7 February 1833 (T. to Charles Feilding).
20. LA(H)33–6 – 20 February 1833 (T. to Charles Feilding).
21. LA(H)33–15.
22. LA(H)34–1 – 12 February 1834 (T. to Constance).
23. LA(H)34–2 – 14 February 1834 (T. to Charles Feilding).
24. 12 February 1834 (Constance to T.) and LA(H)34–5 – 20 February 1834 (T. to Constance).
25. LA(H)34–6 – 29 May 1834.
26. LA(H)34–15 – 11 December 1834.
27. LA34–22 – 7 July 1834 (Constance to Lady Elisabeth) and LA34–28 – 20 July 1834 (Lady Elisabeth to T.).
28. LAM–116 – 'To the independent electors of the Borough of Chippenham' – 1 December 1834.
29. Royal Society Collection: 27 January 1835 (T. to J. W. Lubbock).
30. LA35–42 – 10 December 1835 (Lady Elisabeth to T.).
31. LA32–47 – 27 September 1832.
32. LA31–46 – 1 July 1831.
33. LA33–9 – 8 March 1833.
34. LA33–8 – 7 March 1833.
35. *Science and Industry in the Nineteenth Century* by J. D. Bernal: R&KP, p. 142.
36. *Victorian Science: Self Portrait from the Presidential Addresses of the BAAS* edited by George Basalla, William Coleman and Robert H. Kargon: Anchor Books, New York, 1970, p. 4.
37. For a description of science in Scotland see Bernal, op. cit., and *A History of European Scientific Thought in the Nineteenth Century* 1, by John Theodore Merz: reprinted by Dover Publications, New York, 1965.
38. ibid., p. 17.
39. Quoted ibid., pp. 163–4.
40. Facts relating to optical science, No. 1. *London and Edinburgh Philosophical Magazine and Journal of Science* [*Phil. Mag.*], February 1834, pp. 112–14.
41. Facts relating to optical science, No. III, *Phil. Mag.*, July 1836, pp. 2–4.
42. On the prismatic spectra of the flames of compounds of carbon and hydrogen. *Edinb. Roy. Soc. Trans.*, 1857, pp. 411–30. Quoted McGucken, op. cit., p. 26.
43. McGucken, op. cit., p. 7.
44. Cf. *Nineteenth Century Spectroscopy* by William McGucken: Johns Hopkins Press, 1969, p. 9.
45. Royal Society Collection: 272 – 31 May 1833.
46. For a description of the evolution of spectrum analysis in astronomy see *A Popular History of Astronomy during the Nineteenth Century* by Agnes M. Clerke: Black, 1902 and *Their Majesties' Astronomers* by Colin A. Ronan: Bodley Head, 1967.
47. *Phil. Mag.*, November 1834, pp. 321–34.
48. On the optical phenomena of certain crystals (read to the Royal Society, 5 May 1836). *Philosophical Transactions* Part I, 1837.
49. On Mr Nicol's polarizing eye-piece. *Phil. Mag.*, April 1834, pp. 289–90.
50. LA34–36 – 16 August 1834.
51. LA38–3 – 19 January 1838.
52. On a new principle of crystallization. BAAS Oxford Meeting, June 1847.
53. Facts relating to optical science, No. III, *Phil. Mag.*, July 1836, pp. 1–4.
54. On the optical phenomena of certain crystals. Further observations on the optical phenomena of crystals. *Phil. Trans.*, Part I, 1837, pp. 25–7, 29–35.

55. LA(H)37–5 – 29 November 1837.

56. Facts relating to optical science, No. IV. *Phil. Mag.*, IX, December 1836, pp. 401–7.

57. Facts relating to optical science, No. I, *Phil. Mag.*, February 1834, pp. 112–14.

58. On the nature of light. *Phil. Mag.*, August 1835, pp. 113–18.

59. Remarks on chemical changes of colour. *Phil. Mag.*, May 1833, pp. 359–60; Proposed method of ascertaining the greatest depth of the ocean. *Phil. Mag.*, August 1835, p. 82.

60. Science Museum Collection: 29 April 1837.

61. Science Museum Collection: 29 July 1837.

62. Notebooks I (1831–2) and O (1836–8) respectively.

63. Notebook O (March 1836–July 1838).

64. Cf. *Sir Charles Wheatstone* by Brian Bowers: HMSO, 1975, pp. 189–90.

65. Royal Society Collection: T12 – 14 July 1836.

66. LA(H)38–12 – 17 November 1832.

67. Royal Society Collection: 275 – 11 June 1838.

68. Letter dated 15 August 1836, quoted in *Home Life of Sir David Brewster*, by Mrs Gordon: Edinburgh, 1869, p. 161.

69. LA36–58 – 'Monday'.

70. Notebook K.

71. *Royal Society Proceedings*, III, 1834, p. 258.

72. *Roy. Soc. Proc.*, III, 1834, pp. 287–8.

73. LA34–43.

74. Trinity College Library: 7 October 1835.

75. *Roy. Soc. Phil. Trans.*, 1836, pp. 177–215.

76. The notebooks were those designated C (1821) and D (1825).

77. Researches in the integral calculus, Part 2 (read 17 November 1836). *Roy. Soc. Phil. Trans.*, 1837, pp. 1–18.

78. Royal Society Collection: RR.1.238.

79. LA36–54 – 9 August 1836 (Assistant General Secretary BAAS to T., quoting Peacock).

80. LA(H)38–14 – 1 December 1838.

81. Royal Society Collection: 315 – 29 March 1843.

82. LA44–61 – 13 September 1844.

83. Royal Society Collection: 317 – 8 September 1844.

84. Royal Society Collection: 318 – 16 September 1844.

85. *Literary Gazette*, 19 October 1839, pp. 658–9.

86. 15 August 1838.

87. On the war with the V6ii. *Hermes*, No. 2, p. 187.

88. On the Abaddon of the Revelations. *Hermes*, No. 2, pp. 137–41.

89. LA38–26 – 1 October 1838.

90. *The Antiquity of the Book of Genesis*, p. 5.

91. ibid., pp. 47f.

92. ibid., pp. 21f.

93. Christopher Methuen Campbell Collection, Penrice Castle: 25 January 1840 (T. to Charlotte Traherne).

94. LA35–39 – 27 November 1835.

95. LA(H)35–3 – 16 May 1835 (T. to Lady Elisabeth) and LA(H)38–4 – 5 July 1838.

96. 16 May 1834.

97. LA35–28 – 23 September 1835 and LA35–27 – 18 September 1835 respectively.

98. LA37–17 – 2 April 1837.

99. 19 September 1837.

100. LA37–54 – 6 October 1837.

101. LA37–16 – 2 April 1837 (Lady Elisabeth to T.).

102. LA37–18 – 6 April 1837.

103. LA35–35 – 22 October 1835.

104. LA(H)35–8 – 28 November 1835.

105. LA(H)38–6 – 14 August 1838.
106. Royal Society Collection: 305 – 18 March 1841.
107. LA(H)38–8 – 19 August 1838 (T. to Constance).
108. LA38–17 – 11 June 1838.

CHAPTER 4
PHOTOGENIC DRAWING

The most reliable and comprehensive account of the technical development of photography is *History of Photography* by J. M. Eder, translated by Edward Epstean (Columbia University Press, 1945). Helmut and Alison Gernsheim's *History of Photography* (Thames & Hudson, 1969) is a more recent and extensive treatment which includes interpretation of artistic trends in photography but which is marked by a generally hostile attitude to Henry Talbot. The best short account of the early history of photography is *Latent Image* by Beaumont Newhall (Anchor Books, New York, 1967), although *The Birth of Photography* by Brian Coe (Ash & Grant, 1976) is an attractive popular account with numerous illustrations. A reliable, brief account of the early years of negative–positive photography is contained in *The First Negatives* by David B. Thomas (HMSO, 1964). Detailed aspects of the story were explored by Arthur T. Gill in a series of articles under the general title 'Call back yesterday' which appeared in the *Photographic Journal* between January 1972 and July 1975. Harold White in past years lectured extensively on Talbot – see, for example, 'William Henry Fox Talbot – The first miniaturist,' *Photographic Journal*, November 1949, pp. 247–51. *William Henry Fox Talbot – Father of Photography* by Arthur H. Booth (Arthur Barker, 1964) is a short, attractively written

account of Talbot's photographic activities based, however, entirely on secondary sources. *William H. Fox Talbot* by André Jammes (Macmillan, New York, 1973) contains a useful cross section of Talbot's better known photographs and photo-engravings.

1. *Literary Gazette*, p. 28; *Athenaeum*, p. 69.
2. *Literary Gazette*, 2 February 1839, pp. 74–5.
3. ibid., p. 74. Extract from T.'s letter to the *Literary Gazette* dated 30 January.
4. ibid., p. 73.
5. ibid., p. 72.
6. *Athenaeum*, 2 February, 1839, p. 96.
7. *Comptes Rendus des Séances de l'Académie des Sciences*, 4 February 1839, p. 171.
8. Science Museum Collection: 31 January 1839 (Biot to T.).
9. Science Museum Collection: 13 February 1839.
10. LA39–4 – 'Sunday', presumably in January.
11. *Literary Gazette* – 13 April 1839, pp. 235–6. Letter from T. dated 8 April.
12. The quotations in this account are taken from the text reproduced in full in the *Phil. Mag.*, XIV, 1839, pp. 196–208.
13. See, for example, T. to Herschel – 29 January 1839 (Royal Society Collection) and Herschel to T. – 9 February 1839 (Science Museum Collection). The paper was printed in *Roy. Soc. Proc.*, IV, 1839, pp. 120–21.
14. Letter dated 30 January 1839, pp. 73–4.
15. An account of the processes employed in photogenic drawing, in a letter to Samuel H. Christie Esq., Secretary R.S. from H. Talbot, Esq., F.R.S. The letter was published in the *Roy. Soc. Proceedings*, IV, 1839, pp. 124–6; in the *Phil. Mag.*, XIV, March 1839, pp. 209–11; and details appeared in issues of the

Athenaeum and the *Literary Gazette* of 23 February 1839.

16. 'Note respecting a new kind of sensitive paper' (read 21 March 1839). *Roy. Soc. Proc.*, IV, 1839, p. 134.

17. *The Pencil of Nature*, Part 1, 1844. The pages were not numbered.

18. LAM – 112.

19. Notebook M.

20. Some account of the art of photogenic drawing. *Phil. Mag.*, XIV, 1839, pp. 205–6.

21. ibid., p. 206.

22. Beaumont Newhall, op. cit., p. 47.

23. Letter to Samuel Highley (Jnr), 10 May 1853 – quoted in the *Journal of the Society of Arts*, 13 May 1853, p. 292.

24. Introduction to *The Pencil of Nature* and *Brit. Assoc. Rep.*, 1839, Part 2, pp. 3–5.

25. See also T.'s comment in a letter to Sir John Herschel – Royal Society Collection: 278 – 28 January 1839.

26. LA34–47.

27. LA35–26 – 7 September 1835 (Constance to T.).

28. LA37–51 – 27 September 1837.

29. LA36–58 – 'Monday'.

30. Some account of the art of photogenic drawing. op. cit., p. 203.

31. Royal Society Collection: 287 – 1 March 1839 (T. to Herschel).

32. For a brief and lucid modern explanation of T.'s process, see Beaumont Newhall, op. cit., pp. 53–6.

33. Royal Society Collection: 297 – 12 September 1839 (T. to Herschel).

34. Royal Society Collection: 277 – T. to Herschel.

35. Science Museum Collection.

36. I, 1819, pp. 8, 396; II, 1820, p. 154. The other publication was W. T. Brande's classic *Manual of Chemistry*.

37. Science Museum Collection: Herschel notebook – entry No. 1016 for 1 February 1839.

38. LA39–7 – 4 February 1839 (Brewster to T.).

39. Royal Society Collection: 281 – 8 February 1839.

40. Science Museum Collection: 10 February 1839 (Herschel to T.).

41. Royal Society Collection: 282 – 11 February 1839.

42. Science Museum Collection: 12 February 1839.

43. T.'s general concern early in February 1839 about publishing full details of his process figured in letters to P. M. Roget of the Royal Society. For example see that of 6 February (Royal Society Collection – MC.3.6).

44. Royal Society Collection: 286 – 27 February 1839.

45. *Comptes Rendus*, VIII, 1839, p. 341.

46. Royal Society Collection: 289 – 21 March 1839.

47. Royal Society Collection: 293 – 27 April 1839.

48. Royal Society Collection: T20 – 'Thursday' March 1839 (T. to J. W. Lubbock). This letter indicates that on some occasions Talbot did not wash the paper *at all* after fixing with hypo.

49. Science Museum Collection: entry No. 1032.

50. Science Museum Collection: entry No. 1039.

51. Science Museum Collection – entry No. 1049.

52. On the chemical action of the rays of the solar spectrum on preparations of silver and other substances, both metallic and non-metallic, and on some photographic processes. *Phil. Trans.*, 130, 1840, Part 1, p. 5.

53. Royal Society Collection: 299.

54. *Phil. Trans.*, 130, 1840, Part 1, pp. 1–59.

55. ibid., p. 8.

56. Note on the art of photography, or the application of the chemical rays of light for the purposes of pictorial representation. *Roy. Soc. Proc.* IV, 1837–43, pp. 131–3. Twenty-three photographs were presented with the paper – one (of Herschel's telescope) from the camera, the rest copies of engravings and drawings. Some of the photographs were positives and others negatives.

57. Helmut and Alison Gernsheim (*The History of Photography*, p. 97) are the chief proponents of the argument that Herschel did not wish to belittle T.'s achievements and therefore withdrew the 1839 Royal Society paper. The 'proof' advanced, however, is a statement of opinion by Sir James Murray contained in a letter to Herschel's son and *dated almost seventy years later* – 16 September 1908. (See 'Talbot's and Herschel's experiments in 1839' by Helmut Gernsheim, *Image*, 3, September 1959, p. 137.)

58. Science Museum Collection: Herschel to T.

59. Science Museum Collection: Brewster to T. on 23 October 1840 and 8 November 1840; Biot to T. 14 January 1841.

60. Science Museum Collection.

61. Science Museum Collection.

62. Science Museum Collection: Notebook P.

63. LA39–5.

64. Eder, op. cit., pp. 258–9.

65. LA39–54 – 23 September 1839 (Smith, Elder to T.).

66. Science Museum Collection: 23 October 1851 (Brewster to T.).

67. *Athenaeum*, 6 April 1839, p. 259, and Gernsheim, op. cit., pp. 79–80.

68. LA39–35 – 26 April 1839.

69. Mentioned by Robert Hunt – at this time secretary of the Royal Cornwall Polytechnic Society – in his book *A Popular Treatise on the Art of Photography* (Richard Griffin, 1841) which was the first general manual and history of photography to be published. A facsimile edition, with extensive notes by James Yingpeh Tong, was published in 1973 by the Ohio University Press. See also Arthur T. Gill, 'Call back yesterday', *Photographic Journal*, July 1973.

70. LA39–46 – 1 July 1839 (William Buckmaster to T.).

71. LA39–63.

72. *Athenaeum*, 16 March 1839, p. 204.

73. *Brit. Assoc. Rep.*, 1839, Part 2, pp. 3–5.

74. LA39–44 – 11 June 1839 (Lady Elisabeth to T.).

75. LA39–32 – 13 April 1839 (Theresa Digby to T.).

76. LA40–13 – 2 February 1840 (Lady Elisabeth to T.). See also Eder, op. cit., p. 318.

77. LA39–38 – 17 May 1839 (Constance to T.).

78. LA39–39 – 21 May 1839 (Constance to T.).

79. LA39–18 – 6 March 1839 (Mary Talbot to T.).

80. LA39–16 – 28 February 1839 (T.'s cousin Charlotte Traherne to him).

81. Christopher Methuen Campbell Collection, Penrice Castle: 4 March 1839.

82. LA39–37 – 15 May 1839 (Moore to Lady Elisabeth).

83. Science Museum Collection: 9 May 1839.

84. 8 June 1839, p. 435.

85. LA(H)39–2 – 25 November 1839 (T. to Constance) and LA39–79 – 30 November 1839 (Constance to T.).

86. *Literary Gazette*, 20 July 1839, p. 459.
87. Royal Photographic Society Collection: 146 – 5 October 1839 (T. to Lady Elisabeth).
88. Science Museum Collection: 10 November 1839.
89. Royal Society Collection: 285 – 20 February 1839.
90. Bills – LA39–13, LA40–28, LA42–20, and LA44–37.
91. Royal Society Collection – 293.
92. 13 June 1839, p. 444.
93. Science Museum Collection: 24 (29?) June 1839 (Herschel to T.).
94. Royal Society Collection: 299 – 7 December 1839 (T. to Herschel).
95. Science Museum Collection: Notebook P – entries for 23 September 1839 and 3 April 1840.
96. Issue of March–April 1839. Quoted in Beaumont Newhall, op. cit., p. 102.
97. Royal Society Collection: 302 – 30 August 1840 (note of Herschel letter to T.).
98 Royal Society Collection: 303 – 1 September 1840 (T. to Herschel).
99. LA40–31 – 7 March 1840 (copy letter).
100. Herschel's account of his experiments in reproducing colour was contained in his 1840 paper to the Royal Society (note 52). For a contemporary review of research into colour see Robert Hunt's *Report on the Present State of Our Knowledge of the Chemical Action of the Solar Radiations* (British Association for the Advancement of Science, 1850).
101. Royal Society Collection: 301 – 30 April 1840 (T. to Herschel).
102. *Literary Gazette*, 16 May 1840, pp. 315–16.
103. Science Museum Collection: 3 May 1840 and 19 June 1840 (Herschel to T.).
104. LA40–3 – undated but probably sent at about this time.
105. LA40–61 – 5 August 1840.

CHAPTER 5
THE CALOTYPE

1. LA34–14 – bill dated 10 May 1834.
2. Science Museum Collection: 28 February 1839.
3. Science Museum Collection: Notebook P.
4. Royal Society Collection: T20 – bearing a pencilled date 'March 1839' and 'Thursday'.
5. LA39–25 – bill from Alexander Garden of Oxford Street.
6. All the quotations in this section are drawn from Notebooks P and Q in the Science Museum Collection.
7. T. Frederick Hardwich, *A Manual o, Photographic Chemistry*, 1859, p. 28. It was the first manual of photographic chemistry.
8. Science Museum Collection: Notebook P.
9. Science Museum Collection: 14 January 1841 (Biot to T.).
10. LA40–89 – 15 December 1840 (Wheatstone to T.). See also 'Early stereoscopes' by Arthur T. Gill, *Photographic Journal*, October, November and December 1969.
11. Royal Society Collection: 304 – T. to Herschel.
12. Science Museum Collection: 22 March 1841.
13. Science Museum Collection: 5 and 19 February 1841 (Brewster to T.).
14. Talbot privately reprinted the two letters of 5 and 19 February 1841 under the title *Two Letters on Calotype Photogenic Drawing*. They were also reproduced in The *Phil. Mag.*, XIX, 1841, pp. 88–92.

15. T.'s paper appeared in *Roy. Soc. Proc.* IV, 1841, pp. 312–16, despite an indication from the Society's secretary on 21 March 1841 (LA41–20) that details of the new discovery would be welcomed as 'adorning our Transactions'. A letter from T. to Herschel on 1 July (Royal Society Collection – 309) indicated that this was not to happen because the paper was believed to have been printed elsewhere before being read to the Society – which was not the case.

The paper was privately reprinted by Talbot initially under the title *The Process of Calotype Photogenic Drawing* and subsequently under the title *The Process of Talbotype (Formerly Called Calotype)*.

16. Science Museum Collection: 16 March and 22 March 1841 (Herschel to T.).

17. Science Museum Collection: 12 June 1841 (Brewster to T.).

18. LA40–79 – 1 November 1840 (Lemon to T.).

19. LA41–14 – 4 March 1841.

20. LA40–78 – 28 October 1840.

21. LA41–22 – 25 March 1841.

22. LA41–59 – 24 September 1841 (Lady Elisabeth to Constance).

23. LA41–15 – 12 March 1841; LA41–23 – 28 March 1841; LA41–38 – 14 June 1841.

24. LA41–39 – 15 June 1841.

25. LA40–86 – 14 November 1840 (Lady Elisabeth to T.).

26. Science Museum Collection: 16 March 1841 (Herschel to T.).

27. Science Museum Collection: 14 October 1841.

28. Science Museum Collection: Notebook Q.

29. Patent No. 9,753 dated 1 June 1843.

30. *British Miniatures*, by Basil Long: London, 1829.

31. LA42–59 – 17 August 1842 (West Awdry to T.) and LA54–80 – 29 December 1854 (Collen to T.).

32. LA42–53 – 3 August 1842.

33. Beaumont Newhall: *Latent Image*, p. 108 and *The Daguerreotype in America* (Dover Publications, New York: Third Revised Edition 1976, pp. 24–27). Gernsheim – p. 135. See also 'Call back yesterday: back to the Daguerreotype' by Arthur T. Gill, *Photographic Journal*, September 1973.

34. See *The First Negatives* by D. B. Thomas: HMSO, 1964, pp. 24–5.

35. For example, the *Morning Post* in the spring of 1842 (quoted in D. B. Thomas, op. cit., p. 24) and David Brewster to T. – 22 March 1842 (Science Museum Collection).

36. Correspondence in the Science Museum Collection.

37. LA42–59 – 17 August 1842 (statement sent by West Awdry to T.).

38. LA44–31 – 30 May 1844.

39. LA54–80 – 29 December 1854.

40. Collen estimated in his evidence at the T. versus Laroche trial in 1854 that he 'might have taken a thousand portraits' (*Photographic Journal*, December 1854, p. 89).

41. Lacock Collection: 1842 Misc.

42. 'Early stereoscopes' by Arthur T. Gill, loc. cit.

43. Almost all Claudet's letters to Talbot are in the Science Museum Collection. See also D. B. Thomas, op. cit., pp. 26–30.

44. LA44–62 – 15 September 1844 and LA44–60 – 13 September 1844.

45. Science Museum Collection: 24 August 1844 (Claudet to T.).

46. LA44–85 (statement) and LA45–16 – 29 January 1845 (T. to Constance).

47. LA45–101 – 15 July 1845.

48. For recent introductions to the work of Adamson and Hill see *A Centenary Exhibition of the Work of David Octavius Hill and Robert Adamson*, Scottish Arts Council (Katherine Michaelson) 1970 and *The Hill/Adamson Albums* (Times Newspapers for the N.P.G.) 1973.

49. Many of Brewster's letters to T. are in the Science Museum Collection. The quotations here are from letters dated 27 October 1841 and 29 March 1842 respectively.

50. LA42–77 – 9 November 1842.

51. LA43–53 – 9 May 1843.

52. Science Museum Collection: 3 July 1843 (Brewster to T.).

53. Science Museum Collection: 18 November 1843.

54. 'The first photographic record of a scientific conference' by Katherine Michaelson in *One Hundred Years of Photographic History – Essays in Honor of Beaumont Newhall*, edited by Van Deren Coke: University of New Mexico Press, 1975, pp. 109–16.

55. LA46–65 – 19 May 1846.

56. *Quarterly Review*, LXXVII, cliv, 1846.

57. See one modern appreciation by Ian Jeffrey (pp. 5ff.) in the catalogue to the Arts Council Exhibition *The Real Thing*, 1975.

58. LA45–110 – 29 July 1845.

59. LA42–64 – 24 August 1842.

60. LA44–60 – 13 September 1844.

61. *Literary Gazette*, T.'s letter of 5 February 1841.

62. Royal Society Collection: 319 – 26 October 1847 (T. to Herschel).

63. *Literary Gazette*, 16 May 1840, pp. 315–16.

64. LA41–35 – 4 June 1841 (Jones to T.).

65. LA52–27 – 19 May 1852.

66. *Photographic Journal*, 15 November 1860, p. 33.

67. LA46–76 – 9 June 1846 (Jones to T.).

68. LA46–78 – 14 June 1846 (Jones to T.).

69. LA46–89 – 16 August 1846 (Jones to T.).

70. LA53–24 – 26 May 1853 (Jones to T.).

71. LA54–2 – January 1854.

72. LA52–49 – 26 October 1852.

73. Letters from John Henderson to his son Charles (in 1892) and to Sir Benjamin Stone (2 May 1898) quoted in 'The Talbotype establishment at Reading – 1844 to 1847' by V. F. Snow and D. B. Thomas, *Photographic Journal*, February 1966, pp. 56–67.

74. LA(Am)43–18 – 12 December 1843 (T. to Mlle Amélina).

75. V. F. Snow and D. B. Thomas, op. cit., pp. 59 and 60.

76. LA44–32 – 31 May 1844 (Henneman to T.).

77. LA44–36 – 20 June 1844.

78. LA44–55.

79. LA45–143 – 31 October 1845.

80. Lacock Collection: 1846 Misc.

81. For a later account of the background to the production of the memoir (and the Calotype) see 'Record of C.M.W.' By Arthur T. Gill, *Photographic Journal*, October 1975, pp. 490–91.

82. *The Pencil of Nature:* A Facsimile Edition by D. A. Capo Press, New York, 1969. Introduction by Beaumont Newhall.

83. LA44–8 – 25 February 1844.

84. LAM49.

85. Science Museum Collection: Notebook P.

86. August 1844.

87. March 1845.

88. 22 February 1845.

89. LA44–46 – 6 August 1844.

90. LA45–29 – 4 March 1845 (N. Thompson to T.). The plates referred to are

2B

numbers 7, 8, 10, 2 and 6 respectively in *The Pencil of Nature*.

91. LA45–182 – 12 January 1846. [The code is incorrectly stated as 1845.]

92. LA45–19 – 3 February 1845.

93. Longman sales records: University of Reading Archives.

94. See pp. 162f.

95. Tarrant's bill for mounting and wrapping 150 of Part 1 was £12 10s. od. (LA44–28 – 28 June 1844).

96. Tarrant's bill was for £34 15s. od. (LA45–122 – September 1845) and the charge for Henneman would have been a little over £55. On direct charges and receipts therefore T. may just have broken even.

97. LA45–111 – 31 July 1845.

98. For a specialist view of the publication, see 'The Talbotype applied to hieroglyphics' by Ricardo A. Caminos in *J. Egypt. Arch.*, 52, 1960, pp. 65–70 (with the three illustrations reproduced).

99. *Annals of the Artists of Spain*, 4: *Talbotype Illustrations*, 1847.

100. Science Museum Collection – 5 May 1847 (Henneman to T.).

101. *Amateur's column. Liverpool and Manchester Photographic Journal*, 15 December 1857, p. 270. Malone was editor of the Journal from June 1857 to February 1858.

102. LA45–157 – 7 December 1846. [The code is incorrectly stated as 1845.]

103. LA46–55 – 30 April 1846.

104. LA46–128 – December 1846. (Talbotype Establishment document.)

105. Lacock Collection: 1839–59 Misc.

106. LA45–70 – draft notice. (Other evidence indicates appearance of the notice in 1846.)

107. *Art-Union*, 1 June 1846, pp. 143–4.

108. One print traced measures $3\frac{1}{8} \times 3\frac{5}{8}$

inches and is now badly faded though details of the subject – the deck of a ship – are still clearly visible. The original may have been taken by Nicolaas Henneman aboard H.M.S. *Superb* in September 1845.

109. LA46–84 – a printed leaflet bearing the date 22 July 1846 and the phrase 'The latest edition' in handwriting.

110. LA46–145 – agreement with Benjamin West signed by Cowderoy on 22 December 1846.

111. Science Museum Collection.

112. LA46–77 – 14 June 1846 (T. diary note of a meeting with Cowderoy).

113. LA46–2 – Note on the Reading stock of prints, with quoted prices, e.g. Large Pictures at £2 os. od. per 100.

114. LA46–49 – summary of account.

115. LA46–55 – 30 April 1846 (Cowderoy to T.).

116. LA46–73 – text of agreement.

117. LA46–63 – text of agreement, 18 May 1846.

118. LA47–92.

119. LA46–18 – 27 January 1846 (Cowderoy to T.).

120. LA46–136 – 10 December 1846 (contract between Newman and T.).

121. LA43–24 – 11 February 1843.

122. LA43–22 – 4 February 1843 (Bassano to Mlle Amélina).

123. LA43–30 – 28 January 1843 (Bassano to Mlle Amélina).

124. LA43–45 – 30 March 1843 (Draft agreement signed by T. and Bassano).

125. LA43–62 – 7 June 1843.

126. LA43–66.

127. LA44–76 – 10 October [1844 probably] (Amélina to Caroline).

128. LA46–117 – 6 April 1847 (Bovard to T.).

129. LA48–27 – 9 June 1848 (Bovard to T.).

130. LA46–122 – 2 November 1846.

131. LA47–71 – 30 August 1847 (Anthony to T.).

132. Lacock Collection: 14 November 1870 (from E. & H. J. Anthony of New York).

133. Science Museum Collection: 5 February 1849 (the Langenheims to T.).

134. LA49–13 – 25 April 1849.

135. LA49–14 – 14 May 1849.

136. The Missouri Historical Society in St Louis has a collection of 50 'Views in North America. Taken from nature. July 1850, by the patent Talbotype process, by W. & F. Langenheim . . .' (private communication to author from Beaumont Newhall).

137. Science Museum Collection: 10 June 1849.

138. Science Museum Collection: 21 September 1849.

139. Science Museum Collection: 18 November 1849.

140. LA50–24 – 25 May 1850.

141. Science Museum Collection: 13 June 1854. For an account of the place of the Langenheim brothers in the history of American photography see 'W & F Langenheim – Photographers' in *Pennsylvania Arts and Sciences*, 2, I, 1937, pp. 25–9, 58–9. T. sent them an example of his work and the Talbotype – of Pembroke College, Cambridge – is now in the Smithsonian Institution.

142. LA47–78 – 5 October 1847 (T. to Horatia).

143. LA48–4 – 8 January 1848.

144. LA48–14 – 15 February 1848 (T. to Malone).

145. LA48–29 – 16 June 1848 (text of agreement) and LA48–31 – 17 June 1848 (further elaboration).

146. LA48–25 – 28 April 1848 and LA48–39 – 2 August 1848 (both Malone to T.).

147. LA49–12 – 18 April 1849 (Malone to T.).

148. LA49–20 – 1 October 1849 (Malone to T.).

149. LA50–23 – 25 May 1850 (Malone to T.).

150. Science Museum Collection: 26 July 1849.

151. LA52–48 – 23 October 1852 (Malone to T.).

152. LA49–21 – 2 November 1849 (text of agreement.)

153. In March 1843 (Royal Society Collection: 315 – 29 March 1843) T. suggested the name Amphitype for Herschel's process based on glass plates. Eight years later (Royal Society Collection: 321 – May 1851) T. wrote to Herschel requesting that if the latter had not publicized the name in connection with his original process, he would like to attach it to his recently introduced technique.

154. *Literary Gazette*, 27 November 1852, p. 876 (letter from T.).

155. LA54–19 – 24 April 1854 (T. to Constance).

156. Royal Society Collection: 268 – 4 March 1833 (T. to Herschel) and LA33–8 – 7 March 1833 (Herschel to T.).

157. Notebook M – entry for 7 March 1835.

158. The letter is in *Selected Correspondence of Michael Faraday* (Vol. 2, pp. 636–7), edited by L. Pearce Williams: CUP, 1971. Talbot's note of the letter is in the Lacock Collection: LA51–19.

159. 'On the production of instantaneous photographic images', *Athenaeum*, 6 December 1851, pp. 1286–7.

160. 28 June 1851, p. 443. T. appears not to have conducted any more practical

experiments but in 1854 was seeking W. R. Grove's advice on equipment suitable for single, brilliant discharges of electricity. Two letters from T. to Grove are in the Royal Institution Collection and one from Grove to T. in the Lacock Collection (LA54–55 – 2 November 1854).

161. LA50–17 – 15 March 1850 (Malone to T.).

162. See, for example, advertisement in the *Athenaeum* of 16 March 1850, front page.

163. LA51–53 – 1 October 1851 and LA51–61 – 15 October 1851 (both T. to Constance). See also November 1851 exchanges between T. and the executive committee: LA51–80, LA51–81, and LA51–82.

164. LA51–84 – 17 November 1851 (T. to Constance).

165. Letter from T. to Robert Hunt in the R.P.S. Collection: 141(a) – 7 November 1851 but marked not sent.

166. LA52–24 – 3 May 1852.

167. LA47–73 – 'Mr Henneman's Table of Photographic Portraits taken from 1847 to 1855 inclusive'.

168. LA59–11 – 8 March 1859 (Malone to T.)

169. LA56–36 – 17 October 1856 (J. H. Bolton to T.).

170. LA51–90 – T. account book with Stilwell – 1852–6.

171. Information supplied by Arthur T. Gill.

172. T. gave at least three estimates of his expenditure on photography without defining precisely what activities were included. In 1852 – in a letter from Robert Hunt to Peter Fry quoted in an article in the 23 June 1939 issue of the *Journal of the Royal Society of Arts* (pp.

832–3) – T. was reported to have estimated his expenditure at £7,000. In 1855 – in a letter dated 5 January (LA55–4) to his uncle Lord Lansdowne – he indicated an expenditure of £5–10,000 'more or less'. Finally, on 17 May 1860 (LA60–20) he informed Col. Henry James of the Ordnance Survey that he had spent at least £8–9,000 'on photographic inventions'. It seems fair therefore to take the lowest figure but to allow that his expenditure might have been very much higher.

CHAPTER 6
PHOTOGRAPHY: OF PRIORITY,
PLAGIARISM AND PATENTS

The study of the situation surrounding T.'s photographic patents has benefited greatly in recent years by the scholarly and detailed researches of R. Derek Wood. While the present author does not agree with Mr Wood on some aspects of interpretation, the articles are unhesitatingly recommended to readers wishing to study this particular aspect of T.'s life further:

'J. B. Reade FRS and the early history of photography. Part I, A re-assessment on the discovery of contemporary evidence', *Annals of Science*, 27, I, March 1971, pp. 13–45. 'Part II, Gallic acid and Talbot's Calotype patent', *Annals of Science*, 27, I, March 1971, pp. 47–83, plate XIII.

'The involvement of Sir John Herschel in the photographic patent case, Talbot v Henderson 1854', *Annals of Science*, 27, 3, September 1971, pp. 239–64.

'J. B. Reade's early photographic experiments – recent further evidence on the legend', *British Journal of Photography*, 28 July 1972, pp. 643–7.

The Calotype Patent Law Suit of Talbot v Laroche 1854. Printed privately, 1975, to welcome the opening of the Talbot Museum at Lacock.

While by no means uncritical of T., Mr Wood's research has done much to correct the one-sided account of the patent situation presented in *The History of Photography* by Helmut and Alison Gernsheim (Thames & Hudson, 1969), which account has regrettably been followed by most subsequent writers.

Arthur T. Gill has also unravelled parts of the involved story – for example, see 'A letter by Joseph Bancroft Reade – 1 April 1839'. *Photographic Journal*, January 1961, pp. 10–13.

1. *Art-Journal*, 1 August 1854, pp. 236–8.
2. Science Museum Collection: 31 August 1854 and 16 September 1854 (Brewster to T.).
3. Quoted in 'The patent controversy in the nineteenth century' by Fritz Machlup and Edith Penrose, *Journal of Economic History*, X, 1, May 1950. The article provides an excellent general account of the situation.
4. 28 December 1850, p. 1434: quoted by Machlup and Penrose, op. cit., p. 15.
5. 26 July 1851, p. 812: quoted by Machlup and Penrose, op. cit., p. 18.
6. *An Economic History of England: The 18th Century* by T. S. Ashton: Methuen, 1955, p. 107.
7. 1 February 1851, pp. 114–15: quoted by Machlup and Penrose, op. cit., p. 24.
8. 19 October 1850, pp. 73–5: 'A poor man's tale of a patent'.
9. *The British Patent System (1) Administration*, by Klaus Boehm: CUP, 1967, p. 19.
10. The address of the Rev. William Vernon Harcourt – quoted (p. 37) in *Victorian Science*, edited by George Basalla, William Coleman and Robert H. Kargon: Anchor Books, New York, 1970.
11. *Quarterly Review*, XLIII, 1830, pp. 306ff., from a review by Brewster of Charles Babbage's *Reflexions on the Decline of Science in England, and some of its causes*. Quotation from p. 333.
12. Brewster's address to the 20th Meeting of the BAAS. Quoted in *The Home Life of Sir David Brewster*, by Mrs Gordon: Edinburgh, 1869, pp. 208–9.
13. Brewster review in *Quarterly Review*, loc. cit., p. 341.
14. LA51–98 – 31 December 1851 (draft).
15. Boehm, op. cit., p. 25.
16. *Patent Protection: The Inventor and his Patent*, by Clifford Lees: Business Publications Limited, p. 17.
17. Boehm, op. cit., p. 26.
18. Boehm, op. cit., pp. 26, 28.
19. *Athenaeum*, 8 June 1839, p. 435.
20. LA39–7 – 4 February 1839.
21. *Literary Gazette*, 30 March 1839, pp. 202–4; 6 April 1839, p. 215; and 13 April 1839, pp. 235–6.
22. LA45–39 – 18 April 1845 (T. to Lady Elisabeth).
23. See *The Strutts and the Arkwrights 1758–1830*, by R. S. Fitton and A. P. Wadsworth: Manchester University Press, 1958.
24. *A Popular Treatise on the Art of Photography* by Richard Griffin, 1841 (facsimile edition by Ohio University Press, 1973), pp. 73ff.
25. *Journal of the Photographic Society*, 21 December 1854, p. 94.
26. Science Museum Collection: Notebooks P and Q.
27. Royal Society Collection: 304 – 17 March 1841 (T. to Herschel).

28. Copy of agreement at the Science Museum and the Polytechnic, London.

29. Letter in *Photographic News,* 15 February 1861, pp. 81–2. Sedgfield's letter to the editor resulted from the publication of views critical of T. made at a meeting of the Photographic Society, to which Thomas Malone responded in defence of his former employer. The only reference to a Sedgfield in T.'s legal papers was a brief entry concerning a licence and dated 1 November 1851. LA52–1 – Price & Bolton Bill for 1851–2.

30. *Art-Journal,* 1 August 1849, p. 262.

31. 5 March 1852 letter reprinted in 'The origins of the Photographic Society', by Dudley J. Johnston, *Journal of the Royal Society of Arts,* 23 June 1939, pp. 832–3.

32. LA52–15 – 19 March 1852.

33. Dudley J. Johnston, loc. cit., pp. 833–4. Letter dated 24 March 1852.

34. LA52–19 – 21 April 1852 (Wheatstone to T.).

35. LA52–20 – 23 April 1852 (Hunt to T.).

36. LA52–22 – 26 April 1852.

37. LA52–21 – 28 April 1852 (Hunt to J. H. Bolton).

38. LA52–23 – 28 April 1852 (Hunt to T.).

39. RPS Collection: 141c – 30 April 1852 (T. to Hunt).

40. Science Museum Collection: T. draft note to Wheatstone – 29 May 1852.

41. See *Photographic Journal,* 31 October 1899, p. 43, for reference to Leighton's list of signatories. Also LA52–32 – 1 June 1852 (Caroline to T.).

42. LA52–37 – 11 June 1852 (Eastlake to T.).

43. For example, see again the views expressed in *The Economist* editorial of 1 February 1851 (pp. 177–8).

44. *Journal of the Photographic Society,* 3 March 1853, p. 2.

45. *Photographic News.* The meeting of the Photographic Society Council on 5 February 1861 was reported in the issue of 8 February – but a fuller account of the discussions appeared on pp. 80ff. of the issue of 15 February 1861 and the editorial on p. 74.

46. LA52–12 – 4 February 1852.

47. *Photographic Journal,* 15 February 1860, pp. 166–7.

48. See references at pp. 49ff. in 'J. B. Reade FRS and the early history of photography. Part II, Gallic acid and Talbot's Calotype Patent' by R. Derek Wood, loc. cit.

49. LA45–146 – 10 November 1845 (W. R. King to T.) and LAM22 – copy of a notice served on Willats.

50. LA45–148 – 11 November 1845 (T. to King).

51. LA46–74 – 7 June 1846 (T. to King).

52. The exchanges are contained in LA49–23 – 19 December 1849 (Malone to T.); LA50–4 – 8 January 1850 (Malone to T. containing copy of letter from Harper); LA50–8 – draft agreement with Colls and Bingham; LA50–9 – 2 February 1850 (Malone to T.); LA50–12 – 15 February 1850 (Malone to T.); and LA50–16 – 4 March 1850 (Malone to T.).

53. See R. Derek Wood, op. cit., p. 50.

54. *Athenaeum,* 6 December 1851.

55. LA51–72 – 'Statement of sums received by Messrs Price & Bolton for Patent dues' 1851 to 1854. Twelve definite licence holders appear on the statement over the period.

56. Issue dated 13 May 1853.

57. *British Journal of Photography,* 21 February 1902, p. 149; 13 June 1930, pp. 353–5.

58. LA53–12 – 15 April 1853 and licence notes.

59. LA56–33 covering the period from January 1855 to Midsummer Day 1856.

60. LA52–1 (lawyer's account of work – entry for 10 November 1851) and LA54–52 – 30 September 1854 (signed note in T.'s handwriting in favour of William Brunner to make pictures without payment 'in consideration of his being a refugee from his country, owing to political troubles').

61. LA52–5 – 24 January 1852; LA52–8 – copy of the terms of the injunction. See also R. Derek Wood, op. cit., pp. 52–3.

62. LA52–1 – Price & Bolton account.

63. LA50–12 – 15 February 1850.

64. Charles Wheatstone had been prepared to make a limited affidavit on T.'s behalf but it seems was not called upon to do so finally: LA54–25 – 22 May 1854 (Wheatstone to T.). Copies of the affidavits are in the Lacock Collection, as are the letters dated May 1854 from Herschel to T. which concerned the Henderson case. For a detailed account of Herschel's role in the case, together with source notes and general background, see 'The involvement of Sir John Herschel in the photographic patent case, Talbot v Henderson 1854' by R. Derek Wood, loc. cit.

65. *Athenaeum*, 10 June 1854.

66. LA51–21 – 26 May 1854. [The code is mistakenly attributed to 1851.]

67. *The Times*, 27 May 1854. See also *Liverpool Photographic Journal*, 10 June 1854, p. 78.

68. *The Times*, 21 December 1854; *Journal of the Photographic Society*, 21 December 1854, pp. 84–95, and *Art-Journal*, 1 February 1855, pp. 49–54.

69. LA54–36 – 24 June 1854 (T. to Constance) and Laroche's letter of 27 June 1854 to the Photographic Society published in the Society's *Journal* of 21 July 1854, p. 2.

70. *Journal of the Photographic Society*, 21 July 1854, pp. 2ff.

71. *Liverpool Photographic Journal*, 9 September 1854, pp. 113–14.

72. LA54–60 – 26 November 1854.

73. LA54–66 – 5 December 1854.

74. Probably to be dated to 4 December 1854.

75. LA54–58 – 21 November 1854.

76. Report of the trial in the *Journal of the Photographic Society*, 21 December 1854, p. 86.

77. LA54–48 – Henderson affidavit.

78. See 'J. B. Reade FRS and the early history of photography. Parts I & II' by R. Derek Wood, loc. cit.

79. LAM–142 – Thornthwaite affidavit; [no code] – Hunt/Heisch affidavit and LA52–1 – Price & Bolton account for the period autumn 1851 to autumn 1852.

80. R. Derek Wood, op. cit., Part I, pp. 15ff.

81. Reade letter to Robert Hunt – 13 February 1854. Quoted R. Derek Wood, ibid., p. 20.

82. R. Derek Wood, ibid., pp. 37–9. For other sources see footnotes of Chapter 5.

83. LA54–34. The full text of the letter appeared in this memorandum supplied to Fry and Loxley, and to T., by Brayley on 17 June 1854.

84. *North British Review*, 1847, pp. 465–504. See also R. Derek Wood, ibid., pp. 18ff.

85. Royal Society Collection – MC 3.15. The letter was 'discovered' by R. Derek Wood (ibid., pp. 32–3).

86. 13 November 1854 and 8 December 1854 (both T. to Story-Maskelyne).

87. LA54–69 – 8 December 1854 (Story-Maskelyne to T.). For an outline of Hunt's life and widespread activities see 'Robert Hunt FRS (1807–1887)' by A. Pearson, *Federation of Old Cornwall Societies*, 1976.

88. *Photographic Journal*, April 1907, p. 221 (letter from Charles H. Talbot).
89. *Art-Journal*, 1 February 1855, pp. 49–54.
90. LA54–78 – 28 December 1854 (Bolton to T.).
91. *Art-Journal*, ibid, p. 51.
92. ibid., p. 54.
93. ibid., pp. 53–4.
94. 21 December 1854, p. 95.
95. LA54–73 – 20 December 1854.
96. LA55–4 – 5 January 1855.
97. LA54–75 – 26 December 1854 (Bolton to T.).
98. *Art-Journal*, April 1855, p. 127 (letter from W. H. Thornthwaite, 'Hon. Secretary of the Defence Fund').
99. LA56–33 – Price & Bolton statement for January 1855 to Midsummer Day 1856. For an account of the outcome of the Talbot v Henderson case, see 'The involvement of Sir John Herschel in the photographic patent case, Talbot v Henderson, 1854' by R. Derek Wood, loc. cit., pp. 260ff.
100. LA56–18 – 5 April 1856.
101. 13 January 1855.
102. LA56–33 – Price & Bolton statement.
103. LA55–6 – 22 January 1855.
104. LA58–50 – 20 April 1858 (Mlle Amélina to T.).
105. *The Times*, 25 September 1877.
106. LA57–10 – 11 April 1857.
107. LA57–11 – 14 April 1857.
108. Gernsheim, op. cit., p. 177.
109. ibid., p. 234.
110. *British Economic Growth 1688–1959* by Phyllis Deane and W. A. Cole: CUP, 1967, p. 25.
111. Gernsheim, op. cit., p. 178.
112. For example, see LA54–7 – 4 February 1854 (Fenton to T.).
113. LA55–21 – 27 November 1855.

CHAPTER 7
APPLIED SCIENCE AND ETYMOLOGY

1. *A Manual of Electro-Metallurgy* by James Napier: Griffin & Co., 1851 (part of the *Encyclopaedia Metropolitana*).
2. ibid., p. 99.
3. LA41–26 – 5 April 1841.
4. Napier, op. cit., p. 122.
5. ibid., pp. 122 and 127.
6. 8 May 1843.
7. LA48–20 – 5 April 1848.
8. See, for example, experimental notes from 1843 – LA43–13 and LA43–15.
9. LA46–10 – 9 January 1846 (to T. from the company).
10. A full account of this and other Wheatstone researches is given in *Sir Charles Wheatstone* by Brian Bowers: HMSO, 1975.
11. *Proceedings* of the Institution, 1857, pp. 386–421.
12. LA42–69 – 29 August 1842; LA42–74 – 23 September 1842 and LA42–75 – 24 October 1842 (all Henley to T.). Henley described the motors he constructed for T. and Wheatstone in the *Electrician* of 26 September 1862, p. 244.
13. LA43–3 – 10 January 1843.
14. Royal Institution, Grove Collection: 12 January 1843 (letter from T.).
15. LA43–6 – 13 January 1843 (Grove to T.). There is a puzzle in that Grove's discourse on 10 February 1843 was not on electricity as a motive power which was the subject of his lecture at the Royal Institution one year later on 9 February 1844. Possibly Grove decided to postpone his review until he had more information and working examples on which to base it.
16. LA46–27 – 10 February 1846.

17. LA47–69.
18. Letter owned by A. C. Davidson and on loan to the National Library of Scotland: 9 January 1843 (to Davidson from W. R. King, T.'s solicitor).
19. LA43–5 – 11 January 1843.
20. *Phil. Mag.*, August 1833, pp. 81–2.
21. *Phil. Mag.*, September 1833, pp. 204–5.
22. *Phil. Mag.*, February 1834, p. 114.
23. LA40–89 – 15 December 1840.
24. LA41–8 – 24 February 1841 (Wheatstone to T.).
25. LA41–12.
26. LA41–44 – 8 July 1841 (King to T.) and LA41–45 – draft agreement.
27. 25 June 1866.
28. 29 March 1874 (Charlotte Traherne to T.).
29. For an account of the general background see *The Making of the Electrical Age*, by Harold I. Sharlin: Abelard-Schuman, 1963. Robert Hunt's paper to the Institution of Civil Engineers is a useful contemporary (and pessimistic) review of developments while a modern outline is contained in 'The early history of the electric motor' by Brain Bowers, *Philips Technical Review*, 35, 4, 1975.
30. *Electrician* of 26 September 1862, p.391.
31. LA53–5.
32. LA43–77 – 4 September 1843 (Fox-Strangways to Lady Elisabeth).
33. LA46–69 – 28 May 1846.
34. *Literary Gazette*, 23 January 1847, pp. 57–8; 30 January, pp. 87–9; and 6 February, pp. 109–11.
35. LA46–130 – 3 December 1846.
36. 9 March 1847 and LA47–36 – 13 March 1847.
37. LA46–134 – 9 December 1846.
38. *Quarterly Review*, LXXXI, clxii, September 1847, pp. 500–25.
39. LA48–6 – 11 January 1848.
40. *Literary Gazette*, 1 January 1848, pp. 1–6.
41. *English Etymologies*, pp. 26, 29, 49 and 9 respectively.
42. LA47–36 – 13 March 1847.

CHAPTER 8

MID-CENTURY: FAMILY, ASTRONOMY AND BOTANY

1. Lacock Collection.
2. ibid.
3. LA51–10 – census return dated 30 March 1851 and return for 1854–5.
4. Note dated 14 February 1839.
5. Notes LA40–75 and LA41–4.
6. 17 March 1852 (Awdry to T.).
7. LA45–119 – 25 August 1845.
8. LA46–22 – 1 February 1846 (T. to Lady Elisabeth).
9. 6 January 1848 (Awdry to T.).
10. LA(H)31–3 – 7 October 1831 (T. to Lady Elisabeth).
11. LA45–108 – 28 July 1845 (T. to Lady Elisabeth) and LA45–110 – 29 July 1845 (T. to Constance).
12. LA53–31 – 5 October 1853.
13. From the *Annual Register* for 1872 quoted in *The Age of Equipoise* by W. L. Burn: Allen & Unwin, 1964, p. 30.
14. 5 December 1842.
15. 3 February 1854.
16. LA46–20 – 30 January 1846 (T. to Lady Elisabeth).
17. January 19 1845.
18. LA(H)41–6 – 26 October 1841.
19. 26 April 1855.
20. LA(H)41–5 – 4 June 1841.
21. LA46–36 – 10 March 1846.
22. 28 April 1847.
23. LA48–50 – 5 December 1848.
24. LA48–18 – 27 March 1848 (T. to Horatia).

25. LA48–18.
26. LA48–50 – 5 December 1848 (T. to Horatia).
27. RPS Collection: 148 (M).
28. LA51–14.
29. LA51–15 – 1 May 1851.
30. LA51–16 – 2 May 1851.
31. LA47–21 – 12 February 1847.
32. 27 March 1843.
33. Date unknown, probably early 1847.
34. 28 September 1859.
35. 18 January 1859 (Constance to T.).
36. LA58–33 – 29 March 1858 (Rosamond to T.).
37. 16 September 1811.
38. LA17–10 – 14 February 1817.
39. LA17–22 – 14 May 1817 (T. to Lady Elisabeth).
40. LA(H)31–1 – 9 January 1831.
41. LA58–25 – 4 March 1858.
42. 3 February 1868.
43. 25 August 1877.
44. Royal Society Collection: 315 – 29 March 1843.
45. Notebook D, p. 69.
46. 'Remarks on M. Foucault's pendulum experiment', 1851.
47. Notebook C – 15 March 1825, p. 29.
48. BAAS Manchester Meeting, June 1842. *Report*, pp. 16–17, 'On the improvement of the Telescope'.
49. *Royal Astronomical Society Memoirs*, XXI, Part I, 1852, pp. 107–15.
50. 3 May 1851.
51. Royal Greenwich Observatory: Mss 717, Section 47 – 2 and 4 May 1851 (T. to Airy).
52. For a general account of the beginnings of astro-photography see *Their Majesties' Astronomers* by Colin A. Ronan: Bodley Head, 1967. De La Rue's own account of the 1860 solar photography

was published in the *Athenaeum*, 25 August 1860, pp. 259–60.
53. BAAS Edinburgh Meeting, August 1871. *Report*, pp. 34–6.
54. *A Popular History of Astronomy during the Nineteenth Century* by Agnes M. Clerke: Black, 1902 (first published 1855).
55. 28 October 1814.
56. 10 November 1816 (Trevelyan to T.).
57. 20 August 1816.
58. Untitled notebook.
59. LA17–28 – 20 July 1817.
60. LA60–39 – 8 July 1860.
61. LA51–29 – 20 July 1851.
62. Small notebook entitled 'The Garden'.
63. LA47–49 – 16 May 1847.
64. LA18–17 – 20 June 1818.
65. 11 July 1849.
66. 2 July 1836.
67. 12 January 1826.
68. Lacock Collection.
69. Archives of the Royal Botanic Gardens, Kew: English Letters, V, 228 – 8 March 1833.
70. Archives of the Royal Botanic Gardens, Kew: English Letters, VI, 233 – 12 February 1833.
71. Archives of the Royal Botanic Gardens, Kew: English Letters, XI, 145 – 8 March 1838.
72. Archives of the Royal Botanic Gardens, Kew: English Letters, XI, 147 – 8 May 1838.
73. 23 August 1845.
74. Archives of the Royal Botanic Gardens, Kew: English Letters, VI, 233 – 12 February 1834.
75. Archives of the Royal Botanic Gardens, Kew: English Letters, VI, 243 – 22 December 1835.
76. Royal Botanic Garden Library, Edinburgh: 24 December 1866.

77. Royal Botanic Garden Library, Edinburgh: 20 June 1867.

78. 1 November 1869.

79. Archives of the Royal Botanic Gardens, Kew: English Letters, XIII, 140 – 26 March 1839.

80. 21 June 1839.

81. 25 December 1847.

CHAPTER 9
PHOTOGRAPHS IN PRINTERS' INK

An extensive account of the evolution of photomechanical printing is contained in the fourth edition of J. M. Eder's *History of Photography* (translated Edward Epstean), Columbia UP, 1945. Chapter 44 of H. & A. Gernsheim's *The History of Photography*, Thames & Hudson, 1969, is devoted to the subject and both books provide extensive source notes. *The Focal Encyclopedia of Photography* (Focal Press) has a succinct account of photomechanical reproduction techniques while *Victorian Book Illustration* by Geoffrey Wakeman: David & Charles, 1973 treats the subject from the point of view of an important end use. 'Etching, engraving and photography' and 'Photography and photogravure: History of photomechanical reproduction', by Eugene Ostroff (*Journal of Photographic Science*, 17, No. 3, 1969, pp. 65–80 and No. 4, pp. 101–15) places T.'s work reliably in its historical context, and is additionally valuable for its selection of illustrations of pre-photography illustrative techniques, etched Daguerreotypes and plates etched by T.'s methods.

1. He described the experiments to the Scottish Society of Arts on 17 April 1839 and an account appeared in the *Edinburgh New Philosophical Journal*, July 1839, p. 153.

2. 'On the application of light and electricity to the production of engravings – photogalvanography'. *Royal Institution*, 13 February 1857.

3. Letter to François Arago, 30 September 1839. *Comptes Rendus*, July–December 1839, pp. 423–7. Quoted Ostroff, op. cit., p. 72.

4. Gernsheim, op. cit., p. 539.

5. Ostroff, op. cit., p. 75. Berres's method received considerable publicity. Two communications from him appeared in *Literary Gazette*, 23 May 1840, pp. 331–2 and 5 September 1840, pp. 581–2.

6. Letter to the *Athenaeum*, published in the issue of 9 April 1853.

7. LA47–95, LA47–97, LA47–102 – work notes, 28 November–31 December 1847.

8. LA52–42 and LA52–44 – 21 August 1852 and 28 August 1852 respectively (Barclay to T.).

9. LA52–44.

10. Notebook I.

11. *Edinburgh New Philosophical Journal*, 29 May 1839, pp. 169–71.

12. Eder, op. cit., pp. 553, 594.

13. LA60–20 – 17 May 1860 (T. to James); LA60–22 – 23 May 1860 (James to T.); LA60–23 – 24 May 1860 (T. to James); and LA60–25 – 8 June 1860 (James to T.).

14. Science Museum Collection: 'Memorandum of copies of Engravings distributed in 1853: May–August'.

15. Science Museum Collection: 14 May 1853.

16. LA53–18 – 11 May 1853.

17. LA54–7 – 4 February 1854.

18. LA53–15 – 4 May 1853.

19. LA53–10 – 8 April 1853.

20. 22 May 1853.

21. LA53–26 – 2 June 1853.

22. 30 September 1854.

23. LA53–22 – 19 May 1853.

24. Eder, op. cit., p. 591.

25. LA53–28 – 18 June 1853; LA53–29 – 7 July 1853 and LA53–32 – 17 October 1853 (all Murray to T.).

26. Science Museum Collection: 3 May 1853 (Biot to T.).

27. On photogalvanography; or engraving by light and electricity. *Journal of the Society of Arts*, 25 April 1856, pp. 385–9.

28. LA56–23 – 28 April 1856.

29. LA56–22 – note of T.'s letter to Pretsch, dated 27 April 1856.

30. LA56–25 – Note of T.'s letter to Pretsch, dated May 1856.

31. LA56–30 – 22 May 1856.

32. LA57–12 – 21 April 1857.

33. LA57–13 – 24 April 1857 and LA57–16 – 6 May 1857; LA57–21 – 5 August 1857; LA57–23 – 13 August 1857; and LA57–34 – 21 October 1857 respectively.

34. LA57–15 – 1 May 1857 (Bolton to T.).

35. LA57–36 – 4 November 1857 (Bolton to T.).

36. LA57–6 – 26 February 1857 and LA57–9 – 11 April 1857.

37. *A History and Handbook of Photography*, by G. Tissandier (second English edition). Sampson Low & Co., 1878, Appendix A, p. 372.

38. See Ostroff, op. cit., p. 114.

39. LA58–75 – 16 September 1858 (T. to William Crookes).

40. LA58–67 – 9 August 1858 (T. to Crookes).

41. LA58–63 – 4 June (1858?) (almost certainly T. to Crookes).

42. LA58–76 – 17 September 1858.

43. *Photographic News*, 12 November 1858.

44. 10 November 1858.

45. LA58–69 – 13 August 1858 (Crookes to T.).

46. LA58–91 – 1 November 1858.

47. LA58–103 – 11 November 1858.

48. LA58–112 – 23 November 1858.

49. LA58–110 – 20 November 1858.

50. LA59–28 – 10 May 1859 (T. to Crookes).

51. LA58–90 – 1 November 1858.

52. LA58–93 – 2 November 1858 and LA58–107 – 18 November 1858 (both Wheatstone to T.).

Wheatstone's suggestion does not seem to have been pursued. The provision of original photographs by T. for Wheatstone's experiments has already been mentioned (p. 131). For a description of Wheatstone's work in stereoscopy and his argument over priority of discovery with David Brewster see *Sir Charles Wheatstone* by Brian Bowers: HMSO, 1975, pp. 191ff., and Arthur T. Gill, *Photographic Journal*, 109, 1969, pp. 546–59, 606–14, 641–5.

53. LA58–91 – 1 November 1858.

54. LA58–105 – 14 November 1858.

55. LA59–50 – 20 October 1859 (Beatty to Crookes).

56. LA58–67 – 9 August 1858 (T. to Crookes).

57. LA59–8 – 20 February 1859.

58. Science Museum Collection: 25 November 1858 (T. to Crookes).

59. *Photographic Journal*, 1 February 1859, p. 29. The illustration was a view of the undercliff at Niton (Isle of Wight) photographed by Roger Fenton. It was heavily retouched and could scarcely be recognized as having been made from a photographic original.

[This Journal underwent some title changes being *Liverpool Photographic Journal* from 1854–6; *Liverpool and Manchester Photographic Journal* from 1857–9; *Photographic Journal* (not to be confused with the organ of the Photographic

Society) in 1859; and *British Journal of Photography* – its present title – from 1860.]

60. LA59–54 – 21 December 1859 (Pretsch to T.).

61. An example was printed in the *Photographic Journal* (of the Photographic Society), 15 November 1861, p. 39, and another in the *British Journal of Photography* of the same date.

62. 2 and 16 April 1861 (Hogarth to T.).

63. 19 April and 1 June 1861 (Pretsch to T.).

64. LA61–1 – 11 March and 9 April 1861 (notes of T.'s letters to Hogarth).

65. 30 July and 16 August 1861 (Banks to T.).

66. LA56–3 – 27 January 1856 (experimental notes).

67. Eder, op. cit., p. 594.

68. In *Edinburgh Astronomical Observations*, XII, 1863.

69. 20 April 1863.

70. Science Museum Collection: undated, probably 1863 (letters to T.). For Piazzi Smyth's photographic work in Egypt see 'Photography at the Great Pyramid in 1865' by Arthur T. Gill, *Photographic Journal*, April 1965, pp. 109–18.

71. 5 February 1862 (George Lumley to T.).

72. 30 November 1863.

73. 27 July 1865. The woodcut appeared in the *British Journal of Photography* on 12 August 1864.

74. 28 June 1866 and 29 August 1866.

75. 15 May 1867.

76. 27 August 1866.

77. Science Museum Collection: note in Talbot's handwriting dated 25 October.

78. See *A Treatise on Photogravure in Intaglio by the Talbot–Klič Process*, by Herbert Denison: Iliffe, 1895.

79. See Geoffrey Wakeman, op. cit., for an account of the popularity of the different processes.

80. 25 February 1867 (Harriet Mundy to T.).

CHAPTER 10
NUMBERS AND ASSYRIANS

1. 20 May 1847 (letter from Philip Kelland, Professor of Mathematics at Edinburgh University). Kelland was the first Englishman with an entirely English education to be appointed to a Chair at Edinburgh.

2. On Fermat's theorem. *Edinb. Roy. Soc. Trans.*, XXI, 1857, pp. 403–6. The paper was read on 7 April 1856.

3. On the theory of numbers. *Edinb. Roy. Soc. Trans.*, XXIII, 1862, pp. 45–52.

4. On Fagnani's theorem. *Edinb. Roy. Soc. Trans.*, XXIII, 1863, pp. 285–98.

5. Note on confocal conic sections. *Edinb. Roy. Soc. Trans.*, XXIV, 1865, pp. 53–7.

6. Researches on Malfatti's problem. *Edinb. Roy. Soc. Trans.*, XXIV, 1865, pp. 127–38.

7. Some mathematical researches on cubic equations. *Edinb. Roy. Soc. Trans.*, XXIV, 1867, pp. 573–90.

8. Essay towards a general solution of numerical equations of all degrees having integer roots. *Edinb. Roy. Soc. Trans.*, XXVII, 1875, pp. 303–12.

9. 6 April 1875 (Kelland to T.).

10. For general background of the events described in this section see: *Nineveh and Its Remains*, by Austen Henry Layard (edited by H. W. F. Saggs): R & KP, 1970. (The original was published in 1849.) *The Rise and Progress of Assyriology*, by Sir E. A. Wallis Budge: Hopkinson, 1925; and *The Story of Decipherment*, by Maurice Pope: Thames & Hudson, 1975.

11. *Traité de Calcul. Diff. et. Int.* II by J. Bertrand, 1870, pp. 382ff.
12. Wallis Budge, op. cit., p. 50.
13. ibid., p. 73.
14. *Edward Hincks*, by E. F. Davidson: OUP, 1933, p. 231 (letter dated 9 January 1862).
15. ibid., p. 232 (letter dated 20 January 1862).
16. ibid., pp. 232–3 (letter dated 4 March 1862).
17. ibid., p. 190 (letter dated 21 May 1855).
18. 'Inscription of Tiglath Pileser I, King of *Assyria* 1150 B.C. – as translated by Sir Henry Rawlinson, Fox Talbot Esq., Dr Hincks and Dr Oppert'. Royal Asiatic Society, 1857, pp. 3–4.
19. Davidson, op. cit., p. 213 (letter dated 13 May 1857).
20. 'Inscription of Tiglath Pileser I . . .', pp. 6–10.
21. *Journal of the Royal Asiatic Society*, X, Part III, July 1878.
22. Wallis Budge, op. cit., p. 94.
23. Davidson, op. cit., pp. 214–15.
24. *Journal of the Royal Asiatic Society*, 19, 1862, p. 124.
25. Wallis Budge, op. cit., p. 108.
26. 10 January 1870.
27. 21 January, 25 October 1871 (Smith to T.); August 1871 (T. to Smith).
28. LA61–5 – 25 November 1861 (note of T.'s letter to Oppert).
29. 6 March 1875.
30. For example, 'On the Cypriote inscriptions.' *Transactions of the Society of Biblical Archaeology*, V, 1877, p. 447.
31. 23 October 1876 (Birch to T.).
32. 9 February 1871 (Birch to T.).
33. 8 November 1877 (from Robert N. Cust of the Royal Asiatic Society).
34. *Journal of the Royal Asiatic Society*, July 1895, p. 685.

CHAPTER 11
THE FINAL YEARS

1. 7 November 1861.
2. A touching if brief portrait of Talbot through the eyes of his granddaughter Matilda Gilchrist-Clark (later Talbot) is given in her autobiography *My Life and Lacock Abbey*, Allen & Unwin, 1956.
3. 24 December 1867.
4. 18–19 May 1870.
5. 18 March 1876.
6. 14 August 1870.
7. 14 and 20 August 1870 (Rosamond to T.).
8. 27 January 1872 (Rosamond to T.).
9. Trinity College Collection: 26 May (almost certainly 1861) (T. to Whewell).
10. September 1864.
11. 19 November 1864 (Charles to T.).
12. Wiltshire County Record Office: correspondence with Rev. A. Blomfield, 1860.
13. 8 February 1869 (T. to Constance).
14. 30 July 1868.
15. 10 November 1868 (T. to Mlle Amélina).
16. 27 March 1870 (T. to Mlle Amélina).
17. 8 May 1861 (T. to Mlle Amélina).
18. 27 April 1865 (T. to Mlle Amélina).
19. *Edinb. Roy. Soc. Proc.*, VII, November 1969–June 1872, pp. 408–10, 461–70.
20. LA62–1 – 25 July 1862 (Crookes to T.).
21. 9 May 1871.
22. 10 August 1869.
23. 26 August 1865.
24. 9 December 1864 (Charles to T.).
25. *British Journal of Photography*, 28 September 1877.
26. See 'Portraits of Fox Talbot' by Arthur T. Gill, *Photographic Journal*, July 1975.
27. LA59–12 – 9 March 1859 (from the Society).

28. 13 January 1862 (from the Society).
29. LA56–1 – 25 January 1856.
30. 29 May 1868.
31. 20 January 1860.
32. 25 and 29 March 1862.
33. 5 March 1869 (Caroline to T.).
34. Copy of report in *Edinburgh Evening Courant* of 2 April 1863.
35. 3 April 1863.
36. 13 June 1868.
37. *Photographic Journal*, 16 January 1873, pp. 177–8.
38. 5 May 1873 (Baden Pritchard to T.).
39. 11 September 1876.
40. 27 April 1875 (T. to Constance).
41. 10 February 1877.
42. LAM–138 – dated 'August' but no year.
43. Tissandier, op. cit., p. 17.
44. ibid., p. 367. The letter is reprinted.
45. *Wiltshire Telegraph*, 22 September 1877.
46. *The Times*, 16 February 1900.
47. A notable exception was the *Photogram*, a photographic magazine which published a lengthy series of articles on the birth of photography at this time and organized a sale of photoglyphic engravings, with the proceeds going to the Talbot memorial appeal. (*Photogram*, September 1900, pp. 275–81.)
48. *Literary Gazette*, 2 February 1839, p. 74 (letter dated 30 January 1839).

Appendices

I Selected Genealogies

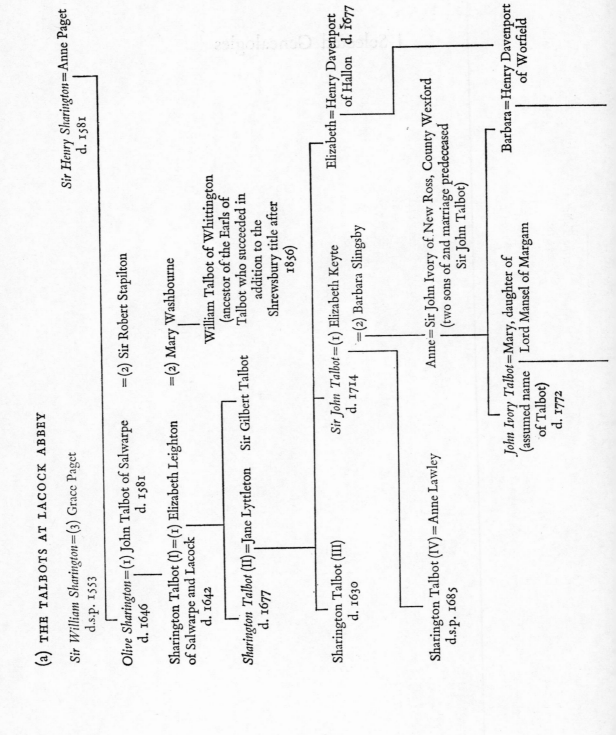

(a) THE TALBOTS AT LACOCK ABBEY

Sir William Sharington=(3) Grace Paget
d.s.p. 1553

Sir Henry Sharington=Anne Paget
d. 1581

Olive Sharington=(1) John Talbot of Salwarpe   =(2) Sir Robert Stapilton
d. 1646   d. 1581

Sharington Talbot (I)=(1) Elizabeth Leighton   =(2) Mary Washbourne
of Salwarpe and Lacock
d. 1642

William Talbot of Whittington
(ancestor of the Earls of
Talbot who succeeded in
addition to the
Shrewsbury title after
1856)

Sharington Talbot (II)=Jane Lyttleton   Sir Gilbert Talbot
d. 1677

Sharington Talbot (III)
d. 1630

Sir John Talbot=(1) Elizabeth Keyte
d. 1714   =(2) Barbara Slingsby

Elizabeth=Henry Davenport d. 1677
of Hallon

Sharington Talbot (IV)=Anne Lawley
d.s.p. 1685

Anne=Sir John Ivory of New Ross, County Wexford
(two sons of 2nd marriage predeceased
Sir John Talbot)

John Ivory Talbot=Mary, daughter of
(assumed name   Lord Mansel of Margam
of Talbot)
d. 1772

Barbara=Henry Davenport
of Worfield

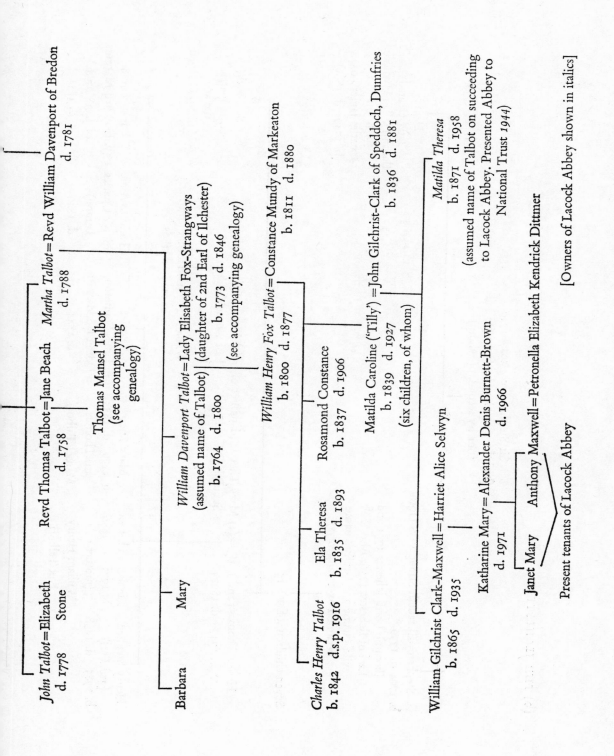

John Talbot = Elizabeth Stone
d. 1778

Revd Thomas Talbot = Jane Beach
d. 1758

Martha Talbot = Revd William Davenport of Bredon
d. 1788   d. 1781

Thomas Mansel Talbot
(see accompanying genealogy)

Barbara

Mary

William Davenport Talbot = Lady Elisabeth Fox-Strangways
(assumed name of Talbot)   (daughter of 2nd Earl of Ilchester)
b. 1764 d. 1800   b. 1773   d. 1846
(see accompanying genealogy)

William Henry Fox Talbot = Constance Mundy of Markeaton
b. 1800   d. 1877   b. 1811   d. 1880

Rosamond Constance
b. 1837   d. 1906

Charles Henry Talbot
b. 1842   d.s.p. 1916

Ela Theresa
b. 1835   d. 1893

Matilda Caroline ('Tilly') = John Gilchrist-Clark of Speddoch, Dumfries
b. 1839   d. 1927   b. 1836   d. 1881
(six children, of whom)

Matilda Theresa
b. 1871   d. 1958
(assumed name of Talbot on succeeding
to Lacock Abbey. Presented Abbey to
National Trust 1944)

William Gilchrist Clark-Maxwell = Harriet Alice Selwyn
b. 1865   d. 1935

Katharine Mary = Alexander Denis Burnett-Brown
d. 1971   d. 1966

Anthony Maxwell = Petronella Elizabeth Kendrick Dittmer

Janet Mary

Present tenants of Lacock Abbey

[Owners of Lacock Abbey shown in italics]

(b) THE ILCHESTERS

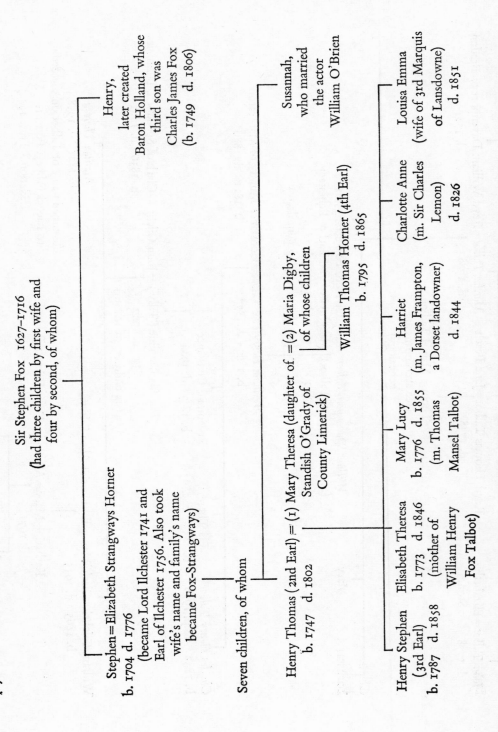

Sir Stephen Fox 1627–1716
(had three children by first wife and four by second, of whom)

Stephen = Elizabeth Strangways Horner
b. 1704 d. 1776
(became Lord Ilchester 1741 and Earl of Ilchester 1756. Also took wife's name and family's name became Fox-Strangways)

Henry, later created Baron Holland, whose third son was Charles James Fox (b. 1749 d. 1806)

Seven children, of whom

Henry Thomas (2nd Earl) = (1) Mary Theresa (daughter of = (2) Maria Digby, of whose children
b. 1747 d. 1802   Standish O'Grady of County Limerick)

William Thomas Horner (4th Earl) b. 1795 d. 1865

Susannah, who married the actor William O'Brien

Henry Stephen (3rd Earl) b. 1787 d. 1858

Elisabeth Theresa b. 1773 d. 1846 (mother of William Henry Fox Talbot)

Mary Lucy b. 1776 d. 1855 (m. Thomas Mansel Talbot)

Harriet (m. James Frampton, a Dorset landowner) d. 1844

Charlotte Anne (m. Sir Charles Lemon) d. 1826

Louisa Emma (wife of 3rd Marquis of Lansdowne) d. 1851

(c) THE TALBOTS IN WALES

John Ivory Talbot=Mary, daughter of Lord Mansel of Margam
of Lacock Abbey
d. 1772

Read Thomas Talbot=Jane Beach
(inherited estate of
4th Lord Mansel in
1750) d. 1758

Thomas Mansel Talbot=Lady Mary Lucy Fox-Strangways
of Oxwich, Penrice (daughter of 2nd Earl
and Margam of Ilchester and sister of
b. 1747 d. 1813 Lady Elisabeth Fox-Strangways)*
b. 1776 d. 1855

Eight children – cousins to William Henry Fox Talbot –
of whom:

Christopher Rice Mansel Talbot=Lady Charlotte Butler
('Kit'): inherited the estate (daughter of 1st Earl of Glengal)
b. 1803 d. 1890 b. 1809 d. 1846
(4 children were born to the
marriage)

Emma Thomasina†=John Dillwyn Llewelyn
b. 1806 d. 1881 b. 1810 d. 1882

Mary Thereza   Jane Harriet=John Nicholl
b. 1795 d. 1861 b. 1796 d. 1874

Charlotte Louisa=Revd J. M.   Isabella Catherine=Richard Franklen
b. 1800 d. 1859 Traherne   b. 1804 d. 1874

*Lady Mary married Sir Christopher Cole in 1815.

†A daughter (Thereza Mary) of these photographic pioneers married Nevil
Story-Maskelyne, F.R.S., M.P.

II Some Major Sources of Original Correspondence, Photographs and Equipment

(a) TALBOT MUSEUM, LACOCK

The major source of letters to and from Talbot is the Lacock Collection. Some of these letters are coded by a reference number, others identified only by date and correspondent. The Notes in this biography contain references to both groups of letters.

The Museum at Lacock contains a wide selection of Henry Talbot's equipment and memorabilia.

(b) THE SCIENCE MUSEUM, LONDON

An important collection of letters including those to Talbot from John Herschel, David Brewster, Jean-Baptiste Biot, and Antoine Claudet. Other correspondents include Charles Chevalier, Charles Piazzi Smyth, W. and F. Langenheim, Thomas A. Malone, Nicolaas Henneman, Warren De La Rue and John Moffat.

The Science Museum has a major collection of photogenic drawings (including the world's earliest surviving paper negative), Calotypes, photo-engravings and of Talbot's cameras and other optical equipment. In addition, it possesses two notebooks covering the period 1839–43 and some of Talbot's Italian sketches dating from 1833.

(c) THE ROYAL SOCIETY, LONDON

In addition to communications from Talbot to the Council of the Royal Society, the collection includes letters from him to Sir John Herschel and Sir John Lubbock.

(d) THE ROYAL SCOTTISH MUSEUM

The Talbot material consists almost exclusively of photographic and other apparatus. It comprises a number of cameras for exposing paper negatives, Daguerreotype cameras and equipment, printing frames, plate holders, microscopes, prisms and electrical apparatus.

(e) THE ROYAL PHOTOGRAPHIC SOCIETY

The Society has a substantial collection of Calotypes and photoglyphic engravings and of cameras (including some of the very small instruments used in the early years of the development of photogenic drawing). Its holdings of miscellaneous written and other original material include two of the sketches made by Talbot at Lake Como in October 1833 after which he commenced his photographic experiments.

III Talbot Notebooks

SCIENCE AND MATHEMATICS

B	1822
C	1825
D	1825–6
E	1827
F	1828–30
I	1831–2
J	1832–3
K	1833–4
M	1834–5
N	1835–6
O	1836–8
P	1839–40 (Science Museum, London)
Q	1840–43 (Science Museum, London)
CC	Mathematical Notebook September 1836
No code	Mathematical Notebook December 1837
No code	Botanical Notebook 1823–6
No code	'The Garden' 1828–9

ETYMOLOGY AND PHILOLOGY

No code	1833
'Called G'	1834
S_2	1836
S_3	1836
S_4	1837
S_5	1837

U	1837
U₂	1837
V	1838
W	1838
X	1838
Y	1838

SEPARATE SERIES

B	1841
C	1841
D	1842
G	1844
J	1845
K	1847
M	1855

[Notebooks are in the Lacock Collection save where indicated.]

IV Published Works of W. H. F. Talbot

Legendary Tales in Verse and Prose, James Ridgway, London, 1830.
Hermes – or Classical and Antiquarian Researches, No. 1, Longman, Orme, Brown, Green &
    Longmans, London, 1838.
Hermes, No. 2, 1839.
The Antiquity of the Book of Genesis – Illustrated by Some New Arguments, Longman, Orme,
    Brown, Green & Longmans, London, 1839.
The Pencil of Nature, Longman, Brown, Green & Longmans, London (issued in six parts
    in the period from June 1844 to April 1846).
Sun Pictures in Scotland, Published by subscription, 1845.
English Etymologies, John Murray, London, 1847.
G. Tissandier, *A History and Handbook of Photography*, containing an Appendix by W. H. F.
    Talbot completed by his son C. H. Talbot, Sampson Low, Marston, Searle & Rivington,
    London, 1878.

[This list does not include works produced at the Reading establishment – e.g. *Annals of
the Artists of Spain* – which contained no original Talbot contribution.]

V Published Papers

SCIENCE, PHOTOGRAPHY AND MATHEMATICS

On the properties of a certain curve derived from the equilateral hyperbola [signed W.H.T.]. Gergonne, *Ann. Math.*, XIII, 1822, pp. 242–7.

Demonstration of a property of the equilateral hyperbola [signed W.H.T.]. Gergonne, *Ann. Math.*, XIII, 1822, pp. 319–20.

Solution of the problem: 'To find the point in a given plane, the sum of whose distances to three given points external to the plane is a minimum' [signed W.H.T.]. Gergonne, *Ann. Math.*, XIII, 1822, pp. 329–30.

On the sums of certain trigonometrical series. Gergonne, *Ann. Math.*, XIV, 1823, pp. 88–95, 187–90.

On a curve, the arcs of which represent Legendre's elliptic functions of the first kind. Gergonne, *Ann. Math.*, XIV, 1823, pp. 380–1.

Theorems concerning a right cone, and the projection of a conic section upon the base of the cone. Gergonne, *Ann. Math.*, XIV, 1823, pp. 123–8.

Some experiments on coloured flames. *Edinb. Journ. Sci.*, V, 1826, pp. 77–82.

On monochromatic light. *Quart. Journ. Sci.*, XXII, 1827, p. 374. [This is a very poor extract from the previous paper.]

Remarks on chemical changes of colour. *Phil. Mag.*, II, May 1833, pp. 359–60.

Remarks upon an optical phenomenon, seen in Switzerland. *Phil. Mag.*, II, June 1833, p. 452.

On a method of obtaining homogeneous light of great intensity. *Phil. Mag.*, III, July 1833, p. 35.

Proposed philosophical experiments (on the velocity of electricity; and proposed method of ascertaining the greatest depth of the ocean). *Phil. Mag.*, III, August 1833, pp. 81–2.

On a new property of the arcs of the equilateral hyperbola. *Roy. Soc. Proc.*, III, 1834, p. 258.

Facts relating to optical science, No. 1. *Phil. Mag.*, IV, February 1834, pp. 112–14.

Facts relating to optical science, No. II. *Phil. Mag.*, IV, April 1834, pp. 289–90.

On the arcs of certain parabolic curves. *Roy. Soc. Proc.*, III, 1834, pp. 287–8.

Experiments on light. *Phil. Mag.*, V, November 1834, pp. 321–34; *Roy. Soc. Proc.*, III, 1834, p. 298.

On the nature of light. *Phil. Mag.,* VII, August 1835, pp. 113–18, 157.

Lettre sur les cristaux de borax. *Comptes Rendus,* II, 1836, pp. 472–3.

On the repulsive power of heat. *Phil. Mag.,* VIII, March 1836, pp. 189–91.

Facts relating to optical science, No. III. *Phil. Mag.,* IX, July 1836, pp. 1–4.

On the optical phenomena of certain crystals. *Phil. Mag.,* IX, October 1836, pp. 288–91; *Phil. Trans.,* 1837, pp. 25–7.

Researches in the integral calculus, Part 1. *Phil. Trans.,* 1836, pp. 177–215.

Further observations on the optical phenomena of crystals (Bakerian Lecture). *Roy. Soc. Proc.,* III, 1836, pp. 455–6; *Phil. Trans.,* 1837, pp. 29–35.

Researches in the integral calculus, Part 2. *Phil. Trans.,* 1837, pp. 1–18.

Facts relating to optical science, No. IV. *Phil. Mag.,* IX, December 1836, pp. 401–7.

An experiment on the interference of light. *Phil. Mag.,* X, May 1837, p. 364.

On a new property of nitre. *Phil. Mag.,* XII, February 1838, pp. 145–8.

On a new property of the iodide of silver. *Phil. Mag.,* XII, March 1838, pp. 258–9.

On analytic crystals. *Phil. Mag.,* XIV, 1839, pp. 19–21.

Some account of the art of photogenic drawing, or the process by which natural objects may be made to delineate themselves without the aid of the artist's pencil. *Roy. Soc. Proc.,* IV, 1839, pp. 120–1; *Phil. Mag.,* XIV, 1839, pp. 196–208.

An account of the processes employed in photogenic drawing. *Roy. Soc. Proc.,* IV, 1839, pp. 124–6.

Note respecting a new kind of sensitive paper. *Roy. Soc. Proc.,* IV, 1839, p. 134.

Remarks on M. Daguerre's photogenic process. *Brit. Assoc. Rep.,* 1839, Part 2, pp. 3–5.

Two letters on Calotype photogenic drawing. *Phil. Mag.,* XIX, 1841, pp. 88–92.

An account of some recent improvements in photography. *Roy. Soc. Proc.,* IV, 1841, pp. 312–16.

Sur la confection des papiers sensibles. *Comptes Rendus,* XII, 1841, pp. 1055–8.

On the improvement of the telescope. *Brit. Assoc. Rep.,* 1842, Part 2, pp. 16–17.

On the coloured rings produced by iodine on silver, with remarks on the history of photography. *Phil. Mag.,* XXII, February 1843, pp. 94–7.

On the iodide of mercury. *Phil. Mag.,* XXII, 1843, pp. 297–8.

On a new principle of crystallization. *Brit. Assoc. Rep.,* 1847, Part 2, pp. 58–9.

Sur la production des images photographiques instantanées. *Comptes Rendus,* XXXIII, 1851, pp. 623–7; *Phil. Mag.,* III, 1852, pp. 73–7; *Roy. Soc. Proc.,* VI, 1851, p. 82.

Remarks on M. Foucault's pendulum experiment. Privately printed, 1851.

Account of a total eclipse of the sun, 28 July 1851, observed at Marienburg in Prussia. *Astron. Soc. Mem.,* XXI, Part I, 1852, pp. 107–15.

Gravure photographique sur acier. *Comptes Rendus,* XXXVI, 1853, pp. 780–4; *Photogr. Soc. Journ.,* I, 1854, pp. 42–4, 62–4. (Copies of Talbot's letters of 9 and 30 April 1853 to the *Athenaeum* on photographic engraving.)

On Fermat's theorem. *Edinb. Roy. Soc. Trans.,* XXI, 1857, pp. 403–6.

Photoglyphic engraving. *Photographic News,* 22 October, 1858.

[All items included had been published before.]

Early researches on the spectra of artificial light from different sources. Some experiments on coloured flames. *Chemical News,* III, 1861, pp. 261–2.

On the theory of numbers. *Edinb. Roy. Soc. Trans.,* XXIII, 1862, pp. 45–52.

On Fagnani's theorem. *Edinb. Roy. Soc. Trans.,* XXIII, 1863, pp. 285–98.

Note on confocal conic sections. *Edinb. Roy. Soc. Trans.,* XXIV, 1865, pp. 53–7.

Researches on Malfatti's problem. *Edinb. Roy. Soc. Trans.,* XXIV, 1865, pp. 127–38.

Some mathematical researches on cubic equations. *Edinb. Roy. Soc. Trans.,* XXIV, 1867, pp. 573–90.

Note on Vellozia elegans, from the Cape of Good Hope. *Edinb. Bot. Soc. Trans.,* IX, 1868, p. 79.

On a method of estimating the distances of some of the fixed stars. *Brit. Assoc. Rep.,* XLI, 1871, pp. 34–6.

Note on some anomalous spectra. *Edinb. Roy. Soc. Proc.,* VII, 1872, pp. 408–10.

Note on the early history of spectrum analysis. *Edinb. Roy. Soc. Proc.,* VII, 1872, pp. 461–6.

On some optical experiments. (1 – On a new mode of observing certain spectra; 2 – On the Nicol prism.) *Edinb. Roy. Soc. Proc.,* VII, 1872, pp. 466–70.

Essay towards a general solution of numerical equations of all degrees having integer roots. *Edinb. Roy. Soc. Trans.,* XXVII, 1875, pp. 303–12.

[This list has been arranged as far as possible in chronological order, with duplications removed and some papers added that were not included in previous lists.]

TRANSLATIONS FROM THE ASSYRIAN

Notes on the Assyrian inscriptions. Privately printed, 1854.

Bellino's Cylinder. The Cylinder of Esarhaddon. A Portion of the Annals of Ashurakhbal. Privately printed, 1856.

Inscription of Tiglath Pileser I King of Assyria 1150 B.C. – As translated by Sir Henry Rawlinson, Fox Talbot Esq., Dr Hincks and Dr Oppert. Published by Royal Asiatic Society, 1857.

Journal of Sacred Literature,

    II, 1856, On the Assyrian inscriptions [No. 1].

    III, 1856, — Nos. 2, 3.

    IV, 1856, — No. 4.

    V, 1857, On the origin of the word sabbath.

    IX, 1859, The annals of Esarhaddon, translated from two cylinders in the British Museum.

Journal of the Royal Asiatic Society, VII, second series, 1863,

    (i) On Assyrian antiquities, p. 169.

    (ii) Preliminary translation of Assyrian inscriptions, p. 183.

    (iii) Translation of inscription of Nebuchadnezzar, from the clay cylinder in the possession of Sir Thomas Phillipps, p. 341;

    (iv) Translation of the annals of Esarhaddon, p. 551.

Society of Antiquaries of Scotland, Proceedings, VI, Part 1, 1866, Standard inscription of Asshur-akh-bal.

Journal of the Royal Society of Literature, VIII, second series, 1866,

    (i) Translation of Assyrian inscriptions, p. 105.

    (ii) On a battle scene in the British Museum, p. 230; Hammurabi, p. 234; Clay tablet in the British Museum, p. 244; Siege of Madakta, p. 258; War in Syria (a fragment), p. 264; On ineffable names, p. 274; Further remarks on inscription of Esarhaddon, p. 281; On the antiquity of coined money, p. 285; On the eastern origin of the name and worship of Dionysus, p. 296;

    (iii) A new translation of Bellino's cylinder; the annals of Sennacherib, p. 369.

Transactions of the Society of Biblical Archaeology, I, 1872.

    (i) On an ancient eclipse, p. 13.

    (ii) Note on the religious belief of the Assyrians, Part I, p. 106.

    (iii) A fragment of ancient Assyrian mythology, p. 271.

    (iv) On the Mazzaroth of Job xxxviii, 32, p. 339.

    (v) A prayer and a vision, from the annals of Assurbanipal, p. 346.

    (vi) Addition to the paper on eclipses, p. 348.

—, II, 1873.

    (i) On the religious belief of the Assyrians, Part II, p. 29.

    (ii) On the religious belief of the Assyrians, Part III, p. 50.

    (iii) Legend of Ishtar descending to Hades, p. 179.

    (iv) On the religious belief of the Assyrians, Part IV, p. 346.

    (v) Illustrations of the prophet Daniel from the Assyrian writings, p. 360.

—, III, 1874.

    (i) Revised translation of Ishtar's descent, with a further commentary, p. 118.

    (ii) Addenda to above, p. 357.

    (iii) Assyrian notes, No. 1, p. 430.

    (iv) Four new syllabaries, &c., p. 496.

—, IV, 1876.

    (i) Commentary on the Deluge tablet, p. 49.

    (ii) A tablet relating apparently to the Deluge, p. 129.

    (iii) Notice of a very ancient comet, p. 257.

    (iv) The revolt in Heaven, p. 349.

—, V, 1877.

    (i) The fight between Bel and the Dragon, &c., p. 1.

    (ii) Ishtar and Isdubar, p. 97.

    (iii) The Chaldean account of the Creation, p. 426.

    (iv) On the Cypriote inscriptions, p. 447.

—, VI, 1878.

    (i) The defence of a magistrate falsely accused, p. 289.

Records of the Past,

    I, Inscription of Khammurabi, p. 5; Bellino's cylinder of Sennacherib, p. 23; Taylor's cylinder of Sennacherib, p. 23; Legend of Ishtar descending into Hades, p. 141.

    III, Inscription of Esarhaddon, p. 101; Second inscription of Esarhaddon, p. 109; Assyrian sacred poetry, p. 131; Assyrian talismans and exorcisms, p. 139.

VI Talbot Patents

Short Title	Number	Date	
Obtaining Motive Power	8,650	1 October	1840
Photographic Pictures	8,842	8 February	1841
Coating and Coloring Metallic Surfaces	9,167	9 December	1841
Gilding and Silvering Metals	9,528	25 November	1842
Photography	9,753	1 June	1843
Obtaining and Applying Motive Power	10,539	3 March	1845
Obtaining and Applying Motive Power	11,475	7 December	1846
Photography (with Thomas A. Malone)	12,906	19 December	1849
Photography	13,664	12 June	1851
Engraving	565	29 October	1852
Obtaining Motive Power	1,046	13 December	1852
Engraving	875	21 April	1858

Index